AYFAIR
BALL
1982-83

Edited by Peter Dunk and Lionel Francis

Queen Anne Press
Macdonald & Co
London & Sydney

Photography courtesy of Sporting Pictures (UK) Ltd

First published in Great Britain in 1982 by
Queen Anne Press
Macdonald & Co (Publishers) Ltd
Maxwell House
74 Worship Street
London EC2A 2EN

ISBN 0 356 07889 2

Typeset in Times by SIOS Limited, London NW6

Printed in England by Hazell, Watson and Viney Limited, Aylesbury

CONTENTS

WORLD CUP 1982

The 24-nation World Cup final tournament in Spain was a qualified success, and the criticisms which have to be made can be classified into three main groups. The first concerns the format of the competition. Even before the finalists were known, FIFA officials were quoted as saying that changes were in the air for 1986, but at the time of writing it doesn't seem as though these changes are likely to produce a better format. The idea of having a league system in the early stages is understandable. It would be unreasonable to expect teams to travel perhaps thousands of miles, only to go home after one game, but the knock-out element which is the essence of cup football has to be introduced after the first phase. With 24 finalists, it would seem to make good sense to have four groups of six teams in the first round, with the top two teams from each group going forward to knock-out quarter-finals. This would reduce the opportunity for teams to indulge in the sort of blatant cheating that was seen in this World Cup, the most obvious example being the game between Austria and West Germany. Having reached half-time with a score which suited both teams, they clearly made no real effort to play football in the second half, which is totally inexcusable. Unfortunately, no actual rules were broken and FIFA, which claims a larger membership than the United Nations, showed itself to be equally ineffective in sorting out injustice, and nothing was done. Unless football remains entertaining, it will die – the writing is already on the wall in our domestic game – and whilst the decline of the game cannot be blamed entirely on the people who run it, they should be seen to be doing something more positive to reverse the trend.

Another major source of disappointment in Spain was the standard of the refereeing. The World Cup is supposed to represent the best in the game, but too often the referees were clearly not reaching these high standards. The examples are well-known (Spain's penalty against Yugoslavia, the non-punishment of Schumacher for his horrendous foul on Battiston etc.) and unfortunately the final itself was plagued with refereeing which could only be described as weak. Very bad fouls early in the game went unbooked by the strutting Brazilian referee, whilst such bookings as did occur were given for relatively minor offences. Of course, refereeing is an extremely difficult job – much more difficult than most people realise – but it should be a simple matter to get a defensive wall back ten yards, and Coelho failed to do this on several occasions during the final. In the earlier game between Italy and Brazil, it was noticeable that suddenly the Brazilian free kicks from outside the Italian penalty area were totally ineffective, but how far back was the wall? Perhaps FIFA's policy of selecting no more than one official per country is partly to blame for this situation. Referees should be chosen on merit, and if this means that at the end of the day there are, for example, six English referees and none from Bolivia is this necessarily a bad thing?

The third major criticism centres on the way in which the Spanish authorities mishandled the entire affair from beginning to end. The signs were there as far back as January, when we were treated to the pantomime of the draw. If they were unable to do that properly, what chance did they stand of succeeding in the real business later on? We are now told that a very substantial proportion of the package deals that were on offer to fans from all over the world went unsold. Indeed, for most games tickets were available outside the stadiums – in many cases for less than their face value. This makes a total nonsense of the claims that, by selling tickets only in conjunction with package deals including travel and accomodation, the problems which might be caused by thousands of fans turning up 'on spec' would be avoided. The truth of the matter is that huge sums of money have been made by a few people to the detriment of the fans. Is it really necessary, or even moral, for hotels to double their prices just because of the World Cup? FIFA must take the blame for their lack of supervision, and we can but hope that they have learned their lesson in this respect.

The behaviour of the Spanish police cannot be allowed to pass without comment. British fans were warned in advance to behave themselves, mainly because the uncompromising nature of the Spanish police was well-known, and to the credit of the fans, they did indeed behave themselves. Therefore the way in which English fans were singled out in Madrid and gratuitously beaten up by the police while the locals stood by and cheered is something which although clearly acceptable in Spain, should be condemned by the civilised world. It is now clear that FIFA made a mistake in awarding the World Cup finals to a country that still has one foot in the Third World, and it is pleasing at least to note that they are now having second thoughts about Colombia for 1986. In fact it is astounding that Colombia should ever have been considered in the first place. She has only ever qualified for one final tournament (Chile, 1962) and then finished bottom of her first round group with one draw and two defeats to her 'credit'. The idea that Colombia could organise a 24-nation tournament was always preposterous, and it is to be hoped that the decision is reversed as quickly as possible. Remember Bogota, Bobby Moore? Enlarging the tournament to 24 teams in order to bring in more qualifiers from the Third World was a fine idea, and thoroughly justified by the entertaining football these teams produced in Spain, but organising the tournament itself should be left to those who are good at it.

These criticisms aside, there was a great deal to enjoy on the football fields of Spain this summer, in the biggest-ever World Cup feast. The three British representatives performed at least as well as could be expected, and the Northern Irish surpassed themselves. Their first phase victory over the hosts was a moment that will live for ever in Irish soccer memories. Scotland, on the other hand, always knew what they were up against. A couple of defensive lapses against New Zealand did nothing to help their cause, but Brazil looked unbeatable at the time, and the Soviet Union are well-known as a well-organised and skilful outfit. At least the ghosts of Argentina '78 were buried.

England went out at the end of the second phase because they weren't quite good enough to go any further. They had started with a heartening victory against France, followed this with a victory against Czechoslovakia which, although it owed much to two lucky goals, could not possibly have been said to be an unfair result, and then went through the motions against Kuwait, knowing that they would in any case finish at the top of the group. It was in the second phase that the shortcomings of the England squad were exposed, and principally their inability to score goals when it really matters. This has been worrying England fans for more than a decade, and the over-cautious approach to the game with West Germany didn't help. Perhaps if Brooking had been fit, perhaps if Keegan had not missed an open goal against Spain, but it is no use relying on 'if'. Ron Greenwood has retired after a creditable spell as England manager, and we wish him well in his retirement. Hopefully, his successor will have a similar effect on England's fortunes to that of the last Ipswich manager to land the job!

FINAL HONOURS 1981-82

British Championship:
England

European Cup:
Aston Villa

European Cup-Winners' Cup:
Barcelona

UEFA Cup:
IFK Gothenburg

Football League
Division One: Liverpool
Division Two: Luton
Division Three: Burnley
Division Four: Sheffield United

Scottish League:
Premier Division: Celtic
Division One: Motherwell
Division Two: Clyde

FA Cup:
Tottenham Hotspur

League Cup:
Liverpool

League Group One:
Grimsby Town

Charity Shield:
Shared by Aston Villa and Tottenham H.

FA Challenge Vase:
Forest Green Rovers

FA Challenge Trophy:
Enfield

Scottish Cup:
Aberdeen

Scottish League Cup:
Rangers

Welsh Cup:
Swansea City

Alliance Premier League:
Runcorn

Northern Premier League:
Bangor City

Southern League Midland Division:
Nuneaton Borough

Southern League Southern Division:
Wealdstone

Irish Cup:
Linfield

Irish League:
Linfield

FA Youth Cup:
Watford

FA Sunday Cup:
Dingle Rail

FOOTBALL LEAGUE CLUBS AND THEIR PLAYERS

ALDERSHOT DIV. 4

Briley, Leslie
Brodie, Murray
Fielder, Colin M.R.
Johnson, Glenn W.
Jopling, Joseph
Lucas, Brian A.
McDonald, Ian C.
Robinson, Stuart A.
Sanford, Mark A.
Scott, Peter W.

League Appearances: Bennett, P.R. 46; Briley, L. 37; Brodie, M. 26(3); Crosby, M. 14; Edwards, N.S. 42; Fielder, C.M.R. 1; French, M.J. 28(3); Garwood, C.A. 30; Hampshire, P. 1; Horn, G.R. 2; Johnson, G.W. 44; Jopling, J. 34; Lucas, B.A. 33(2); McDonald, I.C. 31; McGregor, A.G.P. 7; Robinson, S.A. 28(2); Sanford, M.A. 27(6); Scott, P.W. 33(1); Wanklyn, E.W. 15(3); Wooler, A.T. 27.
Goals – League (57): Sanford 11, French 10 (1 pen), Lucas 9, Garwood 7 (1 pen), Brodie 3, Jopling 3, McDonald 3, Briley 2, Crosby 2, Robinson 2, Wanklyn 2, Bennett 1, Edwards 1, Scott 1.
League Cup (5): Garwood 2, Crosby 1, Lucas 1, Robinson 1.
FA Cup (6): Garwood 2, Brodie 1, French 1, McDonald 1, Robinson 1.
Ground: Recreation Ground, High St., Aldershot GU11 1TW (Aldershot 20211)
Nearest station: Aldershot
Manager: Len Walker **Secretary/Commercial Manager:** M. A. Cosway
Colours: Red and blue striped shirts with blue trim; blue shorts
Record home gate: 19,138 v Carlisle, January 1970 (FA Cup)
Honours – Champions: Nil
FA Cup winners: Nil

ARSENAL DIV. 1

Cork, David
Davis, Paul V.
Devine, John A.
Gorman, Paul A.
Hawley, John E.
Hill, Colin F.
Hollins, John W.
Jennings, Patrick A.
Kay, John
McDermott, Brian J.
Meade, Raphael J.
Nicholas, Peter
O'Leary, David A.
O'Shea, Daniel E.
Rix, Graham
Robson, Stewart I.
Sansom, Kenneth G.
Sparrow, Brian E.
Sunderland, Alan
Talbot, Brian
Vaessen, Paul L.
Whyte, Christopher A.
Wilmot, Rhys J.
Wood, George
Woodcock, Anthony S.

League Appearances: Davis, P.V. 37(1); Devine, J.A. 10(1); Gorman, P.A. 4; Hawley, J.E. 12(2); Hollins, J.W. 40; Jennings, P.A. 16; McDermott, B.J. 9(4); Meade, R.J. 8(8); Nicholas, P. 28(3); O'Leary, D.A. 40; Rix, G. 39; Robson, S.I. 20; Sansom, K.G. 42; Sunderland, A. 38; Talbot, B. 42; Vaessen, P.L. 9(1); Whyte, C.A. 32; Wood, G. 26; Young, W.D. 10.
Goals – League (48): Sunderland 11, Rix 9, Talbot 7, Davis 4, Meade 4, Hawley 3, Robson 2, Vaessen 2, Whyte 2, Hollins 1, McDermott 1, O'Leary 1, own goal 1.

League Cup (3): Nicholas 1, Sunderland 1, Young 1.
FA Cup: Nil.
Ground: Arsenal Stadium, Avenell Road, N5 1BU (01-226 0304)
Nearest stations: Arsenal (Piccadilly Line), Drayton Park (British Rail) or Finsbury Park (BR, Piccadilly Line or Victoria Line)
Manager: Terry Neill **Secretary:** Ken Friar
Colours: Red shirts with white sleeves; white shorts
Record home gate: 73,295 v Sunderland, March 1935 (League)
Honours – Champions: Division 1: 1930-31, 1932-33, 1933-34, 1934-35, 1937-38, 1947-48, 1952-53, 1970-71
FA Cup winners: 1929-30, 1935-36, 1949-50, 1970-71, 1978-79
Fairs Cup winners: 1969-70

ASTON VILLA — DIV. 1

Birch, Paul
Blair, Andrew
Blake, Noel L. G.
Bremner, Desmond G.
Bullivant, Terence P.
Cowans, Gordon S.
Deacy, Eamonn S.
Evans, Allan
Geddis, David
Gibson, Colin J.
Glover, Dean V.
Heard, Timothy P.
Hopkins, Robert
Hutchinson, Mark C.
Jones, Mark A.
Kendall, Mark I.
McKenzie, Martin A.
McNaught, Kenneth
Morley, Anthony W.
Mortimer, Dennis G.
Ormsby, Brendan T. C.
Poole, Kevin
Rimmer, John J.
Rogers, Kevin P.
Shaw, Gary R.
Spink, Nigel P.
Swain, Kenneth
Walker, Raymond
Williams, Gary
Withe, Peter

League Appearances: Blair, A. 9(9); Blake, N.L.G. 1; Bremner, D.G. 38; Bullivant, T.P. 4(3); Cowans, G.S. 42; Deacy, E.S. 4; Donovan, T.C. 8; Evans, A. 38; Geddis, D. 14; Gibson, C.J. 23; Heard, T.P. 6(2); Jones, M.A. 2; Linton, I. –(1); McNaught, K. 22; Morley, A.W. 36(1); Mortimer, D.G. 32; Ormsby, B.T.C. 12; Rimmer, J.J. 42; Shaw, G.R. 26; Shelton, G. 1; Swain, K. 39; Walters, M. –(1); Williams, G. 28; Withe, P. 35.
Goals – League (55): Shaw 9, Withe 9, Cowans 6 (2 pens), Geddis 6, Morley 6, Donovan 4, own goals 4, Bremner 3, Evans 2, Heard 2, McNaught 2, Mortimer 2.
League Cup (9): Cowans 4 (3 pens), Withe 2, Blair 1, Bremner 1, Morley 1.
FA Cup (7): Geddis 3, Shaw 2, Cowans 1 (pen), own goal 1.
Ground: Villa Park, Birmingham B6 6HE (021-327 6604)
Nearest station: Birmingham, New Street
Manager: Tony Barton **Secretary:** Steven Stride
Colours: Claret shirts with light blue sleeves; white shorts
Record home gate: 76,588 v Derby, March 1946 (FA Cup)
Honours – Champions: Division 1: 1893-94, 1895-96, 1896-97, 1898-99, 1899-1900, 1909-10, 1980-81; Division 2: 1937-38, 1959-60; Division 3: 1971-72
FA Cup winners: 1886-87, 1894-95, 1896-97, 1904-05, 1912-13, 1919-20, 1956-57. (Seven wins stands as the record)
League Cup winners: 1960-61, 1974-75, 1976-77
European Champions Cup: 1981-82

BARNSLEY DIV. 2

Aylott, Trevor K.C.
Banks, Ian F.
Barrowclough, Stewart J.
Birch, Alan
Bukavina, John F.
Campbell, Winston R.
Dunstone, Phillip
Evans, Ian P.
Glavin, Ronald M.
Glover, David T.
Horn, Robert I.
Joyce, Joseph P.
Law, Nicholas
Longden, David P.
McCarthy, Michael
McHale, Raymond
Mann, James A.
Martin-Chambers, Philip
New, Martin P.
Parker, Derrick
Pierce, Gary
Walker, Colin
Watkin, Philip
Whitehouse, Dean
Wilkes, David A.

League Appearances: Aylott, T.K.C. 41; Banks, I.F. 41(1); Barrowclough, S.J. 17(1); Birch, A. 17; Campbell, W.R. 7; Cooper, N. 10; Evans, I.P. 40; Glavin, R.M. 26(1); Horn, R.I. 42; Joyce, J.P. 20; Law, N. 19; Longden, D.P. 4; McCarthy, M. 42; McHale, R. 39(1); Mann, J.A. 9(1); Martin-Chambers, P. 42; Parker, D. 18; Riley, G. 7(8); Walker, C. 19; Wilkes, D.A. 2.
Goals – League (59): Banks 15 (3 pens), Walker 12, Aylott 11, Glavin 7, Parker 6, Birch 5 (1 pen), Cooper 1, Evans 1, McCarthy 1.
League Cup (19): Glavin 6, Aylott 4, Parker 2, Barrowclough 1, Cooper 1, Evans 1, Joyce 1, McCarthy 1, Riley 1, Walker 1.
FA Cup: Nil.
Ground: Oakwell, Grove Street, Barnsley S71 1ET (0226-84113)
Nearest station: Barnsley
Manager: Norman Hunter **Secretary:** Michael Spinks
Colours: Red shirts; white shorts
Record home gate: 40,255 v Stoke 1936 (FA Cup)
Honours – Champions: Division 3 North: 1933-34, 1938-39, 1954-55
FA Cup winners: 1911-12

BIRMINGHAM CITY DIV. 1

Broadhurst, Kevan
Brocken, Budde J.P.M.
Coles, David A.
Coton, Anthony P.
Curbishley, Llewellyn C.
Dennis, Mark E.
Dillon, Kevin P.
Evans, Anthony
Francis, Carl E.
Gibson, Alexander S.
Handysides, Ian R.
Harford, Michael G.
Hawker, Philip N.
Langan, David F.
MacDowall, Duncan J.
McGarr, Anthony R.
McKay, Derek C.
Phillips, Leslie M.
Scott, Geoffrey S.
Stevenson, William B.
Stewart, Brian
Sturridge, Michael A.
Todd, Colin
Van Den Hauwe, Patrick W.R.
Van Mierlo, Antonius W.M.T.
Wealands, Jeffrey A.
Whatmore, Neil
Winterburn, Nigel

League Appearances: Broadhurst, K. 35; Brocken, B.J.P.M. 17; Coton, A.P. 15; Curbishley, L.C. 29; Dennis, M.E. 17; Dillon, K.P. 35(1); Evans, A. 29; Gemmill, A. 19; Handysides, I.R. 8(12); Harford, M.G. 12; Hawker, P.N. 19(1); Jones, R. 4; Langan, D.F. 36; Linney, D.W. –(1); MacDowall, D.J. 2; Phillips, L.M. 7(4); Scott, G.S. 14(1); Stevenson, W.B. 12; Todd, C. 19; Van Den Hauwe, P.W.R. 30(1); Van

Mierlo, A.W.M.T. 40; Wealands, J.A. 23; Whatmore, N. 22(2); Worthington, F.S. 18(2).
Goals – League (53): Evans 15 (1 pen), Harford 9, Worthington 9 (3 pens), Whatmore 6, Broadhurst 4, Van Mierlo 4, Curbishley 1, Dillon 1, Gemmill 1, Hawker 1, Langan 1, Phillips 1.
League Cup (3): Evans 1, Whatmore 1, Worthington 1.
FA Cup (2): Curbishley 1, Worthington 1 (pen).
Ground: St Andrews, Birmingham B9 4NH ((021-772 0101 and 2689)
Nearest station: Birmingham, New Street
Manager: Ron Saunders **Secretary:** A. G. Instone
Colours: Royal blue shirts with 3 white vertical stripes on sleeves; white shorts with blue trim.
Record home gate: 66,844 v Everton, February 1939 (FA Cup)
Honours – Champions: Division 2: 1892-93, 1920-21, 1947-48, 1954-55; League South: 1945-46
FA Cup winners: Nil
League Cup winners: 1962-63

BLACKBURN ROVERS — DIV. 2

Bell, Norman
Branagan, James P.S.
Brotherston, Noel
Burke, Marshall
Comstive, Paul T.
Fazackerley, Derek W.
Garner, Simon
Gennoe, Terence W.
Hamilton, David
Keeley, Glen W.
Lowey, John A.
Mail, David
Marshall, Julian P.
Miller, Ian
Murphy, Donal P.
Rathbone, Michael J.
Salmon, Michael B.
Speight, Michael
Stonehouse, Kevin

League Appearances: Arnott, K. 17; Bell, N. 25; Branagan, J.P.S. 40; Brotherston, N. 38; Burke, M. 16(3); Butcher, J.M. 6; Comstive, P.T. 1(1); Crawford, A. 8; Fazackerley, D.W. 39; Garner, S. 35(1); Gennoe, T.W. 35; Hamilton, D. 16(1); Keeley, G.M. 41; Lowey, J.A. 12(2); Miller, I. 42; Murphy, D.P. 1(2); Rathbone, M.J. 41; Speight, M. 13; Stonehouse, K. 35(2); Williamson, P.J. –(1); Salmon, M.B. 1.
Goals – League (47): Garner 14, Stonehouse 11 (5 pens), Bell 4, Keeley 3, Miller 3, Arnott 2, Brotherston 2, Crawford 2, Branagan 1, Burke 1, Fazackerley 1, Lowey 1, Rathbone 1, own goal 1.
League Cup (3): Garner 2, Lowey 1.
FA Cup (2): Garner 2.
Ground: Ewood Park, Blackburn BB2 4JF (Blackburn 55432/3)
Nearest station: Blackburn
Manager: Bobby Saxton **Secretary:** John W. Howarth
Colours: Blue and white shirts; white shorts
Record home gate: 61,783 v Bolton Wanderers, March 1929 (FA Cup)
Honours – Champions: Division 1: 1911-12, 1913-14; Division 2: 1938-39; Division 3: 1974-75
FA Cup winners: 1883-84, 1884-85, 1885-86, 1889-90, 1890-91, 1927-28

BLACKPOOL DIV. 4

Bamber, John D.
Blair, Ronald V.
Brockbank, Andrew
Deary, John S.
Greenall, Colin A.
Hart, Nigel
Hesford, Iain
Hockaday, David
McAvoy, Alan J.
Pashley, Terence
Simmonite, Gordon
Stewart, Paul A.

League Appearances: Bamber, J.D. 38; Bardsley, D.J. 1; Blair R.V. 35(1); Brockbank, A. 19; Butler, J.P. 1; Deary, J.S. 22(5); Entwistle, W.P. 11(1); Fletcher, P.J. –(1); Gardner, P.A. 12; Goddard, H.J. 4; Greenall, C.A. 16(2); Harrison, W.M. 31(4); Hart, N. 27(1); Hesford, I. 39; Hockaday, D. 37(4); McAvoy, A.J. 6; McEwan, S. 24(1); Morgan, W. 11(1); Morris, C. 22; Noble, P. 44; Pashley, T. 46; Pollard, B. –(1); Rush, J. 7; Sbragia, R. 2(1); Simmonite, G. 29; Stewart, P.A. 9(5); Wann, J.D. 13(6).
Goals – League (66): Bamber 15, Morris 10, Noble 9, Hockaday 7, McEwan 5 (4 pens), Blair 3, Entwistle 3, Stewart 3, Goddard 2, Harrison 2, Morgan 2, own goals 2, Brockbank 1, Pashley 1, Simmonite 1.
League Cup (1): Bamber 1.
FA Cup (7): Harrison 2, Morris 2, Bamber 1, Entwistle 1, Wann 1.
Ground: Bloomfield Road, Blackpool FY1 6JJ (Blackpool (0253) 46118)
Nearest station: Blackpool North
Manager: Sam Ellis **Secretary:** D. Johnson
Colours: Tangerine shirts with white stripe on sleeves, white collar and cuffs; white shorts with tangerine stripe
Record home gate: 39,118 v Manchester United, April 1952 (League)
Honours – Champions: Division 2: 1929-30
FA Cup winners: 1952-53
Anglo-Italian Cup winners: 1971

BOLTON WANDERERS DIV. 2

Bennett, Michael
Berry, Neil
Chandler, Jeffrey G.
Doyle, Michael
Farnworth, Simon
Foster, Wayne P.
Henry, Anthony
Hoggan, David M.
McDonagh, James
McElhinney, Gerard A.
Reid, Peter
Thompson, Christopher D.
Whitworth, Stephen

League Appearances: Bailey, I.C. 5; Bennett, M. 35; Berry, N. 2(1); Brennan, I. 4; Cantello, L. 34; Carter, M. 11(2); Chandler, J.G. 32(1); Doyle, M. 10; Foster, W.P. 20(3); Gowling, A.E. 40; Hebberd, T.N. 6; Henry, A. 39; Hoggan, D.M. 25(4); Jones, P.B. 41; Kidd, B. 10; Langley, G.R. 3(3); McDonagh, J. 39; McElhinney, G.A. 18(1); Nicholson, P. 6(2); Nikolic, D. 1; Peacock, D. 3; Reid, P. 12; Thomas, J.W. 3(2); Thompson, C.D. 34(2); Whitworth, S. 29.
Goals – League (39): Henry 13 (2 pens), Thompson 12, Chandler 2, Foster 2, Gowling 2, Cantello 1, Carter 1, Hoggan 1, Jones 1 (pen), Kidd 1, McElhinney 1, Reid 1, Thomas 1.
League Cup (4): Berry 1, Kidd 1, Thomas 1, Thompson 1.
FA Cup (3): Foster 1, Gowling 1, Thompson 1.

Ground: Burnden Park, Manchester Rd., Bolton BL3 2QR (0204-389200)
Nearest station: Bolton
Player/Manager: John McGovern **Secretary:** Des McBain
Colours: White shirts; navy blue shorts
Record home gate: 69,912 v Manchester City, February 1933 (FA Cup)
Honours – Champions: Division 2: 1908-09, 1977-78; Division 3: 1972-3
FA Cup winners: 1922-23, 1925-26, 1928-29, 1957-58

AFC BOURNEMOUTH DIV. 3

Allen, Kenneth
Brignull, Philip A.
Compton, Paul D.
Crawford, Andrew
Dawkins, Derek A.
Dawtry, Kevin A.
Funnell, Anthony
Goddard, Howard J.
Graham, Milton M.
Heffernan, Thomas P.
Impey, John E.
Leigh, Ian R.
Mooney, Dean F.
Morgan, Trevor J.
Mundee, Brian G.
O'Donnell, Brian F.
Spackman, Nigel J.
Sulley, Christopher S.
Williams, Keith D.

League Appearances: Allen, K. 10; Brignull, P.A. 29; Carter, S.C. 15; Compton, P.D. 20; Crawford, A. 27(1); Dawkins, D.A. 3(2); Dawtry, K.A. 27(2); Edmunds, P. 13(1); Funnell, A. 40(3); George, C. 2; Goddard, H.J. 6(3); Graham, M.M. 5; Heffernan, T.P. 45; Impey, J.E. 43; Kelly, E.P. 13; Leigh, I.R. 36; Mooney, D.F. 6; Morgan, T.J. 25; O'Donnell, B.F. 3(4); Smith, B. 22; Spackman, N.J. 34(1); Sulley, C.S. 46; Williams, K.D. 36(1).
Goals – League (64): Funnell 16, Crawford 10, Heffernan 7 (1 pen), Morgan 7, Dawtry 5, Graham 3, Spackman 3, Brignull 2, Edmunds 2, Goddard 2, Impey 2, Carter 1, Smith 1, Williams 1 (pen).
League Cup: Nil.
FA Cup (4): Funnell 2, Crawford 1, Williams 1.
Ground: Dean Court, Bournemouth, Dorset BH7 7AF (0202-35381)
Nearest station: Bournemouth
Manager: David Webb **Secretary:** G. H. MacKrell
Colours: Red shirts; red shorts with white stripe
Record home gate: 28,799 v Manchester United, March 1957 (FA Cup)
FA Cup winners: Nil

BRADFORD CITY DIV. 3

Black, John
Campbell, Robert M.
Cooke, Joseph
Ellis, Mark E.
Gallagher, Barry P.
Jackson, Peter A.
Lester, Michael J.A.
McFarland, Roy L.
McNiven, David S.
Podd, Cyril M.
Ramsbottom, Neil
Watson, Garry
Wood, Michael J.

League Appearances: Black, J. 16(1); Campbell, R.M. 45; Chapman, L. 32(2); Cooke, J. 22; Ellis, M.E. 16(2); Gallagher, B.P. 40(2); Ingham, W.C. 36; Jackson, P.A. 30(2); Lester, M.J.A. 15(3); McFarland, R.L. 30; McNiven, D.S. 46; Podd, C.M. 46; Ramsbottom, N. 34; Smith, S.J. 12; Staniforth, D.A. 31(3); Thompson, W.A. 2; Watson, G. 40(1); Wood, M.J. 13(2).
Goals – League (88): Campbell 24 (1 pen), McNiven 19, Gallagher 16 (6 pens), Jackson 8, Staniforth 8, Black 5 (2 pens), own goals 3, Ingham 1, Lester 1, McFarland 1, Wood 1.
League Cup (11): Campbell 3, Black 2 (1 pen), Gallagher 2 (1 pen), own goals 2, Ingham 1, Watson 1.
FA Cup: Nil.
Ground: Valley Parade, Bradford BD8 7DY (0274-306062)
Nearest station: Bradford Exchange
Player/Manager: Roy McFarland **Secretary:** T. F. Newman
Colours: White shirts with claret and amber shoulder panels, claret trim; claret shorts
Record home gate: 39,146 v Burnley, March 1911 (FA Cup)
Honours – Champions: Division 2: 1907-08; Division 3 North: 1928-29
FA Cup winners: 1910-11 (first holders of present trophy)

BRENTFORD DIV. 3

Booker, Robert
Bowen, Keith B.
Bowles, Stanley
Hurlock, Terence A.
Johnson, Gary J.
Kamara, Christopher
McKellar, David
McNichol, James A.
Priddy, Paul J.
Roberts, Gary P.M.
Salmon, Denis M.M.
Tucker, William B.
Walker, James P.
Whitehead, Alan

League Appearances: Booker, R. 27(11); Bowen, K.B. 37(1); Bowles, S. 31; Crown, D.I. 7(1); Harris, R. 19(1); Hill, M.S. 17(1); Hurlock, T.A. 40; Johnson, G.J. 29(1); Johnson, R.N. 1; Kamara, C. 31; Kemp, D.M. 3; Kruse, P.K. 1; McKellar, D. 45; McNichol, J.A. 26; Priddy, P.J. 1; Roberts, G.P.M. 39(1); Rowe, N.T.S. 10; Salmon, D.M.M. 40; Shrubb, P.J. 4; Spencer, A.R. 3; Sweetzer, G.E.P. 8(1); Tonge, K.A. –(1); Tucker, W.B. 38; Walker, J.P. 7(2); Whitehead, A. 42(1).
Goals – League (56): Bowen 9, Johnson, G. 8, Bowles 5 (2 pens), Kamara 5, Booker 4, Tucker 4 (2 pens), McNichol 3, Whitehead 3, Crown 2, Hurlock 2, Kemp 1, Sweetzer 1, own goal 1.
League Cup: Nil.
FA Cup (3): Bowen 2, Roberts 1.
Ground: Griffin Park, Braemar Road, Brentford TW8 0NT (01-560 2021)
Nearest stations: Brentford (BR) or South Ealing (Piccadilly line)
Manager: Fred Callaghan **Chief administrator/Secretary:** D. R. Piggott
Colours: Red and white striped shirts; black shorts
Record home gate: 39,626 v Preston North End, March 1968 (FA Cup)
Honours – Champions: Division 2: 1934-35; Division 3 South: 1932-33; Division 4: 1962-63.
FA Cup winners: Nil

BRIGHTON & HOVE ALBION — DIV. 1

Case, James R.
Clark, Paul P.
Deans, Daniel
Digweed, Perry M.
Fleet, Mark
Foster, Stephen B.
Gatting, Stephen P.
Grealish, Anthony P.
McNab, Neil
Moseley, Graham
Nelson, Samuel
Pearce, Graham
Ramsey, Christopher L.
Ring, Michael P.
Ritchie, Andrew T.
Robinson, Michael J.
Ryan, Gerard J.
Shanks, Donald
Smith, Gordon D.
Stevens, Gary A.
Stille, Giles K.
Thomas, Michael R.
Williams, Peter G.
Wiltshire, Matthew J.

League Appearances: Case, J.R. 33; Digweed, P.M. 12; Foster, S.B. 40; Gatting, S.P. 39; Grealish, A.P. 34(3); McNab, N. 38(2); Moseley, G. 30; Nelson, S. 27; Ring, M.P. 1; Ritchie, A.T. 38(1); Robinson, M.J. 34(1); Ryan, G.J. 17(3); Shanks, D. 35(1); Smith, G.D. 24(3); Stevens, G.A. 25(7); Stille, G.K. 3(2); Thomas, M.R. 18(2); Williams, P.G. 14.

Goals – League (43): Ritchie 12, Robinson 11, Case 3, Gatting 3, McNab 3 (3 pens), own goals 3, Foster 2, Smith 2, Grealish 1, Ryan 1, Stille 1, Williams 1.

League Cup (3): Gatting 1, Grealish 1, Ritchie 1.

FA Cup (3): Case 1, McNab 1 (pen), Thomas 1.

Ground: Goldstone Road, Old Shoreham Road, Hove, Sussex BN3 7DE (0273-739 535)

Nearest station: Hove

Manager: Mike Bailey **Secretary:** Kenneth J. Calver

Colours: Blue shirts with white trim, blue shorts with white trim

Record home gate: 36,747 v Fulham, December 1958 (League)

Honours – Champions: Division 3 South: 1957-58; Division 3: 1971-72; Division 4: 1964-65

FA Cup winners: Nil

BRISTOL CITY — DIV. 4

Boyle, Terence D.J.
Bray, Wayne
Carter, Leslie A.
Chandler, Ricky D.
Mogg, David M.
Musker, Russell
Newman, Robert N.
Nicholls, Alan
Perlee, Raymond
Stevens, Paul D.
Thompson, Steven J.
Wherry, Stephen
Williams, Gary A.

League Appearances: Aitken, P.G. 19; Boyle, T.D.J. 22(1); Bray, W. 19; Carter, L.A. 16; Chandler, R.D. 30; Devine, P. 19(2); Down, W.F. 1; Economou, J. 17(2); Garland, C.S. 1(1); Gooding, R. 3; Harford, M.G. 30; Hay A.B. 33(1); McCaffery, A. 6; Mabbutt, K.R. 11; Mann, J.A. 22; Marshall, J.P. 3; Merrick, G. 3; Moller, J.B. 31; Musker, R. 32(1); Newman, R.N. 15(6); Nicholls, A. 27; Rodgers, D.M. 18; Shaw, J. 15; Smith, M. 1(4); Stevens, P.D. 46; Sweeney, G. 8(2); Tainton, T.K. 19; Thompson, S.J. –(1); Whitehead, C.R. 6; Williams, G.A. 33.

Goals – League (40): Harford 11, Chandler 7, Mann 6 (1 pen), Newman 3 (1 pen), Bray 2, Devine 1, Economou 1, Garland 1, MacCaffery 1, Mabbutt 1, Nicholls 1, Stevens 1, Tainton 1, Thompson 1, Williams 1, own goal 1.
League Cup (4): Mann 2 (1 pen), Harford 1, Rodgers 1.
FA Cup (6): Harford 2, Mann 2, Chandler 1, Tainton 1.
Ground: Ashton Gate, Bristol BS3 2EJ (Bristol 632812)
Nearest stations: Bristol Temple Mead or Parson Street
Player/Manager: Terry Cooper **Secretary:** J. Lillington
Colours: Red shirts; black shorts
Record home gate: 43,335 v Preston, February 1935 (FA Cup)
Honours – Champions: Division 2: 1905-06; Division 3 South: 1922-23, 1926-27, 1954-55
FA Cup winners: Nil

BRISTOL ROVERS — DIV. 3

Bailey, Stephen J.
Barratt, Michael J.
Curle, Keith
Gillies, Donald G.
Holloway, Ian S.
Hughes, Mark
Kite, Philip D.
McCaffery, Aidan
Mabbutt, Gary V.
Parkin, Timothy J.
Randall, Paul
Stephens, Arthur
Thomas, Martin R.
Williams, Brian
Williams, David G.
Williams, David M.

League Appearances: Bailey, S.J. 15(1); Barratt, M.J. 29(3); Cooper, T. 5(3); Curle, K. 10(10); Gillies, D.G. 26(2); Holloway, I.S. 1; Hughes, M. 22; Jones, V. 34; Kelly, E.E. 3(2); Kite, P.D. 27; McCaffery, A. 28(1); Mabbutt, G.V. 45; Parkin, T.J. 39(1); Pendrey, G.J.S. 1; Penny, S. 5(1); Randall, P. 34(3); Slatter, N.J. 28; Smith, D.J. –(1); Stephens, A. 35(4); Thomas, M.R. 19; Westaway, K.D. 1; Williams, B. 37; Williams, D.G. 16; Williams, D.M. 46.
Goals – League (58): Randall 12, Stephens 11, Williams, D. 11 (1 pen), Mabbutt 5, Williams, B. 4 (2 pens), McCaffery 3, Barrett 2, Curle 2, Hughes 2, Parkin 2, Bailey 1, Penny 1, Slatter 1, own goal 1.
League Cup (4): Mabbutt 1, Parkin 1, Stephens 1, Williams, D. 1.
FA Cup (1): Williams, D. 1 (pen).
Ground: Bristol Stadium, New Stadium, Eastville Rd, Bristol BS5 6NN (Bristol (0272) 511050)
Nearest stations: Bristol Temple Mead or Stapleton Road
Manager: Bobby Gould **Secretary:** Peter Terry
Colours: Blue and white shirts; blue shorts
Record home gate: 38,472 v Preston, January 1960 (FA Cup)
Honours – Champions: Division 3 South: 1952-53
FA Cup winners: Nil

BURNLEY DIV. 2

Allen, Mark S.
Cassidy, Thomas
Cavener, Philip
Dixon, Paul K.
Dobson, John M.
Hamilton, William R.
Holt, David
Laws, Brian
McGee, Paul G.
Miller, David B.
O'Rourke, William J.
Overson, Vincent D.
Phelan, Michael C.
Scott, Derek E.
Steven, Trevor M.
Stevenson, Alan
Taylor, Steven J.
Wharton, Andrew
Wright, William H.R.
Young, Kevin

League Appearances: Allen, M.S. –(2); Anderson, C.R. 2(2); Cassidy, T. 27; Cavener, P. 6(3); Dixon, P.K. 8(1); Dobson, J.M. 44; Flynn, B. 2; Hamilton, W.R. 44; Holt, D. 30; Laws, B. 44; McGee, P.G. 19; Overson, V.D. 36; Phelan, M.C. 22(1); Potts, E.T. 14(7); Robertson, S. 5(1); Scott, D.E. 29(1); Steven, T.M. 36; Stevenson, A. 46; Taylor, S.J. 21(1); Wharton, A. 34; Young, K. 37(2).
Goals – League (66): Hamilton 11, Taylor 9, McGee 7 (1 pen), Young 7, Laws 6 (2 pens), Wharton 5, Overson 4, Cassidy 3, Dobson 3 (1 pen), Steven 3, own goals 3, Scott 2, Allen 1, Phelan 1, Potts 1.
League Cup (5): Holt 2, Cassidy 1, Hamilton 1, Potts 1.
FA Cup (11): Hamilton 4, Taylor 3, McGee 2, Steven 2.
Ground: Turf Moor, Burnley BB10 4BX (0282 27777 and 38021)
Nearest station: Burnley Central
Manager: Brian Miller **Secretary:** A. Maddox
Colours: Claret shirts with light blue sleeves; white shorts
Record home gate: 54,775 v Huddersfield, February 1924 (FA Cup)
Honours – Champions: Division 1: 1920-21, 1959-60; Division 2: 1897-98, 1972-73; Division 3: 1981-82
FA Cup winners: 1913-14

BURY DIV. 4

Bramhall, John
Brown, David J.
Cruickshank, John P.
Cutler, Christopher P.
Gore, John T.
Hilton, Paul
Jakub, Yanek
Johnson, Stephen A.
Kenworthy, Stephen
Madden, Craig
Platt, John

League Appearances: Baines, S.J. 7; Bradley, N.B. 15(3); Bramhall, J. 9; Brown, D.J. 27; Butler, M.A. 43; Constantine, D. 15(2); Cruickshank, J.P. 33(5); Cutler, C.P. –(2); Gore, J.T. 44(1); Hilton, M.G. 27(3); Hilton, P. 41; Howard, P. 44(1); Hughes, J.M. 1; Jakub, Y. 44(2); Johnson, S.A. 31; Kennedy, K.V. 45; Madden, C. 46; Mullen, S.A. 9(13); Platt, J. 19; Smith, B. 6.
Goals – League (80): Madden 35, Johnson 12 (1 pen), Butler 8, Hilton, P. 8, Gore 4, Hilton, M. 3, own goals 3, Cruickshank 2, Howard 2, Jakub 2, Bradley 1.
League Cup (4): Madden 3, Johnson 1 (pen).
FA Cup (6): Madden 4, Johnson 2.
Ground: Gigg Lane, Bury BL9 9HR (061-764 4881/2)
Nearest station: Bury
Player/Manager: Jim Iley **Secretary:** John Heap

Colours: White shirts; royal blue shorts
Record home gate: 35,000 v Bolton, January 1960 (FA Cup)
Honours – Champions: Division 2: 1894-95; Division 3: 1960-61
FA Cup winners: 1899-1900, 1902-03

CAMBRIDGE UNITED DIV. 2

Beattie, Andrew H.
Cartwright, Leslie
Christie, Derrick H.M.
Donaldson, David
Fallon, Stephen P.
Finney, Tom
Goldsmith, Martin S.
Key, Richard M.
Mayo, Joseph
Murray, James G.
O'Neill, Thomas
Pyle, Stephen
Reilly, George G.
Smith, Lindsay J.
Spriggs, Stephen
Streete, Floyd A.
Turner, Christopher J.
Watson, Graham S.
Webster, Malcolm W.

League Appearances: Cartwright, L. 14(3); Christie, D.H.M. 15; Donaldson, D. 37; Fallon, S.P. 42; Finney, T. 26(1); Gibbins, R.G. 35; Goldsmith, M.S. 6(1); Key, R.M. 18; Lockhart, K.S. 1(1); Lyons, J.P. 1(1); Mayo, J. 20(1); Murray, J.G. 42; Nicholls, R.I. 5; O'Neill, T. 29(4); Polycarpou, A. 1(4); Reilly, G.G. 37; Smith, L.J. 27(1); Spriggs, S. 33; Streete, F.A. 29(2); Taylor, A.D. 9(1); Turner, C.J. 11(2); Webster, M.W. 24.
Goals – League (48): Mayo 8, Reilly 7, Spriggs 7 (4 pens), Fallon 5, Streete 5, Gibbins 4, Finney 2, Goldsmith 2, O'Neill 2, Smith 2 (1 pen), Christie 1, Taylor 1, Turner 1, own goal 1.
League Cup (4): Gibbins 3, Reilly 1.
FA Cup (1): Taylor 1.
Ground: Abbey Stadium, Newmarket Road, Cambridge CB5 8LL (02205-2170)
Nearest station: Cambridge
Manager: John Docherty **Secretary:** L. S. Holloway
Colours: Amber shirts with black trim; amber shorts
Record home gate: 14,000 v Chelsea (friendly), May 1970
Honours – Champions: Division 4: 1976-77
FA Cup winners: Nil

CARDIFF CITY DIV. 3

Bennett, David A.
Bennett, Gary E.
Healey, Ronald
Jones, Linden
Lewis, John
Maddy, Paul M.
Micallef, Constantinous
Polycarpou, Andrew
Pontin, Keith
Sanders, Alan J.
Stevens, Gary M.

League Appearances: Bennett, D.A. 35(1); Bennett, G.E. 19; Buchanan, J. 3; Dibble, A. 1; Dwyer, P.J. 21(1); Francombe, P. 2(1); Gilbert, T.H. 28; Giles, P.A. 3(3); Grapes, S.P. 24(1); Grotier, P.D. 9; Healey, R. 32; Henderson, M.R. 11; Hughes, B.W. 22(2); Jones, L. 36; Kitchen, M.P. 25(2); Lewis, J. 19; Maddy, P.M. 23(4); Micallef, C. 29(4); Mullen, J. 12; Polycarpou, A. 7; Pontin, K. 40; Ronson, W. 7; Sanders, A.J. 1(1); Sayer, P.A. 4; Stevens, G.M. 38; Sugrue, P.A. 2(3); Sullivan, C.J. 7; Thomas, R.J. 2(2).

Goals – League (45): Stevens 13, Micallef 9, Kitchen 8 (1 pen), Bennett, D. 6, Dwyer 2, Bennett, G. 1, Gilbert 1, Lewis 1, Maddy 1, Mullen 1, Sayer 1, own goal 1.
League Cup (3): Stevens 2, Sugrue 1.
FA Cup (1): Maddy 1.
Ground: Ninian Park, Sloper Road, Cardiff CF1 8SX (0222-398636/8)
Nearest station: Cardiff Central
Manager: Len Ashurst **Secretary:** L. G. Hayward
Colours: Blue shirts with white trim; blue shorts with white stripe
Record home gate: 61,655 Wales v England, October 1961 (Club record); 57,800 v Arsenal, Division 1: 22 April, 1953
Honours – Champions: Divison 3 South: 1946-47
FA Cup winners: 1926-27

CARLISLE UNITED — DIV. 2

Ashurst, Jack
Coughlin, Russell
Crabbe, Steven A.J.
Haigh, Paul
Houghton, Keith
Larkin, Anthony G.
Lee, Robert G.
Parker, Robert
Robson, Bryan S.
Rushbury, David
Staniforth, Gordon
Swinburne, Trevor

League Appearances: Ashurst, J. 46; Bannon, P.A. 23(2); Beardsley, P.A. 19(3); Campbell, A.J. 6(2); Coady, M.L. 4(2); Collins, A.B. 2(1); Coughlin, R. 33(4); Crabbe, S.A.J. 26; Craig, T.B. 18; Haigh, P. 21(2); Hamilton, J. -(1); Houghton, K. 18; Larkin, A.G. 30(1); Lee, R.G. 40(1); Parker, R. 43; Ritchie, T.G. 14(1); Robson, B.S. 39; Rushbury, D. 45; Staniforth, G. 33(4); Swinburne, T. 46.
Goals – League (65); Robson 15, Staniforth 11, (3 pens), Lee 10, Bannon 9, Coughlin 5, Beardsley 4, Crabbe 3 (1 pen), own goals 3, Craig 2, Ashurst 1, Houghton 1, Ritchie 1.
League Cup (6): Lee 2, Coady 1, Haigh 1, Staniforth 1, own goal 1.
FA Cup (7): Robson 3, Bannon 2, Beardsley 1, Staniforth 1.
Ground: Brunton Park, Carlisle CA1 1LL (0228-26237)
Nearest station: Carlisle
Manager: Bob Stokoe **Secretary:** R. Helm
Colours: Blue shirts with red and white trim; blue shorts
Record home gate: 27,500 v Birmingham, January 1957 (FA Cup) and v Middlesbrough, February 1970 (FA Cup)
Honours – Champions: Division 3: 1964-65
FA Cup winners: Nil

CHARLTON ATHLETIC — DIV. 2

Ambrose, Anthony L.
Berry, Leslie D.
Curtis, Paul A.E.
Dickenson, Kevin J.
Elliott, Paul M.
Ferns, Philip D.
Gritt, Stephen J.
Hales, Derek D.
Johns, Nicholas P.
Kay, Paul T.
Lansdowne, William
McAllister, Donald
Mehmet, David
Naylor, Terence M.P.
Phillips, John T.
Phillips, Leighton
Robinson, Martin J.
Smith, Kevin P.
Walker, Philip
Walsh, Paul A.

League Appearances: Ambrose, A.L. 18(4); Berry, L.D. 24(1); Browne, S.L. -(1); Dickenson, K.J. 5(2); Elliott, P.M. 36(2); Ferns, P.D. 26(2); Gritt, S.J. 33(1); Hales, D.D. 35; Harrison, S.J. 3; Johns, N.P. 40; Lansdowne, W. 24(3); McAllister, D. 26; Madden, L.D. 6(1); Mehmet, D. 16; Naylor, T.M.P. 42; Phillips, J.T. 2; Phillips, L. 42; Robinson, M.J. 37(2); Smith, K.P. 6(4); Walker, P. 3; Walsh, P.A. 38.
Goals – League (50): Walsh 13, Hales 11, Robinson 5, Lansdowne 4, McAllister 4, Gritt 3, Madden 2 (1 pen), Smith 2, own goals 2, Ambrose 1, Elliott 1, Mehmet 1, Phillips 1.
League Cup (5): Hales 2 (1 pen), Elliott 1, Lansdowne 1, Robinson 1.
FA Cup: Nil
Ground: The Valley, Floyd Road, Charlton, SE7 8AW (01-858 3711/2)
Nearest station: Charlton (SR)
Manager: Ken Craggs **Secretary:** W. A. Stevens
Colours: Red shirts; white shorts
Record home gate: 75,031 v Aston Villa, February 1938 (FA Cup)
Honours – Champions: Division 3 South: 1928-29, 1934-35
FA Cup winners: 1946-47

CHELSEA — DIV. 2

Britton, Ian	Francis, Stephen S.	Nutton, Michael W.
Bumstead, John	Hales, Kevin P.	Pates, Colin G.
Canoville, Paul K.	Hutchings, Christopher	Rhoades-Brown, Peter
Chivers, Gary	Iles, Robert J.	Viljoen, Colin
Driver, Philip A.	Jasper, Dale W.	Walker, Clive
Droy, Michael R.	Lee, Colin	Ward, Paul T.
Elmes, Timothy	Locke, Gary R.	Wilkins, Graham G.
Fillery, Michael C.	Mayes, Alan	Williams, Paul J.

League Appearances: Borota, P. 12; Britton, I. 17(1); Bumstead, J. 21; Canoville, P.K. 1(2); Chivers, G. 28(1); Driver, P.A. 4(4); Droy, M.R. 20(3); Fillery, M.C. 39(1); Francis, S.S. 29; Hales, K.P. 10; Hutchings, C. 35; Iles, R.J. 1; Lee, C. 40; Locke, G.R. 31; Mayes, A. 35(4); Nutton, M.W. 17(2); Pates, C.G. 42; Rhoades-Brown, P. 24(3); Rofe, D. 6(1); Viljoen, C. 9; Walker, C. 31(5); Wilkins, G.G. 10(1).
Goals – League (60): Walker 16, Mayes 12, Lee 11, Fillery 6, Bumstead 4 (1 pen), Driver 3, Droy 2, Hales 2, Hutchings 1, Locke 1, Pates 1, Rhoades-Brown 1.
League Cup (5): Fillery 3, Bumstead 1, Walker 1.
FA Cup (9): Mayes 4, Bumstead 1, Droy 1, Fillery 1, Lee 1, Rhoades-Brown 1.
Ground: Stamford Bridge, Fulham Road, London SW6 1HS (01-385 5545/6), also information service 381 0111.
Nearest station: Fulham Broadway (District Line)
Manager: John Neal **Secretary:** Miss S. F. Marson
Colours: Blue shirts; blue shorts with white stripe
Record home gate: 82,905 v Arsenal, October 1935 (League)
Honours – Champions: Division 1: 1954-55
FA Cup winners: 1969-70
League Cup winners: 1964-65
European Cup Winners' Cup: 1970-71

CHESTER DIV. 4

Allen, John
Blackwell, Paul
Cooke, Terence A.
Cottam, John E.
Harrington, Phillip
Ludlam, Steven J.
Millington, Grenville R.
Moffatt, Gregory T.
Needham, Paul A.
Phillips, Trevor
Simpson, Gary
Storton, Trevor G.
Zelem, Peter R.

League Appearances: Allen, J. 15(7); Blackwell, P. 21(2); Burns, D. 29(3); Cooke, T.A. 11(2); Cottam, J.E. 30(3); Dean, M.C. 4; Harrington, P. 10; Henderson, P. 28; Hornsby, B.G. 4; Howat, I.S. 3(2); Jones, B. 33(1); Ludlam, S.J. 33; Millington, G.R. 36; Needham, P.A. 27; Oakes, A.A. 25; Phillips, T. 17(4); Raynor, P.E. 40; Simpson, G. 33(4); Storton, T.G. 42; Sutcliffe, P.D. 32(1); Williams, M. 2; Zelem, P.R. 31.

Goals – League (36): Simpson 12, Cooke 5, Henderson 5, Jones 3, Phillips 2, Storton 2, Sutcliffe 2, Ludlam 1, Needham 1, Oakes 1, Raynor 1, Zelem 1.

League Cup (1): Jones 1.

FA Cup: Nil

Ground: The Stadium, Sealand Road, Chester CH1 4LW (0244 371376)

Nearest station: Chester

Manager: Alan Oakes **Secretary:** S. Gandy

Colours: Royal blue shirts with white stripes; royal blue shorts with red and white trim

Record home gate: 20,500 v Chelsea, January 1952 (FA Cup)

Honours – Champions: Nil

FA Cup winners: Nil

CHESTERFIELD DIV. 3

Athersych, Russell
Bellamy, Gary
Bonnyman, Phillip
Carroll, Michael
Green, William
Gregory, Paul G.
Henderson, William M.M.
Henson, Anthony H.
Hunter, Leslie
Kowalski, Andrew M.
O'Neill, James J.
Partridge, John T.
Pollard, Gary
Stirk, John
Turner, John G.
Walker, Philip A.
Wilson, Daniel
Windridge, David H.

League Appearances: Athersych, R. 6(4); Bellamy, G. 23(2); Bonnyman, P. 46; Carroll, M. 2(1); Crawford, A.P. 40(1); Green, W. 35; Gregory, P.G. 1; Henderson, W.M.M. 44; Henson, A.H. 4(2); Hunter, L. 12; Kowalski, A.M. 37; O'Neill, J.J. 42; Partridge, J.T. 3(1); Pollard, G. 17; Ridley, J. 36(2); Robinson, S.M. 3; Salmons, G. 3(1); Stirk, J. 20; Tartt, C. 4; Turner, J.G. 45; Walker, P.A. 15(10); Wilson, D. 43; Windridge, D.H. 25(9).

Goals – League (57): Bonnyman 14 (5 pens), Henderson 13, Windridge 6, Crawford 5, Ridley 4, Walker 4, Wilson 3, Green 2, Kowalski 2. Own goals 2, Carroll 1, Hunter 1.

League Cup (1): Green 1.

FA Cup (4): Bonnyman 2, Henderson 1, Walker 1.

Ground: Recreation Ground, Saltergate, Chesterfield S40 4SX (Chesterfield 32318)

Nearest station: Chesterfield
Manager: Frank Barlow **General manager/Secretary:** A. G. Sutherland
Colours: Royal blue shirts; white shorts
Record home gate: 30,968 v Newcastle United, April 1939 (League)
Honours – Champions: Division 3 North: 1930-31, 1935-36; Division 4: 1969-70
FA Cup winners: Nil

COLCHESTER UNITED — DIV. 4

Adcock, Anthony C.
Allinson, Ian J.R.
Bremner, Kevin J.
Coleman, Phillip
Cook, Michael
Foley, Stephen P.
Hunter, Allan
Leslie, Steven R.W.
Longhorn, Dennis
Lyons, John P.
McDonough, Roy
Osborne, Roger C.
Packer, Michael D.
Rowles, Edward A.J.
Walker, Michael S.G.
Ward, Wayne W.
Wignall, Steve L.
Wright, Stephen P.

League Appearances: Adcock, A.C.31(9); Allinson, I.J.R. 41(1); Bremner, K.J. 46; Coleman, P. 34(3); Cook, M. 46; Cotton, R.A. 9(2); Foley, S.P. 1(1); Groves, P. 9; Hunter, A. 1; Leslie, S.R.W. 31(3); Longhorn, D. 14(7); Lyons, J.P. 16(2); McDonough, R. 40; Osborne, R.C. 39; Packer, M.D. 14; Rowles, E.A.J. 4(2); Walker, M.S.G. 46; Ward, W.W. 3(2); Wignall, S.L. 43; Wright, S.P. 38.
Goals – League (82): Allinson 21 (6 pens), Bremner 21, McDonough 14, Adcock 5, Osborne 5, Coleman 4, Cook 4, Lyons 3, Leslie 2, own goals 2, Packer 1 (pen).
League Cup (8): Bremner 3, Allinson 2 (1 pen), McDonough 2, Cook 1.
FA Cup (8): Allinson 3 (2 pens), Adcock 1, Cook 1, Leslie 1, Wignall 1, own goal 1.
Ground: Layer Road, Colchester CO2 7JJ (0206-74042)
Nearest station: Colchester
Player/Manager: Allan Hunter **Secretary:** M. R. Bennet
Colours: Blue and white vertical striped shirts; blue shorts
Record home gate: 19,072 v Reading, November 1948 (FA Cup)
Honours – Champions: Nil
FA Cup winners: Nil

COVENTRY CITY — DIV. 1

Blyth, James A.
Butterworth, Ian S.
Daly, Gerard A.
Dyson, Paul I.
English, Thomas S.
Francis, Gerald C.J.
Gillespie, Gary T.
Hateley, Mark W.
Hendrie, John G.
Hormantschuk, Peter A.
Jacobs, Stephen D.
Kaiser, Rudolph H.
Roberts, Brian L.F.
Sealey, Leslie J.
Singleton, Martin D.
Thomas, Daniel J.
Thompson, Garry L.
Whitton, Stephen P.

League Appearances: Barnes, D. 6; Blyth, J.A. 27; Bodak, P.J. 9; Bradford, D.W. 6; Butterworth, I.S. 13(1); Daly, G.A. 19; Dyson, P.I. 40; English, T.S. 8; Francis, G.C.J. 18; Gillespie, G.T. 40; Gooding, R. 1; Hagan, J. 3; Hateley, M.W. 31(3); Hendrie, J.G. 6; Hormantschuk, P.A. -(5); Hunt, S.K. 36; Jacobs, S.D. 37(2); Kaiser, R.H. 11(5); Roberts, B.L.F. 33(1); Sealey, L.J. 15; Singleton, M.D. 3; Thomas, D.J. 39; Thompson, G.L. 35(1); Whitton, S.P. 26(2).
Goals – League (56): Hateley 13, Thompson 10, Hunt 9, Whitton 9, Daly 4, Kaiser 3, Bodak 2, Gillespie 2, Bradford 1, Francis 1, Singleton 1, Thomas 1.

League Cup (1): Hateley 1.
FA Cup (10): Hateley 4, Hunt 3, Thompson 2, Bodak 1.
Ground: Highland Road, Coventry CV2 4GU (0203-57171)
Nearest station: Coventry
Manager: Dave Sexton **Secretary:** J. D. Dent
Colours: Sky blue shirts and shorts, with navy blue and white trim
Record home gate: 51,457 v Wolverhampton, April 1967 (League)
Honours – Champions: Division 2: 1966-67; Division 3: 1963-64; Division 3 South: 1935-36
FA Cup winners: Nil

CREWE ALEXANDRA DIV. 4

Entwistle, Wayne P.
Haslegrave, Sean M.
Palios, Markos
Salathiel, David N.
Scott, Robert W.

League Appearances: Bowers, I. 17(1); Callaghan, I.R. 15; Chesters, C.W. 28(8); Cooke, A.J. 2(1); Entwistle, W.P. 11; Griffiths, N. 32(2); Gwyther, D. 7; Hanlon, S.H. 14(1); Haslegrave, S.M. 40; Heath, D.N. 17(6); Henderson, P. 6(1); Howat, I.S. 16(1); Keighley, J.P. 25(4); Lewis, K.W. 46; Longley, N. 3; Mulhearn, K.J. 42; Palios, M. 42(2); Ricketts, A. 14(3); Salathiel, D.N. 43(1); Scott, R.W. 46; Waller, D.H. 1; Williams, P.J. 39.
Goals – League (29): Palios 12, Scott 3, Williams 3, Chesters 2 (1 pen), Lewis 2, Ricketts 2, Griffiths 1 (pen), Gwyther 1, Haslegrave 1, Howat 1, own goal 1.
League Cup (1): Ricketts 1.
FA Cup (2): Haslegrave 1, Scott 1.
Ground: Gresty Road, Crewe CW2 6EB (Crewe (0270) 213014)
Nearest station: Crewe
Manager: Arfon Griffiths **Secretary:** Mrs G. C. Palin
Colours: Red shirts; white shorts
Record home gate: 20,000 v Tottenham, January 1960 (FA Cup)
Honours – Champions: Nil
FA Cup winners: Nil

CRYSTAL PALACE DIV. 2

Allen, Gary A.
Barron, Paul G.
Bason, Brian
Baxter, Paul A.
Boulter, David A.
Brooks, Shaun
Cannon, James A.
Fry, David P.
Galliers, Steven
Gilbert, William A.
Giles, David C.
Hillaire, Vincent M.
Hinshelwood, Paul A.
Langley, Thomas W.
Lovell, Stephen J.
Mabbutt, Kevin R.
Murphy, Jeremiah M.
Nebbeling, Gavin M.
Oakley, Keith
Price, David J.
Smillie, Neil
Smith, Graeme K.
Wilkins, Paul

League Appearances: Barron, P.G. 40; Bason, B. 17(1); Baxter, P.A. 1; Boulter, D.A. 16; Brooks, S. 22(3); Cannon, J.A. 42; Dare, K.J. 4; Fry, D.P. 2; Galliers, S. 8(5); Gilbert, W.A. 31; Giles, D.C. 20(1); Hilaire, V.M. 33(3); Hinshelwood, P.A. 27; Hughes, S.J. 3(4); Langley, T.W. 25(1); Leahy, S.D. 1(1); Lovell, S.J. 28(2);

Mabbutt, K.R. 31; Murphy, J.M. 24(1); Nebbeling, G.M. 1; Price D.J. 17(2); Smillie, N. 41; Walsh, I.P. 12(1); Wicks, S.J. 14; Wilkins, P. 2(3).
Goals – League (34): Mabbutt 8, Hilaire 5, Smillie 3, Brooks 2, Hinshelwood 2 (2 pens), Langley 2, Murphy 2 (1 pen), Walsh 2, Wilkins 2, own goals 2, Cannon 1 (pen), Giles 1, Lovell 1, Wicks 1.
League Cup (4): Cannon 2 (1 pen), Langley 1, Murphy1.
FA Cup (5): Hilaire 2, Cannon 1 (pen), Price 1, Smillie 1.
Ground: Selhurst Park, SE25 6PU (01-653 3338)
Nearest stations: Selhurst, Norwood Junction or Thornton Heath
Manager: Alan Mullery MBE **Secretary:** Alan J. Leather
Colours: Shirts, white with 4 inch diagonal band red over blue from left shoulder; white shorts
Record home gate: 51,801 v Burnley, May 1979 (League)
Honours – Champions: Division 2: 1978-79; Division 3 South: 1920-21
FA Cup winners: Nil

DARLINGTON DIV. 4

Barber, Frederick
Cuff, Patrick J.
Kamara, Alan
McFadden, Anthony
McLean, David J.
Skipper, Peter D.
Smith, Kevan
Speedie, David R.
Stalker, John A.H.I.
Walsh, Alan
Wicks, Roger
Wilson, Harry

League Appearances: Ball, D. 4; Charlton, H. 1; Cuff, P.J. 46; Hamilton, I.W. 38; Hawker, D. 37(1); Honour, B. –(1); Kamara, A. 43; Liddle, G. 12; McFadden, A. 17(3); McLean, D.J. 46; Mitchell, K. 12(1); Skipper, P.D. 45; Smith, K. 45; Speedie, D.R. 44; Stalker, J.A.H.I. 25(9); Walsh, A. 45; Wicks, R. 17(5); Wilson, H. 29.
Goals – League (61): Speedie 17, Walsh 13 (3 pens), Hamilton 8, McLean 7 (2 pens), Stalker 5, McFadden 3, Wicks 3, Skipper 2, Mitchell 1, Smith 1, own goal 1.
League Cup (2): Charlton 1, Walsh 1.
FA Cup (3): Speedie 1, Smith 1, Walsh 1.
Ground: Feethams Ground, Darlington DL1 5JB (0325-65097 and 67712)
Nearest station: Darlington
Manager: Billy Elliott **Secretary:** D. A. Thorne
Colours: White shirts with black trim; black shorts
Record home gate: 21,023 v Bolton, November 1960 (League Cup)
Honours – Champions: Division 3 North: 1924-25
FA Cup winners: Nil

DERBY COUNTY DIV. 2

Attley, Brian R.
Banovic, Vjekoslav
Barton, John S.
Buckley, Steven
Cherry, Steven R.
Clayton, John
Dalziel, Ian
Emery, Stephen R.
Emson, Paul
Foster, George W.
Gamble, Francis
Hill, Andrew R.
Lovatt, John
McAlle, John
Powell, Stephen
Reid, Anthony J.
Skivington, Glenn
Swindlehurst, David
Wilson, Kevin J.

League Appearances: Attley, B.R. 19; Banovic, V. 21; Barton, J.S. 10; Buckley, S. 40; Cherry, S.R. 4; Clayton, J. 13(1); Coop, M.A. 17(1); Dalziel, I. 4; Emery, S.R. 15(1); Emson, P. 39(2); Gamble, F. 1(1); George, C.F. 11; Gibson, A.M. –(1); Hector, K. 27(4); Hill, A.R. 6; Jones, R. 17; Lovatt, J. 2(2); McAlle, J. 18; Money, R. 5; Osgood, K. 4(3); Powell, B.I. 32; Powell, S. 16; Ramage, A. 9; Reid, A.J. 12; Richards, W. 8(1); Sheridan, F.M. 31(1); Skivington, G. 21(3); Spooner, S.A. 4; Swindlehurst, D. 36; Wilson, K.J. 20(4).
Goals – League (53): Wilson 9, Swindlehurst 6, Buckley 5, Emson 5, Hector 5, Clayton 3, Osgood 3, George 2, Hill 2, Powell, B. 2, Ramage 2, Sheridan 2, Skivington 2, own goals 2, Attley 1, Emery 1, Powell, S. 1.
League Cup (2): Hector 1, own goal 1.
FA Cup (1): Powell, B. 1.
Ground: The Baseball Ground, Shaftesbury Crescent, Derby DE3 8NB (Derby 40105)
Nearest station: Derby
Manager: John Newman **General secretary:** M. J. Dunford
Colours: White shirts; blue shorts
Record home gate: 41,826 v Tottenham, September 1969 (League)
Honours – Champions: Division 1: 1971-72, 1974-75; Division 2: 1911-12, 1914-15, 1968-69; Division 3 North: 1956-57
FA Cup winners: 1945-46.

DONCASTER ROVERS — DIV. 3

Boyd, William
Cawthorne, Graham J.
Cooper, Terence
Douglas, Colin F.
Harle, David
Humphries, Steven R.
Liddell, Garry
Lister, Stephen H.
Little, Alan
Mell, Stewart A.
Nimmo, Ian W.
Pugh, Daral J.
Russell, William M.
Snodin, Glynn
Snodin, Ian
Swan, Carl
Warboys, Alan

League Appearances: Allanson, G.E. 1; Bennett, D.A. –(1); Bremner, W.J. –(1); Boyd, W. 33; Cawthorne, G.J. 12; Cooper, T. 20; Dawson, R. 28(2); Douglas, C.F. 38(4); Dowd, H.O. 27; Harle, D. 21(5); Humphries, G. 12(2); Humphries, S.R. 13(1); Lally, P.A.M. 30(2); Liddell, G. 13; Lister, S.H. 40(1); Little, A. 19(1); Mell, S.A. 12(6); Nimmo, I.W. 4(4); Parkinson, K.J. 5; Pugh, D.J. 42(3); Russell, W.M. 35(2); Snodin, G. 40; Snodin, I. 33; Swan, C. 1; Warboys, A. 14; Wigginton, C.A. 13.
Goals – League (55): Dawson 8, Lister 7 (2 pens), Snodin, G. 7, Mell 6, Pugh 6, Warboys 4, Douglas 3, Russell 3, Harle 2, Little 2, Snodin, I. 2, Cawthorne 1, Dowd 1, Liddell 1, Nimmo 1, Wigginton 1.
League Cup (2): Douglas 2, Mell 1.
FA Cup (7): Warboys 3, Dawson 1, Douglas 1, Little 1, own goal.
Ground: Belle Vue Ground, Doncaster DN4 5HT (Doncaster (0302) 55281)
Nearest station: Doncaster
Manager: Billy Bremner **Secretary:** R. W. Reade
Colours: White shirts with red sleeves; white shorts with red stripes
Record home gate: 37,149 v Hull City, October 1948 (League)

Honours – Champions: Division 3 North: 1934-35, 1946-47, 1949-50; Division 4: 1965-66, 1968-69
FA Cup winners: Nil

EVERTON DIV. 1

Ainscow, Alan
Arnold, James A.
Bailey, John A.
Biley, Alan P.
Borrows, Brian
Eastoe Peter R.
Ferguson, Michael J.
Heath, Adrian P.
Higgins, Mark M.
Hodge, Martin J.
Irvine, James A.
Kearney, Mark J.
Leonard, Mark A.
Lodge, Paul
Lyons, Michael
McBride, Joseph
McMahon, Stephen
Ratcliffe, Kevin
Richardson, Kevin
Ross, Trevor W.
Sharp, Graeme M.
Southall, Neville
Steele, Simon P.
Stevens, Michael G.
Tierney, Keith
Walsh, Michael
Wright, William

League Appearances: Ainscow, A. 15(2); Arnold, J.A. 16; Bailey, J.A. 12; Biley, A.P. 16(3); Borrows, B. 15; Eastoe, P.R. 17(2); Ferguson, M.J. 7(1); Hartford, R.A. 7; Heath, A.P. 22; Higgins, M.N. 29; Irvine, J.A. 25; Kendall, H. 4; Lodge, P. 12(1); Lyons, M. 26(1); McBride, J. 7(1); McMahon, S. 31(1); O'Keefe, E.G. 8(3); Ratcliffe, K. 25; Richardson, K. 15(3); Rimmer, S.A. 2; Ross, T.W. 27(1); Sharp, G.M. 27(2); Southall, N. 26; Stevens, M.G. 19; Thomas, M.R. 10; Walsh, M. 18; Wright, W. 24.
Goals – League (56): Sharp 15 (1 pen), Heath 6, Eastoe 5, Ferguson 5, Biley 3, Higgins 3, Irvine 3, Lyons 3, O'Keefe 3, Ainscow 2, McMahon 2, Richardson 2, Wright 2, McBride 1, Ross 1, Stevens 1.
League Cup (5): Ferguson 2, McMahon 2, O'Keefe 1.
FA Cup (1): Eastoe 1.
Ground: Goodison Park, Liverpool L4 4EL (051-521 2020)
Nearest station: Liverpool Lime Street
Manager: Howard Kendall **Secretary:** Jim Greenwood
Colours: Royal blue shirts with blue and white stripe down seam; white shorts with blue and white stripe down seam
Record home gate: 78,299 v Liverpool, September 1948 (League)
Honours – Champions: Division 1: 1890-91, 1914-15, 1927-28, 1931-32, 1938-39, 1962-63, 1969-70; Division 2: 1930-31
FA Cup winners: 1905-06, 1932-33, 1965-66

EXETER CITY DIV. 3

Bond, Leonard A.
Delve, John F.
Giles, Paul A.
Kellow, Tony
Pratt, Raymond E.
Pullar, David H.
Roberts, Lee J.
Rogers, Martyn
Rogers, Peter P.
Sparrow, John P.

League Appearances: Bond, L.A. 31; Cooke, J. 17; Davey, S.G.R. 15; Delve, J.F. 40; Fisher, P.J. 6(2); Foster, G.W. 28; Giles, P.A. 9; Hatch, P.D. 20(2); Howarth, F. 1(1); Kellow, T. 46; Kirkup, G.S. 8; Lester, M.J.A. 18(1); Main, I. 15; Marker, N.R.T. 11(3); Mitchell, A.J. 13; Pratt, R.E. 23(7); Prince, F.A. 6(4); Pullar, D.H. 27(3); Roberts, L.J. 23(2); Roberts, P.S. 26(1); Robertson, S. 5(1); Rogers, M. 35(1); Rogers, P.P. 42; Shaw, P.K. 3; Sparrow, J.P. 38.
Goals – League (71): Kellow 21 (8 pens), Rogers, P. 10, Pratt 9, Lester 6, Roberts L. 4, Rogers, M. 4, Cooke 3, Delve 3, Hatch 3, Pullar 2, Fisher 1, Giles 1, Marker 1, Prince 1, Sparrow 1, own goal 1.
League Cup (4): Cooke 2, Fisher 1, Kellow 1 (pen).
FA Cup: Nil
Ground: St James' Park, Exeter, Devon EX4 6PX (Exeter (0392) 54073)
Nearest stations: Exeter Central or St David's
Manager: Brian Godfrey **Secretary:** P. R. Wakeham
Colours: Red and white vertical striped shirts; black shorts with white trim
Record home gate: 20,984 v Sunderland, March 1931 (FA Cup)
Honours – Champions: Nil
FA Cup winners: Nil

FULHAM DIV. 2

Beck, John
Brown Roger W.
Coney, Dean H.
Davies, Gordon J.
Day, Clive A.
Gale, Anthony P.
Greenaway, Brian J.
Hatter, Steven
Hopkins, Jeffrey
Lewington, Raymond
Lock, Kevin J.
Mahoney, Anthony J.
O'Driscoll, Sean M.
O'Sullivan, Peter
Parker, Paul A.
Peters, Gary D.
Peyton, Gerald J.
Reeves, John C.
Scott, Peter R.
Stannard, James
Strong, Leslie
Tapley, Steven
Tempest, Dale M.
Wilson, Robert J.

League Appearances: Banton, G. 1; Beck, J. 4(1); Brown, R.W. 46; Coney, D.H. 42; Davies, G.J. 41; Day, C.A. 1(3); Gale, A.P. 44; Hopkins, J. 31(4); Lewington, R. 31; Lock, K.J. 25(1); O'Driscoll, S.M. 42; O'Sullivan, P. 45; Parker, P.A. 2(3); Peters, G.D. -(1); Peyton, G.J. 44; Reeves, J.C. 7; Scott, P.R. 1; Stannard, J. 2; Strong, L. 46; Tempest, D.M. 9(5); Wilson, R.J. 42(1).
Goals – League (77): Davies 24, Coney 13, Brown 12, O'Driscoll 7, Lock 5 (4 pens), Wilson 5, Lewington 4 (3 pens), Tempest 2, own goals 2, Beck 1, Gale 1, O'Sullivan 1.

League Cup (11): Coney 4, Wilson 3, Beck 1, Davies 1, Hopkins 1, Lewington 1.
FA Cup (2): Coney 2.
Ground: Craven Cottage, Stevenage Road, Fulham SW6 6HH (01-736 6561)
Nearest stations: Putney Bridge (District) or Hammersmith (Metropolitan, District and Piccadilly)
Manager: Malcolm Macdonald **Secretary:** George Noyce
Colours: White shirts; black shorts
Record home gate: 49,335 v Millwall, October 1938 (League)
Honours – Champions: Division 2: 1948-49; Division 3, South: 1931-32.
FA Cup winners: Nil

GILLINGHAM DIV. 3

Adams, Michael R.
Bottiglieri, Antonio
Bowman, Richard D.
Bruce, Stephen R.
Cascarino, Anthony G.
Duncan, Colin J.
Hillyard, Ronald W.
Lee, Trevor C.
Miller, Mark J.
Overton, John
Powell, Colin D.
Price, Kenneth G.
Sage, Melvyn
Sharpe, John W.H.
Shaw, Peter K.
Sitton, John E.
Sutton, Gary
Tydeman, Richard
Weatherly, Colin M.
White, Dean

League Appearances: Adams, M.R. 29(2); Bottiglieri, A. 2(2); Bowman, R.D. 18; Bruce, S.R. 45; Cascarino, A.G. 19(5); Donn, N. -(1); Duncan, C.J. 24(1); Ford, A.C. 20; Grewcock, N. 12(1); Hillyard, R.W. 44; Kemp, D.M. 9; Lee, T.C. 24(3); Miller, M.J. 4(1); Ovard, F.C. 4(2); Powell, C.D. 34; Price, K.G. 39; Sage, M. -(1); Sharpe, J.W.H. 37(2); Shaw, P.K. 16; Sitton, J.E. 29(1); Sutton, G. 2; Tydeman, R. 32(1); Weatherly, C.M. 32(1); Westwood, D.R. 3; White, D. 27(5); Young, C.F. 1(1).
Goals – League (64): Price 12, White 12 (3 pens), Lee 8, Bruce 6, Bowman 5 (2 pens), Cascarino 5, Adams 2, Duncan 2, Kemp 2, Sitton 2, own goals 2, Grewcock 1, Powell 1, Sharpe 1, Tydeman 1, Weatherly 1, Westwood 1.
League Cup (1): Price 1.
FA Cup (7): White 2 (1 pen), Bowman 1, Bruce 1, Kemp 1, Powell 1, Price 1.
Ground: Priestfield Stadium, Gillingham, Kent ME7 4DD (0634-51854)
Nearest station: Gillingham
Manager: Keith Peacock **Secretary:** R. J. Dennison
Colours: Blue shirts with white trim; white shorts with blue trim
Record home gate: 23,002 v Queens Park Rangers, January 1948 (FA Cup)
Honours – Champions: Division 4: 1963-64
FA Cup winners: Nil

GRIMSBY TOWN DIV. 2

Batch, Nigel A.
Beacock, Gary C.
Brolly, Michael J.
Cooper, Neil
Crombie, Dean M.
Crosby, Philip A.
Cumming, Robert
Drinkell, Kevin S.
Ford, Tony
Grotier, Peter D.
Kilmore, Kevin
Moore, David
Moore, Kevin T.
O'Dell, Andrew
Steeples, John
Stone, John G.
Waters, Joseph J.
Whymark, Trevor J.

League Appearances: Batch, N.A. 42; Beacock, G.C. 10(3); Brolly, M.J. 35(3); Cooper N. 16; Crombie, D.M. 38; Crosby, P.A. 14(1); Cumming, R. 23(1); Czuczman, M. 3; Drinkell, K.S. 23(5); Ford, T. 25(10); Kilmore, K. 23(7); Mitchell, R. 30; Moore, D. 34; Moore K.T. 36; O'Dell, A. 3; Steeples, J. 1(1); Stone, J.G. 21; Ward, J.P. 2(1); Waters, J.J.W. 35(1); Whymark, T.J. 28(5); Wigginton, C.A. 20.
Goals – League (53): Whymark 11 (1 pen), Ford 7, Waters 7 (4 pens), Drinkell 6, Kilmore 6, Moore, K. 4, Brolly 3, Cumming 2, Mitchell 2, Moore, D. 2, Cooper 1, Crosby 1, Wigginton 1.
League Cup (2): Moore, K. 1, Whymark 1.
FA Cup (9): Drinkell 3, Cumming 2, Brolly 1, Kilmore 1, Moore, K. 1, Whymark 1.
Ground: Blundell Park, Cleethorpes, DN35 7PY (0472-61420 and 61803)
Nearest stations: Cleethorpes or Grimsby Town
Manager: Dave Booth **Secretary:** D. J. Dowse
Colours: Black and white striped shirts; black shorts
Record home gate: 31,657 v Wolverhampton, February 1937 (FA Cup)
Honours – Champions: Division 2: 1900-01, 1933-34; Division 3 North: 1925-26, 1955-56; Division 3: 1979-80; Division 4: 1971-72
FA Cup winners: Nil

HALIFAX TOWN DIV. 4

Ayre, Willaim
Davison, Robert
Evans, David G.
Goodman, Malcolm J.
Hendrie, Paul
Smelt, Lee A.
Spooner, Stephen
Ward, Stephen C.

League Appearances: Allatt, V. 22(2); Ayre, W. 44; Bullock, S.J. 7(1); Carr, E.D. 35(3); Chamberlain, G. 35; Davison, R. 46; Evans, D.G. 46; Firth, F.M. 29(8); Goodman, M.J. 10; Graham, T. 36(1); Hendrie, P. 45; Kendall, P.S. 9(4); Keys, P. 1(1); Kilner, J.I. 12; McIlwraith, J.M. 4(3); O'Neill, T.P. 8(1); Smelt, L.A. 34; Spooner, S. 29; Walker, S. -(1); Ward, S.C. 44; Whiteley, A.M. 10(5).
Goals – League (51): Davison 19, Graham 8, Ward 7, Allatt 4, Ayre 4, Evans 3, Hendrie 2, Spooner 2, Firth 1, McIlwraith 1.
League Cup (1): Davison 1.
FA Cup: Nil
Ground: The Shay, Halifax HX1 2YS (Halifax 53423)
Nearest station: Halifax
Manager: Micky Bullock **Secretary:** M. G. Firth
Colours: Royal blue shirts with white trim; white shorts with blue trim
Record home gate: 36,885 v Tottenham, February 1953 (FA Cup)

Honours – Champions: Nil
FA Cup winners: Nil

HARTLEPOOL UNITED DIV. 4

Bird, John C.
Brown, Phillip
Burleigh, Martin S.
Clarke, Harry
Dobson, Paul
Fagan, Michael J.
Harding, Alan
Hogan, Roy D.
Howard, David F.
Johnson, Kevin P.
Lawrence, Mark
Linacre, John
Linacre, Phillip
Linighan, Andrew
Linighan, David
Loadwick, Derek
Lowe, Kenneth
McNamee, Gerard
Newton, Robert
Ramshaw, Trevor J.
Richardson, Graham
Staff, Paul
Stimpson, Barrie G.
Sweeney, Alan
Watson, John

League Appearances: Bainbridge, T. 9(1); Bird, J.C. 42; Brown, P. 42(2); Burleigh, M.S. 36; Clarke, H. 5(2); Dobson, P. 2(3); Fagan, M.J. 11; Hampton, D. 15(2); Harding, A. 10(3); Hogan, R.D. 36(3); Houchen, K. 32; Howard, D.F. 4(2); Johnson, K.P. 29(3); Kerr, R. 2(1); Lawrence M. 3(3); Linacre, J. 42; Linacre, P. 31(1); Linighan, A. 17; Linighan, D. 6; Lowe, K. 3(1); Newton, R. 34; Staff, P. 24(3); Stimpson, B.G. 29(1); Sweeney, A. 32; Watson, J. 10.
Goals – League (73): Houchen 18 (4 pens), Newton 15 (1 pen), Bird 5, Staff 5, Brown 4, Hampton 4, Hogan 4, Linacre, P. 4, Howard 3, Linacre, J. 3, Harding 2, Johnson 2, Bainbridge 1, Clarke 1, Fagan 1, Stimpson 1.
League Cup (2): Houchen 1, Newton 1.
FA Cup (3): Newton 2, Linacre, P. 1.
Ground: Victoria Ground, Clarence Road, Hartlepool (Hartlepool 72584)
Office: 18 Scarborough Street, Hartlepool TS24 7DA (Hartlepool 73492)
Nearest station: Hartlepool
Manager: Billy Horner **Secretary:** W. P. Hillan
Colours: Blue shirts with white stripes; white shorts
Record home gate: 17,426 v Manchester United, January 1957 (FA Cup)
Honours – Champions: Nil
FA Cup winners: Nil

HEREFORD UNITED DIV. 4

Brand, Andrew S.
Harvey, James
Hicks, Keith
Laidlaw, Joseph D.
Pejic, Melvyn
Phillips, Stewart G.
Price, Christopher J.
Showers, Derek
White, Eric W.

League Appearances: Ames, T. -(2); Bartley, D.R. 17; Binney, F. -(4); Brand, A.S. 32; Bray, I.M. 16; Cornes, J.S. 7; Dobson, I. 24; Dungworth, J.H. 7; Harvey, J. 42; Hicks, K. 42; Hughes, T.A. 14; Laidlaw, J.D. 42; Lane, S.B. 2(3); McGrellis, F. 6(3); Musial, A. 24; Overson, R.J. 5(3); Pejic, M. 27; Phillips, S.G. 43; Price, C.J. 41; Showers, D. 35; Spiring, P.J. 26(3); Sullivan, C. 8; White, E.W. 46.
Goals – League (64): Phillips 12, Price 10, White 8 (1 pen), Laidlaw 7, Showers 7, Harvey 5 (1 pen), Dobson 3, Dungworth 3, Bartley 2, Binney 2, Bray 2, McGrellis 1, Overson 1, Spiring 1.

League Cup (1): Phillips 1.
FA Cup (9): Harvey 2, Laidlaw 2, Phillips 2, Showers 2, Overson 1.
Ground: Edgar Street, Hereford HR4 9JU (Hereford (0432) 4037)
Nearest station: Hereford
Manager: F. Lord **Secretary:** J. Finney
Colours: White shirts with navy trim; navy blue shorts with white side stripe
Record home gate:-18,114 v Sheffield Wednesday, 1958 (FA Cup)
Honours – Champions: Division 3: 1975-76
FA Cup winners: Nil

HUDDERSFIELD TOWN — DIV. 3

Austin, Terence W.
Brown, Malcolm
Burke, David I.
Cowling, David R.
Hanvey, Keith
Kennedy, Michael F.M.
Lillis, Mark A.
Stanton, Brian
Starling, Alan
Sutton, David
Valentine, Peter
Wilson, Philip

League Appearances: Austin, T.W. 20(1); Bell, G.T.A. 2; Brown, M. 46; Burke, D.I. 41; Cowling, D.R. 36(2); Cox, B.R. 14; Fletcher, P. 22(4); Hanvey, K. 43; Hotte, T.M. 13(1); Kennedy, M.F.M. 39; Kindon, S.M. 10; Laverick, M.G. 4; Lillis, M.A. 42; Purdie, B.C. 11(4); Rankin, A.G. 19; Robins, I. 26(6); Stanton, B. 31; Sutton, D. 29; Taylor, R.H. 13; Valentine, P. 14; Wilson, P. 31(3).
Goals – League (64): Cowling 8, Fletcher 7, Kennedy 7 (4 pens), Robins 7, Lillis 5, own goals 5, Hanvey 4, Hotte 4, Kindon 3 (3 pens), Laverick 3, Stanton 3, Austin 2, Wilson 2, Brown 1, Burke 1, Purdie 1, Valentine 1.
League Cup (8): Fletcher 4, Austin 1, Kindon 1, Robins 1, Wilson 1.
FA Cup (11): Fletcher 3, Brown 2, Laverick 2, Austin 1, Cowling 1, Lillis 1, Robins 1.
Ground: Leeds Road, Huddersfield HD1 6PE (Huddersfield (0484) 20335/6)
Nearest station: Huddersfield
Team manager: Mick Buxton **Secretary:** G. S. Binns
Colours: Blue/white striped shirts; white shorts
Record home gate: 67,037 v Arsenal, February 1932 (FA Cup)
Honours – Champions: Division 1: 1923-24, 1924-25, 1925-26; Division 2: 1969-70; Division 3: 1979-80
FA Cup winners: 1921-22

HULL CITY — DIV. 4

Booth, Dennis
Davies, John G.
McClaren, Stephen
Marwood, Brian
Mutrie, Leslie A.M.
Richards, Stephen C.
Roberts, Garreth W.
Roberts, James D.

League Appearances: Booth, D. 37; Davies, J.G. 10; Davis, I. 18(2); Deacy, N.S. 25(5); Ecccleston, S.I. 13(1); Edwards, K. 5; Ferguson, J.B. 12(3); Flounders, A.J. 12(1); Hoolickin, S. 9; Horswill, M.F. 17(1); Kynman, D.J. 8; McClaren, S. 35(2); McNeil, R.M. 21; Marwood, B. 40(2); Mutrie, L.A.M. 43; Norman, A.J. 36; Norrie, C.T. 1; Parkinson, K.J. -(1); Richards, S.C. 28(1); Roberts, G.W. 29; Roberts, J.D. 34; Swann, G. 18(2); Thompson, N. 21(2); Whitehurst, W. 34(2).

Goals – League (70): Mutrie 27 (3 pens), Marwood 11, Whitehurst 7, Roberts (G) 6, Flounders 4, McClaren 4, Booth 2, Deacy 2, Ferguson 2, own goals 2, Davis 1, Edwards 1, Richards 1.
League Cup (1): Ferguson 1.
FA Cup (7): McClaren 2, Whitehurst 2, Marwood 1, Mutrie 1, Swann 1.
Ground: Boothferry Park, Hull HU4 6EU (0482-52195)
Nearest stations: Hull or Boothferry Park Halt
Manager: Colin Appleton **Secretary:** M. T. Stone
Colours: Black and amber striped shirts; black shorts
Record home gate: 55,019 v Manchester United, February 1949 (FA Cup)
Honours – Champions: Division 3 North: 1932-33, 1948-49; Division 3: 1965-66
FA Cup winners: Nil

IPSWICH TOWN DIV. 1

Barnes, David
Brazil, Alan B.
Burley, George E.
Burns, Ronald
Butcher, Terry I.
Cooper, Paul D.
D'Avray, Jean M.
Gates, Eric L.
Gernon, Frederick A.J.
Irving, Russell
Jackson, John K.
King, James R.
Kinsella, Anthony
Klug, Bryan P.
Linford, John R.
McCall, Stephen H.
Mariner, Paul
Mills, Michael D.
Osman, Russell C.
O'Callaghan, Kevin
Parkin, Thomas A.
Putney, Trevor A.
Sivell, Laurance
Steggles, Kevin P.
Templeton, Ian A.
Thijssen, Fransiscus J.
Turner, Robin D.
Wark, John
Westwood, Gary M.
Yallop, Frank W.

League Appearances: Brazil, A.B. 35; Burley, G.E. 29; Butcher, T.I. 27; Cooper, P.D. 32; D'Avray, J.M. 12(1); Gates, E.L. 38; Gernon, F.A.J. 4; Jackson, J.K. 1; McCall, S.H. 42; Mariner, P. 25; Mills, M.D. 42; Muhren, A.J.H. 42; O'Callaghan, K. 7(12); Osman, R.C. 39; Parkin, T.A. 5(1); Sivell, L. 9; Steggles, K.P. 18; Thijssen, F.J. 12; Turner, R.D. 1(2); Wark, J. 42.
Goals – League (75): Brazil 22, Wark 18 (5 pens), Gates 9, Mariner 8, Muhren 4, Mills 3, D'Avray 2, Osman 2, own goals 2, Butcher 1, McCall 1, O'Callaghan 1, Steggles 1, Thijssen 1.
League Cup (15): Gates 4, Brazil 3, Wark 3, Mariner 1, Muhren 1, O'Callaghan 1, Steggles 1, Turner 1.
FA Cup (7): Brazil 3, Gates 2, D'Avray 1, Wark 1.
Ground: Portman Road, Ipswich IP1 2DA (Ipswich 219211)
Nearest station: Ipswich
Manager: Bobby Ferguson **Secretary:** D. C. Rose
Colours: Blue shirts with white trim; white shorts with three blue stripes
Record home gate: 38,010 v Leeds United, March 1975 (FA Cup)
Honours – Champions: Division 1: 1961-62; Division 2: 1960-61, 1967-68; Division 3 South: 1953-54, 1956-57
FA Cup winners: 1977-78

LEEDS UNITED DIV. 2

Barnes, Peter S.
Burns, Kenneth
Butterworth, Aidan J.
Cherry, Trevor J.
Connor, Terence F.
Dickinson, Martin J.
Firm, Neil J.
Flynn, Brian
Graham, Arthur
Gray, Edwin
Gray, Francis T.
Hamson, Gary
Harris, Carl S.
Hart, Paul A.
Hill, Gerald A.
Hinchcliffe, Mark
Hird, Kevin
Lukic, Jovan
MacRae, Keith A.
Parlane, Derek J.
Peel, Robert
Seaman, David A.
Sheridan, John J.
Thacker, Colin
Thomas, David G.
Worthington, Frank S.

League Appearances: Arins, A.F. –(1); Aspin, N. 1; Balcombe, S.W. 1; Barnes, P.S. 30; Burns, K. 22(1); Butterworth, A.J. 13(1); Cherry, T.J. 38; Connor, T.F. 23(4); Firm, N.J. 3; Flynn, B. 16(1); Graham, A. 38; Gray, E. 29; Gray, F.T. 36(1); Greenhoff, B. 10(2); Hamson, G. 17(1); Harris, C.S. 16(3); Hart, P.A. 32; Hird, K. 35(3); Lukic, J. 42; Parlane, D.J. 12; Stevenson, W.B. 18(1); Thomas, D.G. 13(2); Worthington, F.S. 17.
Goals – League (39): Graham 9, Worthington 9 (2 pens), Connor 4, Butterworth 3, Cherry 2, Hamson 2, Hird 2 (1 pen), Parlane 2, Balcombe 1, Barnes 1, Flynn 1, Gray, E. 1, Hart 1, Stevenson 1.
League Cup: Nil.
FA Cup (3): Gray, E. 1, Hamson 1, Hird 1.
Ground: Elland Road, Leeds LS11 0ES (0532-716037/9)
Nearest station: Leeds
Player-Manager: Frank Gray **General manager/Secretary:** K. Archer
Colours: White shirts, blue and yellow trim; white shorts with blue and yellow trim
Record home gate: 57,892 v Sunderland, March 1967 (FA Cup)
Honours – Champions: Division 1: 1968-69, 1973-74; Division 2: 1923-24, 1963-64
FA Cup winners: 1971-72
League Cup winners: 1967-68
European Fairs Cup winners: 1967-68, 1970-71

LEICESTER CITY DIV. 2

Buchanan, David
Cliff, Barry
Friar, John P.
Gibson, William
Grewcock, Neil
Hamill, Stewart
Hill, Richard
Kelly, Edward P.
Leet, Norman D.
Lineker, Gary W.
Lynex, Stephen C.
MacDonald, Kevin D.
May, Lawrence C.
Melrose, James M.
O'Neill, John P.
Peake, Andrew M.
Pell, Richard T.
Ramsey, Paul
Robson, Keith
Sherwood, Ian
Smith, Robert
Thomson, Derek
Walker, Joseph N.
Wallington, Francis M.
Welsh, Peter M.
Williams, Thomas E.
Wilson, Ian W.
Young, Alexander F.

League Appearances: Buchanan, D. –(1); Friar, J.P. 23; Gibson, W. 8; Hamill, S. 2;

Hebberd, T.N. 4; Kelly, E.P. 14; Leet, N.D. 17; Lineker, G.W. 37(2); Lynex, S.C. 37(4); MacDonald, K.D. 24(1); May, L.C. 34; Melrose, J.M. 24(11); O'Neill, J.P. 41; Peake, A.M. 31; Ramsey, P. 10; Robson, K. 8; Scott, G.S. 7; Smith, R. 2(2); Walker, J.N. 6; Wallington, F.M. 36; Welsh, P.M. 7(9); Williams, T.E. 31; Wilson, I.W. 35; Young, A.F. 24.
Goals – League (56): Lineker 17, Melrose 11, Lynex 10 (5 pens), Young 5, Welsh 4 (1 pen), May 3, Hamill 2, Peake 2, Hebberd 1, MacDonald 1.
League Cup (4): Lynex 1, Melrose 1, Robson 1, own goal 1.
FA Cup (11): Young 3, Lineker 2, May 2, Melrose 1, O'Neill 1, own goal 1.
Ground: City Stadium, Filbert Street, Leicester LE2 7FL (Leicester 555000/2; match information 551155)
Nearest station: Leicester
Manager: Jock Wallace **General secretary:** A. K. Bennett
Colours: Blue shirts with white collar and cuffs; white shorts
Record home gate: 47,298 v Tottenham Hotspur, February 1928 (FA Cup)
Honours – Champions: Division 2: 1924-25, 1936-37, 1953-54, 1956-57, 1970-71, 1979-80
FA Cup winners: Nil
League Cup winners: 1963-64

LINCOLN CITY — DIV. 3

Beavon, David
Bell, Derek M.
Carr, David
Cockerill, Glenn
Creane, Gerard M.
Cunningham, Anthony E.
Felgate, David W.
Hibberd, Stuart
Hobson, Gordon
Naylor, Stuart W.
Neale, Phillip A.
Peake, Trevor
Rodgers, David M.
Shipley, George M.
Thompson, Steven P.
Turner, Philip

League Appearances: Beavon, D. 7; Bell, D.M. 11(3); Cammack, S.R. 18; Carr, D. 46; Cockerill, G. 43(1); Creane, G.M. 2; Cunningham, A.E. 46; Felgate, D.W. 43; Gilbert, D.J. 15(14); Hibberd, S. 23(2); Hobson, G. 31(1); McVay, D.R. 13; Naylor, S.W. 3; Neale, P.A. 31(1); Peake, T. 37; Rodgers, D.M. 3; Shipley, G.M. 43; Smith, L.J. 5; Thompson, J.T. 12; Thompson, S.P. 30; Turner, P. 27(1); Turner, W.L. 16; Ward, J.P. 1.
Goals – League (66): Cockerill 11, Cunningham 11, Shipley 11 (7 pens), Hobson 7, Cammack 6, Bell 5, Peake 4, Hibberd 3 (2 pens), Thompson, S. 2, own goals 2, Carr 1, Gilbert 1, Neale 1, Turner, P. 1.
League Cup (12): Cunningham 4, Shipley 3, Carr 1, Cockerill 1, Hobson 1, Peake 1, Turner, P. 1.
FA Cup (2): Cammack 1, Thompson, S. 1.
Ground: Sincil Bank, Lincoln LN5 8LD (Lincoln 222245)
Nearest stations: Lincoln Central and St Mark's
Manager: Colin Murphy **Secretary:** J. H. Sorby
Colours: Red and white striped shirts; black shorts
Record home gate: 23,196 v Derby, November 1967 (League Cup)
Honours – Champions: Division 3 North: 1931-32, 1947-48, 1951-52; Division 4: 1975-76
FA Cup winners: Nil

LIVERPOOL DIV. 1

Dalglish, Kenneth M.
Foley, Stephen
Gayle, Howard
Grobbelaar, Bruce D.
Halsall, Michael
Hansen, Alan D.
Harper, Alan
Johnson, David E.
Johnston, Craig P.
Kennedy, Alan P.
Lawrenson, Mark T.
Lee, Samuel
McDermott, Terence
Neal, Philip G.
Nicol, Stephen
Ogrizovic, Steven
Rush, Ian J.
Russell, Colin
Savage, Robert J.
Sheedy, Kevin M.
Souness, Graeme J.
Thompson, Philip B.
Whelan, Ronald A.

League Appearances: Dalglish, K.M. 42; Grobbelaar, B.D. 42; Hansen, A.D. 35; Johnson, D.E. 10(5); Johnston, C.P. 13(5); Kennedy, A.P. 32(2); Kennedy, R. 15; Lawrenson, M.T. 37(2); Lee, S. 35; McDermott, T. 28(1); Neal, P.G. 42; Rush, I.J. 32; Sheedy, K.M. –(2); Souness, G.J. 34(1); Thompson, P.B. 34; Whelan, R.A. 31(1).
Goals – League (80): Rush 17, McDermott 14 (4 pens), Dalglish 13, Whelan 10, Johnston 6, Souness 5, Kennedy, A. 3, Lee 3, Johnson 2, Kennedy, R. 2, Lawrenson 2, Neal 2 (2 pens), own goal 1.
League Cup (28): Rush 8, Dalglish 5, Johnson 3, McDermott 3 (1 pen), Whelan 3, Sheedy 2, Johnston 1, Neal 1, Souness 1, own goal 1.
FA Cup (7): Rush 3, Dalglish 2, Hansen 1, Lawrenson 1.
Ground: Anfield Road, Liverpool L4 0TH (051-263 2361/2)
Nearest stations: All stations, Liverpool
Manager: Bob Paisley **Secretary:** P. Robinson
Colours: Red shirts with white trim; red shorts
Record home gate: 61,905 v Wolverhampton, February, 1952 (FA Cup)
Honours – Champions: Division 1: 1900-1, 1905-06, 1921-22, 1922-23, 1946-47, 1963-64, 1965-66, 1972-73, 1975-76, 1976-77, 1978-79 1981-82; Division 2: 1893-94, 1895-96, 1904-05, 1961-62
FA Cup winners: 1964-65, 1973-74
League Cup winners: 1980-81, 1981-82
European Champions Cup: 1976-77, 1977-78, 1980-81
UEFA Cup winners: 1972-73, 1975-76
Super Cup winners: 1977

LUTON TOWN DIV. 1

Aizlewood, Mark
Antic, Radomir
Beasley, Andrew
Bunn, Frankie S.
Donaghy, Malachy
Findlay, John W.
Fuccillo, Pasquale
Goodyear, Clive
Heath, Seamus J.M.P.
Hill, Ricky A.
Horton, Brian
Johnson, Robert S.
Judge, Alan G.
Money, Richard
Moss, David J.
Saxby, Michael W.
Small, Michael A.
Stein, Brian
Stephens, Kirk W.
Turner, Wayne L.
White, Stephen J.

League Appearances: Aizelwood, M. 26; Aleksic, M.A. 4; Antic, R. 17(13); Bunn, F.S. –(2); Donaghy, M. 42; Findlay, J.W. 34; Fuccillo, P. 27(2); Goodyear, C. 32; Hill, R.A. 38; Horton, B. 41; Ingram, G.P.A. 3; Jennings, W.J. –(2); Judge, A.G. 4; Money, R. 13; Moss, D.J. 36; Saxby, M.W. 12; Small, M.A. –(3); Stein, B. 42; Stephens, K.W. 42; Turner, W.L. 7; White, S.J. 42.
Goals – League (86): Stein 21 (2 pens), White 19, Moss 16 (11 pens), Donaghy 9, Antic 5, Hill 5, Aizelwood 3, Horton 2, own goals 2, Jennings 1, Money 1, Saxby 1, Turner 1.
League Cup (1): White 1.
FA Cup (2): Horton 1, Moss 1 (pen).
Ground: 70-72 Kenilworth Road, Luton LU1 1DH (Luton (0582) 411622)
Nearest station: Luton
Manager: David Pleat **Secretary:** John Wilkinson
Colours: White shirts with orange collar and cuffs with three navy blue and two orange vertical stripes; white shorts with two orange and three navy blue vertical stripes
Record home gate: 30,069 v Blackpool, March 1959 (FA Cup)
Honours – Champions: Division 2: 1981-82; Division 3 South: 1936-37; Division 4: 1967-68
FA Cup winners: Nil

MANCHESTER CITY — DIV. 1

Bond, Kevin J.
Boyer, Philip J.
Caton, Thomas
Corrigan, Joseph T.
Francis, Trevor J.
Hareide, Age F.
Hartford, Richard A.
Hutchison, Thomas
Jackson, Gary
Kinsey, Stephen
Lomax, Geoffrey W.
McDonald, Robert W.
May, Andrew
Power, Paul C.
Ranson, Raymond
Reeves, Kevin P.
Ryan, John G.
Tueart, Dennis
Wiffill, David P.
Williams, Alexander
Wilson, Clive

League Appearances: Bond, K.J. 32(1); Booth, T.A. 1; Boyer, P.J. 10(2); Caton, T. 39; Corrigan, J.T. 39; Elliott, A. 1; Francis, T.J. 26; Gow, G. 6; Hareide, A.F. 9(7); Hartford, R.A. 30; Henry, A. –(2); Hutchison, T. 20(2); Jackson, G. 6(2); Kinsey, S. 13(3); McDonald, R.W. 36; May, A. 3(3); O'Neill, M.H.M. 12(1); Power, P.C. 25; Ranson, R. 36; Reeves, K.P. 42; Reid, N.S. 36; Ryan, J.G. 19; Tueart, D. 15; Williams, A. 3; Wilson, C. 3(1).
Goals – League (49): Reeves 13, Francis 12, Tueart 9 (2 pens), McDonald 4, Bond 3 (2 pens), Hartford 3, Boyer 1, Caton 1, Hutchison 1, Power 1, own goal 1.
League Cup (5): Tueart 2, Hartford 1, McDonald 1, own goal 1.
FA Cup (4): Francis 2, Bond 1 (pen), McDonald 1.
Ground: Maine Road, Moss Side, Manchester M14 7WN (061-226 1191/2)
Nearest station: Manchester Piccadilly
Manager: John Bond **Secretary:** J. B. Halford
Colours: Sky blue shirts with white trim; sky blue shorts
Record home gate: 84,569 v Stoke City, March 1934 (FA Cup)
Honours – Champions: Division 1: 1936-37, 1967-68; Division 2: 1898-99, 1902-03, 1909-10, 1927-28, 1946-47, 1965-66

FA Cup winners: 1903-04, 1933-34, 1955-56, 1968-69
League Cup winners: 1969-70, 1975-76
European Cup Winners' Cup: 1969-70

MANCHESTER UNITED — DIV. 1

Albiston, Arthur R.
Bailey, Gary R.
Birtles, Garry
Buchan, Martin M.
Coppell, Stephen J.
Davies, Alan
Dempsey, Mark J.
Duxbury, Michael
Gidman, John
Grimes, Augustine A.
Hughes, Leslie M.
Jovanovic, Nikola
Keough, Daniel P.
Macari, Luigi
McGarvey, Scott T.
McGrath, Paul
McQueen, Gordon
Moran, Kevin B.
Moses, Remi M.
Muhren, Arnoldus J.H.
Pears, Stephen
Reynolds, Michael A.
Robson, Bryan
Sloan, Thomas
Stapleton, Francis A.
Whelan, Anthony G.
Wilkins, Raymond C.
Worrall, Garry G.
Wynn, David

League Appearances: Albiston, A.R. 42; Bailey, G.R. 39; Birtles, G. 32(1); Buchan, M.M. 27; Coppell, S.J. 35(1); Davies, A. 1; Duxbury, M. 19(5); Gidman, J. 36(1); Grimes, A.A. 9(2); McGarvey, S.T. 10(6); McIlroy, S.B. 12; McQueen, G. 21; Macari, L. 10(1); Moran, K.B. 30; Moses, R.M. 20(1); Nicholl, J.M. –(1); Robson, B. 32; Roche, P.J. 3; Stapleton, F.A. 41; Whiteside, N. 1(1); Wilkins, R.C. 42.
Goals – League (59): Stapleton 13 (1 pen), Birtles 11, Coppell 9 (1 pen), Moran 7, Robson 5, McIlroy 3, McGarvey 2, Macari 2, Moses 2, Albiston 1, Gidman 1, Grimes 1, Whiteside 1, Wilkins 1.
League Cup: Nil.
FA Cup: Nil.
Ground: Old Trafford, Manchester M16 0RA (061-872 1661/2)
Nearest stations: All stations Manchester
Manager: Ron Atkinson **Secretary:** R. L. Olive
Colours: Red shirts with red and white trim; white shorts
Record home gate: 76,962, FA Cup semi-final (Wolverhampton v Grimsby Town) March 1939; **Club:** 70,504 v Aston Villa, December 1920 (League)
Honours – Champions: Division 1: 1907-08, 1910-11, 1951-52, 1955-56, 1956-57, 1964-65, 1966-67; Division 2: 1935-36, 1974-75
FA Cup winners: 1908-09, 1947-48, 1962-63, 1976-77
European Champions Cup: 1967-68

MANSFIELD TOWN — DIV. 4

Arnold, Roderick J.
Bell, Ian C.
Bird, Kevin
Boam, Stuart
Calderwood, Colin
Caldwell, David W.
Cannell, Paul A.
Nicholson, Gary A.
Parkinson, Noel D.
Woodhead, Simon C.

League Appearances: Arnold, R.J. 45; Bell, I.C. 45; Bird, K. 25(1); Boam, S. 4(4); Brown G.C. 1; Burrows, A.M. 41; Calderwood, C. 1; Caldwell, D.W. 31(2); Cannell, P.A. 23; Foster, B. 28; Lumby, J.A. 38(1); McJannett, W.L. 37(1); Mann, A.F. 35(2); Morgan, T.J. 12; Nicholson, G.A. 37(1); Parkinson, N.D. 31(4); Thomson, B.L. 25(4); Wood, I.N. 36; Woodhead, S.C. 11(1).
Goals – League (63): Lumby 14, Caldwell 9, Parkinson 9 (4 pens), Morgan 6, Bell 5, Nicholson 5, Cannell 4, Wood 4, Burrows 3, Bird 2, Boam 1, Mann 1.
League Cup (6): Lumby 3, Bird 1, Wood 1, own goal 1.
FA Cup: Nil.
Ground: Field Mill, Quarry Lane, Mansfield (Mansfield 23567)
Nearest stations: Alfreton and Mansfield Parkway
Player/Manager: Stuart Boam **Secretary:** J. D. Eaton
Colours: Amber shirts with blue trim; blue shorts
Record home gate: 24,467 v Nottingham Forest, January 1953 (FA Cup)
Honours – Champions: Division 3: 1976-77; Division 4: 1974-75
FA Cup winners: Nil

MIDDLESBROUGH DIV. 2

Angus, Michael A.
Bailey, Ian C.
Baxter, Michael J.
Bolton, Joseph
Cochrane, George T.
Currie, David M.
Hodgson, David J.
Jankovic, Bozo
McAndrew, Anthony
McClurg, David B.
MacDonald, Garry
Mowbray, Anthony M.
Nattrass, Irving
O'Hanlon, Kelham G.
Otto, Hendrikus M.
Platt, James A.
Ross, Colin
Shearer, David J.
Thomas, David
Thomson, Robert
Wood, Darren T.

League Appearances: Angus, M.A. 14; Ashcroft, W. 14(7); Askew, W. 6; Bailey, I.C. 26; Baxter, M.J. 40; Bell, S. 1; Bolton, J. 27; Cochrane, G.T. 22(3); Craggs, J.E. 23; Currie, D.N. –(1); Hedley, G. 3; Hodgson, D.J. 31(3); McAndrew, A. 39; McCreesh, A. 2; MacDonald, G. 4(4); Nattrass, I. 27; Otto, H.M. 40; Platt, J.A. 42; Ross, C. 22; Shearer, D.J. 20(4); Thomas, D. 13; Thomson, R. 18(2); Wood, D.T. 11; Woof, W. 17(6).
Goals – League (34): Ashcroft 4, McAndrew 4 (4 pens), Otto 4, Woof 4, Hodgson 3, Shearer 3, Baxter 2, Thomson 2, (1 pen), own goals 2, Angus 1, Bailey 1, Bolton 1, Cochrane 1, MacDonald 1, Thomas 1.
League Cup (3): Ashcroft 1, Shearer 1, Thomson 1.
FA Cup (3): Thomson 2, Otto 1.
Ground: Ayresome Park, Middlesbrough TS1 4PB (Middlesbrough 89659 and 85996)
Nearest station: Middlesbrough
Manager: Bobby Murdoch **Secretary:** T. H. C. Green
Colours: Red shirts with 3 narrow white stripes down sleeve; red shorts with 3 narrow white stripes
Record home gate: 53,596 v Newcastle United, December 1949 (League)
Honours – Champions: Division 2: 1926-27, 1928-29, 1973-74
FA Cup winners: Nil

MILLWALL DIV. 3

Allardyce, Samuel
Anderson, Peter T.
Chatterton, Nicholas J.
Gleasure, Peter
Hayes, Austin W.P.
Horrix, Dean V.
Kitchener, Barry R.
McCleary, Alan T.
Madden, Lawrence D.
Martin, David
Massey, Andrew
Neal, Dean J.
Roberts, Paul A.
Robinson, Paul
Sansome, Paul E.
Shinton, Robert T.
Stevens, Keith
Warman, Philip R.
West, Alan

League Appearances: Allardyce, S. 36; Anderson, P.T. 17(1); Bartley, J.R. 12; Chatterton, N.J. 44(1); Dibble, C. 19(7); Gleasure, P. 38; Hayes, A.W.P. 19(4); Horrix, D.V. 42(2); Kitchener, B.R. 3; McKenna, A.M. 6; Madden, L.D. 10; Martin, D. 36(2); Massey, A. 25(4); Neal, D.J. 18(4); Paddon, G.C. 5; Roberts, P.A. 41; Robinson, P. 5; Sansome, P.E. 8; Shinton, R.T. 18; Slough, A.P. 14; Stevens, K. 7; Tagg, A.P. 11; Warman, P.R. 27; West, A. 45.
Goals – League (62): Horrix 15, Chatterton 12 (6 pens), Tagg 5, Neal 4, West 4, Anderson 3, Dibble 3, Shinton 3, own goals 3, Hayes 2, Massey 2, Allardyce 1, Bartley 1, McKenna 1, Martin 1, Paddon 1, Warman 1.
League Cup (7): Horrix 3, Dibble 2, Chatterton 1, West 1.
FA Cup (7): Chatterton 3 (1 pen), Allardyce 2, Hayes 1, Neal 1.
Ground: The Den, Cold Blow Lane, London SE14 5RH (01-639 3143/4)
Nearest stations: New Cross or New Cross Gate (SR and Metropolitan line)
Manager: Peter Anderson **Secretary:** G. I. S. Hortop
Colours: Blue shirts with white trim; white shorts with blue trim
Record home gate: 48,672 v Derby County, February 1937 (FA Cup)
Honours – Champions: Division 3 South: 1927-28, 1937-38; Division 4: 1961-62
FA Cup winners: Nil

NEWCASTLE UNITED DIV. 2

Barton, David
Bell, Derek S.
Brownlie, John
Carney, Stephen
Carr, Kevin
Cartwright, Peter
Haddock, Peter M.
Halliday, Bruce
Hardwick, Steven
Hedworth, Christopher
Johnson, Peter E.
Martin, Michael P.
Robson, Justin
Saunders, Wesley
Todd, Kevin
Tredwick, John
Varadi, Imre
Waddle, Christopher R.
Wharton, Kenneth
Withe, Christopher

League Appearances: Barton, D. 20; Bell, D.S. 2; Brownlie, J. 38; Brown, A. 5; Carney, S. 27(1); Carr, K. 42; Cartwright, P. 16(1); Davies, I.C. 13; Ferris, P.J. -(2); Haddock, P.M. 28(2); Halliday, B. 13; Martin, M.P. 37(2); Mills, D.J. 23; Pugh, K.J. -(1); Saunders, W. 29; Shinton, R.T. 8(1); Shoulder, A. 3(7); Todd, K. 1(1); Trewick, J. 40; Varadi, I. 42; Waddle, C.R. 42; Walker, N.S. 5; Wharton, K. 28(5).
Goals – League (52): Varadi 18, Waddle 7, Trewick 6, (3 pens), Wharton 5, Mills 4 (1 pen), Brown 3, Brownlie 2, Davies 2 (1 pen), Shinton 2, Todd 2, Barton 1.
League Cup (1): Barton 1.
FA Cup (6): Varadi 2, Brownlie 1, Saunders 1, Waddle 1, own goal 1.

Ground: St James' Park, Newcastle-upon-Tyne NE1 4ST (Newcastle (0632) 28361 answer service 611571)
Nearest station: Newcastle
Manager: Arthur Cox **Secretary:** R. Cushing
Colours: Black and white vertical striped shirts; black shorts
Record home gate: 68,386 v Chelsea, September 1930 (League)
Honours – Champions: Division 1: 1904-5, 1906-07, 1908-09, 1926-27; Division 2: 1964-65
FA Cup winners: 1909-10, 1923-24, 1931-32, 1950-51, 1951-52, 1954-55
European Fairs' Cup winners: 1968-69
Anglo-Italian Cup winners: 1973

NEWPORT COUNTY — DIV. 3

Aldridge, John W.
Bailey, Neil
Bishop, Raymond J.
Davies, Grant
Elsey, Karl W.
Gwyther, David W.J.
Johnson, Jeffrey D.
Kendall, Mark
Lees, Terrence
Lowndes, Stephen R.
Moore, Kevin J.
Oakes, Keith B.
Relish, John D.
Thomas, Roderick J.
Tynan, Thomas E.
Vaughan, Nigel M.
Watson, Ian

League Appearances: Aldridge, J.W. 32(4); Bailey, N. 17(1); Bishop, R.J. 5(6); Davies, G. 41; Elsey, K.W. 40; Goddard, H.J. 4; Gwyther, D.W.J. 20(6); Johnson, J.D. 34; Kendall, M. 46; Lees, T. 25; Lowndes, S.R. 28(3); Moore, K.J. 28(1); Oakes, K.B. 45; Relish, J.D. 27; Thomas, R.J. 3; Tynan, T.E. 32(6); Vaughan, N.M. 44; Waddle, A. 11(7); Walden, R.F. 23.
Goals – League (54): Tynan 13 (5 pens), Aldridge 11, Elsey 7, Waddle 4, Gwyther 3, Lowndes 3, Vaughan 3, Bishop 2, Johnson 2, Moore 2, own goals 2, Goddard 1, Oakes 1.
League Cup (3): Aldridge 1, Moore 1, Oakes 1.
FA Cup: Nil
Ground: Somerton Park, Newport, Gwent NPT OHZ (Newport 277543 and 277271)
Nearest station: Newport
Manager: Colin Addison **Secretary:** P. Dauncey
Colours: Amber shirts; black shorts
Record home gate: 24,268 v Cardiff, October 1937 (League)
Honours – Champions: Division 3 South: 1938-39
FA Cup winners: Nil

NORTHAMPTON TOWN — DIV. 4

Belfon, Frank
Brady, Paul J.
Buchanan, John
Coffill, Peter T.
Denyer, Peter R.
Gage, Wakeley A.J.
Massey, Stephen
Sandy, Adam V.C.
Saunders, Paul B.
Saxby, Gary P.

League Appearances: Alexander, J.E. 21(1); Belfon, F. 1; Bowen, K. 3; Brady, P.J. 38(1); Bryant, S.P. 10; Buchanan, J. 34; Carlton, D.G. 37; Coffill, P.T. 34(2);

Denyer, P.R. 22; Farmer, K.J. 4; Gage, W.A.J. 43; Heeley, D.M. 23(3); Kruse, P.K. 18; Mahoney, A.J. 6; Massey, S. 18; Muir M.M. -(1); Perrin, S. 18; Phillips, S.E. 30; Poole, A.J. 46; Russell, R.F. -(1); Sandy, A.V.C. 30(9); Saunders, P.B. 21(3); Saxby, G.P. 32(2); Taylor, A.I. 17.

Goals – League (57): Phillips 10 (2 pens), Saxby 7, Denyer 5 (2 pens), Massey 5 (1 pen), Perrin 5, Alexander 4, Buchanan 4, Sandy 4, own goals 4, Heeley 3, Brady 2, Coffill 2, Gage 2.

League Cup (9): Denyer 2, Mahoney 2, Alexander 1, Heeley 1, Phillips 1, Sandy 1, Saxby 1.

FA Cup (6): Gage 2, Carlton 1, Mahoney 1, Phillips 1, Sandy 1.

Ground: County Ground, Abington Avenue, Northampton NN1 4PS (Northampton (0604) 31553)

Nearest station: Northampton

Manager: Clive Walker **Secretary/General manager:** Dave Bowen

Colours: White shirts with claret trim; claret shorts

Record home gate: 24,523 v Fulham, April 1966 (League)

Honours – Champions: Division 3: 1962-63

FA Cup winners: Nil

NORWICH CITY — DIV. 1

Alexander, Philip J.
Baker, Clive E.
Barham, Mark F.
Bennett, David P.
Bertschin, Keith E.
Deehan, John
Fashanu, John
Haylock, Paul
Jack, James R.
McGuire, Michael
Mendham, Peter S.
Mountford, Peter
Muzinic, Drazen
O'Neill, Martin H.M.
Reid, Grant J.
Royle, Joseph
Shepherd, Jamie G.
Symonds, Richard
Walford, Stephen J.
Watson, David
Woods, Christopher

League Appearances: Barham, M.F. 25(2); Bennett, D.P. 21(1); Bertschin, K.E. 35(1); Deehan, J. 22; Donachie, W. 11; Downs, G. 28; Fashanu, J. 4(1); Hart, A. -(1); Haylock, P. 21; Hoadley, P.H.W. 3(1); Jack, J.R. 24(11); McGuire, M. 39; Mendham, P.S. 25(4); Mountford, P. -(2); Muzinic, D. 6(1); Nightingale, M.B.D. 8(1); O'Neill, M.H.M. 20; Paddon, G.C. 8; Royle, J. 2; Shepherd, J.G. 12(3); Symonds, R. 18; Walford, S.J. 42; Watson, D. 38; Woods, C. 42; Woods, C.R. 8.

Goals – League (64): Bertschin 12 (1 pen), Deehan 10 (1 pen), Jack 10 (2 pens), Mendham 6, O'Neill 6, Barham 4, Bennett 3, Watson 3, McGuire 2, Shepherd 2, own goals 2, Downs 1, Fashanu 1, Walford 1, Woods, (Clive) 1.

League Cup (2): Jack 2.

FA Cup (3): Jack 2, Watson 1.

Ground: Carrow Road Stadium, Norwich NR1 1JE (Norwich 612131)

Nearest station: Norwich

Manager: Ken Brown **Secretary:** A. E. Westwood

Colours: Yellow shirts, green collar and cuffs; green shorts with yellow trim

Record home gate: 43,984 v Leicester, March 1963 (FA Cup)

Honours – Champions: Division 2: 1971-72; Division 3 South: 1933-34

FA Cup winners: Nil

League Cup winners: 1961-62

NOTTINGHAM FOREST DIV. 1

Aas, Einar J.
Anderson, Vivian A.
Bowyer, Ian
Davenport, Peter
Fairclough, Courtney H.
Fashanu, Justinus S.
Gray, Stuart
Gunn, Brynley C.
Hodge, Stephen B.
Kendal, Stephen J.
McKechnie, James G.
Plummer, Calvin A.
Proctor, Mark G.
Röber, Hans J.
Robertson, John N.
Shilton, Peter L.
Sutton, Stephen J.
Thrower, Nigel J.
Wallace, Ian A.
Walsh, Colin D.
Wigley, Steven
Young, William D.

League Appearances: Aas, E.J. 14; Anderson, V.A. 39; Bowyer, I. 23(1); Burns, K. 7; Davenport, P. 5; Fashanu, J.S. 31(1); Francis, T.J. 2; Gray, S. 32(1); Gunn, B.C. 36(1); Hodge, S.B. 1; Kendal, S.J. 1; McGovern, J.P. 26(4); Mills, G.R. 13(1); Needham, D.W. 17; Plummer, C.A. 7(2); Proctor, M.G. 35(2); Röber, H-J. 21(1); Robertson, J.N. 36; Shilton, P.L. 41; Sutton, S.J. 1; Wallace, I.A. 28(1); Walsh, C.D. 7(8); Ward, P.D. 14(1); Young, W.D. 25.
Goals – League (42): Wallace 9, Ward 5 (1 pen), Davenport 4, Fashanu 3, Röber 3, Walsh 3, Francis 2, Gray 2, Needham 2, Plummer 2, Robertson 2 (2 pens), Bowyer 1, Burns 1, Mills 1, Proctor 1, Young 1.
League Cup (8): Wallace 3, Fashanu 1, Needham 1, Proctor 1, Röber 1, Robertson 1.
FA Cup (1): Proctor 1.
Ground: City Ground, Nottingham NG2 5FJ (Nottingham (0602) 868236/8; Information Desk 860232)
Nearest station: Nottingham
Manager: Brian Clough **Secretary:** K. Smales
Colours: Red shirts; white shorts
Record home gate: 49,945 v Manchester United, October, 1967 (League)
Honours – Champions: Division 1: 1977-78; Division 2: 1906-07, 1921-22; Division 3 South: 1950-51
FA Cup winners: 1897-98, 1958-59
League Cup winners: 1977-78, 1978-79
European Champions Cup: 1978-79, 1979-80

NOTTS COUNTY DIV. 1

Avramovic, Radojko
Benjamin, Tristan
Chiedozie, John O.
Christie, Trevor
Goodwin, Mark A.
Harkouk, Rachid P.
Hooks, Paul
Hunt, David
Kilcline, Brian
Lahtinen, Aki A.
Leonard, Michael C.
McCulloch, John
McParland, John
Mair, Gordon
Manns, Paul
O'Brian, Raymond
Richards, Peter
Wood, Gary T.
Worthington, Nigel

League Appearances: Avramovic, R. 42; Benjamin, T. 41; Chiedozie, J.O. 32; Christie, T. 24(11); Goodwin, M.A. 36(2); Harkouk, R.P. 17(1); Hooks, P. 28; Hunt, D. 26(4); Kilcline, B. 36; Lahtinen, A.A. 5(3); McCulloch, J. 39(1); McParland, J. 7(5); Mair, G. 32(2); Masson, D.S. 16; O'Brien, R. 39; Richards, P. 40; Worthington, N. 2.

Goals – League (61): McCulloch 16, Christie 13 (1 pen), Mair 9, Goodwin 4, Harkouk 4 (1 pen), Hooks 3, Hunt 3, Kilcline 3, own goals 2, Chiedozie 1, Masson 1, O'Brien 1 (pen), Richards 1.
League Cup (3): Hooks 1, Mair 1, Masson 1.
FA Cup: Nil
Ground: Meadow Lane, Nottingham NG2 3HJ (Nottingham (0602) 868494, information service 864152)
Nearest station: Nottingham
Manager: Jimmy Sirrel **Secretary:** Dennis Marshall
Colours: Black and white striped shirts; black shorts
Record home gate: 47,310 v York, March 1955 (FA Cup)
Honours – Champions: Division 2: 1896-97, 1913-14, 1922-23; Division 3 South: 1930-31, 1949-50; Division 4: 1970-71
FA Cup winners: 1893-94

OLDHAM ATHLETIC — DIV. 2

Anderson, Douglas E.
Atkinson, Paul G.
Bowden, John
Brand, David F.
Clements, Kenneth H.
Edwards, Stephen G.
Futcher, Paul
Goram, Andrew L.
Heaton, Paul J.
Hoolickin, Garry J.
Keegan, Gerard A.
McDonough, Darron K.
Palmer, Roger N.
Ryan, John B.
Sinclair, Nicholas J.T.
Steel, William J.
Wylde, Rodger

League Appearances: Anderson, D.E. 1(1); Atkinson, P.G. 33; Bowden, J. 3(2); Clements, K.H. 27; Edwards, S.G. 20(2); Firm, N.J. 9; Futcher, P. 37; Goram, A.L. 3; Heaton, P.J. 38(1); Hoolickin, G.J. 28; Keegan, G.A. 40; McDonnell, P.A. 39; McDonough, D.K. 33(3); Nuttall, M. 1(5); Palmer, R.N. 35(2); Ryan, J.B. 37; Sinclair, N.J.T. 9; Steel, W.J. 35(2); Wylde, R. 34(1).
Goals – League (50): Wylde 16 (4 pens), Heaton 12 (1 pen), Palmer 7, Steel 7, Keegan 3, Bowden 2, Clements 1, McDonough 1, own goal 1.
League Cup (7): Palmer 3, Atkinson 1, Heaton 1, Steel, Wylde 1.
FA Cup (1): Heaton 1 (pen).
Ground: Boundary Park, Oldham OL1 2PA (061-624 4972)
Nearest station: Oldham, Werneth
Manager: **Secretary:** T. M. Finn
Colours: Blue shirts, with white trim; white shorts with blue stripe
Record home gate: 47,671 v Sheffield Wednesday, January 1930 (FA Cup)
Honours – Champions: Division 3 North: 1952-53; Division 3: 1973-74
FA Cup winners: Nil

ORIENT DIV. 3

Blackhall, Mark C.
Cunningham, Thomas E.
Day, Mervyn R.
Fisher, Robert P.
Foster, Colin J.
Godfrey, Kevin
Gray, Nigel R.
Houchen, Keith
Hurley, William H.
McNeil, Mark J.
Moores, Ian R.
Osgood, Keith
Parsons, Stephen P.J.
Peach, David S.
Roffey, William R.
Silkman, Barry
Taylor, Peter J.
Taylor, Thomas F.

League Appearances: Banjo, T.B. 3; Blackhall, M.C. 1(3); Bowles, S. 7; Cornwell, J.A. 3; Cunningham, T.E. 18; Day, M.R. 42; Fisher, R.P. 31; Foster, C.J. 23; Giles D.C. 3; Godfrey, K. 42; Gray, N.R. 38; Hallybone, J.M. 5(3); Houchen, K. 14; Hughton, H.T. 23(4); Jennings, W.J. 10; McNeil, M.J. 20(4); Margerrison, J.W. 34; Mayo, J. -(1); Moores, I.R. 23(1); Osgood, K. 6; Peach, D.S. 13; Roffey, W.R. 18; Silkman, B. 33(2); Sussex, A.R. 8; Taylor, P.J. 10(3); Taylor, T.F. 33; Vincent, R.G. 1.

Goals – League (36): Godfrey 7, Silkman 5 (2 pens), Moores 4, Jennins 3, McNeil 3, Foster 2, Giles 2, Margerrison 2, Taylor (P) 2, own goals 2, Bowles 1 (pen), Cunningham 1, Hughton 1, Sussex 1.

League Cup (3): Moores 2, Jennings 1.

FA Cup (4): Moores 3, Foster 1.

Ground: Leyton Stadium, Brisbane Road, Leyton, E10 5NE (01-539 2223/4)

Nearest station: Leyton (Central line)

Manager: Ken Knighton **Secretary:** Peter Barnes

Colours: White shirts with a red vertical stripe on each side of chest; white shorts

Record home gate: 34,345 v West Ham United, January 1964 (FA Cup)

Honours – Champions: Division 3: 1969-70; Division 3 South: 1955-56

FA Cup winners: Nil

OXFORD UNITED DIV. 3

Briggs, Gary
Brock, Kevin S.
Burton, Royston
Doyle, John J.
Fogg, David
Foley, Peter J.
Hebberd, Trevor N.
Jones, Mark
Shotton, Malcolm
Smithers, Timothy
Thomas, Andrew M.
Train, Raymond

League Appearances: Berry, P.A. 4; Briggs, G. 45; Brock, K.S. 26(2); Burton, R. 46; Cassells, K.B. 27; Doyle, J.J. 30; Fogg, D. 45(1); Foley, P.J. 37; Hebberd, T.N. 15; Jeffrey, W.G. 35; Jones, M. 20(1); Kearns, O.A. 9(9); Kingston, A.K. 1(2); Lawrence, G. 15; Lythgoe, P. 2(3); Page, M.E. 7; Seacole, J.P. 4; Shotton, M. 40; Smithers, T. 44; Thomas, A.M. 31(8); Train, R. 15; Wright, M. 8(2).

Goals – League (63): Thomas 14, Cassells 10 (3 pens); Foley 7, Brock 5, Kearns 4, Lawrence 4, Shotton 4, Fogg 3 (3 pens), Jeffrey 3, Jones 3, Hebberd 2, Briggs 1, Seacole 1, Smithers 1, own goal 1.
League Cup (7): Cassells 4 (1 pen), Foley 1, Thomas 1, own goal 1.
FA Cup (13): Cassells 7 (1 pen), Thomas 3, Foley 2, Smithers 1.
Ground: Manor Ground, Beech Road, Headington, Oxford OX3 7RS (0865 61503)
Nearest station: Oxford
Manager: Jim Smith **Secretary:** Jim A. Hunt
Colours: Yellow shirts with blue trim; blue shorts with yellow trim
Record home gate: 22,730 v Preston, February 1964 (FA Cup)
Honours – Champions: Division 3: 1967-68
FA Cup winners: Nil

PETERBOROUGH UNITED DIV. 4

Chard, Phillip
Clarke, Colin
Cliss, Tony
Collins, Stephen M.
Cooke, Robert L.
Freeman, Neil
Gynn, Michael
Kellock, William
Phillips, Ian A.
Quow, Trevor
Rodaway, William V.
Slack, Trevor C.
Smith, Anthony
Winters, John M.

League Appearances: Barnard, L. 1(3); Butler, G. 39; Chard, P. 31(8); Clarke, C. 22(5); Cliss, T. 2(2); Collins, S.M. 34; Cooke, R.L. 46; Freeman, N. 41; Gynn, M. 46; Hodgson, G.H. 38(1); Kellock, W. 43; Massey, S. 13(5); Phillips, I.A. 17; Quow, T. 10; Rayment, P.J. 2; Rodaway, W.V. 42; Slack, T.C. 7; Smelt, L.A. 5; Smith, A. 39; Smith, R. 5; Syrett, D.K. 16(1); Winters, J.M. 7.
Goals – League (71): Cooke 24 (2 pens), Kellock 11 (1 pen), Syrett 9, Gynn 6, Clarke 4, Chard 3, Hodgson 3, Smith, T. 3, Massey 2, Phillips 2, Slack 2, Collins 1, Quow 1.
League Cup (2): Cooke 1, Slack 1.
FA Cup (5): Cooke 3, Chard 1, Syrett 1.
Ground: London Road Ground, Peterborough PE2 8AL (0733 63947)
Nearest station: Peterborough
Manager: Peter Morris **Secretary:** A. V. Blades
Colours: Blue shirts with white trim; white shorts with blue trim
Record home gate: 30,096 v Swansea, February 1965 (FA Cup)
Honours – Champions: Division 4: 1960, 1973-74
FA Cup winners: Nil

PLYMOUTH ARGYLE DIV. 3

Cook, Jeffrey W.
Cooper, Leigh V.
Crudgington, Geoffrey
Dennis, John A.
Ham, Michael T.
Hards, Neil A.
Harrison, Christopher C.
Hodges, Kevin
James, Tyrone S.
Kemp, David M.
McCartney, Michael
Nisbet, Gordon J.M.
Phillips, David O.
Phillipson-Masters, Forbes E.
Randell, Colin W.
Rogers, Andrew
Rowe, Mark T.
Sims, John
Uzzell, John E.

League Appearances: Collins, J.D. 1; Cook, J.W. 35; Cooper, L.V. 43; Crudgington, G. 46; Dennis, J.A. 4(2); Foster, G.W. 10; Ham, M.T. 1; Harrison, C.C. 43; Hodges, K. 46; James, T.S. 6; Kemp, D.M. 9; McCartney, M. 16; Murphy, D.P. 4(2); Nisbet, G.J.M. 45; Phillips, D.O. 6(2); Phillipson-Masters, F.E. 31; Randell, C.W. 38; Rogers, A. 40; Rowe, M.T. 2(2); Sims, J. 46; Uzzell, J.E. 34(1).
Goals – League (64): Sims 18, Cook 16 (2 pens), Hodges 11, Cooper 5, Rogers 4, Nisbet 3, Randell 3, Uzzell 2, Harrison 1 (pen), Phillips 1.
League Cup (3): Dennis 1 (pen), Kemp 1, own goal 1.
FA Cup: Nil.

Ground: Home Park, Plymouth, Devon PL2 1BQ (0752 5261/3)
Nearest station: Plymouth
Manager: Bobby Moncur **Secretary:** Graham Little
Colours: Green shirts; white shorts
Record home gate: 43,596 v Aston Villa, October 1936 (League)
Honours – Champions: Division 3 South: 1929-30, 1951-52; Division 3: 1958-59
FA Cup winners: Nil

PORTSMOUTH DIV. 3

Aizlewood, Steven
Berry, Stephen A.
Cropley, Alexander J.
Crown, David I.
Doyle, Robert
Ellis, Peter J.
Gosney, Andrew R.
Knight, Alan E.
McLaughlin, John
Rafferty, William H.
Rogers, Alan J.
Rollings, Andrew N.
Senior, Trevor
Sullivan, Colin
Tait, Michael P.
Wimbleton, Paul P.

League Appearances: Aizlewood, S. 36; Barnard, L.K. 16(1); Bason, B. 9; Bartlett, K.F. –(1); Berry, S.A. 26(1); Bryant, S.P. 11; Cropley, A.J. 8(2); Crown, D.I. 25(2); Doyle, R. 43; Ellis, P.J. 31(1); Garner, A.H. 10; Gosney, A.R. 1; Gregory, D.H. 12(2); Hemmerman, J.L. 29(5); Kamara, C. 11; Knight, A.E. 45; Leworthy, D.J. –(1); McLaughlin, J. 36; Rafferty, W.H. 35(4); Rogers, A.J. 14(4); Rollings, A.N. 19; Senior, T. 9; Sullivan, C. 18; Tait, M.P. 34(1); Viney, K.B. 24; Wimbleton, P.P. 4(4).
Goals – League (56): Rafferty 17, Hemmerman 10, Tait 9, Doyle 8 (7 pens), Aizlewood 3, Berry 2, Cropley 2, Crown 2, Senior 2, Rollings 1.
League Cup (6): Doyle 2, Rafferty 2, Berry 1, Kamara 1.
FA Cup (3): Hemmerman 2, Tait 1.
Ground: Fratton Park, Frogmore Road, Portsmouth, PO4 8RA (Portsmouth 731204/5)
Nearest stations: Fratton or Portsmouth and Southsea
Manager: Bobby Campbell **Secretary:** W. J. B. Davis
Colours: Blue shirts with white trim; white shorts
Record home gate: 51,385 v Derby County, February 1949 (FA Cup)
Honours – Champions: Division 1: 1948-49, 1949-50; Division 3 South: 1923-24; Division 3: 1961-62
FA Cup winners: 1938-39

PORT VALE — DIV. 4

Armstrong, Terrence
Bromage, Russel
Chamberlain, Mark V.
Chamberlain, Neville
Greenhoff, James
Harrison, Mark S.
Healy, Patrick J.
Hunter, Geoffrey
Moss, Ernest
Shankland, Andrew J.
Sproson, Philip J.
Tartt, Colin

League Appearances: Armstrong, T. 32(2); Bennett, P. 3(1); Bowles, P.M.A. 44; Bright, M.A. 1(1); Brissett, T.A. 10(4); Bromage, R. 44(1); Chamberlain, M.V. 46; Chamberlain, N. 28(2); Deakin, R.J. 21(2); Farrell, P. 2(2); Greenhoff, J. 31(2); Harrison, M.S. 46; Higgins, A.M. 3(1); Hunter, G. 39(2); Keenan, G.P. 20(1); Moss, E. 44; Sealy, A.J. 6; Shankland, A.J. 6(6); Sproson, P.J. 42; Tartt, C. 38.
Goals – League (56): Moss 13, Chamberlain, M. 8, Deakin 6 (4 pens), Sproson 6, Chamberlain, N. 4, Sealy 4 (2 pens), Greenhoff 3, Hunter 3, Bowles 2, Armstrong 1, Keenan 1, Shankland 1.
League Cup (3): Moss 2, Chamberlain, N. 1, Deakin 1.
FA Cup (8): Chamberlain, N. 4, Moss 2, Armstrong 1, Chamberlain, M. 1.
Ground: Vale Park, Hamil Road, Burslem, Stoke-on-Trent ST6 1AW (Stoke (0782) 814134)
Nearest station: Stoke-on-Trent
Manager: John McGrath **Secretary:** Andrew Waterhouse
Colours: White shirts with black trim; black shorts
Record home gate: 50,000 v Aston Villa, February 1960 (FA Cup)
Honours – Champions: Division 3 North: 1929-30, 1953-54; Division 4: 1958-59
FA Cup winners: Nil

PRESTON NORTH END — DIV. 3

Bell, Graham T.A.
Booth, Thomas A.
Bruce, Alexander R.
Buckley, Gary
Clark, Jonathan
Coleman, Gordon M.
Elliott, Stephen B.
Farelly, Michael J.
Hanson, Neil
Houston, Graham R.
Hunter, Christopher P.
Kelly, John
Litchfield, Peter
McAteer, Andrew W.
Naughton, William B.S.
O'Riordan, Donald J.
Sayer, Peter A.
Walsh, Mark
Westwell, Simon

League Appearances: Anderson, J.C.P. 35(3); Bell, G.T.A. 22; Blackley, J.H. 3; Booth, T.A. 27; Bruce, A.R. 46; Buckley, G. 20(2); Clark, J. 18; Coleman, G.M. 15; Doyle, S.C. 36; Dunn, B. 8; Elliott, S.B. 34(1); Farelly, M.J. 3(4); Hodge, M.J. 28; Houston, G.R. 9(9); Kelly, J. 28(2); Litchfield, P. 18; McAteer, A.W. 41; McGee, P.G. 10; Mullen, J. 1; Naughton, W.B.S. 31(2); O'Riordan, D.J. 46; Sayer, P.A. 1; Taylor, B.J. 10(2); Walsh, M. 4(6); Westwell, S. 12.
Goals – League (50): Bruce 17 (2 pens), Elliott 10 (2 pens), Kelly 5, Doyle 4, Naughton 3, O'Riordan 3, Buckley 2 (1 pen), Dunn 2, Bell 1, McGee 1, Walsh 1, own goal 1.

League Cup (3): Bruce 1, Clark 1, Naughton 1.
FA Cup (1): Doyle 1.
Ground: Deepdale, Preston PR1 6RU (Preston (0772) 795919)
Nearest station: Preston
Manager: Gordon Lee **Secretary:** Ron Severs
Colours: White shirts with blue collars and cuffs; blue shorts with white trim
Record home gate: 42,684 v Arsenal, April 1938 (League)
Honours – Champions: Division 1: 1888-89, 1889-90; Division 2: 1903-04, 1912-13, 1950-51; Division 3: 1970-71
FA Cup winners: 1888-89, 1937-38

QUEEN'S PARK RANGERS — DIV. 2

Allen, Clive D.
Benstead, Graham M.
Burke, Steven J.
Burridge, John
Currie, Anthony W.
Dawes, Ian R.
Duffield, Martin J.
Fenwick, Terence W.
Fereday, Wayne
Flanagan, Michael A.
Gillard, Ian T.
Gregory, John C.
Hazell, Robert J.
Hucker, Peter I.
Howe, Ernest J.
McDonald, Alan
Micklewhite, Gary
Muir, Ian J.
Neill, Warren A.
O'Connor, Mark A.
Roeder, Glenn V.
Sealy, Anthony J.
Stainrod, Simon A.
Stewart, Ian E.
Waddock, Gary P.
Wicks. Stephen J.
Wilkins, Dean M.

League Appearances: Allen, C.D. 36(1); Burke, S.J. 2(10); Burridge, J. 10; Currie, A.W. 20; Dawes, I.R. 5; Fenwick, T.W. 36; Fereday, W. 2(2); Flanagan, M.A. 36(1); Francis, G.C.J. 7; Gillard, I.T. 33(2); Gregory, J.C. 34; Hazell, R.J. 23(1); Howe, E.J. 16; Hucker, P.I. 22; King, A.E. 4; Micklewhite, G. 24(2); Neill, W.A. 11; O'Connor, M.A. 1; Roeder, G.V. 41; Sealy, A.J. 4(3); Stainrod, S.A. 39; Stewart, I.E. 2(1); Waddock, G.P. 35; Wicks, S.J. 9; Wilkins, D.M. -(1).
Goals – League (65): Stainrod 17, Allen 13, Flanagan 10, Gregory 9, Fenwick 5 (2 pens), King 3, Hazell 2, Micklewhite 2, Roeder 2, Currie 1, Gillard 1.
League Cup (10): Micklewhite 3, Flanagan 2, Gregory 2, Stainrod 2, Allen 1.
FA Cup (15): Allen 7, Stainrod 5, Fenwick 1, Howe 1, Neill 1.
Ground: Rangers Stadium, South Africa Road, Shepherds Bush, W12 7PA (01-743 0262)
Nearest stations: Shepherds Bush (Metropolitan and Central lines); White City (Central line)
Manager: Terry Venables **Secretary:** R. J. Phillips
Colours: Blue and white hooped shirts; white shorts
Record home gate: 35,353 v Leeds United, April 1974 (League)
Honours – Champions: Division 3: 1966-67; Division 3 South: 1947-48
FA Cup winners: Nil
League Cup winners: 1966-67

READING DIV. 3

Barnes, Michael F.
Beavon, Michael S.
Dixon, Kerry M.
Donnellan, Gary
Earles, Patrick J.
Fearon, Ronald T.
Heale, Gary J.
Henderson, James S.
Hetzke, Stephen E.R.
Hicks, Martin
Kearney, Michael J.
Sanchez, Lawrence P.
Webb, Neil J.
White, Mark I.
Williams, Jeremy S.
Wood, Stephen A.

League Appearances: Barnes, M.F. 4(2); Beavon, M.S. 38(2); Clark, P.P. 2; Court, C.C. 1; Cullen, S.J.R. 12(5); Death, S.V. 3; Dixon, K.M. 38(4); Donnellan, G. 19(3); Earles, P.J. 32(1); Fearon, R.T. 42; Heale, G.J. 18; Henderson, J.S. 2; Hetzke, S.E.R. 31(1); Hicks, M. 43(1); Joslyn, R.D.W. -(1); Kearney, M.J. 26(1); Lewis, A.T. 34(2); Matthews, M. 1; Moore, A.D. -(1); Sanchez, L.P. 34(1); Webb, N.J. 40; White, M.I. 9; Williams, J.S. 45; Wood, S.A. 32.
Goals – League (67): Webb 15 (6 pens), Dixon 12, Heale 8, Kearney 8, Earles 7, Beavon 5, Donnellan 3, Hicks 3, Sanchez 3, Hetzke 2 (1 pen), own goal 1.
League Cup (3): Earles 1, Heale 1, Hetzke 1 (pen).
FA Cup: Nil
Ground: Elm Park, Norfolk Road, Reading RG3 2EF (Reading 57878/80)
Nearest station: Reading
Manager: Maurice Evans **Secretary:** R. Bentley
Colours: Blue and white hooped shirts; white shorts
Record home gate: 33,042 v Brentford, February 1927 (FA Cup)
Honours – Champions: Division 3 South: 1925-26; Divison 4: 1978-79
FA Cup winners: Nil

ROCHDALE DIV. 4

Hamilton, Neville R.
Hilditch, Mark
Martinez, Eugene
Snookes, Eric
Taylor, Brian
Warriner, Stephen W.
Weir, Alan
Wellings, Barry

League Appearances: Burke, P. 27; Cooper T. 35; Crawford, P.G. 19; Dolan, T.P. 42(1); Esser, E.D. 20(4); Goodwin, D. 34(5); Hamilton, N.R. 20(1); Hilditch, M. 38(2); Martinez, E. 42(1); O'Loughlin, N. 32(1); Poole, M.D. 27; Snookes, E. 44; Taylor, B. 37; Thompson, D.S. 1(1); Warriner, S.W. 7(1); Weir, A. 32(2); Wellings, B. 45(1); Williams, W.R. 4(2).
Goals – League (50): Hilditch 14, Wellings 11 (5 pens), Martinez 9, Goodwin 6, O'Loughlin 5, Cooper 2, Dolan 1 (pen), Hamilton 1, Warriner 1.
League Cup (3): Cooper 1, Hilditch 1, Wellings 1.
FA Cup (4): Esser 2, Burke 1, Dolan 1.
Ground: Spotland, Sandy Lane, Rochdale OL11 5DS (Rochdale 44648/9)
Nearest station: Rochdale
Manager: Peter Madden **Secretary:** Mrs W. Rawlinson
Colours: Royal blue shirts with white trim; white shorts with blue trim
Record home gate: 24,231 v Notts County, December 1949 (FA Cup)
Honours – Champions: Nil
FA Cup winners: Nil

ROTHERHAM UNITED DIV. 2

Alexander, Ian
Breckin, John
Carr, Peter
Fern, Rodney
Fleetwood, Steven R.
Forrest, Gerald
Gooding, Michael C.
Gow, Gerald
Green, John R.
Henson, Philip W.
Hughes, Emlyn W.
McEwan, Williams J.
Mimms, Robert A.
Moore, Ronald D.
Mountford, Raymond
Mullen, James
Rhodes, Mark N.
Seasman, John
Stancliffe, Paul I.
Taylor, Ashely
Towner, Antony J.
Vaughan, Ian

League Appearances: Alexander, I. 3(5); Breckin, J. 33; Carr, P. -(2); Fern, R. 26(2); Forrest, G. 35; Gooding, M.C. 16(6); Gow, G. 21; Green, J.R. 41; Henson, P.M. 16(1); Hughes, E.W. 23(1); McEwan, W.J. 21; Mimms, R.A. 2; Moore, R.D. 40; Mountford, R. 40; Mullen, J. 6; Rhodes, M.N. 25; Seasman, J. 21(4); Stancliffe, P.I. 42; Taylor, A. 9; Towner, A.J. 42.
Goals – League (66): Moore 22 (2 pens), Fern 13, Seasman 10, Towner 4 (1 pen), Green 3, McEwan 3, Hughes 2 (1 pen), Breckin 1, Forrest 1, Gooding 1, Gow 1, Henson 1, Stancliffe 1, own goals 3.
League Cup (8): Fern 2, Moore 2, Breckin 1, Gooding 1, Henson 1, own goal 1.
FA Cup (1): Towner 1.
Ground: Millmoor, Rotherham S60 1HR (Rotherham (0709) 2434)
Nearest station: Rotherham
Player/Manager: Emlyn Hughes **Secretary:** J. E. Bennison
Colours: red shirts with white trim; white shorts
Record home gate: 25,000 v Sheffield United, December 1952 and Sheffield Wednesday, January 1952 (League)
Honours – Champions: Division 3: 1980-81; Division 3 North: 1950-51
FA Cup winners: Nil

SCUNTHORPE UNITED DIV. 4

Cammack, Stephen R.
Cowling, Christopher
Duncan, John P.
Grimes, Vincent
Keeley, Andrew J.
Moss, Paul M.
Neenan, Joseph P.
Oates, Robert A.
O'Berg, Paul J.
Telfer, George A.

League Appearances: Arins, A.F. 20; Botham, I.T. 4; Boyd, G. 10(1); Cammack, S.R. 9(1); Cowling, C. 23(3); Dall, D.G. 28; Davy, S.J. 25(3); De Vries, R.S. 6; Duffy, V.G. 3(4); Duncan, J.P. –(3); Goodlass, R. 9; Green, R. 18; Grimes, V. 34; Hamill, S.P. 4; Hughes, D.T. 17(4); Johnson, P. 2; Keeley, A.J. 42; Lambert, A.J. 13(2); Moss, P.M. 42; Neenan, J.P. 44; Oates, R.A. 37; O'Berg, P.J. 7(3); Partridge, M. 10(3); Pilling, A.S. 17(1); Pointon, N.G. 5; Stewart, C.D. 37(3); Telfer, G.A. 28(1); Thompson, W.A. 11; Walker, D. 1.
Goals – League (43): Telfer 9, Moss 7 (1 pen), Stewart 6, Cowling 4, Cammack 3, Green 3, Dall 2, Grimes 2, Oates 2, Partridge 2 (2 pens), Arins 1, Devries 1, Keeley 1 (pen).
League Cup: Nil.
FA Cup (6): Cowling 2, Dall 1, Grimes 1, Stewart 1, Telfer 1.

Ground: Old Show Ground, Scunthorpe DN15 7RH (Scunthorpe 842954)
Nearest station: Scunthorpe
Manager: Ron Ashman **Secretary:** Mrs S. Louth
Colours: Red shirts with white trim; red shorts
Record home gate: 23,935 v Portsmouth, January 1954 (FA Cup)
Honours – Champions: Division 3 North: 1957-58
FA Cup winners: Nil

SHEFFIELD UNITED — DIV. 3

Brazil, Gary N.
Burke, John
Charles, Stephen
Conroy, Stephen H.
Dey, Geoffrey
Edwards, Keith
Garner, Paul
Hatton, Robert J.
Houston, Stewart M.
Kenworthy, Anthony D.
King, Jeffrey
McPhail, John
Matthews, John
Morris, Colin
Neville, Stephen F.
Peters, Martin S.
Richardson, Paul
Tibbott, Leslie
Trusson, Michael S.
Waugh, Keith

League Appearances: Brazil, G.N. –(1); Broddle, J.R. 1; Casey, P. 12; Charles, S. 28(2); Conroy, S.H. 1; Edwards, K. 41; Garner, P. 34; Hatton, R.J. 45; Houston, S.M. 27; Kenworthy, A.D. 45; King, J. 22(1); McAlle, J.E. 18; McPhail, J. 26; Matthews, J. 24(1); Moore, A.P. 4; Morris, C. 23; Neville, S.F. 22(8); Richardson, P. 19(1); Ryan J.G. 19; Tibbott, L. 3; Trusson, M.S. 44; Waugh, K. 45; Wiggan, T.A. 3(2).
Goals – League (94): Edwards 35, Hatton 15, Kenworthy 15 (9 pens), Trusson 11, King 4, Morris 4, Neville 4, Matthews 3, Charles 1, McPhail 1, Richardson 1.
Goals – League (3): Hatton 2, Kenworthy 1 (pen).
FA Cup (2): Edwards 1, Hatton 1.
Ground: Bramhall Lane, Sheffield S2 4SU (0742 738955)
Nearest station: Sheffield
Manager: Ian Porterfield **Secretary:** R. H. Chester
Colours: Red and white striped shirts; red shorts with white stripe down seam
Record home gate: 68,287 v Leeds, February 1936 (FA Cup)
Honours – Champions: Division 1: 1897-98; Division 2: 1952-53; Division 3 North: 1945-46; Division 4: 1981-82
FA Cup winners: 1898-99, 1901-02, 1914-15, 1924-25

SHEFFIELD WEDNESDAY — DIV. 2

Bannister, Gary
Beaumont, Richard T.
Bolder, Robert J.
Cox, Brian R.
Curran, Edward
Holton, James A.
McCulloch, Andrew
Matthewson, Trevor
Megson, Gary J.
Mirocevic, Anton
Oliver, Gavin R.
Owen, Gordon
Pearson, John S.
Pickering, Michael J.
Redfern, David
Shelton, Gary
Shirtliff, Paul R.
Shirtliff, Peter A.
Smith, Mark C.
Sterland, Melvyn
Taylor, Kevin
Williamson, Charles H.

League Appearances: Bannister, G. 42; Blackhall, R. 18; Bolder, R.J. 42; Curran, E. 35(1); Grant, D. 4; Hornsby, B.G. –(1); King, J.D. 2; Leman, D. 2; McCulloch, A. 28; Matthewson, T. 1; Megson, G.J. 40; Mellor, I. 9(5); Mirocevic, A. 20; Owen, G. 3(3); Pearson, J.S. 13(11); Pickering, M.J. 24; Shelton, G. 7(2); Shirtliff, P.R. 6; Shirtliff, P.A. 31; Simmons, A.J. –(1); Smith, M.C. 41; Sterland, M. 27; Taylor, K. 35; Williamson, C.H. 32.
Goals – League (55): Bannister 21 (2 pens), McCulloch 7 (1 pen), Pearson 7, Taylor 7, Megson 5, Curran 3, Shirtliff, P.A. 2, Pickering 1, Shelton 1, Williamson 1.
League Cup (2): Bannister 1, Taylor 1.
FA Cup (1): McCulloch 1.
Ground: Hillsborough, Sheffield S6 1SW (0742 343123, Box Office 343122)
Nearest station: Sheffield
Manager: Jack Charlton **Secretary:** Eric England
Colours: Royal blue and white striped shirts; royal blue shorts
Record home gate: 72,841 v Manchester City, February 1934 (FA Cup)
Honours – Champions: Division 1: 1902-03, 1903-04, 1928-29, 1929-30; Division 2: 1899-1900, 1925-26, 1951-52, 1955-56, 1958-59
FA Cup winners: 1895-96, 1906-07, 1934-35

SHREWSBURY TOWN — DIV. 2

Atkins, Ian L.
Bates, Philip D.
Cross, Stephen C.
Griffin, Colin R.
Johnson, Paul
Keay, John P.
McClaren, Ross
McNally, Bernard A.
Pearson, Nigel G.
Perks, Stephen J.
Petts, Paul A.
Sankey, Martin A.
Turner, Graham J.
Wardle, Robert I.
Williams, Wayne

League Appearances: Atkins, I.L. 40; Bates, P.D. 39(1); Biggins, S.J. 22; Blake, N.L.G. 6; Cross, S.C. 30(4); Dungworth, J.H. 21(3); Edwards, D.S. –(3); Gibson, C. 2(4); Griffin, C.R. 36; Johnson, P. 41; Keay, J.P. 23(1); King, J. 2; Leonard, C.C. 26; McClaren, R. 34(1); McNally, B.A. 31(2); Petts, P.A. 17(4); Tong, D.J. 38(2); Turner, G.J. 12(1); Wardle, R.I. 42.
Goals – League (37): Atkins, 17 (4 pens), Dungworth 5, Bates 4, Biggins 3, Cross 3, Johnson 1, McNally 1, Petts 1, Tong 1, own goal 1.
League Cup (4): Atkins 2 (1 pen), Biggins 1, McClaren 1.
FA Cup (6): Bates 3, Cross 1, Keay 1, King 1.
Ground: Gay Meadow, Shrewsbury SY2 6AB (Shrewsbury (0743) 60111)
Nearest station: Shrewsbury
Manager: Graham Turner **Secretary:** M. J. Starkey
Colours: Amber shirts with blue stripes; blue shorts
Record home gate: 18,917 v Walsall, April 1961 (League)
Honours – Champions: Division 3: 1978-79
FA Cup winners: Nil

SOUTHAMPTON DIV. 1

Agboola, Reuben O.F.
Armstrong, David
Baird, Ian J.
Baker, Graham E.
Baker, Stephen
Ball, Alan J.
Cassells, Keith B.
Golac, Ivan
Holmes, Nicholas C.
Juryeff, Ian M.
Katalinic, Ivan
Keegan, Joseph K.
Lawrence, George R.
Moran, Stephen J.
Nicholl, Christopher J.
Puckett, David C.
Stagg, Jeremy
Waldron, Malcolm R.
Wallace, David L.
Wells, Peter A.
Whitlock, Mark
Williams, Steven C.
Wiltshire, Paul
Wright, Mark

League Appearances: Agboola, R.O.F. 5; Armstrong, D. 41; Baker, G.E. 26; Baker, S. 5; Ball, A.J. 41; Cassells, K.B. 4(2); Channon, M.R. 40; Golac, I. 36; Hebberd, T.N. 4; Holmes, N.C. 40; Katalinic, I. 32; Keegan, J.K. 41; Lawrence, G.R. 2(2); Moran, S.J. 18; Nicholl, C.J. 34; Puckett, D.C. 8(9); Rogers, A. –(2); Waldron, M.R. 34; Wallace, D.L. 3(4); Watson, D.V. 5; Wells, P.A. 10; Whitlock, M. 9; Williams, S.C. 21; Wright, M. 3.
Goals – League (72): Keegan 26 (7 pens), Armstrong 15, Moran 9, Channon 7, Baker, G. 4, Puckett 3, Cassells 2, Waldron 2, own goals 2, Ball 1, Whitlock 1.
League Cup (2): Keegan 1, Moran 1.
FA Cup (1): Keegan 1.
Ground: The Dell, Milton Road, Southampton SO9 4XX (Southampton (0703) 39633/5)
Nearest station: Southampton
Manager: Lawrie McMenemy **Secretary:** B. Truscott
Colours: Red and white vertical striped shirts; black shorts
Record home gate: 31,044 v Manchester United, October 1969 (League)
Honours – Champions: Division 3 South: 1921-22; Division 3: 1959-60
FA Cup winners: 1975-76

SOUTHEND UNITED DIV. 3

Cawston, Mervyn W.
Cusack, David S.
Dudley, Philip W.
Greaves, Daniel T.
Hadley, Antony P.F.
Keeley, John H.
Mercer, Keith
Moody, Alan
Nelson, Garry P.
Otulakowski, Antoni
Pennyfather, Glenn J.
Phillips, Stephen E.
Pountney, Ronald A.
Spence, Derek W.
Stead, Michael J.
Walker, John
Yates, Stephen

League Appearances: Cawston, M.W. 19; Cusack, D.S. 43; Dudley, P.W. 6(1); Gray, T.I. 22(1); Greaves, D.T. 13(12); Hadley, A.P.F. 22(6); Keeley, J.H. 27; Mercer, K. 44; Moody, A. 44; Nelson, G.P. 36(4); Otulakowski, A. 38; Pennyfather, G.J. 33; Phillips, S.E. 18; Pountney, R.A. 33(1); Spence, D.W. 32(4); Stead, M.J. 38(1); Walker, J. –(1); Yates, S. 38.
Goals – League (63): Mercer 13, Phillips 10 (2 pens), Greaves 6, Spence 6, Cusack 5 (3 pens), Gray 4, Nelson 4, Pennyfather 4, Pountney 4, Yates 3, Moody 2, Hadley 1, Otulakowski 1.

League Cup (1): Spence 1.
FA Cup (1): Gray 1.
Ground: Roots Hall Ground, Victoria Avenue, Southend SS2 6NQ (Southend 40707)
Nearest stations: Prittlewell or Southend Central
Manager: Davis Smith **Secretary:** K. Holmes
Colours: White shirts with blue sleeves and blue V neck; blue shorts
Record home gate: 31,033 v Liverpool, January 1979 (FA Cup)
Honours – Champions: Division 4: 1980-81
FA Cup winners: Nil

STOCKPORT COUNTY DIV. 4

Coyle, Anthony
Lloyd, Brian W.
Park, Terence
Power, Michael, D.
Rutter, John T.
Sherlock, Steven E.
Smith, Nigel G.
Sword, Thomas W.
Thorpe, Andrew
Wardrobe, Michael
Williams, Oshar J.

League Appearances: Connor, J. 1; Coyle, A. 36; Dwyer, A.R. 4; Emerson, D. 23; Fowler, M. 29(1); Lloyd, B.W. 45; Park, T. 46; Phillips, T. 13; Power, M.D. 22; Rutter, J.T. 39; Seddon, A.J. 2; Sherlock, S.E. 46; Smith, N.G. 31; Stafford, A.G. 21(4); Sunley, D. 27(4); Sword, T.W. 16; Thorpe, A. 46; Uzelac, S. 5; Vaughan, I. 2; Wardrobe, M. 7(4); Williams, O.J. 45.
Goals – League (48): Williams 9, Coyle 7, Power 6, Park 5, Phillips 4, Fowler 3, Sherlock 3 (2 pens), Sword 3, Sunley 2, Uzelac 2, Emerson 1, Lloyd 1, Stafford 1, Vaughan 1.
League Cup (1): Fowler 1.
FA Cup (4): Williams 2, Park 1, Smith 1.
Ground: Edgeley Park, Stockport SK3 9DD (061-480 8888/9)
Nearest station: Stockport
Manager: Eric Webster **Secretary:** T. R. McCreery
Colours: Sky blue shirts with white stripes; black shorts with sky blue trim
Record home gate: 27,833 v Liverpool, February 1950 (FA Cup)
Honours – Champions: Division 3 North: 1921-22, 1936-37; Division 4: 1966-67
FA Cup winners: Nil

STOKE CITY DIV. 1

Bould, Stephen A.
Bracewell, Paul W.
Chapman, Lee R.
Dodd, Alan
Ford, Stephen D.
Fox, Peter D.
Griffiths, Peter J.
Hampton, Peter J.
Lennox, Stephen J.M.
Lumsden, John W.
McAughtrie, David
McIlroy, Samuel B.
McManus, Eric C.
Maguire, Paul B.
O'Callaghan, Brendan R.
Parkin, Derek
Ronan, Kevin, P.
Ursem, Loek A.J.M.
Watson, David V.

League Appearances: Biley, A.P. 8; Bould, S.A. 1(1); Bracewell, P.W. 42; Chapman, L.R. 40(1); Cook, J. –(1); Dodd, A. 41; Doyle, M. 8; Evans, R.L. 22; Ford,

S.D. 1(1); Fox, P.D. 38; Griffiths, P.J. 27(4); Hampton, P.J. 33; Heath, A.P. 17; Johnson, P.A. 12(1); Kirk, S.D. 12; Lumsden, J.W. 2(3); McAughtrie, D. 13; McIlroy, S.B. 18; McManus, E.C. 4; Maguire, P.B. 32(3); O'Callaghan, B.R. 39(2); Parkin, D. 10; Smith, D. 17; Ursem, L.A.J.M. 1(2); Watson, D.V. 24.
Goals – League (44): Chapman 16, Maguire 7 (3 pens), Heath 5, O'Callaghan 5, Griffiths 3, McIlroy 3, Watson 3, Biley 1, Bracewell 1.
League Cup (2): Chapman 1, Evans 1.
FA Cup: Nil.
Ground: Victoria Ground, Stoke-on-Trent ST4 4EG (Stoke 413511)
Nearest station: Stoke-on-Trent
Manager: Richie Barker **Secretary:** M. J. Potts
Colours: Red and white striped shirts; white shorts with black and red stripes down seam
Record home gate: 51,380 v Arsenal, March 1937 (League)
Honours – Champions: Division 2: 1932-33, 1962-63: Divison 3 North: 1926-27
FA Cup winners: Nil
League Cup winners: 1971-72

SUNDERLAND DIV. 1

Brown, Alan	Hinnigan, Joseph P.	Rowell, Gary
Buckley, Michael J.	McCoist, Alistair	Tait, Simon E.B.
Chisholm, Gordon W.	Munro, Alexander I.F.	Turner, Christopher R.
Cooke, John	O'Donnell, Patrick	Venison, Barry
Cummins, Stanley	Pickering, Nicholas	Wardrobe, Thomas B.
Elliott, Shaun	Prudhoe, Mark	West, Colin
Hindmarch, Robert	Ritchie, Thomas G.	Whitfield, Michael

League Appearances: Arnott, K.W. 6; Bowyer, I. 6; Brown, A. 5(2); Buckley, M.J. 37; Chisholm, G.W. 20(2); Clarke, J.D. 25(1); CPOOKE, J.8(2); Cummins, S. 35; Elliott, S. 36; Hindmarch, R. 36; Hinnigan, J.P. 30; McCoist, A. 19(9); McGinley, J. 3; Munro, A.I.F. 34; Nicholl, J.M. 3; Pickering, N. 37; Ritchie, T.G. 18(2); Rowell, G. 30; Siddall, B. 23; Turner, C.R. 19; Ursem, L.A.J. –(4); Venison, B. 17(3); West, C. 13(5); Whitworth, S. 2.
Goals – League (38): Rowell 9 (3 pens), West 6, Buckley 4, Cummins 4, Ritchie 4 (1 pen), Pickering 3, Hindmarch 2, McCoist 2, Brown 1, Cooke 1, Elliott 1, Venison 1.
League Cup (5): Ritchie 3, Cummins 1, Rowell 1 (pen).
FA Cup (2): Buckley 1, Rowell 1.
Ground: Roker Park, Sunderland SR6 9SW (Sunderland 72077 and 58638)
Nearest stations: Sunderland or Seaburn
Manager: Alan Durban **Secretary:** R. M. Linney
Colours: White shirts with red and black stripes; red shorts
Record home gate: 75,118 v Derby, March 1933 (FA Cup)
Honours – Champions: Division 1: 1891-92, 1892-93, 1894-95, 1901-02, 1912-13, 1935-36; Division 2: 1975-76
FA Cup winners: 1936-37, 1972-73

SWANSEA CITY DIV. 1

Charles, Jeremy M.
Curtis, Alan T.
Davies, William D.
Evans, Wyndham E.
Gale, Darren
Guard, Anthony F.
Hadziabdic, Dzemal
Irwin, Colin T.
James, Leighton
James, Robert M.
Kennedy, Raymond
Lake, Huw G.T.
Latchford, Robert D.
Lewis, Dudley K.
Loveridge, James C.
Mahoney, John F.
Marustik, Christopher
Rajkovic, Anto
Richards, Gary V.
Robinson, Neil
Sander, Christopher A.
Stanley, Gary E.
Stevenson, Nigel C.
Thompson, Maxwell
Toshack, John B.
Walsh, Ian P.

League Appearances: Attley, B.R. 2(2); Charles, J.M. 9(4); Curtis, A.T. 40; Davies, W.D. 41; Evans, W.E. 1; Gale, D. –(1); Giles, D.C. –(2); Hadziabdic, D. 25(1); Irwin, C.T. 37; James, L. 34(4); James, R.M. 42; Kennedy, R. 18; Latchford, R.D. 31; Lewis, D.K. 1; Loveridge, J.C. 1; Mahoney, J.F. 25; Marustik, C. 19(3); Rajkovic, A. 40; Richards, G.V. 1; Robinson, N. 27(2); Sander, C.A. 1; Stanley, G.E. 22(7); Stevenson, N.C. 20; Thompson, M. 22(1); Walsh, I.P. 3(2).
Goals – League (58): James, R. 14 (2 pens), Latchford 12, Curtis 10, James, L. 9 (3 pens), Stanley 3, Charles 2, Kennedy 2, Walsh 2, Marustik 1, Rajkovic 1, Robinson 1, Thompson 1.
League Cup (3): Curtis 1, Irwin 1, James, L. 1 (pen).
FA Cup: Nil.
Ground: Vetch Field, Swansea SA1 3SU (Swansea 42855/6)
Nearest station: Swansea
Manager: John Toshack **Secretary:** G. J. Daniels
Colours: White shirts with black trim; white shorts with black trim
Record home gate: 32,796 v Arsenal, February 1968 (FA Cup)
Honours – Champions: Divison 3 South: 1924-25, 1948-49
FA Cup winners: Nil

SWINDON TOWN DIV. 4

Allan, James
Baddeley, Kevin S.
Bailie, Colin J.
Batty, Paul W.
Baverstock, Ray
Beamish, Kenneth G.
Blackler, Martin J.
Carter, Roy W.
Emmanuel, John G.
Graham, Michael A.
Henry, Charles A.
Hughes, Brian D.
Lewis, Russell
Moores, James C.
Pritchard, Howard K.
Quinn, James M.
Rideout, Paul D.
Round, David L.
Rowland, Andrew A.
Stevens, Mark A.
Stroud, Kenneth A.
Williams, Gary

League Appearances: Abbley, S.G. 10(5); Allan, J. 46; Baddeley, K.S. 28; Bailie, C.J. 1; Beamish, K.G. 1(1); Carter, M. 4(1); Carter, R.W. 45; Emmanuel, J.G. 36(1); Graham, M.A. 30; Greenwood, R.T. 22(1); Henry, C.A. 42; Hughes, B.D. 33; Lewis, R. 43; Moores, J.C. 1(1); Peach, D.S. 10; Pritchard, H.K. 24(4); Quinn, J.M. 2(2); Rideout, P.D. 34(1); Rowland, A.A. 27; Stroud, K.A. 30; Williams, G. 37(1).

Goals – League (55): Rideout 14, Carter, R. 13, Rowland 8, Hughes 4, Greenwood 3, Henry 3, Williams 3, Emmanuel 2, Baddeley 1, Graham 1, Lewis 1, Pritchard 1, own goal 1.
League Cup (2): Baddeley 1, Carter, R. 1 (pen).
FA Cup (5): Pritchard 3, Carter, R. 1, Emmanuel 1.
Ground: County Ground, Swindon SN1 2ED (Swindon 22118)
Nearest station: Swindon
Manager: John Trollope **Secretary:** R. Jeffries
Colours: Red shirts; white shorts
Record home gate: 32,000 v Arsenal, January 1972 (FA Cup)
Honours – Champions: Nil
FA Cup winners: Nil
League Cup winners: 1968-69
Anglo-Italian Cup winners: 1970

TORQUAY UNITED — DIV. 4

Brown, Anthony
Cooper, Steven M.
Jones, Graham
O'Keefe, James V.
Rioch, Bruce D.
Wilson, Brian
Young, William J.

League Appearances: Bourne, R.A. -(2); Bowker, K. 12(1); Brown, A. 34; Butler, D. 5(1); Cooper, S.M. 40(3); Cox, M. 23(8); Fell, G.C. 6; Hodge, R.W. 3(1); Johnson, B.F. 2; Jones, G. 45; Keeley, D. 1(2); Larmour, A.A.J. 21(1); Lawrence, L.O. 41(1); Murphy, D. 2(1); Musgrove, M. 1(1); O'Keefe, J.V. 46; Pendrey, G.J.S. 12; Pethard, F.J. 19; Rioch, B.D. 35(1); Rodgers, D.M. 5; Sermanni, T.D. 35(1); Smith, M. 10; Tainton, T. 19; Weston, J. 3; Wheeldon, T. 5(3); Wilson, B. 43; Winn, S. 12(2); Young, W.J. 26.
Goals – League (47): Brown 11, Cooper 8, Lawrence 5, Cox 3, Jones 3 (1 pen), Sermanni 3, Bowker 2, Rioch 2, Winn 2, Bourne 1, Hodge 1, Larmour 1 (pen), Rodgers 1, Tainton 1, Weston 1, Wilson 1, own goal 1.
League Cup (2): Cooper 1, Fell 1
FA Cup (1): Lawrence 1.
Ground: Plainmoor, Torquay, Devon TQ1 3PS (Torquay (0803) 38666/7)
Nearest stations: Torquay or Torre
Manager: Frank O'Farrell **Secretary:** D. J. Easton
Colours: White shirts with blue and yellow trim; white shorts with blue and yellow trim
Record home gate: 21,908 v Huddersfield, January 1955 (FA Cup)
Honours – Champions: Nil
FA Cup winners: Nil

TOTTENHAM HOTSPUR DIV. 1

Archibald, Steven
Ardiles, Osvaldo C.
Bowen, Rossllyn M.
Brooke, Garry J.
Clemence, Raymond N.
Cockram, Allan C.
Corbett, Patrick A.
Crook, Ian S.
Crooks, Garth A.
Dick, Alistair J.
Dixon, Kenneth G.
Falco, Mark P.
Galvin, Anthony
Gibson, Terence B.
Hazard, Michael
Hoddle, Glenn
Hughton, Christopher W.G.
Lacy, John
Mazzon, Georgio
Miller, Paul R.
O'Reilly, Gary M.
Parks, Anthony
Perryman, Steven J.
Price, Paul T.
Roberts, Graham P.
Southey, Peter C.
Villa, Julio R.
Webster, Simon P.

League Appearances: Aleksic, M.A. 2; Archibald, S. 26(1); Ardiles, O.C. 26; Brooke, G.J. 12(4); Clemence, R.N. 38; Corbett, P.A. 3(1); Crook, I.S. 3(1); Crooks, G.A. 27; Dick, A.J. 1; Falco, M.P. 21; Galvin, A. 32; Gibson, T.B. 1; Hazard, M. 26(2); Hoddle, G. 34; Hughton, C.W.G. 37; Jones, C.H. 3(4); Lacy, J. 7(5); Miller, P.R. 35; O'Reilly, G.M. 4(1); Parks, A. 2; Perryman, S.J. 42; Price, P.T. 18(3); Roberts, G.P. 35(2); Smith G.M. 1(1); Villa, J.R. 26(1).
Goals – League (67): Crooks 13, Hoddle 10 (5 pens), Villa 8, Archibald 6, Roberts 6, Falco 5, Hazard 5, Brooke 4 (1 pen), Galvin 3, Ardiles 2, Hughton 2, Corbett 1, Perryman 1, own goal 1.
League Cup (8): Hazard 3, Archibald 2, Ardiles 1, Hoddle 1, Hughton 1.
FA Cup (10): Crooks 3, Hoddle 3 (1 pen), Archibald 1, Falco 1, Hazard 1, own goal 1.
Ground: White Hart Lane, 748 High Road, Tottenham, N17 0AP (01-808 2046)
Nearest stations: White Hart Lane (ER), Northumberland Park (ER) or Seven Sisters (Victoria line) thence by bus
Manager: Keith Burkinshaw **Secretary:** G. W. Jones
Colours: White shirts, navy blue shorts
Record home gate: 75,038 v Sunderland, March 1938 (FA Cup)
Honours – Champions: Division 1: 1950-51, 1960-61; Division 2: 1919-20, 1949-50
FA Cup winners: 1900-01, 1920-21, 1960-61, 1961-62, 1966-67, 1980-81
League Cup winners: 1970-71, 1972-73, 1981-82
European Cup Winners' Cup: 1962-63
UEFA Cup winners: 1971-72

TRANMERE ROVERS DIV. 4

Burgess, David J.
Endersby, Scott G.A.
Griffiths, Ian J.
Hamilton, Bryan
Hutchinson, Robert
Kerr, John
Mathias, Raymond
Mountfield, Derek
Mungall, Stephen H.
Parry, Leslie I.
Powell, Neville D.
Williams, William J.

League Appearances: Bramhall, J. 35; Burgess, D.J. 46; Brown, O.J. 29(8); Craven, S. 36(3); Endersby, S.G.A. 43; Ferguson, M. 4(1); Griffiths, I.J. 36(2); Hamilton, B. 35(3); Hutchinson, R. 26(3); Johnson, R.R. 3; Kelly, J. 7; Kerr, J. 40; Mathias, R. 1; Morley, B. 10(6); Mountfield, D. 21; Mungall, S.H. 43(1); Parry, L.I. 28(1); Powell, N.D. 19(1); Williams, W.J. 44.
Goals – League (51): Kerr 13, Brown 8, Craven 8, Williams 6, Hutchinson 4, Bramhall 3, Hamilton 2, Morley 2, Burgess (1 pen), Ferguson 1, Griffiths 1, Mountfield 1, Mungall 1.
League Cup (12): Brown 5, Kerr 3, Hutchinson 2, Kelly 1, own goal 1.
FA Cup (2): Brown 1, Williams 1.
Ground: Prenton Park, 14 Prenton Road West, Birkenhead, Merseyside, L42 8NR (051-608 3677/4194)
Nearest station: Central Station Birkenhead, Rock Ferry.
Manager: Bryan Hamilton **General Manager/Secretary:** J. Butterfield
Colours: Royal blue shirts with white trim; white shorts
Record home gate: 24,424 v Stoke, February 1972 (FA Cup)
Honours – Champions: Division 3 North: 1937-38
FA Cup winners: Nil

WALSALL DIV. 3

Baines, Stephen J.
Beech, Kenneth
Buckley, Alan P.
Caswell, Brian L.
Conneally, Martin
Green, Ronald R.
Hart, Peter O.
Mower, Kenneth
O'Kelly, Richard F.
Penn, Donald
Preece, David W.
Rees, Mark
Round, Stephen C.
Shakespeare, Craig R.
Teasdale, John S.

League Appearances: Baines, S.J. 10; Beech, K. 38(1); Buckley, A.P. 30(3); Caswell, B.L. 41; Green, R.R. 46; Harrison, C.G. 1; Hart, P.O. 45; Horne, J.R. 4(1); Loveridge, J. 23(3); Lowery, A. 4(2); Macken, A. 40; Mower, K.M. 34; O'Kelly, R.F. 21(8); Penn, D. 38(2); Preece, D.W. 6(2); Rees, M. 38(1); Round, S.C. 4(8); Serella, D.W. 46; Sinnott, L. 4; Smith, C.S. 1; Teasdale, J.S. 8; Waddington, D.P. -(2); Waddington, S.F. 24(2).
Goals – League (51): Penn 14 (1 pen), Buckley 7 (2 pens), O'Kelly 6 (1 pen), Rees 6, Caswell 3, Beech 2, Loveridge 2, Round 2, Serella 2, Waddington S. 2, Baines 1, Hart 1, Horne 1, Lowery 1, Teasdale 1.
League Cup (1): Penn 1.
FA Cup (3): Caswell 1, Macken 1, own goal 1.
Ground: Fellows Park, Walsall WS2 9DB (0922-22791)
Nearest stations: Walsall or Bescot (15 min walk – no public transport)
Manager: Alan Buckley **General Secretary:** W.E. Houghton
Colours: Red shirts with three white stripes on shoulders and sleeves; white shorts with red stripes down sides
Record home gate: 25,453 v Newcastle, August 1961 (League)
Honours – Champions: Division 4: 1959-60
FA Cup winners: Nil

WATFORD DIV. 1

Armstrong, Gerard J.
Barnes, John C.B.
Blissett, Luther L.
Bolton, Ian R.
Callaghan, Nigel I.
Franklin, Paul L.
Gilligan, James M.
Jackett, Kenneth F.
Jenkins, Ross A.
Johnson, David N.
Lohman, Johaanas H.P.
Palmer, Charles A.
Patching, Martin
Poskett, Malcolm
Price, Neil
Pritchett, Keith B.
Rice, Patrick J.
Richardson, Ian P.
Rostron, John W.
Sherwood, Stephen
Sims, Steven F.
Steele, Eric G.
Taylor, Leslie
Terry, Steven G.

League Appearances: Armstrong, G.J. 18(15); Barnes, J.C.B. 35(1); Blissett, L.L. 40; Bolton, I.R. 42; Callaghan, N.I. 34(3); Gilligan, J.M. -(1); Henderson, M.R. 4; Jackett, K.F. 18; Jenkins, R.A. 32(1); Johnson, D.N. -(1); Lohman, J.H.P. 26; Poskett, M. 4(3); Pritchett, K.B. 18; Rice, P.J. 41; Rostron, J.W. 24(3); Sherwood, S. 41; Sims, S.F. 16(1); Steele, E.G. 1; Taylor, L. 42; Terry, S.G. 26.
Goals – League (76): Blissett 19 (8 pens), Barnes 13, Jenkins 13, Armstrong 7, Bolton 5, Callaghan 5, Taylor 4, Jackett 2, Lohman 2, Rostron 2, Terry 2, Poskett 1, own goal 1.
League Cup (13): Blissett 3 (1 pen), Jenkins 2, Taylor 2, Armstrong 1, Barnes 1, Jackett 1, Pritchett 1, Rostron 1, Terry 1.
FA Cup (3): Armstrong 1, Callaghan 1, Lohman 1.
Ground: Vicarage Road, Watford WD1 8ER (Watford 49747/9)
Nearest station: Watford Junction or Watford High Street
Manager: Graham Taylor **General Secretary:** R. E. Rollitt
Colours: Yellow shirts with black/red trim, red shorts
Record home gate: 34,099 v Manchester United, February 1969 (FA Cup)
Honours – Champions: Division 3: 1968-69; Division 4: 1977-78
FA Cup winners: Nil

WEST BROMWICH ALBION DIV. 1

Batson, Brendon M.
Bennett, Martyn
Brown, Alistair
Carlisle, David J.
Childs, Gary P.C.
Cowdrill, Barry
Cross, Nicholas J.R.
Ebanks, Michael W.A.
Frain, Peter A.
Godden, Anthony L.
Grew, Mark S.
Jol, Martin
Jones, Colin M.
King, Andrew E.
Lewis, Michael
Lowery, Anthony W.
Luke, Noel E.
Mackenzie, Stephen
Mills, David J.
Monaghan, Derek J.
Owen, Gary
Perry, Michael A.
Regis, Cyril
Robertson, Alistair
Smith, John G.
Snape, John A.
Statham, Derek J.
Webb, Alan
Whitehead, Clive R.
Wile, John D.
Zondervan, Romeo

League Appearances: Arthur, D.R. 2(1); Batson, B.M. 39; Bennett, M. 23; Brown, A. 22(3); Childs, G.P.C. 2; Cowdrill, B. 6(2); Cross, N.J.R. 11(11); Deehan, J.M. 4; Godden, A.L. 19; Grew, M.S. 23; Jol, M. 9; King, A.E. 21(4); Lewis, M. 3(1); Lowery, A.W. 1; MacKenzie, S. 37; Mills, D.J. 9(2); Monaghan, D.J. 5(3); Moses,

R.M. 4; Owen, G. 39; Regis, C. 37; Robertson, A. 33; Robson, B. 5; Statham, D.J. 35; Summerfield, K. 4; Webb, A. 6; Whitehead, C.R. 8; Wile, J.D. 42; Zondervan, R. 13(1).
Goals – League (46): Regis 17, MacKenzie 5, King 4, Brown 3, Owen 3 (1 pen), Bennett 2, Cross 2, Mills 2 (1 pen), Summerfield 2, own goals 2, Jol 1, Monaghan 1, Robertson 1, Whitehead 1.
League Cup (13): Regis 6, Brown 1, Cross 1, King 1, MacKenzie 1, Monaghan 1, Owen 1, Statham 1.
FA Cup (7): Regis 2, King 1 (pen), MacKenzie 1, Owen 1, Statham 1, Whitehead 1.
Ground: The Hawthorns, West Bromwich B71 4LF (021-553 0095)
Nearest stations: Smethwick Rolfe Street or Birmingham New Street
Manager: Ronnie Allen **Secretary:** Tony Rance
Colours: Navy blue and white striped shirts; white shorts
Record home gate: 64,815 v Arsenal, March 1937 (FA Cup)
Honours – Champions: Division 1: 1919-20; Division 2: 1901-02, 1910-11
FA Cup winners: 1887-88, 1891-92, 1930-31, 1953-54, 1967-68
League Cup winners: 1965-66

WEST HAM UNITED DIV. 1

Allen, Paul K.
Ampofo, Christopher J.K.
Barnes, David O.
Bonds, William A.
Brooking, Trevor D.
Brush, Paul
Burville, Glenn
Cowie, George A.
Cross, David
Devonshire, Alan E.
Goddard, Paul
Holland, Patrick G.
Lampard, Frank R.G.
Laronde, Everald
McAlister, Thomas G.
McGiven, Michael
McPherson, Keith A.
Martin, Alvin E.
Morgan, Nicholas
Neighbour, James E.
Orr, Neil I.
Parkes, Philip B.F.
Pike, Geoffrey A.
Schiavi, Mark A.
Stewart, Raymond S.M.
Van der Elst, Francois J.C.

League Appearances: Allen, P.K. 27(1); Banton, D.C. -(1); Barnes, D.O. 1(2); Bonds, W.A. 29; Brooking, T.D. 34; Brush, P. 10(3); Cowie, G.A. 5(1); Cross, D. 38; Devonshire, A.E. 35; Goddard, P. 38(1); Houghton, R.J. -(1); Lampard, F.R.G. 27(1); Laronde, E. 6(1); McAlister, T.G. 3; Martin, A.E. 28; Neighbour, J.E. 19(4); Orr, N.I. 24; Parkes, P.B.F. 39; Pearson, J.S. 2(2); Pike, G.A. 34; Stewart, R.S.M. 42; Van der Elst, F.J.C. 21(1).
Goals – League (66): Cross 16, Goddard 15, Stewart 10 (10 pens), Brooking 8, Van der Elst 5, Martin 4, Neighbour 2, Pike 2, Bonds 1, Devonshire 1, Orr 1, Pearson 1.
League Cup (8): Stewart 3 (3 pens), Cross 2, Goddard 2, Brooking 1.
FA Cup (2): Bonds 1, Cross 1.
Ground: Boleyn Ground, Green Street, Upton Park, E13 9AZ (01-472 0704)
Nearest station: Upton Park (District line)
Manager: John Lyall **Secretary:** Eddie Chapman
Colours: Claret shirts with blue sleeves; white shorts
Record home gate: 42,322 v Tottenham, October 1970 (League)
Honours – Champions: Division 2: 1957-58, 1980-81
FA Cup winners: 1963-64, 1974-75, 1979-80
European Cup winners' Cup: 1964-65

WIGAN ATHLETIC DIV. 3

Barrow, Graham
Bradd, Leslie J.
Butler, John E.
Cribley, Alexander
Evans, Andrew C.
Glenn, David A.
Houghton, Peter
Lloyd, Laurence V.
McMahon, John
Methven, Colin J.
O'Keefe, Eamon G.
Quinn, Michael
Sheldon, Kevin J.
Tunks, Roy W.
Ward, Robert A.
Weston, James J.
Wignall, Mark

League Appearances: Barrow, G. 40(1); Bradd, L.J. 41; Brown, J.C. 6; Butler, J.E. 1; Cribley, A. 29(2); Evans, A.C. 29(3); Glenn, D.A. 35; Houghton, P.45(1); Langley, K.J. 1(1); Lloyd, L.V. 36; McAdam, S. 1; McMahon, J. 36; Methven, C.J. 46; O'Keefe, E.G. 22; Quinn, M. 20(9); Sheldon, K.J. 15; Taylor, B.J. 7(1); Trunks, R.W. 31; Ward, R.A. 9; Weston, J.J. 22(3); Wignall, M. 25; Wright, J.K. 9(4).
Goals – League (80): Bradd 19, Houghton 15, Barrow 12, Methven 9, O'Keefe 9 (3 pens), McMahon 4, Quinn M. 4 (1 pen), Evans 2, Glenn 2, Lloyd 2, Sheldon 1, Weston 1.
League Cup (13): Barrow 3, Houghton 2, Lloyd 2, Wignall 2, Bradd 1, Evans 1, Methven 1, Quinn (M) 1.
FA Cup (2): Methven 1, Quinn (M) 1.
Ground: Springfield Park, Wigan, WNT 7BAS (0942 44433)
Nearest stations: Wigan Wallgate and Wigan North West
Manager: Larry Lloyd **Secretary:** E. Jones
Colours: Blue and white striped shirts; blue shorts
Record home gate: 27,500 v Hereford United, December 1953 (FA Cup)
Honours – Champions: Northern Premier League 1970-71, 1974-75
Northern Premier League Cup: 1972

WIMBLEDON DIV. 4

Beasant, David
Belfield, Michael R.
Cork, Alan G.
Downes, Walter J.
Evans, Stewart J.
Gage, Kevin W.
Hodges, Glyn P.
Jones, Stephen R.
Joseph, Francis
Ketteridge, Stephen J.
Leslie, John A.
Morris, Mark J.
Smith, Michael
Thomas, Dean

League Appearances: Armstrong, G. 31; Beasant, D. 46; Bellfield, M.R. 9(5); Blochel, J.D. 6; Boyle, T.D.J. 5; Brown, P.R. 27; Clement, D.T. 9; Cork, A.G. 6; Cunningham, T.E. 2; Downes, W.J. 42; Elliott, R.M. 7(4); Evans, S.J. 18; Fishenden, P. 4(1); Gage, K.W. 15(6); Galliers, S. 11; Geddes, P. 2; Hodges, G.P. 32(2); Hubbick, D. 2(2); Hughes, S.J. 2; Jones, S.R. 11; Joseph, F. 38(2); Ketteridge, S.J. 34(2); Lazarus, P. 17(1); Leslie, J.A. 34(4); Morris, M.J. 33; Smith, M. 39; Suddaby, P. 6; Thomas, D. 18.
Goals – League (16): Joseph 13, Leslie 9, Ketteridge 7 (1 pen), Lazarus 6, Belfield 4, Evans 4, Brown 3 (1 pen), Clement 2, Hodges 2, Hubbick 2, Smith 2, Blochel 1, Boyle 1, Elliott 1, Fishenden 1, Gage 1, Morris 1, own goal 1.
League Cup (1): Cork 1 (pen).
FA Cup (3): Brown 1 (pen), Ketteridge 1, Suddaby 1.

Ground: Plough Lane Ground, Durnsford Road, Wimbledon, SW19 (01-946-6311)
Nearest stations: Wimbledon or Haydons Road (BR) South Wimbledon Tube
Manager: Dave Bassett **Secretary:** Adrian Cook
Colours: Blue shirts with yellow trim; blue shorts with yellow trim
Record home gate: 18,000 v HMS Victory, 1934-35 (FA Amateur Cup)
Honours – Champions: Southern League: 1974-75, 1975-76, 1976-77
Southern League Cup: 1970, 1976

WOLVERHAMPTON WANDERERS — DIV. 2

Atkinson, Hugh A.
Beattie, David B.
Bradshaw, Paul W.
Carr, William M.
Clarke, Wayne
Coy, Robert A.
Daniel, Peter W.
Eves, Melvyn J.
Gallagher, Joseph A.
Gray, Andrew M.
Hibbitt, Kenneth
Hollifield, Michael
Humphrey, John
Kernan, Anthony P.
MacLaren, William S.
Matthews, Michael
Palmer, Geoffrey
Pender, John P.
Richards, John P.
Rudge, Dale A.

League Appearances: Atkinson, H.A. 13(3); Bell, N. 3(2); Berry, G.F. 20; Birch, A. 13(2); Bradshaw, P.W. 42; Brazier, C.J. 11(1); Carr, W.M. 19; Clarke, W. 25(4); Coy, R.A. 20; Daniel, P.W. 20; Eves, M.J. 26(1); Gallagher, J.A. 28; Gray, A.M. 28(1); Hibbitt, K. 33; Hollifield, M. 5; Humphrey, J. 23; Kernan, A.P. 1; Matthews, M. 29(3); Moss, C.A. 1; Palmer, G. 33(1); Parkin, D. 21; Pender, J.P. 8; Richards, J.P. 30(4); Teasdale, J. 1; Villazan, R. 9(2).
Goals – League (32): Eves 7, Clarke 6, Gray 5, Hibbitt 4, Richards 3, Daniel 2, Matthews 2, Atkinson 1, Brazier 1, Palmer 1 (pen),
League Cup (3): Gallagher 1, Gray 1, Richards 1.
FA Cup (1): Gray 1.
Ground: Molineux, Wolverhampton WV1 4QR (Wolverhampton (0902) 712181)
Nearest station: Wolverhampton
Manager: Ian Greaves **Secretary:** P. A. Shaw
Colours: Old gold shirts with black trim; black shorts
Record home gate: 61,315 v Liverpool, February 1939 (FA Cup)
Honours – Champions: Division 1: 1953-54, 1957-58, 1958-59; Division 2: 1931-32, 1976-77; Division 3 North: 1923-24
FA Cup winners: 1892-93, 1907-08, 1948-49, 1959-60
League Cup winners: 1973-74, 1979-80

WREXHAM — DIV. 3

Arkwright, Ian
Bater, Philip T.
Buxton, Stephen C.
Davis, Gareth
Dowman, Stephen J.
Fox, Stephen D.
Hill, Alan G.
Hunt, Simon
Jones, Joseph P.
McNeil, Richard
Neidzwiecki, Edward A.
Parker, Stuart E.
Ronson, William
Vinter, Michael

League Appearances: Arkwright, I. 4; Bater, P.T. 36; Buxton, S.C. 7(2); Carrodus F. 41; Cartwright, L. 4; Cegielski, W. 34(1); Davis, G. 13(1); Dowman, S.J. 40; Edwards, R.I. 28(1); Fox, S.D. 38; Hill, A.G. 18(2); Hunt, S. 15(4); Jones, J.P. 35(1); Jones, S.A. 2(2); Leman, D. 17; McNeil, R. 33; Niedzwiecki, E.A. 42; Ronson, W. 31(1); Vinter, M.24(6).
Goals – League (40): Edwards 11, McNeil 9 (4 pens), Vinter 5, Carrodus 4, Buxton 3, Hunt 2, Bater 1 (pen), Fox 1, Hill 1, Leman 1, Ronson 1, own goal 1.
League Cup (7): Vinter 3, Edwards 2, Davis 1, Hunt 1.
FA Cup (5): McNeil 2, Vinter 2, Dowman 1.
Ground: The Racecourse, Mold Road, Wrexham LL1 2AN (Wrexham (0978) 262129)
Nearest station: Wrexham General
Manager: Mel Sutton **Secretary:** C. N. Wison
Colours: Red shirts with white trimmings; white shorts with red stripe
Record home gate: 34,445 v Manchester United, January 1957 (FA Cup)
Honours – Champions: Division 3: 1977-78
FA Cup winners: Nil

YORK CITY — DIV. 4

Aitken, Peter	Crosby, Malcolm	Laverick, Michael G.
Astbury, Michael J.	Dawson, Richard	Pollard, Brian E.
Bentham, John J.	Flood, Edward	Senior, Stephen
Blackburn, Edwin H.	Ford, Gary	Stanley, Thomas
Byrne, John F.	Hood, Derek	Walwyn, Keith I.

League Appearances: Aitken, P. 18; Astbury, M.J. 15; Bentham, J.J. 22(1); Blackburn, E.H. 31; Byrne, J.F. 28(1); Craig, D.M. 7; Croft, S.D. 14; Crosby, M. 19(4); Czuczman, M. 17; Dawson, R. 43; Fell, G.C. 2(3); Flood, E. 13(2); Ford, G. 40(1); Hedley, G. 5; Hood, D. 46; Kay, R. 37; Laverick, M.G. 26; McDonald, I.C. 10; McGhie, W.L. 1(2); Pollard, B.E. 25(1); Senior, S. 14(3); Smith, D. 7; Smith, M. 1; Stanley, T. 6(3); Sweeney, G. 12; Waldron, A. 3; Walwyn, K.I. 44.
Goals – League (69): Walwyn 23, Ford 8, Hood 8 (5 pens), Byrne 6, Kay 4, Laverick 4, Pollard 3, own goals 3, Aitken 2, Crosby 2, McDonald 2 (1 pen), Hedley 1, Senior 1, Smith (D) 1, Waldron 1.
League Cup (1): Byrne 1.
FA Cup (4): Pollard 2, Walwyn 2, Ford 1.
Ground: Bootham Crescent, York YO3 7AQ (York (0904) 24447)
Nearest station: York
Manager: Barry Lyons **Secretary:** S. B. Winship
Colours: Red shirts with red and blue trim; navy blue shorts with red and blue stripe
Record home gate: 28,123 v Huddersfield, March 1938 (FA Cup)
Honours – Champions: Nil
FA Cup winners: Nil

THE LEAGUE – DIVISION I

HOME TEAM	Arsenal	Aston Villa	Birmingham City	Brighton & H.A.	Coventry C.	Everton	Ipswich Town	Leeds United
Arsenal	—	4–3	1–0	0–0	1–0	1–0	1–0	1–0
Aston Villa	0–2	—	0–0	3–0	2–1	1–2	0–1	1–4
Birmingham City	0–1	0–1	—	1–0	3–3	0–2	1–1	0–1
Brighton & Hove Albion	2–1	0–1	1–1	—	2–2	3–1	0–1	1–0
Coventry City	1–0	1–1	0–1	0–1	—	1–0	2–4	4–0
Everton	2–1	2–0	3–1	1–1	3–2	—	2–1	1–0
Ipswich Town	2–1	3–1	3–2	3–1	1–0	3–0	—	2–1
Leeds United	0–0	1–1	3–3	2–1	0–0	1–1	0–2	—
Liverpool	2–0	0–0	3–1	0–1	4–0	3–1	4–0	3–0
Manchester City	0–0	1–0	4–2	4–0	1–3	1–1	1–1	4–0
Manchester United	0–0	4–1	1–1	2–0	0–1	1–1	1–2	1–0
Middlesbrough	1–3	3–3	2–1	2–1	0–0	0–2	0–1	0–0
Nottingham Forest	1–2	1–1	2–1	2–1	2–1	0–1	1–1	2–1
Notts County	2–1	1–0	1–4	4–1	2–1	2–2	1–4	2–1
Southampton	3–1	0–3	3–1	0–2	5–5	1–0	4–3	4–0
Stoke City	0–1	1–0	1–0	0–0	4–0	3–1	2–0	1–2
Sunderland	0–0	2–1	2–0	3–0	0–0	3–1	1–1	0–1
Swansea City	2–0	2–1	1–0	0–0	0–0	1–3	1–2	5–1
Tottenham Hotspur	2–2	1–3	1–1	0–1	1–2	3–0	1–0	2–1
West Bromwich Albion	0–2	0–1	1–1	0–0	1–2	0–0	1–2	2–0
West Ham United	1–2	2–2	2–2	1–1	5–2	1–1	2–0	4–3
Wolverhampton W	1–1	0–3	1–1	0–1	1–0	0–3	2–1	1–0

1981-82 RESULTS

Liverpool	Manchester C.	Manchester U.	Middlesbrough	Nottingham Forest	Notts County	Southampton	Stoke City	Sunderland	Swansea C.	Tottenham H.	W.B.A.	West Ham U.	Wolverhampton W.
1–1	1–0	0–0	1–0	2–0	1–0	4–1	0–1	1–1	0–2	1–3	2–2	2–0	2–1
0–3	0–0	1–1	1–0	3–1	0–1	1–1	2–2	1–0	3–0	1–1	2–1	3–2	3–1
0–1	3–0	0–1	0–0	4–3	2–1	4–0	2–1	2–0	2–1	0–0	3–3	2–2	0–3
3–3	4–1	0–1	2–0	0–1	2–2	1–1	0–0	2–1	1–2	1–3	2–2	1–0	2–0
1–2	0–1	2–1	1–1	0–1	1–5	4–2	3–0	6–1	3–1	0–0	0–2	1–0	0–0
1–3	0–1	3–3	2–0	2–1	3–1	1–1	0–0	1–2	3–1	1–1	1–0	0–0	1–1
2–0	2–0	2–1	3–1	1–3	1–3	5–2	2–0	3–3	2–3	2–1	1–0	3–2	1–0
0–2	0–1	0–0	1–1	1–1	1–0	1–3	0–0	1–0	2–0	0–0	3–1	3–3	3–0
—	1–3	1–2	1–1	2–0	1–0	0–1	2–0	1–0	2–2	3–1	1–0	3–0	2–1
0–5	—	0–0	3–2	0–0	1–0	1–1	1–1	2–3	4–0	0–1	2–1	0–1	2–1
0–1	1–1	—	1–0	0–0	2–1	1–0	2–0	0–0	1–0	2–0	1–0	1–0	5–0
0–0	0–0	0–2	—	1–1	3–0	0–1	3–2	0–0	1–1	1–3	1–0	2–3	0–0
0–2	1–1	0–1	1–1	—	0–2	2–1	0–0	2–0	0–2	2–0	0–0	0–0	0–1
0–4	1–1	1–3	0–1	1–2	—	1–1	3–1	2–0	0–1	2–2	1–2	1–1	4–0
2–3	2–1	3–2	2–0	2–0	3–1	—	4–3	1–0	3–1	1–2	0–0	2–1	4–1
1–5	1–3	0–3	2–0	1–2	2–2	0–2	—	0–1	1–2	0–2	3–0	2–1	2–1
0–2	1–0	1–5	0–2	2–3	1–1	2–0	0–2	—	0–1	0–2	1–2	0–2	0–0
2–0	2–0	2–0	1–2	1–2	3–2	1–0	3–0	2–0	—	2–1	3–1	0–1	0–0
2–2	2–0	3–1	1–0	3–0	3–1	3–2	2–0	2–2	2–1	—	1–2	0–4	6–1
1–1	0–1	0–3	2–0	2–1	2–4	1–1	1–2	2–3	4–1	1–0	—	0–0	3–0
1–1	1–1	1–1	3–2	0–1	1–0	4–2	3–2	1–1	1–1	2–2	3–1	—	3–1
1–0	4–1	0–1	0–0	0–0	3–2	0–0	2–0	0–1	0–1	0–1	1–2	2–1	—

THE LEAGUE – DIVISION II

HOME TEAM	Barnsley	Blackburn R.	Bolton W.	Cambridge U.	Cardiff City	Charlton Ath.	Chelsea	Crystal P.
Barnsley	—	0–1	3–0	0–0	0–1	1–0	2–1	2–0
Blackburn Rovers	2–1	—	0–2	1–0	1–0	0–2	1–1	1–0
Bolton Wanderers	2–1	2–2	—	3–4	1–0	2–0	2–2	0–0
Cambridge United	2–1	1–0	2–1	—	2–1	4–0	1–0	0–0
Cardiff City	0–0	1–3	2–1	5–4	—	0–1	1–2	0–1
Charlton Athletic	2–1	2–0	1–0	0–0	2–2	—	3–4	2–1
Chelsea	1–2	1–1	2–0	4–1	1–0	2–2	—	1–2
Crystal Palace	1–2	1–2	1–0	2–1	1–0	2–0	0–1	—
Derby County	0–1	1–1	0–2	2–1	0–0	1–1	1–1	4–1
Grimsby Town	3–2	1–1	1–1	1–2	0–1	3–3	3–3	0–1
Leicester City	1–0	1–0	1–0	4–1	3–1	3–1	1–1	1–1
Luton Town	1–1	2–0	2–0	1–0	2–3	3–0	2–2	1–0
Newcastle United	1–0	0–0	2–0	1–0	2–1	4–1	1–0	0–0
Norwich City	1–1	2–0	0–0	2–1	2–1	5–0	2–1	1–0
Oldham Athletic	1–1	0–0	1–1	2–0	2–2	1–0	1–0	0–0
Orient	1–3	0–0	3–0	0–0	1–1	1–1	0–2	0–0
Queens Park Rangers	1–0	2–0	7–1	2–1	2–0	4–0	0–2	1–0
Rotherham United	2–4	4–1	2–0	1–0	1–0	2–1	6–0	2–0
Sheffield Wednesday	2–2	2–2	0–1	2–1	2–1	1–1	0–0	1–0
Shrewsbury Town	0–2	1–2	2–0	1–0	1–1	1–1	1–0	1–0
Watford	3–1	3–2	3–0	0–0	0–0	2–2	1–0	1–1
Wrexham	0–0	1–0	2–1	0–0	3–1	1–0	1–0	0–1

1981-82 RESULTS

Derby County	Grimsby Town	Leicester C.	Luton Town	Newcastle U.	Norwich C.	Oldham Ath.	Orient	Q.P.R.	Rotherham U.	Sheffield W.	Shrewsbury T.	Watford	Wrexham
0–0	3–2	0–2	4–3	1–0	0–1	3–1	1–0	3–0	3–0	1–0	4–0	0–0	2–2
4–1	2–0	0–2	0–1	4–1	3–0	3–0	2–0	2–1	2–0	0–1	0–0	1–2	0–0
3–2	1–2	0–3	1–2	1–0	0–1	0–2	1–0	1–0	0–1	3–1	1–1	2–0	2–0
1–2	2–2	1–2	1–1	1–0	1–2	0–0	2–0	1–0	3–0	1–2	2–0	1–2	2–3
1–0	2–1	3–1	2–3	0–4	1–0	0–1	2–1	1–2	1–2	0–2	1–1	2–0	3–2
2–1	2–0	0–4	0–0	0–1	0–0	3–1	5–2	1–2	1–2	3–0	1–0	1–1	1–0
0–2	1–1	4–1	1–2	2–1	2–1	2–2	2–2	2–1	1–4	2–1	3–1	1–3	2–0
0–1	0–3	0–2	3–3	1–2	2–1	4–0	1–0	0–0	3–1	1–2	0–1	0–3	2–1
—	1–1	3–1	0–0	2–2	0–2	1–0	1–2	3–1	3–1	3–1	1–1	3–2	2–1
1–0	—	2–2	0–0	1–1	1–2	2–1	1–2	2–1	1–2	0–1	5–1	0–2	1–1
2–1	1–2	—	1–2	3–0	1–4	2–1	0–1	3–2	1–0	0–0	0–0	1–1	1–0
3–2	6–0	2–1	—	3–2	2–0	2–0	2–0	3–2	3–1	0–3	4–1	4–1	0–0
3–0	0–1	0–0	3–2	—	2–1	2–0	1–0	0–4	1–1	1–0	2–0	0–1	4–2
4–1	2–1	0–0	1–3	2–1	—	1–2	2–0	0–1	2–0	2–3	2–1	4–2	4–0
1–1	3–1	1–1	1–1	3–1	2–0	—	3–2	2–0	0–3	0–3	1–1	1–1	2–1
3–2	1–2	3–0	0–3	1–0	1–1	0–3	—	1–1	1–2	3–0	2–0	1–3	0–0
3–0	1–0	2–0	1–2	3–0	2–0	0–0	3–0	—	1–1	2–0	2–1	0–0	1–1
2–1	2–2	1–1	2–2	0–0	4–1	1–2	1–0	1–0	—	2–2	3–0	1–2	2–0
1–1	1–1	2–0	3–3	2–1	2–1	2–1	2–0	1–3	2–0	—	0–0	3–1	0–3
4–1	2–0	1–1	2–2	0–0	0–2	2–1	2–0	2–1	2–1	0–1	—	0–2	1–1
6–1	0–2	3–1	1–1	2–3	3–0	1–1	3–0	4–0	1–0	4–0	3–1	—	2–0
1–1	2–0	0–0	0–2	4–2	2–3	0–3	0–1	1–3	3–2	0–1	1–0	0–1	—

THE LEAGUE – DIVISION III

HOME TEAM	Brentford	Bristol C.	Bristol R.	Burnley	Carlisle U.	Chester	Chesterfield	Doncaster R.	Exeter City	Fulham
Brentford	—	0–1	1–0	0–0	1–2	1–0	2–0	2–2	2–0	0–1
Bristol City	0–1	—	1–2	2–3	1–1	1–0	0–0	2–2	3–2	0–0
Bristol Rovers	1–2	1–0	—	2–1	0–1	2–2	1–0	3–0	3–2	1–2
Burnley	0–0	2–0	4–0	—	1–0	1–0	1–1	0–1	3–3	2–2
Carlisle United	1–0	2–2	1–2	1–0	—	3–0	3–0	2–0	3–2	1–2
Chester	1–2	0–0	1–1	0–1	0–1	—	0–2	1–1	0–2	0–2
Chesterfield	0–2	1–0	2–0	1–2	1–0	3–5	—	3–1	2–1	3–0
Doncaster Rovers	1–0	2–2	4–2	0–1	1–1	4–3	0–0	—	3–0	2–1
Exeter City	3–1	4–0	1–3	2–1	2–1	3–0	0–3	2–1	—	1–0
Fulham	1–2	2–1	4–2	1–1	4–1	2–0	1–0	3–1	4–1	—
Gillingham	1–1	1–1	2–0	3–1	0–0	0–1	3–2	3–0	2–3	2–0
Huddersfield Town	1–1	5–0	0–2	1–2	2–1	1–2	1–1	1–2	1–1	1–0
Lincoln City	1–0	1–2	1–0	1–1	0–0	3–0	2–1	5–0	2–0	1–1
Millwall	0–1	2–0	0–0	4–3	1–2	2–1	3–2	0–2	5–1	4–3
Newport County	0–1	1–1	1–1	0–0	2–0	0–1	1–0	1–0	1–1	1–3
Oxford United	1–2	1–0	1–1	0–0	2–1	3–1	1–1	3–1	0–0	2–0
Plymouth Argyle	1–0	2–1	4–0	1–1	1–0	5–1	0–2	4–2	2–1	3–1
Portsmouth	2–2	2–0	0–0	1–2	1–2	2–0	5–1	0–0	2–0	1–1
Preston North End	1–3	1–3	0–1	1–1	0–1	0–1	2–0	3–1	1–0	1–3
Reading	4–1	3–1	0–3	1–1	2–2	4–1	0–2	3–3	4–0	0–3
Southend United	1–1	3–0	1–0	1–4	1–1	2–0	0–2	1–1	2–1	0–0
Swindon Town	0–3	0–0	5–2	1–2	2–1	3–0	1–2	2–2	3–2	1–4
Walsall	3–0	0–1	2–1	1–1	1–1	2–1	1–1	0–0	2–1	1–1
Wimbledon	1–2	0–0	1–0	0–0	3–1	1–0	3–1	0–1	1–1	1–3

1981-82 RESULTS

Gillingham	Huddersfield T.	Lincoln C.	Millwall	Newport County	Oxford United	Plymouth Arg.	Portsmouth	Preston N.E.	Reading	Southend U.	Swindon Town	Walsall	Wimbledon
0–1	0–1	3–1	4–1	2–0	1–2	0–0	2–2	0–0	1–2	0–1	4–2	0–0	2–3
2–1	0–0	0–1	4–1	2–1	0–2	3–2	0–1	0–0	2–0	0–2	0–3	0–1	1–3
2–0	3–2	0–2	0–1	2–0	1–0	2–3	1–1	2–0	1–1	2–1	1–4	2–1	2–2
1–0	0–0	1–0	1–1	2–1	2–1	1–0	3–0	2–0	3–0	3–5	0–2	2–1	2–2
2–0	2–2	1–0	2–1	2–2	2–1	3–1	2–0	1–0	2–1	3–2	1–1	2–1	2–1
0–0	3–1	1–2	0–0	0–2	2–2	0–3	3–2	0–1	2–3	1–1	0–0	0–0	1–1
1–3	1–0	0–2	0–1	1–0	2–2	2–2	2–2	0–0	2–1	1–2	2–1	1–0	2–0
1–1	1–2	4–1	1–0	0–2	1–1	2–2	0–0	1–0	0–1	1–1	0–0	1–0	1–3
1–1	1–0	1–2	5–4	1–0	1–2	1–1	3–3	4–3	4–3	1–1	1–2	2–0	2–1
0–0	2–2	1–1	0–0	3–1	0–0	1–3	1–1	3–0	2–2	2–1	2–0	1–1	4–1
—	3–2	1–0	1–1	1–1	2–1	3–2	4–2	0–2	2–1	2–0	1–0	1–4	6–1
2–0	—	0–2	1–2	2–0	2–0	0–0	0–1	2–3	6–1	3–2	3–0	2–1	1–1
2–0	2–0	—	0–1	2–2	2–1	2–0	1–1	1–2	2–1	1–1	2–0	1–1	5–1
1–2	1–3	1–1	—	1–0	1–2	2–1	1–0	2–1	0–1	1–1	0–0	2–0	2–1
4–2	1–0	0–0	1–1	—	3–2	0–1	1–1	1–1	3–1	3–2	1–0	2–2	0–0
1–1	1–0	1–1	0–0	1–1	—	1–0	0–2	3–0	1–0	0–2	5–0	0–1	0–3
1–2	1–1	0–2	2–1	1–2	0–1	—	0–0	0–3	1–1	0–0	2–1	4–1	2–0
1–0	2–1	1–1	2–2	0–0	1–1	1–0	—	1–1	3–0	0–0	3–0	1–0	1–0
1–1	1–1	1–1	1–0	2–1	2–2	1–0	1–0	—	0–0	1–0	0–0	1–0	3–2
3–2	1–2	3–2	4–0	2–1	0–3	2–2	2–1	2–1	—	0–2	1–1	0–0	2–1
3–0	4–0	0–2	2–2	0–4	0–1	3–0	2–0	2–2	2–0	—	0–0	3–2	2–0
0–1	1–5	1–0	1–2	1–1	3–2	0–2	2–0	4–0	0–2	0–0	—	2–2	4–1
1–0	1–1	2–1	1–1	3–1	1–3	0–1	3–1	0–3	1–2	0–1	5–0	—	1–0
0–2	2–0	1–1	1–3	2–3	2–3	2–1	3–2	3–2	0–0	3–0	1–1	2–0	—

THE LEAGUE – DIVISION IV

HOME TEAM	Aldershot	Blackpool	Bournemouth	Bradford City	Bury	Colchester U.	Crewe Alexandra	Darlington	Halifax Town	Hartlepool
Aldershot	—	3–2	2–0	0–2	1–2	1–1	3–0	0–0	3–1	1–2
Blackpool	0–2	—	0–3	1–0	1–1	0–0	5–0	1–0	7–1	2–2
Bournemouth	2–2	1–0	—	0–2	3–2	1–1	2–0	2–0	1–1	5–1
Bradford City	4–1	1–0	2–2	—	1–1	2–1	4–1	3–0	5–2	1–0
Bury	1–1	0–1	2–2	1–1	—	4–3	2–1	2–0	1–1	1–1
Colchester United	1–1	2–1	1–2	1–2	1–1	—	1–1	1–0	1–1	3–3
Crewe Alexandra	2–3	1–1	0–0	0–1	1–2	1–3	—	1–0	0–1	1–2
Darlington	0–1	2–2	0–1	1–5	2–3	1–2	1–0	—	1–1	5–2
Halifax Town	2–2	0–0	1–1	0–0	2–1	0–2	2–1	3–3	—	2–0
Hartlepool	2–2	2–2	1–1	0–2	1–0	1–3	1–2	1–2	3–2	—
Hereford United	0–1	2–1	1–2	1–2	3–0	2–2	4–1	1–1	2–2	1–1
Hull City	1–2	1–0	0–0	2–1	3–2	2–3	1–0	1–3	2–0	5–2
Mansfield Town	1–0	2–2	0–1	0–2	1–1	1–3	0–1	2–3	3–2	3–2
Northampton Town	0–0	0–1	1–0	0–2	1–0	1–2	3–0	0–1	0–1	2–1
Peterborough United	7–1	3–1	1–0	2–0	1–0	2–2	3–0	3–1	0–0	4–4
Port Vale	1–0	2–0	1–1	1–1	0–0	2–1	0–0	2–2	0–0	5–2
Rochdale	0–0	0–0	0–1	1–1	1–1	1–2	1–0	3–2	0–1	2–1
Scunthorpe United	1–1	1–1	0–2	1–3	2–2	2–1	0–1	1–1	0–0	2–1
Sheffield United	2–0	3–1	0–0	1–1	1–1	1–0	4–0	0–0	2–2	1–1
Stockport County	4–2	2–3	1–2	2–3	2–1	0–0	2–0	1–0	2–1	0–2
Torquay United	2–1	1–1	1–2	2–0	1–1	1–0	1–1	1–2	2–2	1–1
Tranmere Rovers	1–0	3–1	0–1	1–1	1–3	2–1	3–0	1–1	1–1	1–0
Wigan Athletic	1–0	2–1	0–0	4–1	3–2	3–2	3–0	2–1	2–0	1–1
York City	4–0	0–4	0–1	0–3	0–0	3–0	6–0	2–2	4–0	1–2

1981-82 RESULTS

Hereford United	Hull City	Mansfield T.	Northampton T.	Peterborough U.	Port Vale	Rochdale	Scunthorpe U.	Sheffield United	Stockport County	Torquay United	Tranmere Rovers	Wigan Athletic	York City
2–2	0–3	2–3	2–1	0–1	1–2	2–2	4–0	1–1	1–1	1–1	2–1	2–0	0–1
1–0	3–1	2–3	1–0	2–2	2–3	1–1	2–0	0–1	2–0	2–1	1–2	1–2	3–1
1–1	1–0	1–0	1–1	1–1	1–1	1–0	2–0	0–0	1–0	4–0	1–1	0–0	5–1
0–0	1–1	3–4	2–1	2–0	1–0	2–0	0–0	0–2	5–1	3–0	1–1	3–3	6–2
1–1	0–2	3–2	7–1	3–1	3–2	3–0	4–0	1–1	2–0	0–1	4–0	5–3	3–1
4–0	2–0	0–1	5–1	1–1	1–0	3–2	2–1	5–2	0–1	3–0	4–0	1–2	4–0
1–0	1–1	0–2	2–2	0–1	0–2	1–2	3–0	2–3	0–2	0–1	1–1	0–1	1–1
0–1	2–1	1–0	3–0	0–0	1–1	2–0	4–1	0–2	2–0	1–1	1–2	3–1	3–1
1–2	2–2	2–1	2–1	1–1	1–1	0–0	1–2	1–5	4–1	1–2	0–2	0–0	0–0
2–1	3–2	3–0	3–1	0–1	3–1	1–1	3–3	2–3	2–2	0–0	0–0	2–1	3–2
—	2–2	3–1	2–1	2–1	1–0	0–0	2–1	1–1	0–0	0–3	1–1	3–0	2–1
2–1	—	2–0	0–1	1–1	3–1	2–1	2–0	2–1	0–0	1–0	1–2	0–2	2–0
2–1	3–3	—	4–1	1–2	1–3	4–3	1–1	1–1	2–2	3–1	3–0	1–2	0–2
2–3	1–1	1–1	—	1–0	3–5	2–1	1–1	1–2	0–0	2–0	3–2	2–3	5–0
3–1	3–0	1–0	1–0	—	1–0	5–1	2–1	0–4	2–0	1–0	1–2	0–3	0–1
1–1	2–1	0–0	1–0	1–3	—	1–1	2–1	0–2	1–0	2–0	0–0	1–1	0–0
0–1	0–1	1–1	5–3	1–1	1–2	—	1–1	0–1	4–1	1–0	0–0	1–1	2–0
2–2	4–4	1–0	2–1	0–1	0–0	1–0	—	2–1	0–0	0–2	2–1	2–7	0–3
2–2	0–0	4–1	7–3	4–0	2–1	3–1	1–0	—	4–0	4–1	2–0	1–0	4–0
1–1	1–2	3–0	0–0	3–0	1–2	0–4	1–1	1–0	—	2–1	1–1	0–1	4–1
1–2	2–1	2–0	2–2	1–2	0–1	2–1	1–0	1–1	1–0	—	1–2	0–0	3–2
0–0	2–2	2–2	0–2	1–2	1–2	2–0	0–1	2–2	2–0	1–1	—	0–0	0–2
1–1	2–1	3–1	3–1	5–0	2–0	1–1	2–1	0–1	2–1	1–0	0–0	—	4–2
3–4	1–3	2–1	2–1	4–3	2–0	1–2	3–1	3–4	2–2	1–1	1–3	0–0	—

FOOTBALL LEAGUE

FINAL TABLES 1981-82

First Division

		Home			Goals		Away			Goals			
	P	W	D	L	F	A	W	D	L	F	A	Pt	Dif
Liverpool	42	14	3	4	39	14	12	6	3	41	18	87	+48
Ipswich Town	42	17	1	3	47	25	9	4	8	28	28	83	+22
Manchester United	42	12	6	3	27	9	10	6	5	32	20	78	+30
Tottenham Hotspur	42	12	4	5	41	26	8	7	6	26	22	71	+19
Arsenal	42	13	5	3	27	15	7	6	8	21	22	71	+11
Swansea City	42	13	3	5	34	16	8	3	10	24	35	69	+7
Southampton	42	15	2	4	49	30	4	7	10	23	37	66	+5
Everton	42	11	7	3	33	21	6	6	9	23	29	64	+6
West Ham United	42	9	10	2	42	29	5	6	10	24	28	58	+9
Manchester City	42	9	7	5	32	23	6	6	9	17	27	58	−1
Aston Villa	42	9	6	6	28	24	6	6	9	27	29	57	+2
Nottingham Forest	42	7	7	7	19	20	8	5	8	23	28	57	−6
Brighton & H.A.	42	8	7	6	30	24	5	6	10	13	28	52	−9
Coventry City	42	9	4	8	31	24	4	7	10	25	38	50	−6
Notts County	42	8	5	8	32	33	5	3	13	29	36	47	−8
Birmingham City	42	8	6	7	29	25	2	8	11	24	36	44	−8
West Bromwich A.	42	6	6	9	24	25	5	5	11	22	32	44	−11
Stoke City	42	9	2	10	27	28	3	6	12	17	35	44	−19
Sunderland	42	6	5	10	19	26	5	6	10	19	32	44	−20
Leeds United	42	6	11	4	23	20	4	1	16	16	41	42	−22
Wolverhampton W.	42	8	5	8	19	20	2	5	14	13	43	40	−31
Middlesbrough	42	5	9	7	20	24	3	6	12	14	28	39	−18

Second Division

		Home			Goals		Away			Goals			
	P	W	D	L	F	A	W	D	L	F	A	Pt	Dif
Luton Town	42	16	3	2	48	19	9	10	2	38	27	88	+40
Watford	42	13	6	2	46	16	10	5	6	30	26	80	+34
Norwich City	42	14	3	4	41	19	8	2	11	23	31	71	+14
Sheffield W.	42	10	8	3	31	23	10	2	9	24	28	70	+4
Q.P.R.	42	15	4	2	40	9	6	2	13	25	34	69	+22
Barnsley	42	13	4	4	33	14	6	6	9	26	27	67	+18
Rotherham U.	42	13	5	3	42	19	7	2	12	24	35	67	+12
Leicester City	42	12	5	4	31	19	6	7	8	25	28	66	+9
Newcastle U.	42	14	4	3	30	14	4	4	13	22	36	62	+2
Blackburn R.	42	12	3	6	29	15	4	8	9	18	28	59	+4
Oldham Ath.	42	9	10	2	28	20	6	4	11	22	31	59	−1
Chelsea	42	10	5	6	37	30	5	7	9	23	30	57	0
Charlton Ath.	42	11	5	5	32	22	2	7	12	17	43	51	−16
Cambridge U.	42	11	4	6	31	19	2	5	14	17	34	48	−5
Crystal Palace	42	9	2	10	25	26	4	7	10	9	19	48	−11
Derby County	42	9	8	4	32	23	3	4	14	21	45	48	−15
Grimsby Town	42	5	8	8	29	30	6	5	10	24	35	46	−12
Shrewsbury T.	42	10	6	5	26	19	1	7	13	11	38	46	−20
Bolton W.	42	10	4	7	28	24	3	3	15	11	37	46	−22
Cardiff City	42	9	2	10	28	32	3	6	12	17	29	44	−16
Wrexham	42	9	4	8	22	22	2	7	12	18	34	44	−16
Orient	42	6	8	7	23	24	4	1	16	13	37	39	−25

Third Division

		Home			Goals		Away			Goals			
	P	W	D	L	F	A	W	D	L	F	A	Pt	Dif
Burnley	46	13	7	3	37	20	8	10	5	29	25	80	+21
Carlisle U.	46	17	4	2	44	21	6	7	10	21	29	80	+15
Fulham	46	12	9	2	44	22	9	6	8	33	29	78	+26
Lincoln City	46	13	7	3	40	16	8	7	8	26	24	77	+26
Oxford U.	46	10	8	5	28	18	9	6	8	35	31	71	+14
Gillingham	46	14	5	4	44	26	6	6	11	20	30	71	+8
Southend U.	46	11	7	5	35	23	7	8	8	28	28	69	+12
Brentford	46	8	6	9	28	22	11	5	7	28	25	68	+9
Millwall	46	12	4	7	36	28	6	9	8	26	34	67	0
Plymouth Arg.	46	12	5	6	37	24	6	6	11	27	32	65	+8
Chesterfield	46	12	4	7	33	27	6	6	11	24	31	64	−1
Reading	46	11	6	6	43	35	6	5	12	24	40	62	−8
Portsmouth	46	11	10	2	33	14	3	9	11	23	37	61	+5
Preston N.E.	46	10	7	6	25	22	6	6	11	25	34	61	−6
Bristol Rovers*	46	12	4	7	35	28	6	5	12	23	37	61	−7
Newport Co.	46	9	10	4	28	21	5	6	12	26	33	58	0
Huddersfield T.	46	10	5	8	38	25	5	7	11	26	34	57	+5
Exeter City	46	14	4	5	46	33	2	5	16	25	51	57	−13
Doncaster R.	46	9	9	5	31	24	4	8	11	24	44	56	−13
Walsall	46	10	7	6	32	23	3	7	13	19	32	53	−4
Wimbledon	46	10	6	7	33	27	4	5	14	28	48	53	−14
Swindon T.	46	9	5	9	37	36	4	8	11	18	35	52	−16
Bristol City	46	7	6	10	24	29	4	7	12	16	36	46	−25
Chester	46	2	10	11	16	30	5	1	17	20	48	32	−42

Fourth Division

		Home			Goals		Away			Goals			
	P	W	D	L	F	A	W	D	L	F	A	Pt	Dif
Sheffield U.	46	15	8	0	53	15	12	7	4	41	26	96	+53
Bradford City	46	14	7	2	52	23	12	6	5	36	22	91	+43
Wigan Ath.	46	17	5	1	47	18	9	8	6	33	28	91	+34
Bournemouth	46	12	10	1	37	15	11	9	3	25	15	88	+32
Peterborough U.	46	16	3	4	46	22	8	7	8	25	35	82	+14
Colchester U.	46	12	6	5	47	23	8	6	9	35	34	72	+25
Port Vale	46	9	12	2	26	17	9	4	10	30	32	70	+7
Hull City	46	14	3	6	36	23	5	9	9	34	38	69	+9
Bury	46	13	7	3	53	26	4	10	9	27	33	68	+21
Hereford U.	46	10	9	4	36	25	6	10	7	28	33	67	+6
Tranmere R.	46	7	9	7	27	25	7	9	7	24	31	60	−5
Blackpool	46	11	5	7	40	26	4	8	11	26	34	58	+6
Darlington	46	10	5	8	36	28	5	8	10	25	34	58	−1
Hartlepool	46	9	8	6	39	34	4	8	11	34	50	55	−11
Torquay U.	46	9	8	6	30	25	5	5	13	17	34	55	−12
Aldershot	46	8	7	8	34	29	5	8	10	23	39	54	−11
York City	46	9	5	9	45	37	5	3	15	24	54	50	−22
Stockport Co.	46	10	5	8	34	28	2	8	13	14	39	49	−19
Halifax T.	46	6	11	6	28	30	3	11	9	23	42	49	−21
Mansfield T.*	46	8	6	9	39	39	5	4	14	24	42	47	−18
Rochdale	46	7	9	7	26	22	3	7	13	24	40	46	−12
Northampton T.	46	9	5	9	32	27	2	4	17	25	57	42	−27
Scunthorpe U.	46	7	9	7	26	35	2	6	15	17	44	42	−36
Crewe Alex.	46	3	6	14	19	32	3	3	17	10	52	27	−55

**Two points deducted for fielding an unregistered player.*

DIVISION ONE LEAGUE POSITIONS (1950-82)

	1981–82	1980–81	1979–80	1978–79	1977–78	1976–77	1975–76	1974–75	1973–74	1972–73	1971–72	1970–71	1969–70	1968–69	1967–68	1966–67
Arsenal	5	3	4	7	5	8	17	16	10	2	5	1	12	4	9	7
Aston Villa	11	1	7	8	8	4	16	—	—	—	—	—	—	—	—	21
Birmingham City	16	13	—	21	11	13	19	17	19	10	—	—	—	—	—	—
Blackburn Rovers	—	—	—	—	—	—	—	—	—	—	—	—	—	—	—	—
Blackpool	—	—	—	—	—	—	—	—	—	—	—	22	—	—	—	22
Bolton Wanderers	—	—	22	17	—	—	—	—	—	—	—	—	—	—	—	—
Brighton & H.A.	13	19	16	—	—	—	—	—	—	—	—	—	—	—	—	—
Bristol City	—	—	20	13	17	18	—	—	—	—	—	—	—	—	—	—
Burnley	—	—	—	—	—	—	21	10	6	—	—	21	14	14	13	14
Cardiff City	—	—	—	—	—	—	—	—	—	—	—	—	—	—	—	—
Carlisle United	—	—	—	—	—	—	—	22	—	—	—	—	—	—	—	—
Charlton Athletic	—	—	—	—	—	—	—	—	—	—	—	—	—	—	—	—
Chelsea	—	—	—	22	16	—	—	21	17	12	7	6	3	5	6	9
Coventry City	14	16	15	10	7	19	14	14	16	19	18	10	6	20	20	—
Crystal Palace	—	22	13	—	—	—	—	—	—	21	20	18	20	—	—	—
Derby County	—	—	21	19	12	15	4	1	3	7	1	9	4	—	—	—
Everton	8	15	19	4	3	9	11	4	7	17	15	14	1	3	5	6
Fulham	—	—	—	—	—	—	—	—	—	—	—	—	—	—	22	19
Grimsby	—	—	—	—	—	—	—	—	—	—	—	—	—	—	—	—
Huddersfield Town	—	—	—	—	—	—	—	—	—	—	22	15	—	—	—	—
Ipswich Town	2	2	3	6	18	3	6	3	4	4	13	19	18	12	—	—
Leeds United	20	9	11	5	9	10	5	9	1	3	2	2	2	1	4	4
Leicester City	—	21	—	—	22	11	7	18	9	16	12	—	—	21	12	8
Liverpool	1	5	1	1	2	1	1	2	2	1	3	5	5	2	3	5
Luton Town	—	—	—	—	—	—	—	20	—	—	—	—	—	—	—	—
Manchester City	10	12	17	15	4	2	8	8	14	11	4	11	10	13	1	15
Manchester United	3	8	2	9	10	6	3	—	21	18	8	8	8	11	2	1
Middlesbrough	22	14	9	12	14	12	13	7	—	—	—	—	—	—	—	—
Newcastle United	—	—	—	—	21	5	15	15	15	9	11	12	7	9	10	20
Northampton Town	—	—	—	—	—	—	—	—	—	—	—	—	—	—	—	—
Norwich City	—	20	12	16	13	16	10	—	22	20	—	—	—	—	—	—
Nottingham F.	12	7	5	2	1	—	—	—	—	—	21	16	15	18	11	2
Notts Co.	15	—	—	—	—	—	—	—	—	—	—	—	—	—	—	—
Orient	—	—	—	—	—	—	—	—	—	—	—	—	—	—	—	—
Portsmouth	—	—	—	—	—	—	—	—	—	—	—	—	—	—	—	—
Preston North End	—	—	—	—	—	—	—	—	—	—	—	—	—	—	—	—
Queen's Park Rangers	—	—	—	20	19	14	2	11	8	—	—	—	—	22	—	—
Sheffield United	—	—	—	—	—	—	22	6	13	14	10	—	—	—	21	10
Sheffield Wednesday	—	—	—	—	—	—	—	—	—	—	—	—	22	15	19	11
Southampton	7	6	8	14	—	—	—	—	20	13	19	7	19	7	15	19
Stoke City	18	11	18	—	—	21	12	5	5	15	17	13	9	19	18	12
Sunderland	19	17	—	—	—	20	—	—	—	—	—	—	21	17	16	17
Swansea City	6	—	—	—	—	—	—	—	—	—	—	—	—	—	—	—
Tottenham Hotspur	4	10	14	11	—	22	9	19	11	8	6	3	11	6	7	3
West Bromwich A.	17	4	10	3	6	7	—	—	—	22	16	17	16	10	8	13
West Ham United	9	—	—	19	20	17	18	13	18	6	14	30	17	8	14	16
Wolverhampton W.	21	18	6	—	15	—	20	12	12	5	9	4	13	16	17	—

1965–66	1964–65	1963–64	1962–63	1961–62	1960–61	1959–60	1958–59	1957–58	1956–57	1955–56	1954–55	1953–54	1952–53	1951–52	1950–51	1949–50	
14	13	8	7	10	11	13	3	12	5	5	9	12	1	3	5	6	Arsenal
16	16	19	15	7	9	—	21	14	10	20	6	13	11	6	15	12	Aston Villa
—	22	20	20	17	18	19	9	13	12	6	—	—	—	—	—	22	Birmingham City
22	10	7	11	16	8	17	10	—	—	—	—	—	—	—	—	—	Blackburn Rovers
13	17	18	13	13	20	11	8	7	4	2	19	6	7	9	3	7	Blackpool
—	—	21	18	11	18	6	4	15	9	8	18	5	14	5	8	16	Bolton Wanderers
—	—	—	—	—	—	—	—	—	—	—	—	—	—	—	—	—	Brighton & H.A.
—	—	—	—	—	—	—	—	—	—	—	—	—	—	—	—	—	Bristol City
3	12	9	3	2	4	1	7	6	7	7	10	7	6	14	10	10	Burnley
—	—	—	21	15	—	—	—	21	17	20	10	12	—	—	—	—	Cardiff City
—	—	—	—	—	—	—	—	—	—	—	—	—	—	—	—	—	Carlisle United
—	—	—	—	—	—	—	—	—	22	14	15	9	5	10	17	20	Charlton Athletic
5	3	5	—	22	12	18	14	11	13	16	1	8	19	19	20	13	Chelsea
—	—	—	—	—	—	—	—	—	—	—	—	—	—	—	—	—	Coventry City
—	—	—	—	—	—	—	—	—	—	—	—	—	—	—	—	—	Crystal Palace
—	—	—	—	—	—	—	—	—	—	—	—	—	22	17	11	11	Derby County
11	4	3	1	4	5	15	16	16	15	15	11	—	—	—	22	18	Everton
20	20	15	16	20	17	10	—	—	—	—	—	—	—	22	18	17	Fulham
—	—	—	—	—	—	—	—	—	—	—	—	—	—	—	—	—	Grimsby
—	—	—	—	—	—	—	—	—	—	21	12	3	—	21	19	15	Huddersfield Town
—	—	22	17	1	—	—	—	—	—	—	—	—	—	—	—	—	Ipswich Town
2	2	—	—	—	—	21	15	17	8	—	—	—	—	—	—	—	Leeds United
7	18	11	4	14	6	12	19	18	—	—	21	—	—	—	—	—	Leicester City
1	7	1	8	—	—	—	—	—	—	—	—	22	17	11	9	8	Liverpool
—	—	—	—	—	—	22	17	8	16	10	—	—	—	—	—	—	Luton Town
—	—	—	21	12	13	16	20	5	18	4	7	17	20	15	—	21	Manchester City
4	1	2	19	15	7	7	2	9	1	1	5	4	8	1	2	4	Manchester United
—	—	—	—	—	—	—	—	—	—	—	—	21	13	18	6	9	Middlesbrough
15	—	—	—	—	21	8	11	19	17	11	8	15	16	8	4	5	Newcastle United
21	—	—	—	—	—	—	—	—	—	—	—	—	—	—	—	—	Northampton Town
—	—	—	—	—	—	—	—	—	—	—	—	—	—	—	—	—	Norwich City
18	5	13	9	19	14	20	13	10	—	—	—	—	—	—	—	—	Nottingham Forest
—	—	—	—	—	—	—	—	—	—	—	—	—	—	—	—	—	Notts County
—	—	—	22	—	—	—	—	—	—	—	—	—	—	—	—	—	Orient
—	—	—	—	—	—	—	22	20	19	12	3	14	15	4	7	1	Portsmouth
—	—	—	—	—	22	9	12	2	3	19	14	11	2	7	—	—	Preston North End
—	—	—	—	—	—	—	—	—	—	—	—	—	—	—	—	—	Queen's Park R.
9	19	12	10	5	—	—	—	—	—	22	13	20	—	—	—	—	Sheffield United
17	8	6	6	6	2	5	—	22	14	—	22	19	18	—	21	—	Sheffield Wednesday
—	—	—	—	—	—	—	—	—	—	—	—	—	—	—	—	—	Southampton
10	11	17	—	—	—	—	—	—	—	—	—	—	21	20	13	19	Stoke City
19	15	—	—	—	—	—	—	21	20	9	4	18	9	12	12	3	Sunderland
—	—	—	—	—	—	—	—	—	—	—	—	—	—	—	—	—	Swansea City
8	6	4	2	3	1	3	18	3	2	18	16	16	10	2	1	—	Tottenham Hotspur
6	14	10	14	9	10	4	5	4	11	13	17	2	4	13	16	14	West Bromwich Albion
12	9	14	12	8	16	14	6	—	—	—	—	—	—	—	—	—	West Ham United
—	21	16	5	18	3	2	1	1	6	3	2	1	3	16	14	2	Wolverhampton W.

DIVISION TWO LEAGUE POSITIONS (1950-82)

	1981–82	1980–81	1979–80	1978–79	1977–78	1976–77	1975–76	1974–75	1973–74	1972–73	1971–72	1970–71	1969–70	1968–69	1967–68	1966–67
Aston Villa	—	—	—	—	—	—	—	2	14	3	—	—	21	18	17	—
Barnsley	6	—	—	—	—	—	—	—	—	—	—	—	—	—	—	—
Birmingham City	—	—	3	—	—	—	—	—	—	—	2	9	18	7	4	10
Blackburn Rovers	10	4	—	22	5	12	15	—	—	—	—	21	8	19	9	4
Blackpool	—	—	—	—	20	5	10	7	5	7	6	—	2	8	3	—
Bolton Wanderers	19	18	—	—	1	4	4	10	11	—	—	22	16	17	12	9
Bradford City	—	—	—	—	—	—	—	—	—	—	—	—	—	—	—	—
Brentford	—	—	—	—	—	—	—	—	—	—	—	—	—	—	—	—
Brighton & H.A.	—	—	—	2	4	—	—	—	—	22	—	—	—	—	—	—
Bristol City	—	21	—	—	—	—	2	5	16	5	8	19	14	16	19	15
Bristol Rovers	—	22	19	16	18	15	18	19	—	—	—	—	—	—	—	—
Burnley	—	—	21	13	11	16	—	—	—	1	7	—	—	—	—	—
Bury	—	—	—	—	—	—	—	—	—	—	—	—	—	21	—	22
Cambridge United	14	13	8	12	—	—	—	—	—	—	—	—	—	—	—	—
Cardiff City	20	19	15	9	19	18	—	21	17	20	19	3	7	5	13	20
Carlisle United	—	—	15	—	—	20	19	—	3	18	10	4	12	12	10	3
Charlton Athletic	13	—	22	19	17	7	9	—	—	—	21	20	20	3	15	19
Chelsea	12	12	4	—	—	2	11	—	—	—	—	—	—	—	—	—
Chesterfield	—	—	—	—	—	—	—	—	—	—	—	—	—	—	—	—
Coventry City	—	—	—	—	—	—	—	—	—	—	—	—	—	—	—	1
Crystal Palace	15	—	—	1	9	—	—	—	20	—	—	—	—	2	11	7
Derby County	16	6	—	—	—	—	—	—	—	—	—	—	—	1	18	17
Doncaster Rovers	—	—	—	—	—	—	—	—	—	—	—	—	—	—	—	—
Everton	—	—	—	—	—	—	—	—	—	—	—	—	—	—	—	—
Fulham	—	—	20	10	10	17	12	9	13	9	20	—	—	22	—	—
Grimsby	17	7	—	—	—	—	—	—	—	—	—	—	—	—	—	—
Hereford United	—	—	—	—	—	22	—	—	—	—	—	—	—	—	—	—
Huddersfield Town	—	—	—	—	—	—	—	—	—	21	—	—	1	6	14	6
Hull	—	—	—	—	22	14	14	8	9	13	12	5	13	11	16	12
Ipswich Town	—	—	—	—	—	—	—	—	—	—	—	—	—	—	1	5
Leeds United	—	—	—	—	—	—	—	—	—	—	—	—	—	—	—	—
Leicester City	8	—	1	17	—	—	—	—	—	—	—	1	3	—	—	—
Lincoln City	—	—	—	—	—	—	—	—	—	—	—	—	—	—	—	—
Liverpool	—	—	—	—	—	—	—	—	—	—	—	—	—	—	—	—
Luton Town	1	5	6	18	13	6	7	—	2	12	13	6	—	—	—	—

1965–66	1964–65	1963–64	1962–63	1961–62	1960–61	1959–60	1958–59	1957–58	1956–57	1955–56	1954–55	1953–54	1952–53	1951–52	1950–51	1949–50	
—	—	—	—	—	—	1	—	—	—	—	—	—	—	—	—	—	Aston Villa
—	—	—	—	—	—	—	22	14	19	18	—	—	22	20	15	13	Barnsley
10	—	—	—	—	—	—	—	—	—	—	1	7	6	3	4	—	Birmingham City
—	—	—	—	—	—	—	—	2	4	4	6	3	9	14	6	16	Blackburn Rovers
—	—	—	—	—	—	—	—	—	—	—	—	—	—	—	—	—	Blackpool
9	3	—	—	—	—	—	—	—	—	—	—	—	—	—	—	—	Bolton Wanderers
—	—	—	—	—	—	—	—	—	—	—	—	—	—	—	—	22	Bradford City·
—	—	—	—	—	—	—	—	—	—	—	—	21	17	10	9	9	Brentford
—	—	—	—	22	16	14	12	—	—	—	—	—	—	—	—	—	Brighton & H.A.
5	—	—	—	—	—	22	10	17	13	11	—	—	—	—	—	—	Bristol City
—	—	—	—	21	17	9	6	10	9	6	9	9	—	—	—	—	Bristol Rovers
—	—	—	—	—	—	—	—	—	—	—	—	—	—	—	—	—	Burnley
19	16	18	8	18	—	—	—	—	21	16	13	17	20	17	20	18	Bury
—	—	—	—	—	—	—	—	—	—	—	—	—	—	—	—	—	Cambridge United
20	13	15	10	—	—	2	9	15	—	—	—	—	—	2	3	10	Cardiff City
14	—	—	—	—	—	—	—	—	—	—	—	—	—	—	—	—	Carlisle United
16	18	4	20	15	10	7	8	3	—	—	—	—	—	—	—	—	Charlton Athletic
—	—	—	1	—	—	—	—	—	—	—	—	—	—	—	—	—	Chelsea
—	—	—	—	—	—	—	—	—	—	—	—	—	—	—	21	14	Chesterfield
3	10	—	—	—	—	—	—	—	—	—	—	—	—	21	7	11	Coventry City
11	7	—	—	—	—	—	—	—	—	—	—	—	—	—	—	—	Crystal Palace
8	9	13	18	16	12	18	7	16	—	—	22	18	—	—	—	—	Derby County
—	—	—	—	—	—	—	—	22	14	17	18	12	13	16	11	11	Doncaster Rovers
—	—	—	—	—	—	—	—	—	—	—	—	2	16	7	—	—	Everton
—	—	—	—	—	—	—	2	5	11	9	14	8	8	—	—	—	Fulham
—	—	21	19	—	—	—	21	13	16	—	—	—	—	—	22	11	Grimsby
—	—	—	—	—	—	—	—	—	—	—	—	—	—	—	—	—	Hereford United
4	8	12	6	7	20	6	14	9	12	—	—	—	2	—	—	—	Huddersfield Town
—	—	—	—	—	—	21	—	—	—	22	19	15	18	18	10	7	Hull City
15	5	—	—	—	1	11	16	8	—	—	21	—	—	—	—	—	Ipswich Town
—	—	1	5	19	14	—	—	—	—	2	4	10	10	6	5	5	Leeds United
—	—	—	—	—	—	—	—	—	1	5	—	1	5	5	14	15	Leicester City
—	—	—	—	—	22	13	19	20	18	8	16	16	15	—	—	—	Lincoln City
—	—	—	—	1	3	3	4	4	3	3	11	—	—	—	—	—	Liverpool
—	—	—	22	3	13	—	—	—	—	—	2	6	3	8	19	17	Luton Town

DIVISION TWO LEAGUE POSITIONS (1950-82)

	1981–82	1980–81	1979–80	1978–79	1977–78	1976–77	1975–76	1974–75	1973–74	1972–73	1971–72	1970–71	1969–70	1968–69	1967–68	1966–67
Manchester City	—	—	—	—	—	—	—	—	—	—	—	—	—	—	—	—
Manchester United	—	—	—	—	—	—	—	1	—	—	—	—	—	—	—	—
Mansfield Town	—	—	—	—	21	—	—	—	—	—	—	—	—	—	—	—
Middlesbrough	—	—	—	—	—	—	—	—	1	4	9	7	4	4	6	—
Millwall	—	—	—	21	16	10	—	20	12	11	3	8	10	10	7	8
Newcastle United	9	11	9	8	—	—	—	—	—	—	—	—	—	—	—	—
Northampton Town	—	—	—	—	—	—	—	—	—	—	—	—	—	—	—	21
Norwich City	3	—	—	—	—	—	—	3	—	—	1	10	11	13	8	11
Nottingham F.	—	—	—	—	—	8	16	7	14	—	—	—	—	—	—	—
Notts County	—	2	17	6	15	8	5	14	10	—	—	—	—	—	—	—
Oldham Athletic	11	15	11	14	8	13	17	18	—	—	—	—	—	—	—	—
Orient	22	17	14	11	14	19	13	12	4	15	17	17	—	—	—	—
Oxford United	—	—	—	—	—	—	20	11	18	8	15	14	15	20	—	—
Plymouth Argyle	—	—	—	—	—	21	16	—	—	—	—	—	—	—	22	16
Portsmouth	—	—	—	—	—	—	22	17	15	17	16	16	17	15	5	14
Port Vale	—	—	—	—	—	—	—	—	—	—	—	—	—	—	—	—
Preston North End	—	20	10	7	—	—	—	—	21	19	18	—	22	14	20	13
Queen's Park R.	5	8	5	—	—	—	—	—	—	2	4	11	9	—	2	—
Rotherham United	7	—	—	—	—	—	—	—	—	—	—	—	—	—	21	18
Scunthorpe	—	—	—	—	—	—	—	—	—	—	—	—	—	—	—	—
Sheffield United	—	—	—	20	12	11	—	—	—	—	—	2	6	9	—	—
Sheffield Wed.	4	10	—	—	—	—	—	22	19	10	14	15	—	—	—	—
Shrewsbury Town	18	14	13	—	—	—	—	—	—	—	—	—	—	—	—	—
Southampton	—	—	—	—	2	9	6	13	—	—	—	—	—	—	—	—
Stoke City	—	—	—	3	7	—	—	—	—	—	—	—	—	—	—	—
Sunderland	—	—	2	4	6	—	1	4	6	6	5	13	—	—	—	—
Swansea City	—	3	12	—	—	—	—	—	—	—	—	—	—	—	—	—
Swindon Town	—	—	—	—	—	—	—	—	22	16	11	12	5	—	—	—
Tottenham Hotspur	—	—	—	—	3	—	—	—	—	—	—	—	—	—	—	—
Walsall	—	—	—	—	—	—	—	—	—	—	—	—	—	—	—	—
Watford	2	9	18	—	—	—	—	—	—	—	22	18	19	—	—	—
West Bromwich Alb.	—	—	—	—	—	—	3	6	8	—	—	—	—	—	—	—
West Ham United	—	1	7	5	—	—	—	—	—	—	—	—	—	—	—	—
Wolverhampton W.	—	—	—	—	—	1	—	—	—	—	—	—	—	—	—	2
Wrexham	21	16	16	15	—	—	—	—	—	—	—	—	—	—	—	—
York City	—	—	—	—	—	—	21	—	—	—	—	—	—	—	—	—

1965–66	1964–65	1963–64	1962–63	1961–62	1960–61	1959–60	1958–59	1957–58	1956–57	1955–56	1954–55	1953–54	1952–53	1951–52	1950–51	1949–50	
1	11	6	—	—	—	—	—	—	—	—	—	—	—	—	2	—	Manchester City
—	—	—	—	—	—	—	—	—	—	—	—	—	—	—	—	—	Manchester United
—	—	—	—	—	—	—	—	—	—	—	—	—	—	—	—	—	Mansfield Town
21	17	10	4	12	5	5	13	7	6	14	12	—	—	—	—	—	Middlesbrough
—	—	—	—	—	—	—	—	—	—	—	—	—	—	—	—	—	Millwall
—	1	8	7	11	—	—	—	—	—	—	—	—	—	—	—	—	Newcastle United
—	2	11	—	—	—	—	—	—	—	—	—	—	—	—	—	—	Northampton Town
13	6	17	13	17	4	—	—	—	—	—	—	—	—	—	—	—	Norwich City
—	—	—	—	—	—	—	—	—	2	7	15	4	7	4	—	—	Nottingham Forest
—	—	—	—	—	—	—	—	21	20	20	7	14	19	15	17	—	Notts County
—	—	—	—	—	—	—	—	—	—	—	—	22	—	—	—	—	Oldham Athletic
22	19	16	—	2	19	10	17	12	15	—	—	—	—	—	—	—	Orient
—	—	—	—	—	—	—	—	—	—	—	—	—	—	—	—	—	Oxford United
18	15	20	12	5	11	19	—	—	—	21	20	19	4	—	—	21	Plymouth Argyle
12	20	9	17	—	21	20	—	—	—	—	—	—	—	—	—	—	Portsmouth
—	—	—	—	—	—	—	—	—	22	12	17	—	—	—	—	—	Port Vale
17	12	3	16	10	—	—	—	—	—	—	—	—	—	—	1	6	Preston North End
—	—	—	—	—	—	—	—	—	—	—	—	—	—	22	16	20	Queen's Park R.
7	14	7	14	9	15	8	20	18	17	19	3	5	12	9	—	—	Rotherham United
—	—	22	9	4	9	15	18	—	—	—	—	—	—	—	—	—	Scunthorpe
—	—	—	—	—	2	—	—	6	7	—	—	—	1	11	8	3	Sheffield United
—	—	—	—	—	—	—	1	—	—	1	—	—	—	1	—	2	Sheffield Wednesday
—	—	—	—	—	—	—	—	—	—	—	—	—	—	—	—	—	Shrewsbury Town
2	4	5	11	6	8	—	—	—	—	—	—	—	21	13	12	4	Southampton
—	—	—	1	8	18	17	5	11	5	13	5	11	—	—	—	—	Stoke City
—	—	2	3	3	6	16	15	—	—	—	—	—	—	—	—	—	Sunderland
—	22	19	15	20	7	12	11	19	10	10	10	20	11	19	18	8	Swansea City
—	21	14	—	—	—	—	—	—	—	—	—	—	—	—	—	—	Swindon Town
—	—	—	—	—	—	—	—	—	—	—	—	—	—	—	—	1	Tottenham Hotspur
—	—	—	21	14	—	—	—	—	—	—	—	—	—	—	—	—	Walsall
—	—	—	—	—	—	—	—	—	—	—	—	—	—	—	—	—	Watford
—	—	—	—	—	—	—	—	—	—	—	—	—	—	—	—	—	West Bromwich Alb
—	—	—	—	—	—	—	—	1	8	16	8	13	14	12	13	19	West Ham United
6	—	—	—	—	—	—	—	—	—	—	—	—	—	—	—	—	Wolverhampton W.
—	—	—	—	—	—	—	—	—	—	—	—	—	—	—	—	—	Wrexham
—	—	—	—	—	—	—	—	—	—	—	—	—	—	—	—	—	York City

DIVISION THREE LEAGUE POSITIONS (1961-82)

	1981–82	1980–81	1979–80	1978–79	1977–78	1976–77	1975–76	1974–75	1973–74	1972–73	1971–72	1970–71	1969–70	1968–69	1967–68	1966–67	1965–66	1964–65	1963–64	1962–63	1961–62	
Aldershot	—	—	—	—	—	—	21	20	8	—	—	—	—	—	—	—	—	—	—	—	—	Aldershot
Aston Villa	—	—	—	—	—	—	—	—	—	—	1	4	—	—	—	—	—	—	—	—	—	Aston Villa
Barnsley	—	2	11	—	—	—	—	—	—	—	22	12	7	10	—	—	—	24	20	18	20	Barnsley
Barrow	—	—	—	—	—	—	—	—	—	—	—	—	23	19	8	—	—	—	—	—	—	Barrow
Blackburn Rovers	—	—	2	—	—	—	—	1	13	3	10	—	—	—	—	—	—	—	—	—	—	Blackburn Rovers
Blackpool	—	23	18	12	—	—	—	—	—	—	—	—	—	—	—	—	—	—	—	—	—	Blackpool
Bolton Wanderers	—	—	—	—	—	—	—	—	—	1	7	—	—	—	—	—	—	—	—	—	—	Bolton Wanderers
AFC Bournemouth	—	—	—	—	—	—	—	21	11	7	3	—	21	4	13	20	18	11	4	5	3	AFC Bournemouth
Bradford	—	—	—	—	—	—	—	—	—	—	—	—	—	—	—	—	—	—	—	21	11	Bradford
Bradford City	—	—	—	—	22	—	—	—	—	—	24	19	10	—	—	—	—	—	—	—	—	Bradford City
Brentford	8	9	19	10	—	—	—	—	—	22	—	—	—	—	—	—	23	5	16	—	23	Brentford
Brighton & Hove Alb.	—	—	—	—	—	2	4	19	19	—	2	14	5	12	11	19	15	—	—	22	—	Brighton & Hove Alb.
Bristol City	23	—	—	—	—	—	—	—	—	—	—	—	—	—	—	—	—	2	5	14	6	Bristol City
Bristol Rovers	15	—	—	—	—	—	—	—	2	5	6	6	3	16	16	5	16	6	12	19	—	Bristol Rovers
Burnley	1	8	—	—	—	—	—	—	—	—	—	—	—	—	—	—	—	—	—	—	—	Burnley
Bury	—	—	21	19	15	7	13	14	—	—	—	22	19	—	2	—	—	—	—	—	—	Bury
Cambridge United	—	—	—	—	2	—	—	—	21	—	—	—	—	—	—	—	—	—	—	—	—	Cambridge United
Cardiff City	—	—	—	—	—	—	2	—	—	—	—	—	—	—	—	—	—	—	—	—	—	Cardiff City
Carlisle United	2	19	6	6	13	—	—	—	—	—	—	—	—	—	—	—	—	—	—	23	—	Carlisle United
Charlton Athletic	—	3	—	—	—	—	—	3	14	11	—	—	—	—	—	—	—	—	—	—	—	Charlton Athletic
Chester	24	18	9	16	5	13	17	—	—	—	—	—	—	—	—	—	—	—	—	—	—	Chester
Chesterfield	11	5	4	20	9	18	14	15	5	16	13	5	—	—	—	—	—	—	—	—	—	Chesterfield
Colchester United	—	22	5	7	8	—	22	11	—	—	—	—	—	—	23	13	—	23	17	12	—	Colchester United
Coventry City	—	—	—	—	—	—	—	—	—	—	—	—	—	—	—	—	—	—	1	4	14	Coventry City
Crewe Alexandra	—	—	—	—	—	—	—	—	—	—	—	—	—	23	—	—	—	—	22	—	—	Crewe Alexandra
Crystal Palace	—	—	—	—	—	3	5	5	—	—	—	—	—	—	—	—	—	—	2	11	15	Crystal Palace
Darlington	—	—	—	—	—	—	—	—	—	—	—	—	—	—	—	22	—	—	—	—	—	Darlington
Doncaster Rovers	19	—	8	—	—	—	—	—	—	—	—	23	11	—	—	23	—	—	—	—	—	Doncaster Rovers
Exeter City	18	11	8	8	17	—	—	—	—	—	—	—	—	—	—	—	22	17	—	—	—	Exeter City
Fulham	3	13	—	—	—	—	—	—	—	—	—	2	4	—	—	—	—	—	—	—	—	Fulham
Gillingham	6	15	16	5	7	12	15	10	—	—	—	24	20	20	12	11	6	7	—	—	—	Gillingham
Grimsby Town	—	—	1	—	—	23	18	16	6	9	—	—	—	—	22	17	11	10	—	—	2	Grimsby Town
Halifax Town	—	—	—	—	—	—	24	17	9	20	17	3	18	—	—	—	—	—	—	24	18	Halifax Town
Hartlepool United	—	—	—	—	—	—	—	—	—	—	—	—	—	22	—	—	—	—	—	—	—	Hartlepool United

Hereford United	—	—	—	—	—	23	—	1	12	18	—	—	—	—	—	—	—	—	—	—	—	Hereford United
Huddersfield Town	17	4	—	—	—	—	—	24	10	—	—	—	—	—	—	—	—	—	—	—	—	Huddersfield Town
Hull City	—	24	20	9	—	—	—	—	—	—	—	—	—	—	—	—	1	4	8	10	10	Hull City
Lincoln City	4	—	—	24	16	9	—	—	—	—	—	—	1	—	—	—	—	—	—	—	22	Lincoln City
Luton Town	—	—	—	—	—	—	—	—	—	—	—	—	2	3	—	—	—	21	18	—	—	Luton Town
Mansfield Town	—	—	23	18	—	1	11	—	—	—	21	7	6	15	21	9	19	3	7	—	—	Mansfield Town
Middlesbrough	—	—	—	—	—	—	—	—	—	—	—	—	—	—	1	2	—	—	—	—	—	Middlesbrough
Millwall	9	16	14	—	—	—	3	—	—	—	—	—	—	—	—	—	2	—	21	16	—	Millwall
Newport County	16	12	—	—	—	—	—	—	—	—	—	—	—	—	—	—	—	—	—	—	24	Newport County
Northampton Town	—	—	—	—	—	22	—	—	—	—	—	—	—	21	18	—	—	—	—	1	8	Northampton Town
Notts County	—	—	—	—	—	—	—	—	—	2	4	—	—	—	—	—	—	—	24	7	13	Notts County
Oldham Athletic	—	—	—	—	—	—	—	—	1	4	11	—	—	24	17	10	20	20	20	9	—	Oldham Athletic
Orient	—	—	—	—	—	—	—	—	—	—	—	—	1	18	19	14	—	—	—	—	—	Orient
Oxford United	5	14	17	11	18	17	—	—	—	—	—	—	—	—	1	15	14	—	—	—	—	Oxford United
Peterborough United	—	—	—	21	4	16	10	7	—	—	—	—	—	—	9*	16	13	8	10	6	5	Peterborough United
Plymouth Argyle	10	7	15	15	19	—	—	2	17	8	8	15	17	5	—	—	—	—	—	—	—	Plymouth Argyle
Portsmouth	13	6	—	—	24	20	—	—	—	—	—	—	—	—	—	—	—	—	—	—	1	Portsmouth
Port Vale	—	—	—	—	21	19	12	6	20	6	15	17	—	—	—	—	22	13	3	12	—	Port Vale
Preston North End	14	—	—	—	3	6	8	9	—	—	—	1	—	—	—	—	—	—	—	—	—	Preston North End
Queen's Park Rangers	—	—	—	—	—	—	—	—	—	—	—	—	—	—	—	1	3	14	15	13	4	Queen's Park Rangers
Reading	12	10	7	—	—	21	—	—	—	—	—	21	8	14	5	4	8	13	6	20	7	Reading
Rochdale	—	—	—	—	—	—	—	—	24	13	18	16	9	—	—	—	—	—	—	—	—	Rochdale
Rotherham United	—	1	13	17	20	4	16	—	—	21	5	8	14	11	—	—	—	—	—	—	—	Rotherham United
Scunthorpe United	—	—	—	—	—	—	—	—	—	24	—	—	—	—	24	18	4	18	—	—	—	Scunthorpe United
Sheffield United	—	21	12	—	—	—	—	—	—	—	—	—	—	—	—	—	—	—	—	—	—	Sheffield United
Sheffield Wednesday	—	—	3	14	14	8	20	—	—	—	—	—	—	—	—	—	—	—	—	—	—	Sheffield Wednesday
Shrewsbury Town	—	—	—	1	11	10	9	—	22	15	12	13	15	17	3	6	10	16	11	15	19	Shrewsbury Town
Southend United	7	—	22	13	—	—	23	18	12	14	—	—	—	—	—	—	21	12	14	8	16	Southend United
Southport	—	—	—	—	—	—	—	—	23	—	—	—	22	8	15	—	—	—	—	—	—	Southport
Stockport County	—	—	—	—	—	—	—	—	—	—	—	—	24	9	14	—	—	—	—	—	—	Stockport County
Swansea City	—	—	—	3	—	—	—	—	—	23	14	11	—	—	—	21	17	—	—	—	—	Swansea City
Swindon Town	22	17	10	4	10	11	19	4	—	—	—	—	—	2	10	8	7	—	—	2	9	Swindon Town
Torquay United	—	—	—	—	—	—	—	—	—	—	23	10	13	6	4	7	—	—	—	—	21	Torquay United
Tranmere Rovers	—	—	—	23	12	14	—	22	16	10	20	18	16	7	20	—	—	—	—	—	—	Tranmere Rovers
Walsall	20	20	—	22	6	15	7	8	15	17	9	20	12	13	7	12	9	19	19	—	—	Walsall
Watford	—	—	—	2	—	—	—	23	7	19	—	—	—	1	6	3	12	9	3	17	17	Watford
Wimbledon	21	—	24	—	—	—	—	—	—	—	—	—	—	—	—	—	—	—	—	—	—	Wimbledon
Workington	—	—	—	—	—	—	—	—	—	—	—	—	—	—	—	24	5	15	—	—	—	Workington
Wrexham	—	—	—	—	24	—	—	3	18	19	—	—	—	—	—	24	—	—	—	—	—	Wrexham
York City	—	—	—	—	5	6	13	4	12	16	9	—	—	—	—	—	—	23	9	—	—	York City

*Relegated by order of the Football League

DIVISION FOUR LEAGUE POSITIONS (1961-82)

	1981–82	1980–81	1979–80	1978–79	1977–78	1976–77	1975–76	1974–75	1973–74	1972–73	1971–72	1970–71	1969–70	1968–69	1967–68	1966–67	1965–66	1964–65	1963–64	1962–63	1961–62	
Accrington Stanley	—	—	—	—	—	—	—	—	—	—	—	—	—	—	—	—	—	—	—	—	R	Accrington Stanley
Aldershot	16	6	10	5	5	17	—	—	—	4	17	13	6	15	9	10	17	18	9	11	7	Aldershot
Barnsley	—	—	—	4	7	6	12	15	13	14	—	—	—	—	2	16	16	—	—	—	—	Barnsley
Barrow	—	—	—	—	—	—	—	—	—	—	22	24	—	—	—	3	12	21	24	9	9	Barrow
Blackpool	12	—	—	—	—	—	—	—	—	—	—	—	—	—	—	—	—	—	—	—	—	Blackpool
AFC Bournemouth	5	13	11	18	17	13	6	—	—	—	—	2	—	—	—	—	—	—	—	—	—	AFC Bournemouth
Bradford	—	—	—	—	—	—	—	—	—	—	—	—	24	24	24	23	11	7	13	—	—	Bradford
Bradford City	2	14	5	15	—	4	17	10	8	16	—	—	—	4	5	11	23	19	5	23	5	Bradford City
Brentford	—	—	—	—	4	15	18	8	19	—	3	14	5	11	14	9	—	—	—	1	—	Brentford
Brighton & Hove Alb.	—	—	—	—	—	—	—	—	—	—	—	—	—	—	—	—	—	1	8	—	—	Brighton & Hove Alb.
Bury	9	12	—	—	—	—	—	—	4	12	9	—	—	—	—	—	—	—	—	—	—	Bury
Cambridge United	—	—	—	—	—	1	13	6	—	3	10	20	—	—	—	—	—	—	—	—	—	Cambridge United
Carlisle United	—	—	—	—	—	—	—	—	—	—	—	—	—	—	—	—	—	—	2	—	4	Carlisle United
Chester	—	—	—	—	—	—	—	4	7	15	20	5	11	14	22	19	7	8	12	21	23	Chester
Chesterfield	—	—	—	—	—	—	—	—	—	—	—	—	1	20	7	15	20	12	16	15	19	Chesterfield
Colchester United	6	—	—	—	—	3	—	—	3	22	11	6	10	6	—	—	4	—	—	—	2	Colchester United
Crewe Alexandra	24	18	23	24	15	12	16	18	21	21	24	15	15	—	4	5	14	10	—	3	10	Crewe Alexandra
Darlington	13	8	22	21	19	11	20	21	20	24	19	12	22	5	16	—	2	17	19	12	13	Darlington
Doncaster Rovers	—	3	22	12	12	8	10	17	22	17	22	—	—	1	10	—	1	9	14	16	21	Doncaster Rovers
Exeter	—	—	—	—	—	2	7	9	10	8	15	9	18	17	20	14	—	—	4	17	18	Exeter
Gillingham	—	—	—	—	—	—	—	—	2	9	13	—	—	—	—	—	—	—	1	5	20	Gillingham
Grimsby Town	—	—	—	2	6	—	—	—	—	—	1	19	16	23	—	—	—	—	—	—	—	Grimsby Town
Halifax Town	19	23	18	23	20	21	—	—	—	—	—	—	—	2	11	12	15	23	10	—	—	Halifax Town
Hartlepool United	14	9	19	13	21	22	14	13	11	20	18	23	23	—	3	8	18	15	23	24	22	Hartlepool United
Hereford United	10	22	21	14	—	—	—	—	—	2	—	—	—	—	—	—	—	—	—	—	—	Hereford United
Huddersfield Town	—	—	1	10	11	9	5	—	—	—	—	—	—	—	—	—	—	—	—	—	—	Huddersfield Town
Hull City	8	—	—	—	—	—	—	—	—	—	—	—	—	—	—	—	—	—	—	—	—	Hull City

R – Resigned from Football League

Lincoln City	—	2	7	—	—	—	1	5	12	10	5	21	8	8	13	24	22	22	11	22	—	Lincoln City
Luton Town	—	—	—	—	—	—	—	—	—	—	—	—	—	—	1	17	6	—	—	—	—	Luton Town
Mansfield Town	20	7	—	—	—	—	—	1	17	6	—	—	—	—	—	—	—	—	—	4	14	Mansfield Town
Millwall	—	—	—	—	—	—	—	—	—	—	—	—	—	—	—	—	—	2	—	—	1	Millwall
Newport County	—	—	3	7	16	19	—	12	9	5	14	22	21	22	12	18	9	16	15	20	—	Newport County
Northampton Town	22	10	13	19	10	—	22	16	5	23	21	7	14	—	—	—	—	—	—	—	—	Northampton Town
Notts County	—	—	—	—	—	—	2	—	—	—	—	1	7	19	17	20	8	13	—	—	—	Notts County
Oldham Athletic	—	—	—	—	—	—	—	—	—	—	—	3	19	—	—	—	—	—	—	2	11	Oldham Athletic
Oxford United	—	—	—	—	—	—	—	—	—	—	—	—	—	—	—	—	—	4	18	18	—	Oxford United
Peterborough United	4	5	8	—	—	—	—	—	1	19	8	16	9	18	—	—	—	—	—	—	—	Peterborough United
Portsmouth	—	—	4	18	—	—	—	—	—	—	—	—	—	—	—	—	—	—	—	—	—	Portsmouth
Port Vale	7	19	20	6	—	—	—	—	—	—	—	—	4	13	18	13	19	—	—	—	—	Port Vale
Reading	—	—	—	20	8	—	12	7	6	7	16	—	—	—	—	—	—	—	—	—	—	Reading
Rochdale	21	15	24	—	24	18	3	19	—	—	—	—	—	3	19	21	21	6	20	7	12	Rochdale
Rotherham United	—	—	—	12	—	—	15	3	15	—	—	—	—	—	—	—	—	—	—	—	—	Rotherham United
Scunthorpe United	23	16	14	—	14	20	—	24	18	—	4	17	12	16	—	—	—	—	—	—	—	Scunthorpe United
Sheffield United	1	—	—	—	—	—	—	—	—	—	—	—	—	—	—	—	—	—	—	—	—	Sheffield United
Shrewsbury Town	—	—	—	—	—	—	19	2	—	—	—	—	—	—	—	—	—	—	—	—	—	Shrewsbury Town
Southend United	—	1	—	—	2	10	—	—	—	—	2	18	17	7	6	6	—	—	—	—	—	Southend United
Southport	—	—	—	17	23	23	—	11	—	1	7	8	—	—	—	2	10	20	21	13	17	Southport
Stockport County	18	20	16	—	18	14	23	20	24	11	23	—	—	—	—	1	13	24	17	19	16	Stockport County
Swansea City	—	—	—	—	3	5	21	22	14	—	—	—	3	10	15	—	—	—	—	—	—	Swansea City
Torquay United	15	17	9	11	9	16	9	14	16	18	—	—	—	—	—	—	3	11	6	6	—	Torquay United
Tranmere Rovers	11	21	15	—	—	—	4	—	—	—	—	—	—	—	—	4	5	5	7	8	15	Tranmere Rovers
Walsall	—	—	2	—	—	—	—	—	—	—	—	—	—	—	—	—	—	—	—	—	—	Walsall
Watford	—	—	—	—	1	7	8	—	—	—	—	—	—	—	—	—	—	—	—	—	—	Watford
Wigan Athletic	3	11	6	6	—	—	—	—	—	—	—	10	—	—	—	—	—	—	—	—	—	Wigan Athletic
Wimbledon	—	4	—	3	13	—	—	—	—	—	—	—	—	—	—	—	—	—	—	—	—	Wimbledon
Workington	—	—	—	—	—	24	24	23	23	13	6	10	20	12	23	—	—	—	3	10	8	Workington
Wrexham	—	—	—	—	—	—	—	—	—	—	—	—	2	9	8	7	24	13	—	—	3	Wrexham
York City	17	24	17	9	22	—	—	—	—	—	—	4	13	21	21	22	—	3	22	14	6	York City

LEADING LEAGUE SCORERS 1981-82

Division One: 26 – Keegan (Southampton); 22 – Brazil (Ipswich T.); 18 – Wark (Ipswich T.), Worthington (Leeds U., inc. 9 for Birmingham C.); 17 – Regis (W.B.A.), Rush (Liverpool); 16 – Chapman (Stoke C.), Cross (West Ham U.), McCulloch (Notts Co.); 15 – Armstrong (Southampton), Evans (Birmingham C.), Goddard (West Ham U.), Sharp (Everton); 14 – Francis (Manchester C., inc. 2 for Nottingham F.), R. James (Swansea C.), McDermott (Liverpool); 13 – Christie (Notts Co.), Crooks (Tottenham H.), Dalglish (Liverpool), Hateley (Coventry C.), Reeves (Manchester C.), Stapleton (Manchester U.); 12 – Latchford (Swansea C.), Ritchie (Brighton & H.A.); 11 – Birtles (Manchester U.), Robinson (Brighton & H.A.), Sunderland (Arsenal); 10 – Curtis (Swansea C.), Hoddle (Tottenham H.), Stewart (West Ham U.), Thompson (Coventry C.), Whelan (Liverpool); 9 – Coppell (Manchester U.), Gates (Ipswich T.), Graham (Leeds U.), Harford (Birmingham C.), Hunt (Coventry C.), L. James (Swansea C.), Mair (Notts Co.), Moran (Southampton), Rowell (Sunderland), Rix (Arsenal), Shaw (Aston Villa), Tueart (Manchester C.), N. Wallace (Nottingham F.), Whitton (Coventry C.), Withe (Aston Villa).

Division Two: 22 – Moore (Rotherham U.); 21 – Bannister (Sheffield W.), Stein (Luton T.); 19 – Blissett (Watford), White (Luton T.); 18 – Varadi (Newcastle U.); 17 – Atkins (Shrewsbury T.), Lineker (Leicester C.), Stainrod (Q.P.R.); 16 – Moss (Luton T.), Walker (Chelsea), Wylde (Oldham Ath.); 15 – Banks (Barnsley); 14 – Garner (Blackburn R.); 13 – Allen (Q.P.R.), Barnes (Watford), Fern (Rotherham U.), Henry (Bolton W.), Jenkins (Watford), Stevens (Cardiff C.), Walsh (Charlton Ath.); 12 – Bertschin (Norwich C.), Heaton (Oldham Ath.), Mayes (Chelsea), Thompson (Bolton W.), Walker (Barnsley); 11 – Aylott (Barnsley), Edwards (Wrexham), Hales (Charlton Ath.), Lee (Chelsea), Melrose (Leicester C.), Stonehouse (Blackburn R.), Whymark (Grimsby T.); 10 – Deehan (Norwich C.), Flanagan (Q.P.R.), Jack (Norwich C.), Lynex (Leicester C.), Seasman (Rotherham U.); 9 – Donaghy (Luton T.), Gregory (Q.P.R.), McNeil (Wrexham), Micallef (Cardiff C.), Wilson (Derby Co.).

Division Three: 24 – Davies (Fulham); 21 – Kellow (Exeter C.); 18 – Sims (Plymouth Arg.); 17 – Bruce (Preston N.E.), Rafferty (Portsmouth); 16 – Cook (Plymouth Arg.); 15 – Horrix (Millwall), Robson (Carlisle U.), Webb (Reading); 14 – Bonnyman (Chesterfield), Penn (Walsall), Rideout (Swindon), Thomas (Oxford U.); 13 – Carter (Swindon T.), Coney (Fulham), Henderson (Chesterfield), Joseph (Wimbledon), Mercer (Southend), Tynan (Newport Co.); 12 – Brown (Fulham), Chetterton (Millwall), Dixon (Reading), Price (Gillingham), Randall (Bristol R.), Simpson (Chester), White (Gillingham); 11 – Aldridge (Newport Co.), Cockerill (Lincoln C.), Cunningham (Lincoln C.), Hamilton (Burnley), Harford (Bristol C.), Hodges (Plymouth Arg.), Shipley (Lincoln C.), Staniforth (Carlisle U.), Stephens (Bristol R.), D. Williams (Bristol R.); 10 – Cassells (Oxford U.), Elliott (Preston N.E.), Hemmerman (Portsmouth), Lee (Carlisle U.), Phillips (Southend U.), P. Rogers (Exeter C.); 9 – Bannon (Carlisle U.), Bowen (Brentford), Leslie (Wimbledon), Pratt (Exeter C.), Tait (Portsmouth), Taylor (Burnley).

Division Four: 36 – Edwards (Sheffield U., inc. 1 for Hull C.); 35 – Madden (Bury); 27 – Mutrie (Hull C.); 24 – Campbell (Bradford C.), Cooke (Peterborough U.); 23 – Walwyn (York C.); 21 – Allinson (Colchester U.), Bremner (Colchester U.); 19 – Bradd (Wigan Ath.), Davison (Halifax T.), McNiven (Bradford C.); 18 – Houchen (Hartlepool); 17 – Speedie (Darlington); 16 – Funnell (Bournemouth), Gallagher (Bradford C.); 15 – Bamber (Blackpool), Hatton (Sheffield U.), Houghton (Wigan Ath.), Kenworthy (Sheffield U.), Newton (Hartlepool); 14 – Hilditch (Rochdale), Lumby (Mansfield T.), McDonough (Colchester U.); 13 – Kerr (Tranmere R.), Moss (Port Vale), Walsh (Darlington); 12 – Barrow (Wigan Ath.), Johnson (Bury),

Palios (Crewe Alex.), Phillips (Hereford U.); 11 – Brown (Torquay U.), Kellock (Peterborough U.), Marwood (Hull C.), Sanford (Aldershot), Trusson (Sheffield U.), Wellings (Rochdale); 10 – Crawford (Bournemouth), French (Aldershot), Morris (Blackpool), Phillips (Northampton T.), Price (Hereford U.); 9 – Caldwell (Mansfield T.), Lucas (Aldershot), Martinez (Rochdale), Methven (Wigan Ath.), Noble (Blackpool), O'Keefe (Wigan Ath.), Parkinson (Mansfield T.), Syrett (Peterborough U.), Telfer (Scunthorpe U.), Williams (Stockport Co.).

TOP LEAGUE SCORERS SINCE 1946-47

1981-82	K. Edwards (Sheffield U., inc. 1 for Hull C.)	36
1980-81	T. Kellow (Exeter C.) and D. Kemp (Plymouth Arg.)	24
1979-80	C. Allen (Queens Park Rangers)	28
1978-79	R. Jenkins (Watford)	29
1977-78	A. Curtis (Swansea City) and S. Phillips (Brentford)	32
1976-77	P. Ward (Brighton & Hove Albion)	32
1975-76	R. McNeil (Hereford United)	35
1974-75	R. McNeil (Hereford United)	31
1973-74	B. Yeo (Gillingham)	31
1972-73	B. Robson (West Ham United) and F. Binney (Exeter)	28
1971-72	E. MacDougall (Bournemouth) and A. Wood (Shrewsbury)	35
1970-71	E. MacDougall (Bournemouth)	42
1969-70	G. Jones (Bury) and A. Kinsey (Wrexham)	26
1968-69	J. Greaves (Tottenham Hotspur)	27
1967-68	G. Best (Manchester United) and R. Davies (Southampton)	28
1966-67	R. Davies (Southampton)	37
1965-66	K. Hector (Bradford)	44
1964-65	A. Jeffrey (Doncaster Rovers)	36
1963-64	H. MacIlmoyle (Carlisle United)	39
1962-63	J. Greaves (Tottenham Hotspur)	37
1961-62	R. Hunt (Liverpool) and B. Thomas (Scunthorpe and Newcastle United)	41
1960-61	T. Bly (Peterborough)	52
1959-60	C. Holton (Watford)	48
1958-59	B. Clough (Middlesbrough)	43
1957-58	T. Johnston (Blackburn Rovers and Leyton Orient)	44
1956-57	A. Rowley (Leicester City)	44
1955-56	R. Collins (Torquay United)	40
1954-55	T. Briggs (Blackburn Rovers)	33
1953-54	J. Charles (Leeds United)	42
1952-53	G. Rowley (Leicester City)	39
1951-52	D. Dooley (Sheffield W.)	46
1950-51	J. Shaw (Rotherham U.)	37
1949-50	T. Briggs (Grimsby T.)	35
1948-49	C. Wyman (Southampton)	32
1947-48	R. Rooke (Arsenal)	33
1946-47	C. Jordan (Doncaster R.)	42

LEAGUE CHAMPIONSHIP HONOURS

Division I

	First	Pt	Second	Pt	Third	Pt
1888–9	*a*Preston NE	40	Aston Villa	29	Wolverhampton W	28
1889–90	Preston NE	33	Everton	31	Blackburn R	27
1890–1	Everton	29	Preston NE	27	Wolverhampton W / Notts County	26
1891–2	*b*Sunderland	42	Preston NE	37	Bolton W	36
1892–3	*c*Sunderland	48	Preston NE	37	Everton	36
1893–4	Aston Villa	44	Sunderland	38	Derby C	36
1894–5	Sunderland	47	Everton	42	Aston Villa	39
1895–6	Aston Villa	45	Derby C	41	Everton	39
1896–7	Aston Villa	47	Sheffield U	36	Derby C	36
1897–8	Sheffield U	42	Sunderland	37	Wolverhampton W	35
1898–9	*d*Aston Villa	45	Liverpool	43	Burnley	39
1899–1900	Aston Villa	50	Sheffield U	48	Sunderland	41
1900–1	Liverpool	45	Sunderland	43	Notts C	40
1901–2	Sunderland	44	Everton	41	Newcastle U	37
1902–3	Sheffield W	42	Aston Villa	41	Sunderland	41
1903–4	Sheffield W	47	Manchester C	44	Everton	43
1904–5	Newcastle U	48	Everton	47	Manchester C	46
1905–6	*e*Liverpool	51	Preston NE	47	Sheffield W	44
1906–7	Newcastle U	51	Bristol C	38	Everton	45
1907–8	Manchester U	52	Aston Villa	43	Manchester C	43
1908–9	Newcastle U	53	Everton	46	Sunderland	44
1909–10	Aston Villa	53	Liverpool	48	Blackburn R.	45
1910–11	Manchester U	52	Aston Villa	51	Sunderland	45
1911–12	Blackburn R	49	Everton	46	Newcastle U	44
1912–13	Sunderland	54	Aston Villa	50	Sheffield W	49
1913–14	Blackburn R	51	Aston Villa	44	Middlesbrough	43
1914–15	Everton	46	Oldham A	45	Blackburn R	43
1919–20	*f*WBA	60	Burnley	51	Chelsea	49
1920–21	Burnley	59	Manchester C	54	Bolton W	52
1921–22	Liverpool	57	Tottenham H	51	Burnley	49
1922–23	Liverpool	60	Sunderland	54	Huddersfield T	53
1923–24	*Huddersfield T	57	Cardiff C	57	Sunderland	43
1924–25	Huddersfield T	58	WBA	56	Bolton W	55
1925–26	Huddersfield T	57	Arsenal	52	Sunderland	48
1926–27	Newcastle U	56	Huddersfield T	51	Sunderland	49
1927–28	Everton	53	Huddersfield T	51	Leicester C	48
1928–29	Sheffield W	52	Leicester C	51	Aston Villa	50
1929–30	Sheffield W	60	Derby C	50	Manchester C	47
1930–31	Arsenal	66	Aston Villa	59	Sheffield W	52
1931–32	Everton	56	Arsenal	54	Sheffield W	50
1932–33	Arsenal	58	Aston Villa	54	Sheffield W	51
1933–34	Arsenal	59	Huddersfield T	56	Tottenham H	49
1934–35	Arsenal	58	Sunderland	54	Sheffield W	49
1935–36	Sunderland	56	Derby C	48	Huddersfield T	48
1936–37	Manchester C	57	Charlton A	54	Arsenal	52
1937–38	Arsenal	52	Wolverhampton W	51	Preston NE	49
1938–39	Everton	59	Wolverhampton W	55	Charlton A	50
1946–47	Liverpool	57	Manchester U	56	Wolverhampton W	56
1947–48	Arsenal	59	Manchester U	52	Burnley	52
1948–49	Portsmouth	58	Manchester U	53	Derby C	53

	First	Pt	Second	Pt	Third	Pt
1949–50	*Portsmouth	53	Wolverhampton W	53	Sunderland	52
1950–51	Tottenham H	60	Manchester U	56	Blackpool	50
1951–52	Manchester U	57	Tottenham H	53	Arsenal	53
1952–53	*Arsenal	54	Preston NE	54	Wolverhampton W	51
1953–54	Wolverhampton W	57	WBA	53	Huddersfield T	51
1954–55	Chelsea	52	Wolverhampton W	48	Portsmouth	48
1955–56	Manchester U	60	Blackpool	49	Wolverhampton W	49
1956–57	Manchester U	64	Tottenham H	56	Preston NE	56
1957–58	Wolverhampton W	64	Preston NE	59	Tottenham H	51
1958–59	Wolverhampton W	61	Manchester U	55	Arsenal	50
1959–60	Burnley	55	Wolverhampton W	54	Tottenham H	53
1960–61	Tottenham H	66	Sheffield W	58	Wolverhampton W	57
1961–62	Ipswich T	56	Burnley	53	Tottenham H	52
1962–63	Everton	61	Tottenham H	55	Burnley	54
1963–64	Liverpool	57	Manchester U	53	Everton	52
1964–65	Manchester U	61	Leeds U	61	Chelsea	56
1965–66	Liverpool	61	Leeds U	55	Burnley	55
1966–67	Manchester U	60	Nottingham F	56	Tottenham H	56
1967–68	Manchester C	58	Manchester U	56	Liverpool	55
1968–69	Leeds U	67	Liverpool	61	Everton	57
1969–70	Everton	66	Leeds U	57	Chelsea	55
1970–71	Arsenal	65	Leeds U	64	Tottenham H	52
1971–72	Derby C	58	Leeds U	57	Liverpool	57
1972–73	Liverpool	60	Arsenal	57	Leeds U	53
1973–74	Leeds U	62	Liverpool	57	Derby C	48
1974–75	Derby C	53	Liverpool	51	Ipswich T	51
1975–76	Liverpool	60	QPR	59	Manchester U	56
1976–77	Liverpool	57	Manchester C	56	Ipswich T	52
1977–78	Nottingham F	64	Liverpool	57	Everton	55
1978–79	Liverpool	68	Nottingham F	60	WBA	59
1979–80	Liverpool	60	Manchester U	58	Ipswich T	53
1980–81	Aston Villa	60	Ipswich T	56	Arsenal	53
1981–1982	*g*Liverpool	87	Ipswich T	83	Manchester U	78

*Won on goal average. Maximum points: *a*, 44; *b*, 56; *c*, 60; *d*, 58; *e*, 76; *f*, 84, *g*, 126.

Division II

	First	Pt	Second	Pt	Third	Pt
1892–3	*a*Small Heath	36	Sheffield U	35	Darwen	30
1893–4	*b*Liverpool	50	Small Heath	42	Notts County	39
1894–5	*c*Bury	48	Notts C	39	Newton Heath	38
1895–6	*Liverpool	46	Manchester C	46	Grimsby T	42
1896–7	Notts C	42	Newton Heath	39	Grimsby T	38
1897–8	Burnley	48	Newcastle	45	Manchester C	39
1898–9	*d*Manchester C	51	Glossop NE	46	Leicester Fosse	45
1899–1900	Sheffield W	54	Bolton W	52	Small Heath	46
1900–1	Grimsby T	49	Small Heath	48	Burnley	44
1901–2	WBA	55	Middlesbrough	51	Preston NE	42
1902–3	Manchester C	54	Small Heath	51	W'lwich Arsenal	48
1903–4	Preston NE	50	W'lwich Arsenal	49	Manchester U	48
1904–5	Liverpool	58	Bolton W	56	Manchester U	53
1905–6	*e*Bristol C	66	Manchester U	62	Chelsea	53
1906–7	Nottingham F	60	Chelsea	57	Leicester Fosse	48
1907–8	Bradford C	54	Leicester Fosse	52	Oldham	50
1908–9	Bolton W	52	Tottenham H	51	WBA	51
1909–10	Manchester C	54	Oldham A	53	Hull C	53
1910–11	WBA	53	Bolton W	51	Chelsea	49
1911–12	*Derby C	54	Chelsea	54	Burnley	52

	First	Pt	Second	Pt	Third	Pt
1912–13	Preston NE	53	Burnley	50	Birmingham	46
1913–14	Notts County	53	Bradford	49	W'lwich Arsenal	49
1914–15	Derby C	53	Preston NE	50	Barnsley	47
1919–20	fTottenham H	70	Huddersfield T	64	Birmingham C	56
1920–21	*Birmingham	58	Cardiff C	58	Bristol C	51
1921–22	Nottingham F	56	Stoke C	52	Barnsley	52
1922–23	Notts C	53	West Ham U	51	Leicester C	51
1923–24	Leeds U	54	Bury	51	Derby C	51
1924–25	Leicester C	59	Manchester U	57	Derby C	55
1925–26	Sheffield W	60	Derby C	57	Chelsea	52
1926–27	Middlesbrough	62	Portsmouth	54	Manchester C	54
1927–28	Manchester C	59	Leeds U	57	Chelsea	54
1928–29	Middlesbrough	55	Grimsby T	53	Bradford C	48
1929–30	Blackpool	58	Chelsea	55	Oldham A	53
1930–31	Everton	61	WBA	55	Tottenham H	51
1931–32	Wolverhampton W	56	Leeds U	54	Stoke C	52
1932–33	Stoke C	56	Tottenham H	55	Fulham	50
1933–34	Grimsby	59	Preston NE	52	Bolton W	51
1934–35	Brentford	61	Bolton W	56	West Ham U	56
1935–36	Manchester U	56	Charlton A	55	Sheffield U	52
1936–37	Leicester C	56	Blackpool	55	Bury	52
1937–38	Aston Villa	57	Manchester U	53	Sheffield U	53
1938–39	Blackburn R	55	Sheffield U	54	Sheffield W	53
1946–47	Manchester C	62	Burnley	58	Birmingham	55
1947–48	Birmingham	59	Newcastle U	56	Southampton	52
1948–49	Fulham	57	WBA	56	Southampton	55
1949–50	Tottenham H	61	Sheffield W	52	Sheffield U	52
1950–51	Preston NE	57	Manchester C	52	Cardiff C	50
1951–52	Sheffield W	53	Cardiff C	51	Birmingham C	51
1952–53	Sheffield U	60	Huddersfield T	58	Luton T	52
1953–54	Leicester C	56	Everton	56	Blackburn R	55
1954–55	*Birmingham C	54	Luton	54	Rotherham U	54
1955–56	Sheffield W	55	Leeds U	52	Liverpool	48
1956–57	Leicester C	61	Nottingham F	54	Liverpool	53
1957–58	West Ham U	57	Blackburn R	56	Charlton A	55
1958–59	Sheffield W	62	Fulham	60	Sheffield U	53
1959–60	Aston Villa	59	Cardiff C	58	Liverpool	50
1960–61	Ipswich T	59	Sheffield U	58	Liverpool	52
1961–62	Liverpool	62	Leyton O	54	Sunderland	53
1962–63	Stoke C	53	Chelsea	52	Sunderland	52
1963–64	Leeds U	63	Sunderland	61	Preston NE	56
1964–65	Newcastle U	57	Northampton T	56	Bolton W	50
1965–66	Manchester C	59	Southampton	54	Coventry C	53
1966–67	Coventry C	59	Wolverhampton W	58	Carlisle U	52
1967–68	Ipswich T	59	QPR	58	Blackpool	58
1968–69	Derby C	63	Crystal P	56	Charlton A	50
1969–70	Huddersfield T	60	Blackpool	53	Leicester C	51
1970–71	Leicester C	59	Sheffield U	56	Cardiff C	53
1971–72	Norwich C	57	Birmingham C	56	Millwall	55
1972–73	Burnley	62	QPR	61	Aston Villa	50
1973–74	Middlesbrough	65	Luton	50	Carlisle	49
1974–75	Manchester U	61	Aston Villa	58	Norwich C	53
1975–76	Sunderland	56	Bristol C	53	WBA	53
1976–77	Wolverhampton	57	Chelsea	55	Nottingham F	52
1977–78	Bolton W	58	Southampton	57	Tottenham H	56

*Won on goal average.

	First	Pt	Second	Pt	Third	Pt
1978–79	Crystal P	57	Brighton & HA	56	Stoke C	56
1979–80	Leicester C	55	Sunderland	54	Birmingham C	53
1980–81	West Ham U	66	Notts Co	53	Swansea C	50
1981–82	*g*Luton T	88	Watford	80	Norwich C	71

Maximum points: *a*, 44; *b*, 56; *c*, 60; *d*, 58; *e*, 76; *f*, 84; *g*, 126

Division III

1958–59	*a*Plymouth Argyle	62	Hull C	61	Brentford	57
1959–60	Southampton	61	Norwich C	59	Shrewsbury	52
1960–61	Bury	68	Walsall	62	QPR	60
1961–62	Portsmouth	65	Grimsby T	62	Bournemouth	59
1962–63	Northampton T	62	Swindon T	58	Port Vale	54
1963–64	*Coventry C	60	Crystal P	60	Watford	58
1964–65	Carlisle U	60	Bristol C	59	Mansfield T	59
1965–66	Hull C	69	Millwall	65	QPR	57
1966–67	QPR	67	Middlesbrough	55	Watford	54
1967–68	Oxford U	57	Bury	56	Shrewsbury T	55
1968–69	*Watford	64	Swindon T	64	Luton T	61
1969–70	Orient	62	Luton T	60	Bristol R	56
1970–71	Preston NE	61	Fulham	60	Halifax	56
1971–72	Aston Villa	70	Brighton & HA	65	Bournemouth	62
1972–73	Bolton W	61	Notts C	57	Blackburn R	55
1973–74	Oldham A	62	Bristol R	61	York C	61
1974–75	Blackburn R	60	Plymouth A	59	Charlton A	55
1975–76	Hereford U	63	Cardiff C	57	Millwall	56
1976–77	Mansfield T	64	Brighton & HA	61	Crystal P	59
1977–78	Wrexham	61	Cambridge U	58	Preston NE	56
1978–79	Shrewsbury T	61	Watford	60	Swansea C	60
1979–80	Grimsby T	62	Blackburn R	59	Sheffield W	58
1980–81	Rotherham U	61	Barnsley	59	Charlton Ath	59
1981–82	*b*Burnley	80	Carlisle U	80	Fulham	78

*Won on goal average. Maximum points *a* 92; *b* 138

Division III (Southern Section)

1920–21	*a*Crystal P	59	Southampton	54	QPR	53
1921–22	*Southampton	61	Plymouth A	61	Portsmouth	53
1922–23	Bristol C	59	Plymouth A	53	Swansea	53
1923–24	Portsmouth	59	Plymouth A	55	Millwall	54
1924–25	Swansea C	57	Plymouth A	56	Bristol C	53
1925–26	Reading	57	Plymouth A	56	Millwall	53
1926–27	Bristol C	62	Plymouth A	60	Millwall	56
1927–28	Millwall	65	Northampton T	55	Plymouth A	53
1928–29	*Charlton A	54	Crystal P	54	Northampton T	52
1929–30	Plymouth A	68	Brentford	61	QPR	51
1930–31	Notts C	59	Crystal P	51	Brentford	50
1931–32	Fulham	57	Reading	55	Southend U	53
1932–33	Brentford	62	Exeter	58	Norwich C	57
1933–34	Norwich C	61	Coventry C	54	Reading	54
1934–35	Charlton A	61	Reading	53	Coventry C	51
1935–36	Coventry C	57	Luton T	56	Reading	54
1936–37	Luton T	58	Notts C	56	Brighton & HA	53
1937–38	Millwall	56	Bristol C	55	QPR	53
1938–39	Newport C	55	Crystal P	52	Brighton & HA	49
1946–47	Cardiff	66	QPR	57	Bristol C	51
1947–48	QPR	61	Bournemouth	57	Walsall	51

*Won on goal average. Maximum points: *a*, 84; *b*, 92

	First	Pt	Second	Pt	Third	Pt
1949–49	Swansea	62	Reading	55	Bournemouth	52
1949–50	Notts C	58	Northampton T	51	Southend U	51
1950–51*b*	Nottingham F	70	Norwich C	64	Reading	57
1951–52	Plymouth A	66	Reading	61	Norwich C	61
1952–53	Bristol R	64	Northampton T	62	Millwall	62
1953–54	Ipswich T	64	Brighton & HA	61	Bristol C	56
1954–55	Bristol C	70	Leyton O	61	Southampton	59
1955–56	Leyton O	66	Brighton & HA	65	Ipswich T	64
1956–57	*Ipswich T	59	Torquay U	59	Colchester U	58
1957–58	Brighton & HA	60	Brentford	58	Plymouth A	58

Division III (Northern Section)

	First	Pt	Second	Pt	Third	Pt
1921–22*a*	Stockport C	56	Darlington	50	Grimsby	50
1922–23	Nelson	51	Bradford	47	Walsall	46
1923–24*b*	Wolverhampton W	63	Rochdale	62	Chesterfield	54
1924–25	Darlington	58	Nelson	53	New Brighton	53
1925–26	Grimsby T	61	Bradford	60	Rochdale	59
1926–27	Stoke C	63	Rochdale	58	Bradford	55
1927–28	Bradford	63	Lincoln C	55	Stockport C	54
1928–29	Bradford C	63	Stockport C	62	Wrexham	52
1929–30	Port Vale	67	Stockport C	63	Darlington	50
1930–31	Chesterfield	58	Lincoln C	57	Wrexham	54
1931–32*c*	*Lincoln C	57	Gateshead	57	Chester	50
1932–33*b*	Hull C	59	Wrexham	57	Stockport C	54
1933–34	Barnsley	62	Chesterfield	61	Stockport C	59
1934–35	Doncaster R	57	Halifax T	55	Chester	54
1935–36	Chesterfield	60	Chester	55	Tranmere R	55
1936–37	Stockport C	60	Lincoln C	57	Chester	53
1937–38	Tranmere R	56	Doncaster R	54	Hull C	53
1938–39	Barnsley	67	Doncaster R	56	Bradford C	52
1946–47	Doncaster R	72	Rotherham U	64	Chester	56
1947–48	Lincoln C	60	Rotherham U	59	Wrexham	50
1948–49	Hull C	65	Rotherham U	62	Doncaster R	50
1949–50	Doncaster R	55	Gateshead	53	Rochdale U	51
1950–51*d*	Rotherham U	71	Mansfield T	64	Carlisle U	62
1951–52	Lincoln C	69	Grimsby T	66	Stockport C	59
1952–53	Oldham A	59	Port Vale	58	Wrexham	56
1953–54	Port Vale	69	Barnsley	58	Scunthorpe	57
1954–55	Barnsley	65	Accrington S	61	Scunthorpe	58
1955–56	Grimsby T	68	Derby C	63	Accrington S	59
1956–57	Derby C	63	Hartlepool	59	Accrington S	58
1957–58	Scunthorpe U	66	Accrington S	59	Bradford C	57

*Won on goal average. Maximum points: *a*, 70; *b*, 84; *c*, 80; *d*, 90.
No championship during the World Wars.

Division IV

	First	Pt	Second	Pt	Third	Pt
1958–59*a*	Port Vale	64	Coventry C	60	York C	60
1959–60	Walsall	65	Notts C	60	Torquay	60
1960–61	Peterborough	66	Crystal P	64	Northampton T	60
1961–62	Millwall	56	Colchester U	55	Wrexham	53
1962–63	Brentford	62	Oldham A	59	Crewe A	59
1963–64	*Gillingham	60	Carlisle U	60	Workington T	59
1964–65	Brighton & HA	63	Millwall	62	York C	62
1965–66	*Doncaster R	59	Darlington	59	Torquay	58
1966–67	Stockport C	64	Southport C	59	Barrow	59

	First	Pt	Second	Pt	Third	Pt
1967–68	Luton T	66	Barnsley	61	Hartlepool	60

*Won on goal average.

1968–69	Doncaster R	59	Halifax T	57	Rochdale	56
1969–70	Chesterfield	64	Wrexham	61	Swansea T	60
1970–71	Notts C	69	Bournemouth	60	Oldham A	59
1971–72	Grimsby T	63	Southend U	60	Brentford	59
1972–73	Southport	62	Hereford U	58	Cambridge U	57
1973–74	Peterborough U	65	Gillingham	62	Colchester	60
1974–75	Mansfield T	68	Shrewsbury T	62	Rotherham U	59
1975–76	Lincoln C	74	Northampton T	68	Reading	60
1976–77	Cambridge U	65	Exeter C	62	Colchester	59
1977–78	Watford	71	Southend U	60	Swansea C	56
1978–79	Reading	65	Grimsby T	61	Wimbledon	61
1979–80	Huddersfield T	66	Walsall	64	Newport Co	61
1980–81	Southend U	67	Lincoln C	65	Doncaster R	56
1981–82	*b*Sheffield U	96	Bradford C	91	Wigan Ath	91

Maximum points *a*, 92; *b*, 138

RELEGATED CLUBS

(Since inception of automatic promotion and relegation in 1898–99)

Season	Division I to Division II	Division II to Division III
1981–82	Leeds U., Middlesbrough, Wolverhampton W.	Cardiff, Wrexham, Orient.
1980–81	Norwich C., Leicester C., Crystal P.	Preston N.E., Bristol C., Bristol R.
1979–80	Bristol C., Derby Co., Bolton W.	Fulham, Burnley, Charlton Ath.
1978–79	QPR, Birmingham, Chelsea	Sheffield U., Millwall, B'burn
1977–78	West Ham, Newcastle, Leicester	Blackpool, Mansfield, Hull C.
1976–77	Sunderland, Stoke, Tottenham	Carlisle, Plymouth, Hereford
1975–76	Wolves, Burnley, Sheffield U.	Oxford, York, Portsmouth
1974–75	Luton, Chelsea, Carlisle	Millwall, Cardiff, Sheff. W.
1973–74	So'ton, Man. U., Norwich	C. Palace, Preston, Swindon
1972–73	Crystal P. and WBA	Huddersfield and Brighton
1971–72	Huddersfield and Nottingham F.	Charlton and Watford
1970–71	Burnley and Blackpool	Blackburn and Bolton
1969–70	Sunderland and Sheffield W.	Aston Villa and Preston
1968–69	Leicester and QPR	Bury and Fulham
1967–68	Sheffield U. and Fulham	Rotherham and Plymouth
1966–67	Aston Villa and Blackpool	Northampton and Bury
1965–66	Blackburn and Northampton	Leyton O. and Middlesbrough
1964–65	Birmingham and Wolverh'pton	Swindon and Swansea
1963–64	Bolton and Ipswich	Grimsby and Scunthorpe
1962–63	Manchester C. and Leyton O.	Walsall and Luton
1961–62	Cardiff and Chelsea	Bristol R. and Brighton
1960–61	Newcastle and Preston	Portsmouth and Lincoln
1959–60	Leeds and Luton	Hull and Bristol C.
1958–59	Aston V. and Portsmouth	Grimsby and Barnsley
1957–58	Sunderland and Sheffield W.	Notts Co. and Doncaster
1956–57	Cardiff and Charlton	Bury and Port Vale
1955–56	Huddersfield and Sheffield U.	Plymouth and Hull
1954–55	Leicester and Sheffield W.	Ipswich and Derby
1953–54	Middlesbrough and Liverpool	Brentford and Oldham
1952–53	Stoke and Derby	Southampton and Barnsley
1951–52	Fulham and Huddersfield	Coventry and QPR
1950–51	Sheffield W. and Everton	Chesterfield and Grimsby
1949–50	Manchester C. and Birmingham	Plymouth and Bradford

1948–49	Preston and Sheffield U.	Lincoln and Nottingham F.
1947–48	Blackburn and Grimsby	Doncaster and Millwall
1946–47	Brentford and Leeds	Swansea and Newport
1938–39	Birmingham and Leicester	Norwich and Tranmere
1937–38	Manchester C. and WBA	Barnsley and Stockport
1936–37	M'chester U. and Sheffield W.	Doncaster and Bradford C.
1935–36	Aston Villa and Blackburn	Port Vale and Hull
1934–35	Leicester and Tottenham	Oldham and Notts Co.
1933–34	Newcastle and Sheffield U.	Millwall and Lincoln
1932–33	Bolton and Blackpool	Chesterfield and Charlton
1931–32	Grimsby and West Ham	Barnsley and Bristol City
1930–31	Leeds and Manchester U.	Reading and Cardiff
1929–30	Burnley and Everton	Hull and Notts Co.
1928–29	Bury and Cardiff	Port Vale and Clapton O.
1927–28	Tottenham and Middlesbro'	Fulham and South Shields
1926–27	Leeds and WBA	Darlington and Bradford C.
1925–26	Manchester C. and Notts Co.	Stoke and Stockport
1924–25	Preston and Nottingham F.	Crystal Palace and Coventry
1923–24	Chelsea and Middlesbro'	Nelson and Bristol City
1922–23	Stoke and Oldham	Rotherham and W'ham'ton
1921–22	Bradford C. and Manchester U.	Bradford and Bristol City
1920–21	Derby and Bradford	Stockport
1919–20	Notts Co. and Sheffield W.	

1916–18 During the War the Football League competition was suspended.
Previously the clubs relegated from Div. I to Div. II were:
1914–15 Tottenham and Chelsea
1913–14 Preston North End and Derby County
1912–13 Notts County and Woolwich Arsenal
1911–12 Preston North End and Bury
1910–11 Bristol City and Nottingham Forest
1909–10 Bolton Wanderers and Chelsea
1908–09 Manchester City and Leicester Fosse
1907–08 Bolton Wanderers and Birmingham
1906–07 Derby County and Stoke
1905–06 Nottingham Forest and Wolverhampton
1904–05 League extended. Bury and Notts County, two bottom clubs in First Division, re-elected.
1903–04 Liverpool and West Bromwich Albion
1902–03 Grimsby and Bolton
1901–02 Small Heath and Manchester City
1900–01 Preston North End and West Bromwich
1899–1900 Burnley and Glossop
1898–99 Bolton and Sheffield Wednesday

Season Relegation from Third to Fourth Division
1981–82 Wimbledon, Swindon T., Bristol C., Chester
1980–81 Sheffield U., Colchester U., Hull C., Blackpool
1979–80 Bury, Southend U., Mansfield T. and Wimbledon
1978–79 Peterborough, Walsall, Tranmere and Lincoln
1977–78 Port Vale, Bradford, Hereford and Portsmouth
1976–77 Reading, Northampton, Grimsby and York
1975–76 Aldershot, Colchester, Southend U., and Halifax T.
1974–75 Bournemouth, Tranmere, Watford and Huddersfield
1973–74 Cambridge, Shrewsbury, Southport and Rochdale
1972–73 Rotherham, Brentford, Swansea and Scunthorpe
1971–72 Mansfield, Barnsley, Bradford C. and Torquay

1970–71 Reading, Bury, Doncaster and Gillingham
1969–70 Bournemouth, Southport, Barrow and Stockport
1968–69 Northampton, Hartlepool, Crewe and Oldham
1967–68 Grimsby, Colchester, Scunthorpe and Peterborough*
1966–67 Swansea, Darlington, Workington and Doncaster
1965–66 Southend, Exeter, Brentford, and York
1964–65 Luton, Port Vale, Colchester and Barnsley
1963–64 Millwall, Crewe, Wrexham and Notts County
1962–63 Bradford, Brighton, Carlisle and Halifax
1961–62 Torquay, Lincoln, Brentford and Newport
1960–61 Tranmere, Bradford C., Colchester and Chesterfield
1959–60 York, Mansfield, Wrexham and Accrington
1958–59 Stockport, Doncaster, Notts County and Rochdale
*Expelled to Fourth Division by League

APPLICATION FOR RE-ELECTION TO THIRD DIVISION UNTIL 1957-58

Seven times: Walsall.
Six: Exeter, Halifax, Newport.
Five: Accrington, Barrow, Gillingham, New Brighton, Southport.
Four: Norwich, Rochdale.
Three: Crewe, Crystal Palace, Darlington, Hartlepool, Merthyr Town, Swindon.
Two: Aberdare Athletic, Aldershot, Ashington, Bournemouth, Brentford, Chester, Colchester, Millwall, Durham City, Nelson, Queen's Park Rangers, Rotherham, Southend, Tranmere, Watford, Workington.
One: Bradford, Bradford City, Brighton, Bristol Rovers, Cardiff, Carlisle, Charlton, Gateshead, Grimsby, Mansfield, Shrewsbury, Thames, Torquay, York.

APPLICATION FOR RE-ELECTION TO FOURTH DIVISION

Nine times: Hartlepool.
Six: Barrow, Crewe, Southport and York.
Five: Darlington, Lincoln, Rochdale and Workington.
Four: Bradford, Chester, Halifax, Newport and Stockport.
Three: Doncaster and Northampton.
Two: Bradford City, Hereford U., Oldham and Scunthorpe.
One: Aldershot, Colchester, Exeter, Gateshead, Grimsby, Port Vale, Swansea City, Tranmere R., and Wrexham.
Gateshead not re-elected, their place being taken by Peterborough in the 1960–61 season.
Accrington resigned March 1962, and Oxford United elected to replace them in 1962–63 season.
Bradford not re-elected, their place being taken by Cambridge United in the 1970–71 season.
Barrow not re-elected, their place being taken by Hereford United in the 1972–73 season.
Workington not re-elected, their place being taken by Wimbledon in the 1977–78 season.
Southport not re-elected, their place being taken by Wigan in the 1978–79 season.

LEAGUE TITLE WINS

League Division I–13–Liverpool; 8–Arsenal; 7–Aston Villa, Everton, Manchester U.; 6–Sunderland; 4–Newcastle, Sheffield Wed.; 3–Huddersfield, Wolves; 2–Blackburn, Burnley, Derby, Leeds, Manchester City, Portsmouth, Preston, Tottenham; 1–Chelsea, Ipswich, Nottingham Forest, Sheffield United, West Bromwich Albion.

League Division II–6–Manchester City, Leicester; 5–Sheffield Wed.; 4–*Birmingham, Liverpool; 3–Derby, Middlesbrough, Notts Co., Preston; 2–Aston Villa, Bolton, Burnley, Grimsby, Ipswich, Leeds, Manchester U., Nottingham Forest, Stoke, Tottenham, West Bromwich, West Ham, Wolverhampton; 1–Blackburn, Blackpool, Bradford City, Brentford, Bristol City, Bury, Coventry, Crystal Palace, Everton, Fulham, Huddersfield, Luton, Newcastle, Norwich, Sheffield United, Sunderland.
*Once as Small Heath.

League Division III–Aston Villa, Blackburn R., Bolton, Burnley, Bury, Carlisle, Coventry, Grimsby T., Hereford U., Hull, Mansfield, Northampton, Oldham Ath., Orient, Oxford U., Plymouth, Portsmouth, Preston, Queen's Park Rangers, Rotherham U., Shrewsbury T., Southampton, Watford, Wrexham.

League Division IV–Doncaster 2, Peterborough 2; Brentford, Brighton, Cambridge, Chesterfield, Gillingham, Grimsby, Huddersfield T., Lincoln C., Luton, Mansfield T., Millwall, Notts Co., Port Vale, Reading, Sheffield U., Southend U., Southport, Walsall, Watford.

To 1957-58
Division III (South): Bristol City, three times; Charlton, Ipswich, Millwall, Notts Co., Plymouth, Swansea, twice; Brentford, Brighton, Bristol R., Cardiff, Coventry, Crystal P., Fulham, Leyton Orient, Luton, Newport, Nottingham Forest, Norwich, Portsmouth, Queen's Park Rangers, Reading, Southampton, once.
Division III (North): Barnsley, Doncaster, Lincoln, three times; Chesterfield, Grimsby, Hull, Port Vale, Stockport, twice; Bradford, Bradford City, Darlington, Derby, Nelson, Oldham, Rotherham, Scunthorpe, Stoke, Tranmere, Wolverhampton, once.

TRANSFER TRAIL

(players with British Clubs)

First four-figure transaction
Alf Common: Sunderland to Middlesborough for £1,000 in February 1905.
First five-figure transaction
David Jack: Bolton Wanderers to Arsenal for £10,340 in October 1928.
First six-figure transaction
Alan Ball: Blackpool to Everton £112,000, August 1966.
First £200,000 transaction
Martin Peters: West Ham United to Tottenham Hotspur £200,000, March 1970.
First seven-figure transaction
Trevor Francis: Birmingham City to Nottingham Forest £1,000,000, February 1979.

Bryan Robson: West Bromwich Albion to Manchester United £1,500,000, in October 1981.
Andy Gray: Aston Villa to Wolverhampton W. £1,469,000, September 1979.
Steve Daley: Wolverhampton W. to Manchester City £1,450,000, September 1979.
Kenny Sansom: Crystal Palace to Arsenal £1,350,000, August 1980.
Clive Allen: Queens Park Rangers to Arsenal £1,250,000, June 1980.
Clive Allen: Arsenal to Crystal Palace, £1,250,000, August 1980.
Gary Birtles: Nottingham Forest to Manchester United £1,250,000, October 1980.
Trevor Francis: Birmingham City to Nottingham Forest £1,000,000, February 1979.
Kevin Reeves: Norwich City to Manchester City £1,000,000, March 1980.
Justin Fashanu: Norwich City to Nottingham Forest £1,000,000, in August 1981.
Trevor Francis: Nottingham Forest to Manchester City £1,000,000, in September 1981.
Peter Barnes: West Bromwich Albion to Leeds United £930,000, in August 1981.
Mark Lawrenson: Brighton & Hove Albion to Liverpool £900,000, in August 1981.
Frank Stapleton: Arsenal to Manchester United £900,000, in August 1981.
Steve Archibald: Aberdeen to Tottenham Hotspur £800,000, May 1980.
Paul Goddard: Queens Park Rangers to West Ham United £800,000 August 1980.
Mick Robinson: Preston North End to Manchester City £756,000, July 1979.
Ray Wilkins: Chelsea to Manchester United £750,000, August 1979.
Mike Flanagan: Charlton Athletic to Crystal Palace £722,000 August 1979.
Adrian Heath: Stoke City to Everton £700,000, in January 1982.
Steve Wicks: Queen's Park Rangers to Crystal Palace £670,000, in June 1981.
Peter Barnes: Manchester City to West Bromwich Albion £650,000, July 1979.
John Gidman: Aston Villa to Everton £650,000, October 1979.
Garth Crooks: Stoke City to Tottenham Hotspur £600,000, July 1980.
David Armstrong: Middlesbrough to Southampton £600,000, in August 1981.
John Chiedozie: Orient to Notts County £600,000, in August 1981.
Craig Johnston: Middlesbrough to Liverpool £575,000, April 1981.
Phil Parkes: Queens Park Rangers to West Ham United £565,000, February 1979.
David Mills: Middlesbrough to West Bromwich Albion £516,000, January 1979.
Asa Hartford: Manchester City to Nottingham Forest £500,000, July 1979.
Asa Hartford: Nottingham Forest to Everton £500,000, August 1979.
Peter Withe: Newcastle United to Aston Villa £500,000, May 1980.
Andrew Ritchie: Manchester U. to Brighton & Hove A. £500,000, October 1980.
Steve McKenzie: Manchester C. to West Bromwich A. £500,000, in August 1981.
Remi Moses: West Bromwich A. to Manchester U. £500,000, in September 1981.
Tony Woodcock: FC Cologne to Arsenal £500,000, in June 1982.
Gerry Francis: Queen's Park Rangers to Crystal Palace £465,000, July 1979.

Gordon McQueen: Leeds United to Manchester United £450,000, February 1978.
Brian Talbot: Ipswich Town to Arsenal £450,000, January 1979.
Garry Owen: Manchester City to West Bromwich Albion £450,000, June 1979.
Kenny Dalglish: Celtic to Liverpool £440,000, May 1979.
Mick Baxter: Preston North End to Middlesbrough £425,000, in August 1981.
Paul Proctor: Middlesbrough to Nottingham Forest £425,000, in August 1981.
Osvaldo Ardiles: Huracan to Tottenham Hotspur £400,000, July 1978.
Charlie George: Derby County to Southampton £400,000, December 1978.
Tony Currie: Leeds United to Queen's Park Rangers £400,000, August 1979.
Frank Gray: Leeds United to Nottingham Forest £400,000, August 1979.
John Deehan: Aston Villa to West Bromwich Albion £400,000, September 1979.
Gordon Smith: Rangers to Brighton & Hove Albion £400,000, May 1980.
Ray Stewart: Dundee United to West Ham United £400,000, September 1979.
Dave Thomas: Everton to Wolverhampton Wanderers £400,000, October 1979.
Dave Swindlehurst: Crystal Palace to Derby County £400,000, April 1980.
Alex Sabella: Sheffield United to Leeds United £400,000, May 1980.
Kevin Keegan: Hamburg to Southampton £400,000, July 1980.
Michael Robinson: Manchester C. to Brighton & Hove Albion £400,000, July 1980.
Paul Barron: Arsenal to Crystal Palace £400,000, August 1980.
Thomas Langley: Chelsea to Queens Park Rangers £400,000, August 1980.
Andrew King: Everton to Queens Park Rangers £400,000, September 1980.
Peter Ward: Brighton & Hove A. to Nottingham Forest £400,000, October 1980.
Peter Nicholas: Crystal Palace to Arsenal £400,000, March 1981.
Clive Allen: Crystal Palace to Queen's Park Rangers £400,000, in June 1981.
Jimmy Case: Liverpool to Brighton & Hove Albion £400,000, in August 1981.
Andy King: Queen's Park Rangers to West Bromwich Albion £400,000 in September 1981.
Kenny Burns: Nottingham Forest to Leeds United £400,000, in October 1981.
Neil Orr: Greenock Morton to West Ham United £400,000, in January 1982.
Alan Curtis: Swansea City to Leeds United £375,000, May 1979.
Irving Nattrass: Newcastle United to Middlesbrough £375,000, August 1979.
Kevin Hird: Blackburn Rovers to Leeds United £360,000, March 1979.
Graeme Souness: Middlesbrough to Liverpool £352,000, January 1978.
Joe Jordan: Leeds United to Manchester United £350,000, January 1978.
Paul Futcher: Luton Town to Manchester City £350,000, June 1978.
Richardo Villa: Racing Club to Tottenham Hotspur £350,000, July 1978.
Len Cantello: West Bromwich Albion to Bolton Wanderers £350,000, June 1979.
Garry Collier: Bristol City to Coventry City £350,000, July 1979.
Brian Greenhoff: Manchester United to Leeds United £350,000, August 1979.
Alan Biley: Cambridge United to Derby County £350,000, January 1980.
David Langan: Derby County to Birmingham City £350,000, July 1980.
Joe Gallagher: Birmingham City to Wolverhampton Wanderers £350,000, in August 1981.
Colin Irwin: Liverpool to Swansea City £350,000, in August 1981.
Kevin Bond: Seattle Sounders to Manchester City £350,000, in September 1981.
Chris Kamara: Portsmouth to Brentford £350,000, in October 1981.
Richard Money: Fulham to Liverpool £333,000, May 1980.
Paul Hart: Blackpool to Leeds United £330,000, March 1978.
Colin Todd: Derby County to Everton £330,000, September 1978.
Mick Walsh: Blackpool to Everton £325,000, August 1978.
John Gidman: Everton to Manchester United £325,000, in August 1981.
Claudio Marangoni: San Lorenzo (Arg.) to Sunderland £320,000, December 1979.
Alan Kennedy: Newcastle United to Liverpool £300,000, August 1978.
Mike Thomas: Wrexham to Manchester United £300,000, November 1978.
Frank McGarvey: St Mirren to Liverpool £300,000, May 1979.

John Gregory: Aston Villa to Brighton & Hove Albion £300,000, July 1979.
Bobby Shinton: Wrexham to Manchester City £300,000, July 1979.
Garry Stanley: Chelsea to Everton £300,000, August 1979.
Terry Yorath: Coventry City to Tottenham Hotspur £300,000, August 1979.
David Geddis: Ipswich Town to Aston Villa £300,000, September 1979.
Steve Wicks: Derby County to Queen's Park Rangers £300,000, September 1979.
Barry Powell: Coventry City to Derby County £300,000, October 1979.
Stan Cummins: Middlesbrough to Sunderland £300,000, November 1979.
Ian Rush: Chester to Liverpool £300,000, May 1980.
Gerrard Daly: Derby County to Coventry City £300,000, August 1980.
Drazen Muzinic: Hadjuk Split to Norwich City £300,000, September 1980.
Alexander Munro: St. Mirren to Stoke City £300,000, October 1980.
Frank Gray: Nottingham Forest to Leeds United £300,000, in May 1981.
John Gregory: Brighton & Hove Albion to Queen's Park Rangers £300,000, in June 1981.
Alan Biley: Derby Co. to Everton £300,000, in July 1981.
Andy Blair: Coventry City to Aston Villa £300,000, in August 1981.
Ray Clemence: Liverpool to Tottenham Hotspur £300,000, in August 1981.
Ally McCoist: St Johnstone to Sunderland £300,000, in August 1981.
Neil Whatmore: Bolton Wanderers to Birmingham City £300,000, in August 1981.
Steve Nicol: Ayr United to Liverpool £300,000, in October 1981.
Ray Hankin: Vancouver Whitecaps to Arsenal £300,000 in November 1981.
Peter Eastoe: Queen's Park Rangers to Everton £280,000, March 1979.
Mick Walsh: Everton to Queen's Park Rangers £280,000, March 1979.
Mick Ferguson: Coventry City to Everton £280,000, in August 1981.
Steve Wicks: Chelsea to Derby County £275,000, January 1979.
Des Bremner: Hibernian to Aston Villa £275,000, September 1979.
Frank McGarvey: Liverpool to Celtic £275,000, March 1980.
Simon Stainrod: Oldham Athletic to Q.P.R. £275,000, November 1980.
Martin O'Neill: Norwich City to Manchester City £275,000, in June 1981.
Micky Thomas: Manchester United to Everton, £275,000, in August 1981.
Paul Maguire: Shrewsbury Town to Stoke City £262,000, September 1980.
Tommy Craig: Newcastle United to Aston Villa £250,000, January 1978.
Gordon Hill: Manchester United to Derby County £250,000, April 1978.
Neil McNab: Tottenham Hotspur to Bolton Wanderers £250,000, November 1978.
David Jones: Everton to Coventry City £250,000, June 1979.
Stephen Mackenzie: Crystal Palace to Manchester City £250,000, July 1979.
Chris Woods: Nottingham Forest to Queen's Park Rangers £250,000, July 1979.
Tony Fitzpatrick: St Mirren to Bristol City £250,000, August 1979.
Mike Pejic: Everton to Aston Villa £250,000, September 1979.
Colin Todd: Everton to Birmingham City £250,000, September 1979.
Stan Bowles: Q.P.R. to Nottingham Forest £250,000, December 1979.
Gary Megson: Plymouth Argyle to Everton £250,000, February 1980.
Roger Van Gool: FC Cologne to Ipswich Town £250,000, March 1980.
James McDonagh: Bolton Wanderers to Everton £250,000, July 1980.
James Melrose: Partick Thistle to Leicester City £250,000, July 1980.
Robert McDonald: Coventry City to Manchester City £250,000, October 1980.
Gerard Armstrong: Tottenham Hotspur to Watford £250,000, November 1980.
John Trewick: West Bromwich A. to Newcastle United £250,000, December 1980.
Martin O'Neill: Nottingham Forest to Norwich City £250,000, February 1981.
Aas Elnar: Bayern Munich to Nottingham Forest £250,000, March 1981.
Paul Price: Luton Town to Tottenham Hotspur £250,000, in June 1981.
Alan Ainscaw: Birmingham City to Everton £250,000, in August 1981.
James McDonagh: Everton to Bolton Wanderers £250,000, in August 1981.
Steve Wicks: Crystal Palace to Queen's Park Rangers £250,000, in March 1982.
Romeo Zondervan: to West Bromwich Albion £250,000, in March 1982.

FA CUP

FA Cup Report 1981-82

Tottenham won the FA Cup for the second successive season, thus emulating their achievement of exactly 20 years ago, but in the end the manner of their victory was not terribly enthralling. Their second Wembley final of the season was a disappointing affair at the first time of asking, and much of the sparkle that seemed to characterise the performances of Spurs in the early part of the season had gone. Eventually, after the anticlimax of a replay, they managed to beat their fellow-Londoners Queen's Park Rangers by a single penalty goal.

Tottenham's route to the final had been marked out by a series of single goal victories, with perhaps the most attractive fixture coming against their greatest rivals, Arsenal, in the third round. Similar 1-0 wins were then recorded against Leeds and Aston Villa before Spurs faced up to some more London opposition in the quarter-finals. This tie, against Chelsea, turned out to be one of the better games of the whole tournament, with Tottenham winning by the odd goal in five. Chelsea had disposed of Liverpool in the previous round, and played with plenty of confidence. It is a great pity that this open-ness is noticeably lacking in so much football today.

Queen's Park Rangers had a more interesting journey to Wembley. They beat Middlesbrough 3-2 in a replay after their third-round tie had finished 1-1, and in the fourth round, after a 0-0 draw at Blackpool, they cruised to a 5-1 victory on their controversial artificial turf at Shepherd's Bush. Their other victims on the way were Grimsby, Crystal Palace and West Bromwich Albion.

The 1981-82 FA Cup tournament will not be one remembered with a great deal of relish by the First Division clubs involved. No fewer than half of the 22 were wiped out in the third round, and by the time the quarter-finals arrived, there were only three left, with two of them playing against each other! Among the more notable exits in the third round were Manchester United (0-1 v Watford), Nottingham Forest (1-3 v Wrexham) and Southampton (1-3 v Leicester). During the past decade there have been five finalists from the Second Division, and victories have been recorded by Sunderland (1973 v Leeds), Southampton (1976 v Manchester United) and West Ham United (1980 v Arsenal). Why the First Division clubs have failed to dominate the competition more fully is hard to understand, but certainly the way in which the game in general has tightened up during the same period, with the avoidance of defeat slowly assuming as much, if not more, importance than winning, must have had an effect. Caution, especially when it is overdone, can carry as much risk as adventurism, and is certainly much less attractive to watch. The FA Cup Final is still playing to a full house, but full houses are rare nowadays.

First Round

Aldershot	2	Leytonstone & Ilford	0
Bedford	0	Wimbledon	2
Bideford	1	Barking	2
Bishop Auckland	4	Nuneaton	1
Bishops Stortford	2 1	Sutton United	2 2
Blyth Spartans	1	Walsall	2
Boston United	0	Kettering	1
Bournemouth	1	Reading	0
Brentford	2	Exeter City	0
Bristol City	0 2	Torquay United	0 1
Bristol Rovers	1	Fulham	2
Burnley	0 2	Runcorn	0 1

First Round (continued)

Chesterfield	4	Preston North End	1
Colchester United	2	Newport County	0
Dagenham	2 1	Yeovil	2 0
Darlington	2 1	Carlisle United	2 3
Dorchester	3 4	Minehead	3 0
Dover	0	Oxford United	2
Enfield	2	Hastings	0
Halifax Town	0	Peterborough United	3
Harlow	0 0	Barnet	0 1
Hendon	1 0	Wycombe Wanderers	1 2
Hereford United	3	Southend United	1
Horden C.W.	0	Blackpool	1*
Lincoln City	2 0 0	Port Vale	2 0 2
Mansfield Town	0	Doncaster Rovers	1
Penrith	1	Chester	0
Plymouth Argyle	0 0	Gillingham	0 1
Portsmouth	1 2	Millwall	1 3
Rochdale	2 2 0	Hull City	2 2 1
Scunthorpe United	1	Bradford City	0
Sheffield United	2 0	Altrincham	2 3
Stafford Rangers	1	York City	2
Stockport County	3	Mossley	1
Taunton	1	Swindon	2**
Tranmere	1 1	Bury	1 3
Weymouth	0 2	Northampton Town	0 6
Wigan Athletic	2 0	Hartlepool	2 1
Willenhall	0	Crewe Alexandra	1
Workington	1 0	Huddersfield	1 5

**At Blackpool*
***At Swindon*

Second Round

Aldershot	2 2	Oxford United	2 4
Barnet	2	Wycombe Wanderers	0
Brentford	1 0	Colchester United	1 1
Bristol City	3	Northampton Town	0
Bury	1 1	Burnley	1 2
Carlisle United	1	Bishop Auckland	0
Chesterfield	0	Huddersfield Town	1
Crewe Alexandra	1	Scunthorpe United	3
Dagenham	1	Millwall	2
Doncaster Rovers	3	Penrith	0
Dorchester	1 1	Bournemouth	1 2
Enfield	4	Wimbledon	1
Gillingham	1 3	Barking	1 1
Hereford United	1	Fulham	0
Hull City	2	Hartlepool	0
Kettering	0	Blackpool	3
Peterborough United	2	Walsall	1
Port Vale	4	Stockport County	1
Swindon Town	2	Sutton	1
York City	0 3	Altrincham	0 4

Third round	Fourth round	Fifth round	Quarter-finals	Semi-finals	Final
Barnsley .0	Blackpool .0 1	Q.P.R. .3	Q.P.R. .1	Q.P.R. .1	**Q.P.R. 1, 0**
Blackpool .2					*Scorer:* Fenwick
Q.P.R. .1 3	Q.P.R. .0 5				Both matches at Wembley. Attendance: 100,000; 92,000.
Middlesbrough .1 2					
Newcastle U. .1 4	Newcastle U. .1	Grimsby T. .1			
Colchester U. .1 3					
Millwall .1	Grimsby T. .2				
Grimsby T. .6					
Enfield .2	Crystal Palace .1	Crystal Palace .0 1	Crystal Palace .0		
Crystal Palace .3					
Bolton W. .3	Bolton W. .0				
Derby Co. .1					
Carlisle U. .2	Huddersfield T. .1 0	Orient .0 0			
Huddersfield T. .3					
Orient .1	Orient .1 2				
Charlton Ath. .0					
Gillingham .2	Gillingham .0	W.B.A. .1	W.B.A. .2	W.B.A. .0	
Oldham Ath. .1					
W.B.A. .3	W.B.A. .1				
Blackburn R. .2					
Stoke C. .0	Norwich C. .2	Norwich C. .0			
Norwich C. .1					
Doncaster R. .2	Doncaster R. .1				
Cambridge U. .1					
Manchester C. .3	Manchester C. .1	Coventry C. .4	Coventry C. .0		
Cardiff C. .1					
Coventry C. .3	Coventry C. .3				
Sheffield W. .1					
Barnet .0 1	Brighton & H.A. .0	Oxford U. .0			
Brighton & Hove A. .0 3					
Bournemouth .0	Oxford U. .3				
Oxford U. .2					

TOTTENHAM H. 1, 1

Scorer: Hoddle; *replay:* Hoddle (pen)

Round 1		Round 2		Round 3		Semi-final		Final
Chelsea .0 2		Chelsea .0 1 2		Chelsea .2		Chelsea .2		Tottenham H. .2
Hull C. .0 0		Wrexham .0 1 1		Liverpool .0		Tottenham H. .3		Leicester C. .0
Nottingham F. .1		Sunderland .0		Tottenham H. .1		Leicester C. .5		
Wrexham .3		Liverpool .3		Aston Villa .0		Shrewsbury T. .2		
Rotherham U. .1 0		Tottenham H. .1		Leicester C. .2				
Sunderland .1 1		Leeds U. .0		Watford .0				
Swansea C. .0		Bristol C. .0		Shrewsbury T. .2				
Liverpool .4		Aston Villa .1		Ipswich T. .1				
Tottenham H. .1		Hereford U. .0						
Arsenal .0		Leicester C. .1						
Wolverhampton W. .1		Watford .2						
Leeds U. .3		West Ham U. .0						
Peterborough U. .0		Shrewsbury T. .1						
Bristol C. .1		Burnley .0						
Notts Co. .0		Luton T. .0						
Aston Villa .6		Ipswich T. .3						
Scunthorpe U. .1 1								
Hereford U. .1 4								
Leicester C. .3								
Southampton .1								
Watford .1								
Manchester U. .0								
West Ham U. .2								
Everton .1								
Shrewsbury T. .1								
Port Vale .0								
Burnley .6								
Altrincham .1								
Luton T. .2								
Swindon T. .1								
Birmingham C. .2								
Ipswich T. .3								

FA CUP WINNERS SINCE 1871

Aston Villa	7	Sunderland	2
Tottenham Hotspur	7	Barnsley	1
Blackburn Rovers	6	Blackburn Olympic	1
Newcastle United	6	Blackpool	1
Arsenal	5	Bradford City	1
Wanderers	5	Burnley	1
West Bromwich Albion	5	Cardiff City	1
Bolton Wanderers	4	Charlton Athletic	1
Manchester City	4	Chelsea	1
Manchester United	4	Clapham Rovers	1
Sheffield United	4	Derby County	1
Wolverhampton Wanderers	4	Huddersfield Town	1
Everton	3	Ipswich Town	1
Sheffield Wednesday	3	Leeds United	1
West Ham United	3	Notts County	1
Bury	2	Old Carthusians	1
Liverpool	2	Oxford University	1
Nottingham Forest	2	Portsmouth	1
Old Etonians	2	Royal Engineers	1
Preston North End	2	Southampton	1

APPEARANCES IN FA CUP FINAL

Arsenal	11	Blackpool	3
Newcastle United	11	Burnley	3
West Bromwich Albion	10	Chelsea	3
Aston Villa	9	Portsmouth	3
Blackburn Rovers	8	Southampton	3
Manchester City	8	Sunderland	3
Manchester United	8	Barnsley	2
Wolverhampton Wanderers	8	Birmingham City	2
Bolton Wanderers	7	Bury	2
Everton	7	Cardiff City	2
Preston North End	7	Charlton Athletic	2
Tottenham Hotspur	7	Clapham Rovers	2
Liverpool	6	Nottingham Forest	2
Old Etonians	6	Notts County	2
Sheffield United	6	Queen's Park (Glasgow)	2
Huddersfield Town	5	Blackburn Olympic	1
Sheffield Wednesday	5	Bradford City	1
Wanderers	5	Bristol City	1
Derby County	4	Fulham	1
Leeds United	4	Ipswich Town	1
Leicester City	4	Luton Town	1
Oxford University	4	Old Carthusians	1
Royal Engineers	4	Queen's Park Rangers	1
West Ham United	4		

FOOTBALL LEAGUE CUP

Liverpool retain trophy

Having won the League Cup for the first time in 1981, Liverpool retained the trophy in 1982 with a determined performance against Tottenham, who had taken the lead after only ten minutes with a goal by Archibald, and then hung on almost to the end of the game. Liverpool forced a late equaliser through Whelan and then, with Spurs noticeably flagging during extra time, powered their way to a 3-1 victory with further goals by Whelan and Rush.

The holders had made a promising start to the competition, thrashing Exeter City 11-0 on aggregate in the Second Round, then cruising to a comfortable 4-1 win over Middlesbrough in the Third. In the Fourth Round they were a little fortunate to survive a 0-0 draw at Highbury, especially after Ray Kennedy had been sent off for apparently striking Peter Nicholas in the first half, but they won the replay easily enough at Anfield. In the quarter finals they were drawn against Barnsley, who had thus far enjoyed a remarkable run against First Division opposition, disposing of Swansea, Brighton and Manchester City. With the match scheduled for Anfield, Liverpool were clear favourites, but were surprisingly held to a 0-0 draw, although they had less trouble in the replay, winning 3-1. Against Ipswich in the semi-finals, Liverpool established a useful 2-0 lead at Portman Road, and although they could only draw 2-2 in the second leg, they were through.

In theory, Tottenham's hardest match prior to the final was their first – a Second Round clash with Manchester United. Spurs played solid football to win both legs 1-0, and were rewarded with a Third Round home tie against Wrexham. This was the only game in the League Cup this season when Spurs managed to score more than one goal, which could have been a pointer to their eventual fate. A single late goal by Liverpool in the final might not have mattered so much had it not been an equaliser.

Apart from Barnsley, the only other non-First Division side in the quarter-finals was Watford, and although they were beaten by the odd goal in three by Ipswich, no doubt their later promotion to the First Division more than made up for that. In contrast, West Bromwich won through to the semi-final stages of both major cup competitions, but found themselves in all sorts of trouble in the League.

And so Tottenham were beaten in a Wembly final for the first time in their history, although in the F.A. Cup they earned themselves a chance to redeem their honour, and the final was also notable for the fact that for the first time it was sponsored – as will be the whole competition for the next three seasons – by the Milk Marketing Board. A sum of around

£2,000,000 for a four-year agreement was reported in the Press, which is good news for the Football League, although it is difficult to imagine people referring to the competition as the 'Milk Cup', and one is left wondering if the milk marketers are going to get their money's-worth. However, it is a bold move by the League, and will be an interesting experiment to watch.

PAST LEAGUE CUP FINALS

Played as two legs up to 1966

1961	Rotherham United	2	Aston Villa	0
	Webster, Kirkman			
	Aston Villa	3	Rotherham United	0
	O'Neill, Burrows, McParland			
1961	Rotherham United	2	Aston Villa	0
	Webster, Kirkman			
	Aston Villa	3	Rotherham United	0
	O'Neill, Burrows, McParland			
1962	Rochdale	0	Norwich City	3
			Lythgoe 2, Punton	
	Norwich City	1	Rochdale	0
	Hill			
1963	Birmingham City	3	Aston Villa	1
	Leek 2, Bloomfield		*Thomson*	
	Aston Villa	0	Birmingham City	0
1964	Stoke City	1	Leicester City	1
	Bebbington		*Gibson*	
	Leicester City	3	Stoke City	2
	Stringfellow, Gibson, Riley		*Viollett, Kinnell*	
1965	Chelsea	3	Leicester City	2
	Tambling, Venables (pen), McCreadie		*Appleton, Goodfellow*	
	Leicester City	0	Chelsea	0
1966	West Ham United	2	West Bromwich Albion	1
	Moore, Byrne		*Astle*	
	West Bromwich Albion	4	West Ham United	1
	Kaye, Brown, Clark, Williams		*Peters*	
1967	Queens Park Rangers	3	West Bromwich Albion	2
	Morgan R., Marsh, Lazarus		*Clark C. 2*	
1968	Leeds United	1	Arsenal	0
	Cooper			
1969	Swindon Town	3	Arsenal	1
	Smart, Rogers 2		*Gould*	
1970	Manchester City	2	West Bromwich Albion	1
	Doyle, Pardoe		*Astle*	
1971	Aston Villa	0	Tottenham Hotspur	2
			Chivers 2	
1972	Chelsea	1	Stoke City	2
	Osgood		*Conroy, Eastham*	
1973	Tottenham Hotspur	1	Norwich City	0
	Coates			
1974	Wolverhampton W.	2	Manchester City	1
	Hibbitt, Richards		*Bell*	
1975	Aston Villa	1	Norwich City	0
	Graydon			

1976	Manchester City *Barnes, Tueart*	2	Newcastle United *Gowling*	1
1977	Aston Villa	0	Everton	0
Replay	Aston Villa *Kenyon (og)*	1	Everton *Latchford*	1
Replay	Aston Villa *Little 2, Nicholl*	3	Everton *Latchford, Lyons*	2
1978	Nottingham Forest *Robertson (pen)*	1	Liverpool	0
1979	Nottingham Forest *Birtles 2, Woodcock*	3	Southampton *Peach, Holmes*	2
1980	Nottingham Forest	0	Wolverhampton W *Gray*	1
1981	Liverpool *Kennedy, R.*	1	West Ham U *Stewart (pen)*	1
Replay	Liverpool *Dalglish, Hansen*	2	West Ham U *Goddard*	1

LEAGUE CUP 1981-82

First Round *(2 legs)*

Aldershot	0	3	Wimbledon	0	1
Bournemouth	0	0	Fulham	1	2
Bolton W.	2	2	Oldham Ath.**	1	4
Bradford C.	3	0	Blackpool	1	0
Bristol C.	2	0	Walsall	0	1
Bury	3	1	Carlisle U.**	3	2
Cardiff C.	2	1	Exeter C.	1	3
Chester	1	0	Plymouth Arg.	1	1
Colchester U.	2	1	Gillingham	0	1
Crewe Alex.	1	0	Bristol R.**	1	1
Darlington	1	1	Rotherham U.	3	2
Doncaster R.	0	1	Chesterfield*	0	1
Halifax T.	1	0	Preston N.E.	2	0
Hereford U.	1	0	Port Vale	1	2
Huddersfield T.	3	4	Rochdale	1	2
Lincoln C.	3	1	Hull C.	0	1
Northampton T.	2	1	Hartlepool	0	2
Orient	1	2	Millwall	1	3
Oxford U.	1	2	Brentford	0	0
Peterborough U.	2	0	Barnsley	3	6
Reading	2	1	Charlton Ath.**	2	3
Scunthorpe U.	0	0	Mansfield T.	0	2
Sheffield U.	1	1	York C.	0	1
Southend U.	0	1	Portsmouth	0	4
Torquay U.	2	0	Newport Co.	3	0
Tranmere R.	4	3	Burnley	2	3
Wigan Ath.	3	2	Stockport Co.	0	1
Wrexham	3	2	Swindon T.	2	0

**After extra time, Doncaster won on away goals rule.*
***After extra time.*

Second round (2 legs)	Third round	Fourth round	Quarter-finals	Semi-finals (2 legs)
Aldershot .2 0	Wigan Ath. .4	Wigan Ath. .1	Aston Villa .0	W.B.A. .0 0
Wigan Ath. .2 1				
Southampton .1 1	Chelsea .2			
Chelsea .1 2				
Preston N.E. .1 0	Leicester C. .0 0	Aston Villa .2		
Leicester C. .0 4				
Aston Villa .3 2	Aston Villa .0 2			
Wolverhampton W. 2 1				
Sunderland .2 3	Sunderland .0	Crystal Palace .1	W.B.A. .1	
Rotherham U. .0 3				
Doncaster R. .1 0	Crystal Palace .1			
Crystal Palace .0 2				
Derby Co. .2 0	West Ham U. .2 1 0	W.B.A. .3		
West Ham U. .3 2				
Shrewsbury T. .3 1	W.B.A. .2 1 1			
W.B.A. .3 2				
Tottenham H. .1 1	Tottenham H .2	Tottenham H. .1	Tottenham H. .1	Tottenham H. .0 1
Manchester U. .0 0				
Luton T. .0 1	Wrexham .0			
Wrexham .2 0				
Oldham Ath. .1 0	Oldham Ath. .1 0	Fulham .0		
Newport Co. .0 0				
Newcastle U. .1 0	Fulham .1 3			
Fulham .2 2				
Blackburn R. .1 2	Blackburn R. .0	Nottingham F. .2	Nottingham F. .0	
Sheffield W. .1 1				
Birmingham C. .2 1	Nottingham F. .1			
Nottingham F. .3 2				
Tranmere R. .2 2	Tranmere R. .1	Tranmere R. .0		
Port Vale .0 1				
Colchester U. .3 2	Colchester U. .0			
Cambridge U. .1 3				

TOTTENHAM H. (1) 1

Scorer: Archibald

Wembley att: 100,000 Receipts: £720,000

LIVERPOOL (0) 3

Scorers: Whelan 2, Rush

(After extra time, 90 mins. – 1-1)

Everton 1 1	Everton 1	Everton 2	Ipswich T. 2	Ipswich T. 0 2
Coventry C 1 0				
Millwall 3 0	Oxford U. 0			
Oxford U. 3 1				
Leeds U. 0 0	Ipswich T.** 1 3	Ipswich T. 3		
Ipswich T. 1 3				
Bradford C. 3 2	Bradford C. 1 2			
Mansfield T. 4 0				
Grimsby T. 1 1	Watford 2 3	Watford 4	Watford 1	
Watford 0 3				
Lincoln C. 1 3	Lincoln C. 2 2			
Notts Co. 1 2				
Q.P.R. 5 2	Q.P.R. 3	Q.P.R. 1		
Portsmouth 0 2				
Carlisle U. 0 1	Bristol C. 0			
Bristol C. 0 2				
Sheffield U. 1 0	Arsenal 1	Arsenal 0 0	Liverpool 0 3	Liverpool 2 2
Arsenal 0 2				
Norwich C. 1 1	Norwich C. 0			
Charlton Ath. 0 0				
Liverpool 5 6	Liverpool 4	Liverpool 0 3		
Exeter C. 0 0				
Middlesbrough 2 0	Middlesbrough 1			
Plymouth Arg. 1 0				
Barnsley 2 2	Barnsley 4	Barnsley 1	Barnsley 0 1	
Swansea C. 0 3				
Huddersfield T. 1 0	Brighton & H.A. 1			
Brighton & H.A. ...0 2				
Manchester C.* 2 0	Manchester C. 3	Manchester C. 0		
Stoke C. 0 2				
Bristol R. 1 1	Northampton T. 1			
Northampton T. ...2 3				

*won 9-8 on penalties **after extra time

SCOTTISH CLUBS

ABERDEEN — PREM. DIV.

Ground: Pittodrie Stadium, Aberdeen (Aberdeen 21428)
Colours: All scarlet.
Goals – League (71): Hewitt 11, McGhee 8, Strachan 7 (3 pens), Rougvie 6, McLeish 5, Watson 5, McCall 4, Simpson 4, Black 3, Cooper 3, Cowan 3, Harrow 2, Jarvie 2, Weir 2, Angus 1, Bell 1, Kennedy 1, McMaster 1, own goals 2.
League Cup (21): Strachan 6 (4 pens), McGhee 4, Bell 2, Hewitt 2, Weir 2, Cooper 1, Harrow 1, Kennedy 1, McCall 1, McMaster 1.
Cup: (14): Strachan 4 (3 pens), McGhee 3, Hewitt 2, Simpson 2, Cooper 1, McLeish 1, Weir 1.

AIRDRIEONIANS — DIV. 1

Ground: Broomfield Park, Gatlea Road, Airdrie (Airdrie 62067)
Colours: White shirts with red diamond, white shorts.
Goals – League (31): Clark 15 (8 pens), McGuire 2, McKeown 2, Flood 2, Rodger 2, Walker T. 2, Anderson N. 1, Campbell 1, Gordon 1, McDonagh 1, Thompson 1, own goal 1.
League Cup (4): Clark 2, Anderson 1, Kerr 1.
Cup (1): McCluskey 1.

ALBION ROVERS — DIV. 2

Ground: Clifton Hill Park, Coatbridge (Coatbridge 21865)
Colours: Yellow shirts with white sleeves, white shorts with red trim.
Goals – League (52): Evans 16 (4 pens), Houston 9, Burgess 5, Craig 4, Gibson 4 (1 pen), Shields 4, Gillespie 3, Leishman 2, Collins 1, Hill 1 pen, McDonough 1, Sinnett 1, 1 own goal.
League Cup (8): Burgess 3 (1 pen), Campbell 1, Craig 1, Gillespie 1, Hill 1, McDonough 1.
Cup (4): Houston 3, 1 own goal.

ALLOA — DIV. 1

Ground: Recreation Park, Alloa (Alloa 2695)
Colours: Gold shirts with black trim, black shorts.
Goals – League (66): Murray 14, McComb 13, Holt 11 (2 pens), Purdie 7 (1 pen), Grant 6, Pattison 6, McNab 4, Smith 2, Oliver 1, Wilson 1, 1 own goal.
League Cup (8): Grant 6 (2 pens), Holt 1, Smith 1.
Cup (6): Holt 2, Pattison 2, Grant 1, 1 own goal.

ARBROATH DIV. 2

Ground: Gayfield Park, Arbroath (Arbroath 2157)
Colours: Maroon shirts, white shorts.
Goals – League (62): Robb 21 (3 pens), Yule 9, Gavine 7, Shaw 6, Docherty 4, Lees 3, Steele 3, Harley 2, Young 2, Burke 1, Casey 1, Forsyth 1, Hislop 1, Powell 1.
League Cup (19): Robb 5, Harley 4, Durno 2, Gavine 2, Yule 2, Casey 2, Docherty 1, Lees 1 pen.
Cup: Nil

AYR UNITED DIV. 1

Ground: Somerset Park, Ayr (Ayr 63435)
Colours: White shirts with black trim, black shorts.
Goals – League (56): Fry 13, McInally 9, Morris 8, Christie 5, Ahern 4 (2 pens), Hendry 3, McAllister 3, Hume 2, Nicol 2, Shanks 2, Board 2, Cashmore 1, Fleeting 1, Keen 1.
League Cup (14): Fry 8, Christie 1, Connor 1, Hendry 1, Keen 1, Nicol 1, 1 own goal.
Cup (1): Connor 1.

BERWICK RANGERS DIV. 2

Ground: Shiefield Park, Berwick-on-Tweed (Berwick 7424)
Colours: Black and gold striped shirts, black shorts.
Goals – League (66): Lawson 16, Davidson 10, Tate 9, McCulloch 6, O'Connor 6, Armstrong 4 (1 pen), Marshall 4, McGlinchey 2, McKenna 2, Moys 2, Dixon 1, McGlynn 1, 3 own goals.
League Cup (12): Davidson 5, Lawson 4, McGlynn 1, Tate 1, 1 own goal.
Cup (6): McGlynn 2, Davidson 1, Lawson 1, McCann 1, Muir 1.

BRECHIN CITY DIV. 2

Ground: Glebe Park, Brechin (Brechin 2856)
Colours: All red.
Goals – League (61): Campbell, I. 16 (2 pens), Graham 9 (1 pen), Paterson 8, Mackie 5, Henderson 4, Lesslie 4, Cormack 3, Stewart 3, Campbell R. 2, Elvin 2, McKay 2, Hay 1 pen, Lorimer 1, Reed 1.
League Cup (11): Campbell I. 3, Graham 2, Mackie 2, Paterson 2, McKay 1, 1 own goal.
Cup (5): Campbell, I. 2, Cormack 1, Lesslie 1, 1 own goal.

CELTIC PREM. DIV.

Ground: Celtic Park, Glasgow (041-554 2710)
Colours: Green and white hooped shirts, white shorts.
Goals – League (79): McCluskey 21 (2 pens), McGarvey 10, MacLeod 10, Burns 9, Crainie 7, McAdam 5, Provan 4, Aitken 3, Nicholas 3, Sullivan 3, Reid 2 (2 pens), Conroy 1, McStay 1.
League Cup (18): McLeod 5, McGarvey 4, McCluskey 3, Nicholas 3, Provan 2, Sullivan 1.
Cup (4): Halpin 1, McCluskey 1 (pen), McGarvey 1, McGrain 1.

CLYDE DIV. 1

Ground: Shawfield Stadium, Glasgow (041-647 6329)
Colours: White shirts with red trim, black shorts.
Goals – League (79): Masterton 23 (1 pen), Nevin 12 (3 pens), O'Neill 11, Reilly 11, McCutcheon 8, Doherty 7, Hood 2, Brogan 1, Dempsey 1, Rae 1, Sinclair 1, 1 own goal.
League Cup (6): Reilly 2, Doherty 1, Evans 1, McCutcheon 1, Masterton 1.
Cup (9): Doherty 2, Nevin 2, Hood 1, O'Neill 1 pen, Reilly 1, Sinclair 1, 1 own goal.

CLYDEBANK DIV. 1

Ground: Kilbowie Park, Clydebank (041-952 2887)
Colours: Red shirts with broad white vertical stripe on front, black shorts.
Goals – League (61): Millar 20, Coyne 9, McCabe 8, Given 6 (3 pens), Ronald 5, Fallon 3, McGorm 3, McKeown 3, Hughes 1, McLaughlan 1, Williamson 1, 1 own goal.
League Cup (9): Millar 2, Ronald 2, Evans 2, Given 1, McCabe 1, McLaughlan 1.
Cup (2): Given 1 pen, Millar.

COWDENBEATH DIV. 2

Ground: Central Park, Cowdenbeath (Cowdenbeath 511205)
Colours: Royal blue shirts with white stripes, white shorts.
Goals – League (51): Forrest 16 (3 pens), Liddle 9, Steele W. 7, Hislop 3, Marshall 3, McFarlane 2, Russell 2, Tierney 2, Gilchrist 1, Hunter 1, MacKintosh 1, Markey 1, Miller 1, Scott 1, 1 own goal.
League Cup (9): Forrest 3, Liddle 2, Steele W. 2, Allison 1, Mercer 1.
Cup (12): Forrest 5 (1 pen), Liddle 3, McFarlane 1, Marshall 1, Park 1, Steele W. 1.

DUMBARTON DIV. 1

Ground: Boghead Park, Dumbarton (Dumbarton 2569)
Colours: White shirts with gold and black trim, white shorts.
Goals – League (49): Blair 9, Dunlop 7, Brown 6, Coyle J. 6, Donnelly 5 (4 pens),

Montgomery 5, McGowan P. 4, Gallacher 1, Kenney 1 pen, McGowan M. 1, McNeil 1, Rankin 1.
League Cup (8): Blair 3 pens, Mailer 2, Campbell 1, Gallacher 1, Rankin 1.
Cup (2): Coyle J. 1, Donnelly 1.

DUNDEE — PREM. DIV.

Ground: Dens Park, Dundee (Dundee 86104)
Colours: White shirts, dark blue shorts.
Goals – League (48): Ferguson 13 (3 pens), Sinclair 7, Fraser 7, Mackie 4, Stephen 4, McGeachie 3, Kidd 2, MacDonald 2, Bell 1, Cameron 1, Fleming 1, Smith 1, own goals 2.
League Cup (7): Fleming 4, Cameron 1, MacDonald 1, Stephen 1.
Cup (4): Ferguson 1, Mackie 1, Smith 1, Stephen 1.

DUNDEE UNITED — PREM. DIV.

Ground: Tannadice Park, Dundee (Dundee 86289)
Colours: Tangerine shirts with black trim, black shorts.
Goals – League (61): Sturrock 15, Dodds 14, Bannon 12 (7 pens), Milne 8, Hegarty 2, Kirkwood 2, Gough 1, Holt 1, Narey 1, Payne 1, Pettigrew 1, Reilly 1, own goals 2.
League Cup (26): Sturrock 6, Bannon 5 (2 pens), Dodds 3, Pettigrew 3, Holt 2, Milne 2, Gough 1, Kirkwood 1, Payne 1, Reilly 1, own goal 1.
Cup (9): Dodds 2, Holt 2, Kirkwood 2, Sturrock 2, Bannon 1 (pen).

DUNFERMLINE ATHLETIC — DIV. 1

Ground: East End Park, Dunfermline (Dunfermline 24295)
Colours: Black and white striped shirts, black shorts.
Goals – League (46): McNaughton 13 (2 pens), Jenkins 7, Stewart 7, McCathey 4, Morrison 4 (1 pen), Concidine 3, Hegarty 3, Bowie 2, Forrest 1, Hamill 1, Nicholl 1.
League Cup (8): Hamill 2, McNaughton 2, Morrison 2, Berry 1, Forrest 1.
Cup (1): McNaughton 1.

EAST FIFE — DIV. 2

Ground: Bayview Park, Methil, Fife (Leven 2323)
Colours: Old gold shirts with black trim, black shorts.
Goals – League (48): Scott 16, Caithness 13, O'Brien 8 (2 pens), Neilson 4, Miller 2, Dury 1, Honeyman 1, McLaren 1, Thomson 1 pen, 1 own goal.
League Cup (8): O'Brien 3, Caithness 1 pen, Mutch 1, Neilson 1, Scott 1, Tate 1.
Cup (7): Caithness 2, Scott 2, Burt 1, Neilson 1, O'Brien 1.

EAST STIRLINGSHIRE DIV. 2

Ground: Firs Park, Falkirk (Falkirk 23583)
Colours: Black shirts with white hoops, black shorts.
Goals – League (38): Blair 4, Edgar 4, Lamont 4, Grant 3, Howitt 3, Kettings 3, McCaig 3, McCulley 2 (1 pen), Lowe 2, McGorm 2 (1 pen), Sharp 2, Ashwood 1, Goodall 1, McCall 1, Rennie 1, Renwick 1, 1 own goal.
League Cup (2): Hunter 1, McCall 1.
Cup (1): Howitt 1.

FALKIRK DIV. 1

Ground: Brockville Park, Falkirk (Falkirk 24121)
Colours: Navy blue shirts with white trim, white shorts.
Goals – League (49): Herd 10, Smith 7, MacKintosh 5, Hogan 4 pens, Mackin 4, Board 4, Stevenson 3, Thompson 3, Brown 2, Conn 2, Perry 2, McRoberts 1, Oliver A. 1, Oliver M. 1.
League Cup (11): Brown 5, Smith 4, Hogan 1 pen, Mackintosh 1.
Cup: Nil.

FORFAR ATHLETIC DIV. 2

Ground: Station Park, Forfar, Angus (Forfar 3576)
Colours: Navy and sky blue striped shirts, sky blue shorts.
Goals – League (59): Clark 9, Hancock 9, Gallacher 7, Porter 6, Farningham 5, Allan 4, Brash 4 (2 pens), McPhee 4, Watt 3, Bennett 2, Craig 2, Alexander 1, Brown 1, Leitch 1, Rankin 1.
League Cup (16): Hancock 4, Morris 3, Allan 2, Clark 2, Rankin 2, Craig 1, Gallacher 1, 1 own goal.
Cup (10) Brash 3 (1 pen), Clark 2, Hancock 2, Gallacher 1, Leitch 1, Mitchell 1.

HAMILTON ACADEMICALS DIV. 1

Ground: Douglas Park, Hamilton (Hamilton 23108)
Colours: Red and white striped shirts, white shorts.
Goals – League (52): Fairley 10 (5 pens), Craig 9, Donnelly 7, McDowell 6, Brown 5, Wright 5, Howie 3, Deeney 2, Wilson 2, McAdams 1, 2 own goals.
League Cup (14): Deeney 6, McDowell 3, Paton 2, Callan 1, Donnelly 1, Howie 1.
Cup (2): Fairley 1, Howie 1.

HEART OF MIDLOTHIAN DIV. 1

Ground: Tyncastle Park, Gorgie Road, Edinburgh (031-337 6132)
Colours: White shirts with maroon centre panel at front, maroon trim, white shorts.
Goals – League (65): Pettigrew 16, McCoy 9, Byrne 8 (2 pens), Robertson C. 7, MacDonald R. 6, Addison 4, O'Connor 4, Hamill 2, Liddell G. 1, Mackay 2,

Marinello 2, Bowman 1, Macdonald A. 1, Shields 1.
League Cup (5): Lidell G. 2, Robertson 2, McCoy 1.
Cup (4): Byrne 1, Macdonald R. 1, Marinello 1, Robertson C. 1.

HIBERNIAN — PREM. DIV.

Ground: Easter Road Park, Edinburgh (031-661 2159)
Colours: Green shirts with white sleeves and collar, white shorts.
Goals – League (38): Rae G. 11, MacLeod 7 (1 pen), Jamieson 5, Murray 5 (1 pen), Callachan 4, Flavell 3, Duncan 1, Paterson 1, Turnbull 1.
League Cup (5): Duncan 1, Flavell 1, Murray 1, Paterson 1, Rodier 1.
Cup (4): Duncan 1, Paterson 1, Rae G. 1, Rodier 1.

KILMARNOCK — PREM. DIV.

Ground: Rugby Park, Kilmarnock (Kilmarnock 25184)
Colours: Royal blue shirts with white trim, royal blue shorts.
Goals – League (60): Bourke 14, Gallagher 10, McDicken 8, Clarke P. 4, Mauchlen 4, Bryson 3 (2 pens), Eadie 3, Armstrong 2, Clark J. 2, McGiven 2, Robertson 2, McBride 1, McCready 1, McLean 1 pen, MacLeod 1, 2 own goals.
League Cup (5): Bourke 2, Clark J. 1, McLean 1, Wilson 1 pen.
Cup (6): Bourke 3, McGiven 2, Gallagher 1.

MEADOWBANK THISTLE — DIV. 2

Ground: Meadowbank Stadium, Edinburgh (031-661 5351)
Colours: Amber with black trim.
Goals – League (49): Jobson 15 (2 pens), Sprott 9, Hendry 7, Godfrey 6, Georgeson 5 (1 pen), Conroy 2, McPhee 2, Brown 1, Leechin 1, Thompson 1.
League Cup (8): Jobson 3, Boyd 1, Dunn 1, Leetion 1, Masterton 1, Sprott 1.
Cup (10): Boyd 3, Jobson 3 (1 pen), Georgeson 2, Godfrey 1, Hendry 1.

MONTROSE — DIV. 2

Ground: Links Park, Montrose (Montrose 498)
Colours: All royal blue.
Goals – League (49): Campbell 9, Taylor 8, Turnbull 8 (3 pens), Allan 5, Fletcher 4 (1 pen), Johnston 4, McManus 3, Oliver 3, Forrest 1, Milne 1, Nicol 1, Sherrin 1, 1 own goal.
League Cup (5): Turnbull 3 (1 pen), McManus 1, Milne 1.
Cup (2): Campbell 1, Johnston 1.

MORTON PREM. DIV.

Ground: Cappielow Park, Greenock (Greenock 23571)
Colours: Blue and white hooped shirts, white shorts.
Goals – League (31): Ritchie 6 (2 pens), Hutchinson 5, McNeil 5, Houston 4, Rooney 4, Docherty 3, Cochrane 2, Slaven 1, Thomson 1.
League Cup (13): Thomson 4, Busby 2, Hutchinson 2, McNeil 2, Rooney 2 (1 pen), Ritchie 1.
Cup (1): Houston 1.

MOTHERWELL PREM. DIV.

Ground: Fir Park, Motherwell (Motherwell 63229)
Colours: All amber with claret trim.
Goals – League (92): Irvine 20, McLaughlin 19 (8 pens), Cleland 15, Gahagan 7, Forbes 6, Rafferty 5, McClair 4, Carson 3, McKeever 3, McLelland 3, Clinging 2, Conn 2, Coyne 2, Mills 1.
League Cup (4): Cleland 1, Clinging 1 (pen), Forbes 1, McLaughlin 1 (pen).
Cup: Nil.

PARTICK THISTLE DIV. 1

Ground: Firhill Park, Glasgow (041-946 2673)
Colours: Yellow shirts with red trim, red shorts.
Goals – League (35): Johnston 9, Park 5, Watson 5 (3 pens), Clark 4, Jardine 4, O'Hara 3, Doyle 2, Higgins 2, Gibson 1.
League Cup (5): Higgins 2, Gibson 1 (pen), Johnston 1, O'Hara 1.
Cup (1): Johnston 1.

QUEEN OF THE SOUTH DIV. 2

Ground: Palmerston Park, Dumfries (Dumfries 4853)
Colours: Royal blue shirts with white trim, white shorts.
Goals – League (44): Phillips 12, Alexander 11, Cloy 4 pens, McCann 4, Coughlin 3, McLeod 3, Clark 2, Gordon 1, McVitie 1, Robertson G. 1, Robertson J. 1, Roddy 1.
League Cup (10): Alexander 5, Robertson J. 2, Clark 1, McVitie 1, Phillips 1.
Cup: Nil.

QUEEN'S PARK DIV. 1

Ground: Hampden Park, Glasgow (041-632 1275)
Colours: Black and white hooped shirts, white shorts.
Goals – League (41): Crawley 10 (4 pens), Gilmour 7, McGregor 4, McNiven 4, Nicholson 4, Verrechia 4, Wood 3, Grant 2, Melrose 1, own goals 2.
League Cup (8): Nicholson 3, McGregor 2, McNiven 1, Wood 1, own goal 1.
Cup (5): McNiven 3, McFarlane 1, Verrechia 1.

RAITH ROVERS DIV. 1

Ground: Stark's Park, Pratt Street, Kirkcaldy (Kirkcaldy 3514)
Colours: All royal blue.
Goals – League (31): Ballantyne 12, Gibson 9 (2 pens), Ford 3, Irvine 2, Robinson 2, Berry 1, Harris 1, Houston 1.
League Cup (7): Russell 4, Ballantyne 2, Forsyth 1.
Cup: Nil.

RANGERS PREM. DIV.

Ground: Ibrox Stadium, Glasgow (041-427 0159)
Colours: Royal blue shirts, white shorts.
Goals – League (57): McDonald 14, Bett 11 (6 pens), Johnstone 9, Dalziel 6, Russell 6, Cooper 3, McAdam 2, Redford 2, Dawson 1, Jardine 1, McKay 1, McLean 1 pen.
League Cup (30): Redford 7, McDonald 5, McAdam 4, Johnstone 3, Russell 3, Bett 1 pen, Cooper 1, Jackson 1, Jardine 1, McLean 1, Miller 1, Stevens 1, 1 own goal.
Cup (16): Johnstone 4, McAdam 3, Jardine 3, McDonald 2, Bett 1, Cooper 1, McPherson 1, Redford 1, Russell 1.

ST JOHNSTONE DIV. 1

Ground: Muirton Park, Perth (Perth 26961)
Colours: Royal blue shirts, white shorts.
Goals – League (69): Morton 17 (2 pens), Brogan 16, Brannigan 11, Rutherford 6, Beedie 5, McNeil 3, Caldwell 2, Docherty 2, McDonald 2, Pelosi 2, Weir 2, Mackay 1.
League Cup (8): McCoist 4, Beedie 1, Brogan 1, McDonald 1, Morton 1 pen.
Cup (3): Beedie 1, Brogan 1, Morton 1 pen.

ST MIRREN PREM. DIV.

Ground: St Mirren Park, Paisley (Paisley 2558)
Colours: White shirts with black vertical stripes, black shorts.
Goals – League (49): McAvennie13, Stark 10 (3 pens), McDougall 7, Scanlon 5 (3 pens), Bone 4, Richardson 4, Somner 2, Fitzpatrick 1, Logan 1, McEachran 1, Speirs 1.
League Cup (20): McDougall 6, Scanlon 4 (2 pens), Logan 2, McAvennie 2, Stark 2, McCormack 1, Richardson 1, Somner 1, own goal 1.
Cup (8): McAvennie 2, Abercromby 1, Bone 1, Fitzpatrick 1, McDougall 1, Scanlon 1, Somner 1.

STENHOUSEMUIR DIV. 2

Ground: Ochilview Park, Stenhousemuir (Larbert 2992)
Colours: Maroon shirts with white trim, white shorts.
Goals – League (41): Jenkins 8 (1 pen), Mullen 7, Murray 7, Meakin 5 (1 pen), Jack 4, Bremner 2, Buchanan 2, Kirkland 2, Campbell 1, Harper 1, Stirling 1, 1 own goal.
League Cup (7): Meakin 2, Mullen 2, Murray 2, Jack 1.
Cup (2): Meakin 1, Murray 1.

STIRLING ALBION DIV. 2

Ground: Annfield Stadium, Stirling (Stirling 3584)
Colours: All red.
Goals – League (39): Colquhoun 13 (3 pens), Torrance 7, Leetion 4, McNeil 3, Steele 3, Cavanagh 2, Kennedy A. 2, Moffat 1, Philliben 1, Steedman 1, 2 own goals.
League Cup (6): Torrance 2, Colquhoun 1, Gibson 1, Morrison 1, Philliben 1.
Cup (1): Torrance 1.

STRANRAER DIV. 2

Ground: Stair Park, Stranraer (Stranraer 3271)
Colours: Royal blue shirts, white shorts.
Goals – League (36): Sweeney 11, Dolan 7, Taylor I. 4, Black 2, Gibb 2, McDonald 2 pens, Neil 2, Armour 1, Devine 1, MacKintosh 1, McLaughlin 1, Murdoch 1 pen, Murphy 1.
League Cup (7): Neil 3, Hamilton 1, Murphy 1, Sweeney 1, 1 own goal.
Cup (2): Harvey 2.

SCOTTISH LEAGUE – PREMIER DIVISION RESULTS 1981-82

	Aberdeen	Airdrieonians	Celtic	Dundee	Dundee United	Hibernian	Morton	Partick Thistle	Rangers	St Mirren
Aberdeen	—	0–0 2–0	1–3 1–3	2–1 0–0	1–1 2–1	1–0 3–1	2–0 0–0	2–1 3–1	3–1 4–0	4–1 5–1
Airdrieonians	0–4 0–3	—	1–3 1–5	4–2 0–2	2–1 2–0	3–1 0–2	1–1 1–1	1–1 3–1	2–2 0–1	3–4 0–2
Celtic	2–1 0–1	5–2 2–0	—	3–1 4–2	1–1 3–1	0–0 6–0	2–1 1–0	2–0 2–2	3–3 2–1	0–0 3–0
Dundee	0–3 0–5	3–1 1–0	1–3 1–3	—	1–3 0–2	0–0 2–2	4–1 2–1	4–2 1–2	2–3 3–1	3–0 0–2
Dundee United	4–1 1–2	4–0 4–0	0–2 3–0	5–2 1–1	—	1–0 0–1	3–0 5–0	0–0 5–1	2–0 1–1	0–2 1–1
Hibernian	1–1 0–3	1–1 1–0	1–0 1–0	2–0 2–1	1–1 0–1	—	4–0 2–2	3–0 1–1	1–2 0–0	0–0 2–1
Morton	2–1 2–1	3–0 1–0	1–1 1–1	2–0 2–0	1–0 1–1	2–1 0–0	—	1–0 0–0	0–0 1–3	0–2 0–1
Partick Thistle	0–2 0–0	4–1 0–0	0–2 0–3	1–2 0–2	2–3 1–2	1–0 1–2	2–2 4–0	—	0–1 2–0	1–1 0–0
Rangers	0–0 1–3	4–1 1–0	0–2 1–0	2–1 4–0	2–0 1–1	2–2 1–1	1–1 3–0	0–2 4–1	—	4–1 3–0
St Mirren	1–2 0–2	1–1 3–0	1–2 2–5	4–0 0–1	1–0 2–2	1–0 2–2	2–0 3–1	2–1 2–0	1–1 2–3	—

SCOTTISH LEAGUE – DIVISION I RESULTS 1981-82

	Ayr United	Clydebank	Dumbarton	Dunfermline Ath.	East Stirling	Falkirk	Hamilton A.	Hearts	Kilmarnock	Motherwell	Queen of the South	Queens Park	Raith Rovers	St Johnstone
Ayr United	—	2–1	3–2	1–1	5–1 1–1	4–1 1–0	2–0 3–2	0–0 0–3	1–1	4–3 1–1	1–0 5–2	2–0	2–0	1–1
Clydebank	2–1 2–0	—	3–0	4–1 1–0	2–1	1–1 0–2	2–1	1–5 2–1	0–0	1–7	2–1 5–1	2–1 1–0	0–1 0–0	2–3
Dumbarton	3–1 3–1	1–3 0–2	—	0–1	0–3	3–1 1–0	1–2	3–1	0–2 0–2	0–6	1–0 3–1	1–0	1–1 0–2	2–1 2–0
Dunfermline Ath	0–0 2–2	3–6	2–2 0–0	—	2–1 1–1	1–1	1–3 1–1	1–1 1–2	1–2	1–2	1–1	2–1	2–3	1–2 1–0
East Stirling	2–1	0–0 0–1	1–1 2–2	1–2	—	2–2	1–5 2–1	0–1	2–1 1–5	0–6 1–2	3–1	0–1	0–1 1–1	1–1
Falkirk	1–2	3–0	1–1	0–0 1–0	0–3 2–0	—	3–0	0–0 3–1	2–2	1–1 1–3	0–0	0–0 1–1	1–2 3–2	1–0 2–1
Hamilton A	1–0	0–2 3–1	0–0 1–0	0–2	1–1	2–0 1–0	—	0–2 0–2	1–2	1–0	2–3	2–1 2–0	1–0	0–0 2–0
Hearts	2–1	1–0	2–1 2–5	1–1	0–1 2–0	3–0	2–1	—	0–1	0–3 0–1	4–1	1–1 1–0	2–1 4–0	3–1 3–0
Kilmarnock	1–1 1–1	2–0 0–0	0–0	0–1 2–0	2–0	2–2 4–1	2–2 0–0	0–0 0–0	—	2–0	0–0 6–0	0–0	1–1	0–2
Motherwell	1–1	3–1 0–0	1–1 1–0	6–1 2–2	3–0	3–2	2–2 3–2	2–2	2–0 1–0	—	2–1	1–0 3–0	3–0	2–2
Queen of the S.	1–2	2–1	0–4	0–3 2–3	1–1 4–0	0–4 1–1	2–4 0–3	1–2 1–5	1–1	0–2 2–5	—	1–1 1–2	2–3	3–3
Queens Park	2–0 0–0	2–2	3–0 3–0	0–1 2–1	2–1 3–0	2–2	2–0	1–0	2–3 0–2	0–1	1–1	—	0–0 2–0	3–2 2–1
Raith R.	0–1 1–0	0–2	1–3	0–0 0–1	1–0	0–3	2–0 1–2	0–3	3–3 0–3	0–1 0–2	2–1 1–2	1–0	—	0–4 0–1
St Johnstone	2–0 3–2	1–3 3–3	5–2	2–1	3–2 7–1	2–0	1–1	2–1	0–2 1–3	1–3 3–2	1–0 3–3	2–0	2–0	—

Note: In the Scottish League Divisions I and II, each team plays each other once and then after a draw made at the beginning of the season, half of the fixtures are repeated.

SCOTTISH LEAGUE – DIVISION II RESULTS 1981-82

	Albion R.	Alloa	Arbroath	Berwick R.	Brechin C.	Clyde	Cowdenbeath	East Fife	Forfar Ath.	Meadowbank	Montrose	Stenhousemuir	Stirling A.	Stranraer
Albion Rovers	—	1–3 1–1	2–0	1–3	1–2 1–2	0–1 2–3	2–0	1–0	3–3	2–0	0–2 2–2	1–4 2–0	1–0 1–0	4–0
Alloa	1–0	—	2–1 2–2	1–0 1–1	1–3	0–3 2–2	3–1 2–2	1–2	1–2	4–3 2–0	3–0	1–0	0–0	3–2 1–1
Arbroath	4–0 2–0	2–1	—	2–1	1–1	0–1 0–5	1–1 3–0	3–1 1–1	1–1	3–2 0–0	1–0 2–0	3–0	1–0	4–1
Berwick Rangers	6–1 4–1	2–0	3–0 2–2	—	3–1	4–0	1–2	2–1 3–0	1–1 2–1	3–1 2–2	4–0	1–0 0–2	1–0	0–0 2–0
Brechin City	3–2	0–4 0–1	2–2 0–2	2–0 1–0	—	2–2	0–1	2–1 1–1	0–0	3–0	3–0	1–1 0–1	2–1	3–0 3–0
Clyde	1–2	1–1	1–1	3–1 1–2	1–0 3–1	—	1–1 2–0	3–2	1–1	1–0	3–0	3–0 1–0	3–3 2–0	3–0 1–1
Cowdenbeath	2–0 2–3	1–2	1–2	2–1 2–0	0–0 0–2	0–4	—	2–2 1–2	1–1 3–1	2–2	6–0 3–2	3–1	0–0 2–0	1–1
East Fife	3–0 1–1	1–2 0–2	0–1	0–1	2–2	2–2 1–1	1–1	—	0–4 1–0	2–0 1–0	0–1	3–2 1–0	3–0 1–2	0–2
Forfar Athletic	3–1 3–0	0–0 0–1	1–1 6–0	2–1	0–1 0–0	1–3 0–0	4–0	1–0	—	1–1	2–1 0–0	2–0	3–1	3–1 3–0
Meadowbank	3–2 0–2	1–1	1–2	2–1	1–0 2–0	2–3 1–3	1–1 1–0	1–1	1–1 2–5	—	2–2	6–1	2–1 0–1	4–1 1–1
Montrose	4–2	2–0 0–3	2–1	0–2 0–0	2–2 1–4	0–3 4–1	2–2	1–2 1–2	2–1	1–0 1–0	—	2–1	1–1 1–2	1–2
Stenhousemuir	2–2	0–1 2–2	1–3 0–2	1–1	0–4	0–3	2–1 3–0	2–0	0–0 0–1	1–2 3–1	2–4 2–1	—	0–0	1–0
Stirling Albion	1–0	0–0 3–2	0–1 3–2	0–1 0–0	5–0 0–2	1–2	0–0	0–2	0–0 2–0	1–0	1–1	2–3 3–1	—	1–0 2–1
Stranraer	0–1 1–4	0–4	4–0 1–3	2–4	0–6	0–2	1–4 1–0	0–3 1–2	2–1	0–1	3–5 2–0	2–1 0–1	2–2	—

Note: In the Scottish League Divisions I and II, each team plays each other once and then after a draw made at the beginning of the seaon, half of the fixtures are repeated.

SCOTTISH FOOTBALL LEAGUE
FINAL TABLES 1981-82

Premier Division		Home			Goals		Away			Goals			
	P	W	D	L	F	A	W	D	L	F	A	Pt	Dif
Celtic	36	12	5	1	41	16	12	2	4	38	17	55	+46
Aberdeen	36	12	4	2	36	15	11	3	4	35	14	53	+42
Rangers	36	10	5	3	34	16	6	6	6	23	29	43	+12
Dundee U.	36	10	4	4	40	14	5	6	7	21	24	40	+23
St Mirren	36	8	4	6	30	23	6	5	7	19	29	37	−3
Hibernian	36	8	7	3	23	14	3	7	8	15	26	36	−2
Morton	36	9	6	3	20	12	0	6	12	11	42	30	−23
Dundee	36	7	2	9	28	34	4	2	12	18	38	26	−26
Partick Th.	36	4	5	9	19	23	2	5	11	16	36	22	−24
Airdrieonians	36	5	4	9	24	36	0	4	14	7	40	18	−45

First Division		Home			Goals		Away			Goals			
	P	W	D	L	F	A	W	D	L	F	A	Pt	Dif
Motherwell	39	12	7	0	41	17	14	2	4	51	19	61	+56
Kilmarnock	39	6	12	2	25	11	11	5	3	35	18	51	+31
Hearts	39	12	2	5	33	19	9	6	5	32	18	50	+28
Clydebank	39	12	3	5	33	27	7	5	7	28	26	46	+8
St Johnstone	39	12	3	4	44	29	5	5	10	25	31	42	+9
Ayr United	39	12	6	1	39	20	3	6	11	17	30	42	+6
Hamilton Academicals	39	10	3	6	20	16	6	5	9	32	33	40	+3
Queens Park	39	11	5	4	32	17	2	5	12	9	24	36	0
Falkirk	39	8	8	4	26	19	3	6	10	23	33	36	−3
Dunfermline Ath.	39	3	9	7	24	31	8	5	7	22	25	36	−10
Dumbarton	39	10	1	9	25	30	3	8	8	24	31	35	−12
Raith Rovers	39	5	2	13	13	32	6	5	8	18	27	29	−28
East Stirling	39	4	6	9	20	35	3	4	13	18	42	24	−39
Queen of the South	39	2	5	13	25	50	2	5	12	19	43	18	−49

Second Division		Home			Goals		Away			Goals			
	P	W	D	L	F	A	W	D	L	F	A	Pt	Dif
Clyde	39	11	6	2	35	16	13	5	2	44	22	59	+41
Alloa	39	9	6	4	31	25	10	6	4	31	17	50	+20
Arbroath	39	12	5	2	34	16	8	5	7	28	34	50	+12
Berwick Rangers	39	14	4	2	46	15	6	4	9	20	23	48	+28
Brechin City	39	9	5	5	28	19	9	5	6	33	24	46	+18
Forfar Athletic	39	11	6	3	35	12	4	9	6	24	23	45	+24
East Fife	39	7	5	8	23	24	7	4	8	25	27	37	−3
Stirling Albion	39	9	5	6	25	18	3	6	10	14	26	35	−5
Cowdenbeath	39	8	6	6	34	26	3	7	9	17	31	35	−6
Montrose	39	8	4	8	28	31	4	4	11	21	41	32	−23
Albion Rovers	39	8	3	8	28	26	5	2	13	24	46	31	−20
Meadowbank	39	8	6	6	34	29	2	4	13	15	33	30	−13
Stenhousemuir	39	6	5	8	22	28	5	1	14	19	37	28	−24
Stranraer	39	5	1	13	22	44	2	5	13	14	41	20	−49

SCOTTISH LEAGUE HONOURS LIST

Premier Division (Maximum points: 72)

	First	Pt	Second	Pt	Third	Pt
1975–76	Rangers	54	Celtic	48	Hibernian	43
1976–77	Celtic	55	Rangers	46	Aberdeen	43
1977–78	Rangers	55	Aberdeen	53	Dundee United	40
1978–79	Celtic	48	Rangers	45	Dundee United	44
1979–80	Aberdeen	48	Celtic	47	St Mirren	42
1980–81	Celtic	56	Aberdeen	49	Rangers	44
1981–82	Celtic	55	Aberdeen	53	Rangers	43

First Division (Maximum points: 78)

1975–76	Partick Thistle	41	Kilmarnock	35	Montrose	30
Maximum points: 52						
1976–77	St Mirren	62	Clydebank	58	Dundee	51
1977–78	*Morton	58	Hearts	58	Dundee	57
1978–79	Dundee	55	Kilmarnock	54	Clydebank	54
1979–80	Hearts	53	Airdrieonians	51	Ayr United	44
1980–81	Hibernian	57	Dundee	52	St Johnstone	51
1981–82	Motherwell	61	Kilmarnock	51	Hearts	50

Second Division (Maximum points: 78)

1975–76	*Clydebank	40	Raith Rovers	40	Alloa	35
Maximum points: 52						
1976–77	Stirling Albion	55	Alloa	51	Dunfermline	50
1977–78	*Clyde	53	Raith Rovers	53	Dunfermline	48
1978–79	Berwick	54	Dunfermline	52	Falkirk	50
1979–80	Falkirk	50	East Stirlingshire	49	Forfar Athletic	46
1980–81	Queen's Park	50	Queen of the S	46	Cowdenbeath	45
1981–82	Clyde	59	Alloa	50	Arbroath	50

First Division to 1974-75

1890–1	*a*††Dumbarton	29	Rangers	29	Celtic	24
1891–2	*b*Dumbarton	37	Celtic	35	Hearts	30
1892–3	*a*Celtic	29	Rangers	28	St Mirren	23
1893–4	*a*Celtic	29	Hearts	26	St Bernards	22
1894–5	*a*Hearts	31	Celtic	26	Rangers	21
1895–6	*a*Celtic	30	Rangers	26	Hibernian	24
1896–7	*a*Hearts	28	Hibernian	26	Rangers	25
1897–8	*a*Celtic	33	Rangers	29	Hibernian	22
1898–9	*a*Rangers	36	Hearts	26	Celtic	24
1899–1900	*a*Rangers	32	Celtic	25	Hibernian	24
1900–1	*c*Rangers	35	Celtic	29	Hibernian	25
1901–2	*a*Rangers	28	Celtic	26	Hearts	22
1902–3	*b*Hibernian	37	Dundee	31	Rangers	29
1903–4	*d*Third Lanark	43	Hearts	39	*Rangers	38
1904–5	*d*‡Celtic	41	Rangers	41	Third Lanark	35
1905–6	*e*Celtic	49	Hearts	43	Airdrieonians	38
1906–7	*f*Celtic	55	Dundee	48	Rangers	45
1907–8	*f*Celtic	55	Falkirk	51	Rangers	50
1908–9	*f*Celtic	51	Dundee	50	Clyde	48
1909–10	*f*Celtic	54	Falkirk	52	Rangers	46
1910–11	*f*Rangers	52	Aberdeen	48	Falkirk	44
1911–12	*f*Rangers	51	Celtic	45	Clyde	42
1912–13	*f*Rangers	53	Celtic	49	*Hearts	41
1913–14	*g*Celtic	65	Rangers	59	*Hearts	54
1914–15	*g*Celtic	65	Hearts	61	Rangers	50

	First	Pt	Second	Pt	Third	Pt
1916–17	*g*Celtic	64	Morton	54	Rangers	53
1917–18	*f*Rangers	56	Celtic	55	Kilmarnock	43
1918–19	*f*Celtic	58	Rangers	57	Morton	47
1919–20	*h*Rangers	71	Celtic	68	Motherwell	57
1920–21	*h*Rangers	76	Celtic	66	Hearts	56
1921–22	*h*Celtic	67	Rangers	66	Raith Rovers	56
1922–23	*g*Rangers	55	Airdrieonians	50	Celtic	46
1923–24	*g*Rangers	59	Airdrieonians	50	Celtic	41
1924–25	*g*Rangers	60	Airdrieonians	57	Hibernian	52
1925–26	*g*Celtic	58	*Airdrieonians	50	Hearts	50
1926–27	*g*Rangers	56	Motherwell	51	Celtic	49
1927–28	*g*Rangers	60	*Celtic	55	Motherwell	55
1928–29	*g*Rangers	67	Celtic	51	Motherwell	50
1929–30	*g*Rangers	60	Motherwell	55	Aberdeen	53
1930–31	*g*Rangers	60	Celtic	58	Motherwell	56
1931–32	*g*Motherwell	66	Rangers	61	Celtic	48
1932–33	*g*Rangers	62	Motherwell	59	Hearts	50
1933–34	*g*Rangers	66	Motherwell	62	Celtic	47
1934–35	*g*Rangers	55	Celtic	52	Hearts	50
1935–36	*g*Celtic	66	*Rangers	61	Aberdeen	61
1936–37	*g*Rangers	61	Aberdeen	54	Celtic	52
1937–38	*g*Celtic	61	Hearts	58	Rangers	49
1938–39	*g*Rangers	59	Celtic	48	Aberdeen	46
1946–47	*f*Rangers	46	Hibernian	44	Aberdeen	39
1947–48	*j*Hibernian	48	Rangers	46	Partick Thistle	36
1948–49	*j*Rangers	46	Dundee	45	Hibernian	39
1949–50	*j*Rangers	50	Hibernian	49	Hearts	43
1950–51	*j*Hibernian	48	*Rangers	38	Dundee	38
1951–52	*j*Hibernian	45	Rangers	41	East Fife	37
1952–53	*j**Rangers	43	Hibernian	43	East Fife	39
1953–54	*j*Celtic	43	Hearts	38	Partick Thistle	35
1954–55	*j*Aberdeen	49	Celtic	46	Rangers	41
1955–56	*f*Rangers	52	Aberdeen	46	*Hearts	45
1956–57	*f*Rangers	55	Hearts	53	Kilmarnock	42
1957–58	*f*Hearts	62	Rangers	49	Celtic	46
1958–59	*f*Rangers	50	Hearts	48	Motherwell	44
1959–60	*f*Hearts	54	Kilmarnock	50	*Rangers	42
1960–61	*f*Rangers	51	Kilmarnock	50	Third Lanark	42
1961–62	*f*Dundee	54	Rangers	51	Celtic	46
1962–63	*f*Rangers	57	Kilmarnock	48	Partick Thistle	46
1963–64	*f*Rangers	55	Kilmarnock	49	*Celtic	47
1964–65	*f**Kilmarnock	50	Hearts	50	Dunfermline Ath.	49
1965–66	*f*Celtic	57	Rangers	55	Kilmarnock	45
1966–67	*f*Celtic	58	Rangers	55	Clyde	46
1967–68	*f*Celtic	63	Rangers	61	Hibernian	45
1968–69	*f*Celtic	54	Rangers	49	Dunfermline Ath.	45
1969–70	*f*Celtic	57	Rangers	45	Hibernian	44
1970–71	*f*Celtic	56	Aberdeen	54	St Johnstone	44
1971–72	*f*Celtic	60	Aberdeen	50	Rangers	44
1972–73	*f*Celtic	57	Rangers	56	Hibernian	45
1973–74	*f*Celtic	53	Hibernian	49	Rangers	48
1974–75	*f*Rangers	56	Hibernian	49	Celtic	45

Maximum points: *a*, 36; *b*, 44; *c*, 40; *d*, 52; *e*, 60; *f*, 68; *g*, 76; *h*, 84; *j*, 60.

Second Division to 1974-75

	First	Pt	Second	Pt	Third	Pt
1921–22	*a*†Alloa	60	Cowdenbeath	47	Armadale	48
1922–23	*a*Queen's Park	57	Clydebank	**50	St Johnstone	**45
1923–24	*a*St Johnstone	56	Cowdenbeath	55	Bathgate	44
1924–25	*a*Dundee United	50	Clydebank	48	Clyde	47
1925–26	*a*Dunfermline A.	59	Clyde	53	Ayr United	52
1926–27	*a*Bo'ness	56	Raith Rovers	49	Clydebank	45
1927–28	*a*Ayr United	54	Third Lanark	45	King's Park	44
1928–29	*b*Dundee United	51	Morton	50	Arbroath	47
1929–30	*a**Leith Athletic	57	East Fife	57	Albion Rovers	54
1930–31	*a*Third Lanark	61	Dundee United	50	Dunfermline A.	47
1931–32	*a**East Stirling	55	St Johnstone	55	*Raith Rovers	46
1932–33	*c*Hibernian	54	Queen of the S.	49	Dunfermline A.	47
1933–34	*c*Albion Rovers	45	*Dunfermline A.	44	Arbroath	44
1934–35	*c*Third Lanark	52	Arbroath	50	St Bernard's	47
1935–36	*c*Falkirk	59	St Mirren	52	Morton	48
1936–37	*c*Ayr United	54	Morton	51	St Bernard's	48
1937–38	*c*Raith Rovers	59	Albion Rovers	48	Airdrieonians	47
1938–39	*c*Cowdenbeath	60	*Alloa	48	East Fife	48
1946–47	*d*Dundee	45	Airdrieonians	42	East Fife	31
1947–48	*e*East Fife	53	Albion Rovers	42	Hamilton A	40
1948–49	*e**Raith Rovers	42	Stirling Albion	42	*Airdrieonians	41
1949–50	*e*Morton	47	Airdrieonians	44	*St Johnstone	36
1950–51	*e**Queen of the S.	45	Stirling Albion	45	*Ayr United	36
1951–52	*e*Clyde	43	Falkirk	33	Ayr United	39
1952–53	*e*Stirling Albion	44	Hamilton A.	43	Queen's Park	37
1953–54	*e*Motherwell	45	Kilmarnock	42	*Third Lanark	36
1954–55	*e*Airdrieonians	46	Dunfermline A.	42	Hamilton A.	39
1955–56	*b*Queen's Park	54	Ayr United	51	St Johnstone	49
1956–57	*b*Clyde	64	Third Lanark	51	Cowdenbeath	45
1957–58	*b*Stirling Albion	55	Dunfermline A.	53	Arbroath	47
1958–59	*b*Ayr United	60	Arbroath	51	Stenhousemuir	46
1959–60	*b*St Johnstone	53	Dundee United	50	Queen of the S.	49
1960–61	*b*Stirling Albion	55	Falkirk	54	Stenhousemuir	50
1961–62	*b*Clyde	54	Queen of the S.	53	Morton	44
1962–63	*b*St Johnstone	55	East Stirling	49	Morton	48
1963–64	*b*Morton	67	Clyde	53	Arbroath	46
1964–65	*b*Stirling Albion	59	Hamilton A	50	Queen of the S.	45
1965–66	*b*Ayr United	53	Airdrieonians	50	Queen of the S.	49
1966–67	*b*Morton	69	Raith Rovers	58	Arbroath	57
1967–68	*b*St Mirren	62	Arbroath	53	East Fife	40
1968–69	*b*Motherwell	64	Ayr United	53	*East Fife	47
1969–70	*b*Falkirk	56	Cowdenbeath	55	Queen of the S.	58
1970–71	*b*Partick Thistle	56	East Fife	51	Arbroath	46
1971–72	*b*†Dumbarton	52	Arbroath	52	Stirling Albion	50
1972–73	*b*Clyde	56	Dunfermline A.	52	*Raith Rovers	47
1973–74	*b*Airdrieonians	60	Kilmarnock	59	Hamilton A.	55
1974–75	*b*Falkirk	54	*Queen of the S.	53	Montrose	53

Maximum points: *a*, 76; *b*, 72; *c*, 68; *d*, 52; *e*, 60.
*On goal average. †Held jointly after indecisive play-off. ‡Won on deciding match. ††Held jointly. **Two points deducted for fielding ineligible player. Competition suspended 1940–45.

RELEGATED CLUBS

From Premier Division

1975–76 Dundee, St Johnstone
1976–77 Hearts, Kilmarnock
1979–80 Dundee, Hibernian
1981–82 Partick Th., Airdrieonians
1977–78 Ayr United, Clydebank
1978–79 Hearts, Motherwell
1980–81 Kilmarnock, Hearts

From Division 1

1975–76 Dunfermline A., Clyde
1976–77 Raith Rovers, Falkirk
1979–80 Arbroath, Clyde
1981–82 East Stirling, Queen of the S.
1977–78 Alloa, East Fife
1978–79 Montrose, Queen of the S.
1980–81 Stirling A., Berwick R.

Relegated from Division 1 to 1973-74

1921–22* Queen's Park, Dumbarton, Clydebank
1922–23 Albion Rovers, Alloa
1923–24 Clyde, Clydebank
1924–25 Third Lanark, Ayr United
1925–26 Raith R., Clydebank
1926–27 Morton, Dundee United
1927–28 Dunfermline Athletic, Bo'ness
1928–29 Third Lanark, Raith R.
1929–30 St Johnstone, Dundee United
1930–31 Hibernian, East Fife
1931–32 Dundee United, Leith Athletic
1932–33 Morton, East Stirling
1933–34 Third Lanark, Cowdenbeath
1934–35 St Mirren, Falkirk
1935–36 Airdrieonians, Ayr United
1936–37 Dunfermline Athletic, Albion Rovers
1937–38 Dundee, Morton
1938–39 Queen's Park, Raith R.
1946–47 Kilmarnock, Hamilton Academicals
1947–48 Airdrieonians, Queen's Park
1948–49 Morton, Albion Rovers
1949–50 Queen of the South, Stirling Albion
1950–51 Clyde, Falkirk
1951–52 Morton, Stirling Albion
1952–53 Motherwell, Third Lanark
1953–54 Airdrieonians, Hamilton Academicals
1954–55 No clubs relegated
1955–56 Stirling Albion, Clyde
1956–57 Dunfermline Athletic, Ayr United
1957–58 East Fife, Queen's Park
1958–59 Queen of the S., Falkirk
1959–60 Arbroath, Stirling Albion
1960–61 Ayr United, Clyde
1961–62 St Johnstone, Stirling Albion
1962–63 Clyde, Raith Rovers
1963–64 Queen of the South, East Stirling
1964–65 Airdrieonians, Third Lanark
1965–66 Morton, Hamilton A.
1966–67 St Mirren, Ayr United
1967–68 Motherwell, Stirling Albion
1968–69 Falkirk, Arbroath
1969–70 Raith Rovers, Partick Thistle
1970–71 St Mirren, Cowdenbeath
1971–72 Clyde, Dunfermline Athletic
1972–73 Kilmarnock, Airdrieonians
1973–74 East Fife, Falkirk
1974–75 League re-organised at end of season

*Season 1921–22—only 1 club promoted, 3 clubs relegated.

SCOTTISH FA CUP 1981-82

Third round	Fourth round	Fifth round	Semi-finals	Final
Motherwell 0	Aberdeen 1	Aberdeen 4	Aberdeen 1 3	**Aberdeen** .... **4** *Scorers:* McLeish, McGhee, Strachan, Cooper
Aberdeen 1				
Celtic 4	Celtic 0			
Queen of the S. 0				
Kilmarnock 1	Kilmarnock 3	Kilmarnock 2		
Montrose 0				
Gala Fairydean 1	St Johnstone 1			
St Johnstone 2				
Clydebank 2	Clydebank 0	St Mirren 1	St Mirren 1 2	
Dunfermline Ath. 1				
St Mirren 2	St Mirren 2			
Morton 1				
Brechin C. 2	Dundee U. 1, 1 3	Dundee U. 0		
Dundee U. 4				
Hibernian 2	Hibernian 1 1 0			
Falkirk 0				
Rangers 6	Rangers 4	Rangers 2	Rangers 0 3	**Rangers** .... **1** *Scorer:* MacDonald After extra time, 90 mins 0-0 Attendance: 53,778
Albion R. 2				
Partick Th. 1	Dumbarton 0			
Dumbarton 2				
Dundee 1	Dundee 3	Dundee 0		
Raith R. 0				
Clyde 2 2	Meadowbank Th. 0			
Meadowbank Th. 2 4				
Airdrieonians 1	Queen's Park 2	Queen's Park 1	Forfar Ath. 0 1	
Queen's Park 2				
Alloa 2	Alloa 0			
Ayr U. 1				
East Stirling 1	Hearts 0	Forfar Ath. 2		
Hearts 4				
Hamilton 0 2	Forfar Ath. 1			
Forfar Ath. 0 3				

SCOTTISH LEAGUE CUP 1981-82

Quarter-finals (2 legs)			Semi-finals (2 legs)			Final	
Hamilton A.	0	0	Dundee U.	0	3	Dundee U. *Milne*	1
Dundee U.	4	5					
Aberdeen	5	3	Aberdeen	1	0		
Berwick R.	0	0					
Forfar Ath.	1	0	St Mirren	2	1	Rangers *Cooper, Redford*	2
St Mirren	1	6					
Brechin C.	0	0	Rangers	2	2		
Rangers	4	1					

PAST SCOTTISH LEAGUE CUP FINALS

1946-47	Hampden Park	Rangers	4	Aberdeen	0
1947-48	Hampden Park	East Fife	1 4	Falkirk	1 1
1948-49	Hampden Park	Rangers		Raith Rovers	0
1949-50	Hampden Park	East Fife	3	Dunfermline	0
1950-51	Hampden Park	Motherwell	3	Hibernian	0
1951-52	Hampden Park	Dundee	3	Rangers	2
1952-53	Hampden Park	Dundee	2	Kilmarnock	0
1953-54	Hampden Park	East Fife	3	Partick Thistle	2
1954-55	Hampden Park	Hearts	4	Motherwell	2
1955-56	Hampden Park	Aberdeen	2	St Mirren	1
1956-57	Hampden Park	Celtic	0 3	Partick Thistle	0 0
1957-58	Hampden Park	Celtic	7	Rangers	1
1958-59	Hampden Park	Hearts	5	Partick Thistle	1
1959-60	Hampden Park	Hearts	2	Third Lanark	1
1960-61	Hampden Park	Rangers	2	Kilmarnock	0
1961-62	Hampden Park	Rangers	1 3	Hearts	1 1
1962-63	Hampden Park	Hearts	1	Kilmarnock	0
1963-64	Hampden Park	Rangers	5	Morton	0
1964-65	Hampden Park	Rangers	2	Celtic	1
1965-66	Hampden Park	Celtic	2	Rangers	1
1966-67	Hampden Park	Celtic	1	Rangers	0
1967-68	Hampden Park	Celtic	5	Dundee	3
1968-69	Hampden Park	Celtic	6	Hibernian	2
1969-70	Hampden Park	Celtic	1	St Johnstone	0
1970-71	Hampden Park	Rangers	1	Celtic	0
1971-72	Hampden Park	Partick Thistle	4	Celtic	1
1972-73	Hampden Park	Hibernian	2	Celtic	1
1973-74	Hampden Park	Dundee	1	Celtic	0
1974-75	Hampden Park	Celtic	6	Hibernian	3
1975-76	Hampden Park	Rangers	1	Celtic	0
1976-77	Hampden Park	Aberdeen	2	Celtic	1
1977-78	Hampden Park	Rangers	2	Celtic	1
1978-79	Hampden Park	Rangers	2	Aberdeen	1
1979-80	Hampden Park	Aberdeen	0 0	Dundee U.	0 3
1980-81	Hampden Park	Dundee	0	Dundee U.	3

ATTENDANCES

The depression continues
Once again, attendances dropped in the Football League during 1981-82, thus continuing a depressing trend which has been going on for some seasons now. The overall drop for the League was 8.7% on the previous season. Some things never change, however – Manchester United are still the best-supported team. The only light in this gloomy picture comes, surprisingly, from the Fourth Division, which shows an increase in attendances of 17.5%. The totals, with last year's figures in brackets, were:

Division One: 10,420,793 (11,392,894)
Division Two: 4,750,463 (5,175,442)
Division Three: 2,836,915 (3,637,854)
Division Four: 1,998,790 (1,701,379)

Total: 20,006,961 (21,907,569)

DIVISION ONE

	League position	Average 1981-82	Average 1980-81	Difference
Arsenal	5	25,494	32,480	−6,986
Aston Villa	11	26,876	33,641	−6,765
Birmingham City	16	17,117	19,248	−2,131
Brighton & Hove Albion	13	18,244	18,984	−740
Coventry City	14	13,100	16,904	−3,804
Everton	8	24,674	26,105	−1,431
Ipswich Town	2	21,925	24,619	−2,694
Leeds United	20	22,109	21,377	+732
Liverpool	1	35,061	37,547	−2,486
Manchester City	10	34,063	33,587	+476
Manchester United	3	44,571	45,071	−500
Middlesbrough	22	13,413	16,432	−3,019
Nottingham Forest	12	19,937	24,483	−4,546
Notts County	15	11,628	9,551	+2,077
Southampton	7	21,835	21,482	+353
Stoke City	18	14,635	15,580	−945
Sunderland	19	19,608	26,477	−6,869
Swansea City	6	18,226	13,143	+5,083
Tottenham Hotspur	4	35,100	30,724	+4,376
West Bromwich Albion	17	16,786	20,331	−3,545
West Ham United	9	26,585	27,140	−555
Wolverhampton W.	21	15,242	21,551	−6,309

DIVISION TWO

	League position	Average 1981-82	Average 1980-81	Difference
Barnsley	6	15,098	12,800	+2,298
Blackburn Rovers	10	8,405	11,684	−3,279
Bolton Wanderers	19	7,597	9,847	−2,250
Cambridge United	14	5,073	5,796	−723
Cardiff City	20	5,574	6,767	−1,193
Charlton Athletic	13	6,649	7,206	−557
Chelsea	12	13,132	17,897	−4,765
Crystal Palace	15	10,381	19,280	−8,899
Derby County	16	11,828	16,682	−4,854
Grimsby Town	17	8,406	10,961	−2,555
Leicester City	8	14,182	19,476	−5,294
Luton Town	1	11,881	10,291	+1,590
Newcastle United	9	17,276	16,001	+1,275
Norwich City	3	14,183	17,140	−2,957
Oldham Athletic	11	7,023	6,510	+513
Orient	22	4,419	6,076	−1,657
Queens Park Rangers	5	12,574	10,936	+1,638
Rotherham United	7	9,857	7,985	+1,872
Sheffield Wednesday	4	19,170	18,624	+546
Shrewsbury Town	18	4,571	5,616	−1,045
Watford	2	14,631	13,108	+1,523
Wrexham	21	4,304	6,495	−2,191

DIVISION THREE

	League position	Average 1981-82	Average 1980-81	Difference
Brentford	8	5,693	6,752	−1,059
Bristol City	23	6,511	9,765	−3,254
Bristol Rovers	15	5,600	5,929	−329
Burnley	1	6,936	6,469	+467
Carlisle United	2	4,409	4,064	+345
Chester	24	2,170	2,892	−722
Chesterfield	11	4,752	7,331	−2,579
Doncaster Rovers	19	5,234	5,412	−178
Exeter City	18	3,858	4,559	−701
Fulham	3	6,938	5,060	+1,878
Gillingham	6	5,241	4,676	+565
Huddersfield Town	17	6,746	11,548	−4,802
Lincoln City	4	4,222	4,715	−493
Millwall	9	4,626	4,494	+132
Newport County	16	4,459	5,683	−1,224
Oxford United	5	5,851	4,132	+1,719
Plymouth Argyle	10	4,792	6,766	−1,974
Portsmouth	13	8,544	13,514	−4,970
Preston North End	14	5,497	7,631	−2,134
Reading	12	4,018	5,439	−1,421
Southend United	7	5,083	6,095	−1,012
Swindon Town	22	5,825	6,933	−1,108
Walsall	20	3,744	4,265	−521
Wimbledon	21	2,596	2,484	+112

DIVISION FOUR

	League position	Average 1981-82	Average 1980-82	Difference
A.F.C. Bournemouth	4	5,933	3,380	+2,553
Aldershot	16	2,168	2,989	−821
Blackpool	12	4,224	5,863	−1,639
Bradford City	2	5,391	2,858	+2,533
Bury	9	3,558	2,748	810
Colchester United	6	2,859	2,645	+214
Crewe Alexandra	24	2,196	2,909	−713
Darlington	13	2,510	2,537	−27
Halifax Town	19	2,407	1,924	+483
Hartlepool United	14	2,055	3,115	−1,060
Hereford United	10	2,592	2,444	+148
Hull City	8	3,993	4,319	−326
Mansfield Town	20	2,685	3,400	−715
Northampton Town	22	2,306	2,305	+1
Peterborough United	5	4,698	4,137	+561
Port Vale	7	3,639	2,738	+901
Rochdale	21	1,837	2,460	−623
Scunthorpe United	23	2,232	2,357	−125
Sheffield United	1	14,892	12,772	+2,120
Stockport County	18	2,547	2,335	+212
Torquay United	15	2,248	2,050	+198
Tranmere Rovers	11	1,735	1,901	−166
Wigan Athletic	3	5,840	4,434	+1,406
York City	17	2,360	2,245	+115

WELSH FA CUP WINNERS (Since 1901)

1900-1 Oswestry
1901-2 Wellington
1902-3 Wrexham
1903-4 Druids
1904-5 Wrexham
1905-6 Wellington
1906-7 Oswestry
1907-8 Chester
1908-9 Wrexham
1909-10 Wrexham
1910-11 Wrexham
1911-12 Cardiff
1912-13 Swansea
1913-14 Wrexham
1914-15 Wrexham
1915-16 Abandoned
1919-20 Cardiff
1920-21 Wrexham
1921-22 Cardiff
1922-23 Cardiff
1923-24 Wrexham
1924-25 Wrexham
1925-26 Ebbw Vale
1926-27 Cardiff
1927-28 Cardiff
1928-29 Connah's Quay
1929-30 Cardiff
1930-31 Wrexham
1931-32 Swansea
1932-33 Chester
1933-34 Bristol City
1934-35 Tranmere
1935-36 Crewe
1936-37 Crewe
1937-38 Shrewsbury
1938-39 S. Liverpool
1939-40 Wellington
1940-46 No contest
1946-47 Chester
1947-48 Lovell's Ath.
1948-49 Merthyr Tydfil
1949-50 Swansea
1950-51 Merthyr Tydfil
1951-52 Rhyl
1952-53 Rhyl
1953-54 Flint
1954-55 Bury
1955-56 Cardiff
1956-57 Wrexham
1957-58 Wrexham
1958-59 Cardiff
1959-60 Wrexham
1960-61 Swansea
1961-62 Bangor
1962-63 Borough Utd
1963-64 Cardiff
1964-65 Cardiff
1965-66 Swansea
1966-67 Cardiff
1967-68 Cardiff
1968-69 Cardiff
1969-70 Cardiff
1970-71 Cardiff
1971-72 Wrexham
1972-73 Cardiff
1973-74 Cardiff
1974-75 Wrexham
1975-76 Cardiff
1976-77 Shrewsbury
1977-78 Wrexham
1978-79 Shrewsbury
1979-80 Newport County
1980-81 Swansea
1981-82 Swansea

EUROPEAN TOURNAMENTS 1981-82

The highlight of the year from the British point of view was, of course, Aston Villa's triumph in the European Champions' Cup – making it six years in a row for English clubs. Although their season at home had not been so successful – they finished in a mid-way position in the table and lost manager Ron Saunders early on – they rose to the occasion every time they took part in a European Cup tie, and won a tight final by the only goal of the game against the favourites Bayern Munich. The other English representatives – holders Liverpool – went out to CSKA Sofia 2-1 on aggregate at the quarter-final stage. No other British team got past the first round except Glentoran, who also lost to CSKA Sofia despite winning the away leg 2-1.

In the Cup-Winners' Cup Tottenham Hotspur could consider themselves unlucky, losing at the semi-final stage to a Barcelona team who displayed all the worst traits of vicious cynicism that have unfortunately come to be expected of latin teams from time to time down the years. Barcelona went on to win the trophy in front of 120,000 of their own fanatical supporters in their home stadium.

From the statistical point of view it was a pity that Spurs didn't make it because it was ten years ago that Glasgow Rangers last put a British club's name on this particular trophy, and we certainly seem to have enjoyed much more success in the other two competitions.

But the biggest surprise of all the European club tournaments in 1981-82 came in the UEFA Cup. British clubs have often done well in this competition in the past, but on this occasion only Dundee United reached the quarter-finals. In the final, however, Kevin Keegan's old club, SV Hamburg, faced the part-timers of IFK Gothenburg. In the first leg, in Sweden, Gothenburg won 1-0 with a finely taken goal from Holmgren, but even then nobody really expected what was to come in Hamburg. The Swedes overran their illustrious opposition and scored three times without reply to the delight of all neutral observers and a rapturous reception from their own people when they got home with the trophy. With some amazing first phase results coming in later from the World Cup, it was certainly the year of the underdog.

Key: A – Austria; B – Bulgaria; BE – Belgium; CY – Cyprus; CZ – Czechoslovakia; D – Denmark; E – Eire; EG – East Germany; FI – Finland; F – France; G – Greece; H – Hungary; I – Italy; IC – Iceland; L – Luxembourg; N – Netherlands; NI – Northern Ireland; NO – Norway; PO – Poland; P – Portugal; R – Rumania; S – Switzerland; SP – Spain; SW – Sweden; T – Turkey; WG – West Germany; Y – Yugoslavia.

**Won on away goals rule*
***After extra time*
†Aggregate score – 2 leg final
‡Won on penalties

EUROPEAN CHAMPIONS' CUP 1981-82

Second round

Austria Memphis (A)	0	1
Dynamo Kiev (USSR)	1	1
Dynamo Berlin (EG)	1	1
Aston Villa*	2	0
RSC Anderlecht (BE)	3	1
Juventus (I)	1	1
Banik Ostrava (CZ)	3	0
Red Star Belgrade (Y)	1	3
AZ67 Alkmaar (N)	2	2
Liverpool	2	3
CSKA Sofia (B)	2	1
Glentoran (NI)	0	2
KB Copenhagen (D)	1	1
Uni. Craiova (R)	0	4
Benfica (P)	0	1
Bayern Munich (WG	0	4

Quarter-finals

Dynamo Kiev	0	0
Aston Villa	0	2
RSC Anderlecht	2	2
Red Star Belgrade	1	1
Liverpool	1	0
CSKA Sofia	0	2
Uni. Craiova	0	1
Bayern Munich	2	1

Semi-finals

Aston Villa	1	0
RSC Anderlecht	0	0
CSKA Sofia	4	0
Bayern Munich	3	4

Final

Aston Villa	**1**
Scorer: Withe	
Bayern Munich	**0**

At Rotterdam, HT — 0-0, Att. 40,000

EUROPEAN CUP-WINNERS' CUP 1981-82

Second round	Quarter-finals	Semi-finals	Final
Legia Warsaw (PO) 2 1	Legia Warsaw 0 0	Dynamo Tbilisi 0 0	**Standard Liege** **1**
SC Lausanne (S) 1 1			*Scorer:* Vandermissen
SEC Bastia (F) 1 1	Dynamo Tbilisi 1 1		
Dynamo Tbilisi .....(USSR)1 3			
Vasas (H) 0 1	Standard Liege 2 2	Standard Liege 1 1	
Standard Liege (BE) 2 2			
FC Porto (P) 2 0	FC Porto 0 2		
AS Roma (I) 0 0			
Dundalk (E) 1 0	Tottenham Hotspur 2 1	Tottenham Hotspur 1 0	**Barcelona** **2**
Tottenham Hotspur 1 1			*Scorers:* Simonsen, Quini
SKA Rostov-on-Don (USSR) 1 0	Eintracht Frankfurt 0 2		
Eintracht Frankfurt (WG) ..0 2			
Lokomotiv Leipzig‡ (EG) ..1 1	Lokomotiv Leipzig 0 2	Barcelona 1 1	
Velez Mostar (Y) 1 1			
Dukla Prague (CZ) 1 0	Barcelona 3 1		
Barcelona (SP) 0 4			

At Barcelona, HT — 1-1, Att. 120,000

UEFA CUP 1981-82

Third round			Quarter-finals			Semi-finals			Final	
Rapid Vienna (A)	0	0	Real Madrid	3	0	FC Kaiserslautern	1	1	**IFK Gothenburg**	**1, 3**
Real Madrid (SP)	1	0							*Scorers:* Holmgren; Corneliusson, Nilsson, Fredericksson (pen).	
KSC Lokeren (BE)	1	1	FC Kaiserslautern	1	5					
FC Kaiserslautern (WG)	0	4								
Valencia (SP)	5	1	Valencia	2	0	IFK Gothenburg	1	2		
Hajduk Split (Y)	1	4								
IFK Gothenburg (SW)	3	1	IFK Gothenburg	2	2					
Dinamo Bucharest (R)	1	0								
KFC Winterslag (BE)	0	0	Dundee United	2	0	FC Radnicki Nis	2	1	**SV Hamburg**	**0, 0**
Dundee United	0	5								
FC Radnicki Nis (Y)	2	0	FC Radnicki Nis	0	3					
Feyenoord (N)	0	1								
Aberdeen	3	1	SV Hamburg	3	0	SV Hamburg	1	5		
SV Hamburg (WG)	2	3								
SC Portugal (P)	0	0	Neuchatel Xamax	2	0					
Neuchatel Xamax (S)	0	1								

At Gothenburg, Att. 42,548; At Hamburg, Att. 62,000

EUROPEAN CUP PAST FINALS

1956	Real Madrid	4	Stade de Rheims	3
1957	Real Madrid	2	Florentina	0
1958	Real Madrid	3	AC Milan	2**
1959	Real Madrid	2	Stade de Rheims	0
1960	Real Madrid	7	Eintracht Frankfurt	3
1961	SL Benfica	3	Barcelona	2
1962	SL Benfica	5	Real Madrid	3
1963	AC Milan	2	SL Benfica	1
1964	Inter Milan	3	Real Madrid	1
1965	Inter Milan	1	SL Benfica	0
1966	Real Madrid	2	Partizan Belgrade	1
1967	Celtic	2	Inter Milan	1
1968	Manchester United	4	SL Benfica	1
1969	AC Milan	4	Ajax Amsterdam	1
1970	Feyenoord	2	Celtic	1**
1971	Ajax Amsterdam	2	Panathinaikos	0
1972	Ajax Amsterdam	2	Inter Milan	0
1973	Ajax Amsterdam	1	Juventus	0
1974	Bayern Munich	1 4	Atlético Madrid	1 0
1975	Bayern Munich	2	Leeds United	0
1976	Bayern Munich	1	St Etienne (Fra)	0
1977	Liverpool	3	Borussia Munchengladbach	1
1978	Liverpool	1	FC Bruges	0
1979	Nottingham Forest	1	Malmoe	0
1980	Nottingham Forest	1	SV Hamburg	0
1981	Liverpool	1	Real Madrid	0

EUROPEAN CUP-WINNERS' CUP PAST FINALS

1961	Florentina	4	Rangers	1†
1962	Atlético Madrid *(After 1–1 draw)*	3	Florentina	0
1963	Tottenham Hotspur	5	Atlético Madrid	1
1964	Sporting Lisbon *(After 3–3 draw)*	1	MTK Budapest	0
1965	West Ham United	2	Munich 1860	0
1966	Borussia Dortmund	2	Liverpool	1**
1967	Bayern Munich	1	Rangers	0**
1968	AC Milan	2	SV Hamburg	0
1969	Slovan Bratislava	3	Barcelona	2
1970	Manchester City	2	Gornik Zabrze	1
1971	Chelsea *(After 1–1 draw)*	2	Real Madrid	1
1972	Rangers	3	Dynamo Moscow	2
1973	AC Milan	1	Leeds United	0
1974	FC Magdeburg	2	AC Milan	0
1975	Dynamo Kiev	3	Ferencvaros	0
1976	RSC Anderlecht	4	West Ham United	2
1977	SV Hamburg	2	Anderlecht	0
1978	RSC Anderlecht	4	Austria Wien	0
1979	Barcelona	4	Fortuna Dusseldorf	3

1980	Valencia	0	Arsenal	0
	(Valencia won on penalties)			
1981	Dinamo Tbilisi	2	Carl Zeiss Jena	1

FAIRS CUP PAST FINALS

(Aggregate Scores)

1958	Barcelona	8	London	2
1960	Barcelona	4	Birmingham City	1
1961	AS Roma	4	Birmingham City	2
1962	Valencia	7	Barcelona	3
1963	Valencia	4	Dynamo Zagreb	1
1964	Real Zaragoza	2	Valencia	1
1965	Ferencvaros	1	Juventus	0
1966	Barcelona	4	Real Zaragoza	3**
1967	Dynamo Zagreb	2	Leeds United	0
1968	Leeds United	1	Ferencvaros	0
1969	Newcastle United	6	Ujpest Dozsa	2
1970	Arsenal	4	Anderlecht	3
1971	Leeds United	3*	Juventus	3

UEFA CUP PAST FINALS

1972	Tottenham Hotspur	3	Wolverhampton Wanderers	2
1973	Liverpool	3	Borussia Munchengladbach	2
1974	Feyenoord	4	Tottenham Hotspur	2
1975	Borussia Munchengladbach	5	Twente Enschede	1
1976	Liverpool	4	FC Bruges	3
1977	Juventus	2	Athletico Bilbao	2‡
1978	PSV Eindhoven	3	SEC Bastia	0
1979	Borussia Munchengladbach	1 1	Red Star Belgrade	1 0
1980	Borussia Munchengladbach	3 0	Eintracht Frankfurt	2 1
	(Eintracht won on away goals)			
1981	Ipswich T.	3 2	AZ 67 Alkmaar	0 4

EUROPEAN SUPER CUP

1972	Ajax	3 3	Glasgow Rangers	1 2
1973	Ajax	0 6	AC Milan	1 0
1974	Not contested			
1975	Dynamo Kiev	1 2	Bayern Munich	0 0
1976	Anderlecht	4 1	Bayern Munich	1 2
1977	Liverpool	1 6	SV Hamburg	1 0
1978	Anderlecht	1 3	Liverpool	1 2
1979	Nottingham Forest	1 1	Barcelona	0 1
1980	Nottingham Forest	2 0	Valencia	1 1
	(Valencia won on away goals)			
1981	Not contested			
1982	Not contested			

EUROPEAN CHAMPIONSHIPS PAST FINALS

1958-60 Paris, 10 July 1960
USSR 2, Yugoslavia 1 (*after extra time*)
USSR: Yachin; Tchekeli, Kroutikov, Voinov, Maslenkin, Netto, Metreveli, Ivanov, Ponedelnik, Bubukin, Meshki.
Yugoslavia: Vidinic; Durkovic, Jusufi, Zanetic, Miladinovic, Perusic, Sekularac, Jerkovic, Galic, Matus, Kostic.
Scorers: *USSR* – Metreveli, Ponedelnik; *Yugoslavia* – Netto og.

1962-64 Madrid, 21 June 1964
SPAIN 2, USSR 1
Spain; Iribar; Rivilla, Calleja, Fuste, Olivella, Zoco, Amancio, Pereda, Marcellino, Suarez, Lapetra.
USSR: Yachin; Chustikov, Mudrik, Voronin, Shesternjev, Anitchkin, Chislenko, Ivanov, Ponedelnik, Kornaev, Khusainov.
Scorers: *Spain* – Peredal Marcellino; *USSR* – Khusainov.

1966-68 Rome, 8 June 1968
ITALY 1, YUGOSLAVIA 1
Italy: Zoff; Burgnich, Facchetti, Ferrini, Guarneri, Castano, Domenghini, Juliano, Anastasi, Lodetti, Prati.
Yugoslavia: Pantelic; Fazlagic, Damjanovic, Pavlovic, Paunovic, Holcer, Petkovic, Acimovic, Musemic, Trivic, Dzajic.
Scorers: *Italy* – Domenghini, *Yugoslavia* – Dzajic.

Replay: Rome, 10 June 1968
ITALY 2, YUGOSLAVIA 0
Italy: Zoff; Burgnich, Facchetti, Rosato, Guarneri, Salvadore, Domenghini, Mazzola, Anastasi, De Sisti, Riva.
Yugoslavia: Pantelic; Fazlagic, Damjanovic, Pavlovic, Paunovic, Holcer, Hosic, Acimovic, Musemic, Trivic, Dzajic.
Scorers: *Italy* – Riva, Anastasi.

1970-72 Brussels, 18 June 1972
WEST GERMANY 3, USSR 0
West Germany: Maier; Hottges, Schwarzenbeck, Beckenbauer, Breitner, Hoeness, Wimmer, Netzer, Heynckes, Muller, Kremers.
USSR: Rudakov; Dzodzuashvili, Khurtislava, Kaplichny, Istomin, Troshkin, Kolotov, Baidachini, Konkov (Dolmatov), Banishevski (Konzinkievits), Onishenko.
Scorers: *West Germany* – Muller 2, Wimmer.

1974-76 Belgrade, 20 June 1976
CZECHOSLOVAKIA 2, WEST GERMANY 2 (*after extra time*)
Czechoslovakia: Viktor; Dobias (Vesely, F.), Pivarnik, Ondrus, Capkovic, Gogh, Moder, Panenka, Svehlik (Jurkemik), Masny, Nehoda.
West Germany: Maier; Vogts, Beckenbauer, Schwarzenbeck, Dietz, Bonhof, Wimmer, (Flohe), Muller, D., Beer (Bongartz), Hoeness, Holzenbein.
Scorers: *Czechoslovakia* – Svehlik, Dobias; *West Germany* – Muller, Holzenbein.
Czechoslovakia won 5-3 on penalties.

1978-80 Rome, 22 June 1980
WEST GERMANY 2, BELGIUM 1
West Germany: Schumacher; Briegel, Foerster, Dietz, Schuster, Rummenigge, Hrubesch, Mueller, Allofs, Stielike, Kaltz.
Belgium: Pfaff; Gerets, Millecamps, Meeuws, Renquin, Cools, Van der Eycken, Van Moer, Mommens, Van der Elst, Ceulemans.
Scorers: *West Germany* – Hrubesch 2; *Belgium* – Van der Eycken.

BRITISH INTERNATIONAL CHAMPIONSHIP 1981-82

The British Championship, no longer played as an end-of-season tournament, was won comfortably by England, who won all three of their fixtures and did not concede a single goal in the process. With three of the four participants through to the World Cup finals, the matches took on more significance than usual, and in this respect it must all have been rather disappointing for the Scots and the Irish. Unfortunately, the football failed to rise above the mediocre in any of the six games, and the attendance figure for the game between Wales and Northern Ireland (2,315) can only be described as desperate.

Things got under way at Wembley in February, where England ran out 4-0 winners against Northern Ireland, and were wrapped up by England's victory at Hampden Park, where even the fervent Scottish supporters were noticeably muted compared with the same fixture four years ago, prior to Scotland's last World Cup campaign. Being beaten by your greatest rivals and then booed off the field in your last home game before Spain could not have been the send-off that the Scots had been hoping for.

England alone were able to salvage some measure of satisfaction from the tournament as a whole. The win at Hampden was England's fifth successive victory since the fiasco in Oslo back in September, and whilst it was not a win which could be described as spectacular, the English did appear to have some cohesion about their team effort, and as Liverpool have proved time and time again, this is a very important factor. If only the home teams were given the same opportunity as some of the other World Cup finalists to play and train together for extended periods of time, we would surely see even better results, but that is something which will remain a dream for the foreseeable future.

Welsh manager Mike England, although often quoted out of context, did make the point that England were unlikely to do well in Spain, and whilst any objective observer of the British game would be likely to draw the same conclusions, Mike's comments that the Scots would probably do better looked a bit strange at the end of this Championship.

The Scotland v England fixture was the 100th between the two countries since this oldest of international fixtures began in 1872, and the teams have now registered 39 wins each with 22 games drawn.

BRITISH INTERNATIONAL CHAMPIONSHIP 1981-82

England (1) 4, N. Ireland (0) 0
Wembley, 23 February 1982, 54,900
England: Clemence; Anderson, Sansom, Wilkins, Watson, Foster, Keegan, Robson, Francis (Regis), Hoddle, Morley (Woodcock).
N. Ireland: Jennings; J. Nicholl, Nelson, Donaghy, C. Nicholl, J. O'Neill, Brotherston (Cochrane), M. O'Neill (McCreery), Armstrong, McIlroy, Hamilton.
Scorers: England – Robson, Keegan, Wilkins, Hoddle.

Wales (0) 0, England (0) 1
Cardiff, 27 April 1982, 23,927
Wales: Davies; Marustik, Ratcliffe, Nicholas, Stevenson, Jones, Curtis, Flynn, Rush, Thomas (L. James), R. James.
England: Corrigan; Neal, Sansom, Thompson, Butcher, Robson, Wilkins, Francis, Withe, Hoddle (McDermott), Morley.
Scorer: England – Francis.

N. Ireland (0) 1, Scotland (1) 1
Belfast, 28 April 1981, 20,000
N. Ireland: Platt; Donaghy, Nelson, J. O'Neill, McClelland, Cleary, Brotherston, M. O'Neill, Campbell, McIlroy, Healey.
Scotland: Wood; McGrain, Albiston, Wark, McLeish, (Hansen), Evans, Provan, Brazil, Dalglish, Hartford, Robertson (Sturrock).
Scorers: N. Ireland – McIlroy; Scotland – Wark.

Scotland (1) 1, Wales (0) 0
Glasgow, 24 May 1982, 25,284
Scotland: Rough; Stewart (Burley), F. Gray, Souness, Hansen, Narey, Dalglish, Brazil, Jordan (Sturrock), Hartford, Burns.
Wales: Davies; Marustik, Jones, Nicholas, N. Stevenson, B. Stevenson, Curtis (Walsh), R. James, Rush, Flynn (Thomas), L. James.
Scorer: Scotland – Hartford.

Wales (1) 3, N. Ireland (0) 0
Wrexham, 27 May 1982, 2,315
Wales: Southall; Marustik, Jones, Nicholas, N. Stevenson, B. Stevenson, R. James, Rush, Curtis (Walsh), Flynn, L. James (Thomas).
N. Ireland: Jennings; J. Nicholl, Donaghy, McClelland, C. Nicholl, Cleary (Campbell), Brotherston, Healey, Armstrong, McIlroy, Hamilton.
Scorers: Wales – Curtis, Rush, Nicholas.

Scotland (0) 0, England (1) 1
Glasgow, 29 May 1982, 85,000
Scotland: Rough; Burley, McGrain, Evans, Hansen, Narey, Dalglish, Souness, Jordan (Sturrock), Hartford (Robertson), Brazil.
England: Shilton; Mills, Sansom, Thompson, Butcher, Robson, Keegan (McDermott), Coppell, Mariner (Francis), Brooking, Wilkins.
Scorer: England – Mariner.

FINAL TABLE	P	W	D	L	F	A	Pts
England	3	3	0	0	6	0	6
Scotland	3	1	1	1	2	2	3
Wales	3	1	0	2	3	2	2
N. Ireland	3	0	1	2	1	8	1

OTHER INTERNATIONALS 1981-82

SPAIN (1) 3, SCOTLAND (0) 0
Valencia, 24 February 1982, 30,000
Spain: Arconada; Camacho, Gordillo, Alonso, Tendillo, Alesanco, Saura, Sanchez, Satrustegui (Quini), Victor (Gallego), Ufarte.
Scotland: Rough; McGrain, F. Gray, Strachan (Archibald), McLeish, Hansen, Brazil, Wark, Dalglish, Hartford, Souness.
Scorers: Spain – Victor, Quini (pen), Gallego.

SCOTLAND (2) 2, NETHERLANDS (1) 1
Glasgow, 23 March 1982, 71,848
Scotland: Rough; McGrain, F. Gray, Narey, Evans, Miller, Dalglish (Brazil), Archibald (Burns), Jordan (Strachan), Bett Wark.
Netherlands: Van Breukelen; Spelbos, Krol, Van der Korput, Metgod, Hovenkamp, Rijkaard, Peters, Kieft, Muhren, Tamahata.
Scorers: Scotland – F. Gray (pen), Dalglish; Netherlands – Kieft.

FRANCE (2) 4, N. IRELAND (0) 0
Paris, 24 March 1982, 34,000
France: Catendas; Amoro, Lopez, Tresor, Bossis, Larios, Genghini, Giresse, Couriol, Bellone, Zenier.
N. Ireland: Platt; J. Nicholl, C. Nicholl, J. O'Neill, Donaghy, M. O'Neill, McCreery (Caskey), McIlroy (Spence), Brotherston, Armstrong, Cochrane (Stewart).
Scorers: France – Zenier, Couriol, Larios (pen), Genghini.

SPAIN (1) 1, WALES (0) 1
Valencia, 24 March 1982, 20,000
Spain: Arconada; Camacho, Gordillo, Sanchez, Tendillo, Alesanco, Saura, Gallego, Satrustegui, Estrella, Ufarte.
Wales: D. Davies; Marustik, Ratcliffe, Price, Jones, R. James, Nicholas, Stevenson, Curtis, Walsh (G. Davies), Thomas (Giles).
Scorers: Spain – Satrustegui; Wales – R. James.

ENGLAND (0) 2, NETHERLANDS (0) 0
Wembley, 25 May 1982, 69,000
England: Shilton; Neal, Sansom, Thompson, Foster, Robson, Wilkins, Devonshire (Rix), Mariner (Barnes), McDermott, Woodcock.
Netherlands: Van Breukelen; Van der Korput, Metgod (Rijkaard), Ophof, Krol, Boeve, La Ling (Van Kooten), Peters (Van der Kerkhof), Kieft, Muhren, Tahamata.
Scorers: England – Woodcock, Mariner.

ICELAND (1) 1, ENGLAND (0) 1
Reykjavik, June 2 1982, 6000
Iceland: Baldursson; Osuarsson, Jonsson, Ceirson, Haraldsson, K. Thordarson, Gudjohnsen, Gudlavesson, T. Thordarson, Gudmundsson, Edvaldsson.
England: Corrigan; Anderson, Watson, Osman, Neal, McDermott, Hoddle, Devonshire (Perryman), Withe, Regis (Goddard), Morley.
Scorers: Iceland – Gudjohnsen; England – Goddard.

FRANCE (0) 0, WALES (0) 1
Toulouse, 2 June 1982, 30,000
France: Castenada; Battiston, Bossis, Lopez, Tresor, Tigana (Larios), Couriol, Giresse, Soler, Platini, Six (Bellone).
Wales: D. Davies; Marustik, Jones, Price, B. Stevenson, Nicholas, R. James, Flynn, Walsh (G. Davies), Rush, L. James.
Scorer: Wales – Rush.

FINLAND (0) 1, ENGLAND (2) 4
Helsinki, 3 June 1982, 21,421
Finland: Alaja; Lahtinen, Ikalainen, Granskog, Pekonen, Turunen, Haaskivi, Rautiainen, Himanka, Ismail, Nieminen.
England: Clemence; Mills, Sansom, Thompson, Martin, Robson (Rix), Keegan, Coppell (Francis), Mariner, Brooking (Woodcock), Wilkins.
Scorers: Finland – Haaskivi (pen); England – Mariner 2, Robson 2.

INTERNATIONAL GOALSCORERS 1946/82

As at 12 July 1982

ENGLAND

Charlton R.	49	Woodcock	7	Neal	3
Greaves	44	Charlton, J.	6	O'Grady	3
Finney	30	Coppell	6	Peacock	3
Lofthouse	30	Johnson	6	Ramsey	3
Hurst	24	Macdonald	6	Sewell	3
Mortensen	23	Mullen	6	Wilkins	3
Channon	21	Robson, B.	6	Wright	3
Keegan	21	Rowley, J.	6	Allen, R.	2
Peters	21	Atyeo	5	Bradley	2
Haynes	18	Baily	5	Broadbent	2
Hunt	18	Brooking	5	Brooks	2
Lawton	16	Carter	5	Eastham	2
Taylor, T.	16	Edwards	5	Froggatt, J.	2
Chivers	13	Hitchens	5	Froggatt, R.	2
Smith, R.	13	Latchford	5	Haines	2
Douglas	11	Pearson, Stan	5	Hancocks	2
Mannion	11	Pearson, Stuart	5	Hunter	2
Mariner	11	Pickering	5	McDermott	2
Clarke	10	Barnes	4	Moore	2
Flowers	10	Hassall	4	Royle	2
Lee, F.	10	Hoddle	4	Perry	2
Milburn	10	Revie	4	Tueart	2
Wilshaw	10	Robson, R.	4	Pointer	2
Bell	9	Watson	4	Taylor, P.	2
Bentley	9	Baker	3	Wignall	2
Ball	8	Currie	3	Worthington	2
Broadis	8	Elliott	3	A'Court	1
Byrne, J.	8	Francis, G.	3	Astall	1
Francis, T.	8	Grainger	3	Beattie	1
Kevan	8	Kennedy	3	Bowles	1
Connelly	7	Matthews	3	Bradford	1
Paine	7	Morris	3	Bridges	1

Crawford	1	Marsh	1	Stiles	1
Goddard	1	Medley	1	Summerbee	1
Hughes	1	Melia	1	Tambling	1
Kay	1	Mullery	1	Thomson	1
Kidd	1	Nicholls	1	Viollet	1
Langton	1	Nicholson	1	Weller	1
Lawler	1	Parry	1		
Lee, J.	1	Shackleton	1		

Own Goals 10

NORTHERN IRELAND

Crossan	10	Nicholl, C.	4	Ferris	1
McIlroy, J.	10	Simpson	4	D'Arcy	1
Armstrong	9	Brotherston	3	Walker	1
Best	9	Hamilton, W.	3	Blanchflower, J.	1
Bingham	9	Harvey	3	Elder	1
Irvine	9	Lockhart	3	Johnston	1
McParland	9	McMordie	3	Nelson	1
Dougan	8	Morgan	3	Ferguson	1
Wilson	7	Spence	3	Jones	1
Cush	7	Doherty	2	McCrory	1
McAdams	7	Clements	2	Barr	1
McLaughlin	6	Finney	2	Humphries	1
Nicholson	6	Tully	2	Hunter	1
O'Neill, M.	6	Peacock	2	Welsh	1
Hamilton, B.	5	Casey	2	Campbell	1
Smyth	5	Harkin	2	O'Kane	1
Walsh	5	Blanchflower, D.	2	Cassidy	1
Anderson	4	Neil	2	Caskey	1
McMorran	4	Stevenson	1	Cochrane	1
McGrath	4	Brennan	1	Moreland	1
McIlroy, S.	4	McGarry	1		

Own Goals 2

SCOTLAND

Law	30	Gemmill	8	Masson	5
Dalglish	26	Leggatt	8	O'Hare	5
Reilly	22	Robertson, J	7	Wark	5
Steel	13	Brown	6	Gray A.	4
Gilzean	12	Liddell	6	Hartford	4
Jordan	11	Waddell	6	McLaren	4
Stein	11	Rioch	6	Lorimer	4
Collins	10	Scott	6	Mason	4
Johnston, R.	10	Young	5	Hamilton	4
Mudie	9	Macari	5	Johnstone, J.	4
St John	9	McQueen	5	Archibald	3
Wilson	9	Murdoch	5	Smith	3
Brand	8	Henderson	5	Caldow	3

Bremner	3
Mackay	3
Herd	3
MacDougall	3
McNeill	3
Morris	3
McPhail	3
Baxter	3
White	3
Gibson	3
Lennox	3
Greig	3
Chalmers	3
Gray, E.	3
Graham, A	3
Bauld	2
Pettigrew	2
Flavell	2
Houliston	2
Graham, A.	2
Johnstone, D.	2
McMillan	2
Harper	2
Fleming	2
Ring	2
Robertson	2
Baird	2
Hewie	2
Holton	2
Gemmell	1
Combe	1
Duncan	1
Herd	1
Howie	1
Linwood	1
Mitchell	1
Orr	1
Thornton	1
Henderson	1
McKenzie	1
Ormond	1
Davidson	1
Buckley	1
Docherty	1
Curran	1
Conn	1
Fernie	1
Hutchison	1
Burns	1
Jackson	1
Parlane	1
Quinn	1
Weir	1
Murray	1
Mulhall	1
Hunter	1
McLintock	1
McCalliog	1
McKinnon	1
Hughes	1
McLean	1
Johnstone	1
Campbell	1
Morgan	1
Bone	1
Jardine	1
Craig	1
Wallace	1
Miller	1
Strachan	1
Provan	1
Gray, F.	1
Souness	1
Sturrock	1
Narey	1

Own Goals 9

WALES

Ford	23
Allchurch	22
Jones, C.	16
Charles J.	15
Toshack	12
James, L.	11
Davies, R.	8
Vernon	8
Walsh	7
Medwin	6
Griffiths, A.	6
Charles, M.	6
Clarke	5
Curtis	5
Leek	5
Deacy	5
Flynn	5
Tapscott	4
Palmer	3
Rees	3
England	3
Woosnam	3
Lowrie	2
Edwards	2
Griffiths, M.	2
Godfrey	2
Jones, Bryn	2
Jones, Barrie	2
Dwyer	2
Reece	2
Durban	2
Nicholas	2
James, R.	2
Rush	2
Thomas	2
Giles	2
Yorath	2
Paul	1
Powell	1
Burgess	1
Foulkes	1
Barnes	1
Bowen	1
Moore	1
Hewitt	1
Powell	1
Kryzwicki	1
Williams	1
Hockey	1
Smallman	1
Roberts	1
Mahoney	1
Evans	1
Jones, D	1
O'Sullivan	1
Harris	1
Price	1
Boyle	1

Own Goals 2

POST-WAR INTERNATIONAL APPEARANCES

As at 12 July, 1982

Abbreviations *A*—Albania; *Arg*—Argentina; *Aust*—Austria; *Au*—Australia; *Bel*—Belgium; *Braz*—Brazil; *Bulg*—Bulgaria; *Ch*—Chile; *Czecho*—Czechoslovakia; *Co*—Colombia; *C*—Cyprus; *D*—Denmark; *Ec*—Ecuador; *E*–England; *E/Germ*—East Germany; *F*—France; *FIFA*—Federation of International Associations; *Fin*—Finland; *G*—West Germany; *Gr*—Greece; *H*–Hungary; *Holl*—Holland; *Hon*—Honduras; *I*—N Ireland; *Ic*—Iceland; *Ir*—Iran; *Isr*—Israel; *It*—Italy; *K*—Kuwait; *Lux*—Luxembourg; *M*—Malta; *Mex*—Mexico; *N*—Norway; *NZ*—New Zealand; *P*—Paraguay; *Per*—Peru; *Pol*—Poland; *Port*—Portugal; *Ru*—Rumania; *Rus*—Russia; *S*—Scotland; *Sp*—Spain; *Swdn*—Sweden; *Switz*—Switzerland; *T*—Turkey; *U*—Uruguay; *UK*—Rest of United Kingdom; *US*—United States of America; *W*—Wales; *Y*—Yugoslavia; Z—Zaire.

ENGLAND

A'court, A. (5) (Liverpool) 1957/8 *I, Braz, Aust, Rus;* 1958/9 *W*.
Allen, R. (5) (West Bromwich Albion) 1951/2 *Switz*; 1953/4 *US, Y*; 1954/5 *W, G*.
Allen, T. (3) (Stoke City) 1959/60 *W, Swdn, I*.
Anderson, S. (2) (Sunderland) 1961/2 *Aust, S*.
Anderson, V. (9) (Nottingham Forest) 1978/9 *Czecho, Swdn;* 1979/80 *Bulg, Sp;* 1980/81 *N, Ru, W, S;* 1981/82 *I, Ic*.
Angus, J. (1) (Burnley) 1960/1 *Aust*.
Armfield, J. (43) (Blackpool) 1958/9 *Braz, Per, Mex, US*; 1959/60 *S, Y, Sp, H*; 1960/1 *Lux, Sp, W, S, Mex, Port, It, Aust*; 1961/2 *Lux, W, Port, I, Aust, S, Switz, Per, H, Arg, Bulg, Braz*; 1962/3 *F, I, W, F, S, Braz, E/Germ, Switz*; 1963/4 *W, FIFA, I, S*; 1965/6 *Y, Fin*.
Armstrong, D. (1) (Middlesbrough) 1979/80 *Au*.
Armstrong, K. (1) (Chelsea) 1954/5 *S*.
Astall, G. (2) (Birmingham) 1955/6 *Fin, G*.
Astle, J. (5) (West Bromwich Albion) 1968/9 *W;* 1969/70 *Port, S, Braz, Czecho*.
Aston, J. (17) (Manchester United) 1948/9 *W, S, D, Switz, Swdn, N, F;* 1949/50 *W, I, S, Eire, It, Port, Bel, Ch, US;* 1950/1 *I*.
Atyeo, J. (6) (Bristol City) 1955/6 *Sp, Braz, Swdn;* 1956/7 *Eire, D, Eire*.

Bailey, M. (2) (Charlton) 1963/4 *US*; 1964/5 *W*.
Baily, E. (9) (Tottenham Hotspur) 1949/50 *Sp*; 1950/1 *I, W, Y*; 1951/2 *W, Aust* (2), *Switz*; 1952/3 *I*.
Baker, J. (8) (Hibernian) 1959/60 *I, S, Y, Sp, H;* 1965/6 (Arsenal) *I, Sp, Pol*.
Ball, A. (72) (Blackpool) 1964/5 *Y, G, Swdn*; 1965/6 *Sp, Pol, G, S, Fin, D, Pol, U, Arg, Port, G*; 1966/7 (Everton) *I, Czecho, W, S, Sp, Aust*; 1967/8 *W, Rus, S, Sp* (2), *G, Y*; 1968/9 *Ru* (2), *I, W, S, Mex, U, Braz*; 1969/70 *Port, Bel, W, S, Co, Ec, Ru, Braz, Czecho, G*; 1970/1 *E/Germ, M, Gr, M, I, S*; 1971/2 *Switz, Gr* (Arsenal), *G*(2), *S*; 1972/3 *Y, W* (2), *S, I, W, S, Czecho, Pol*; 1973/4 *Port*; 1974/5 *G, C* (2), *I, W, S*.
Banks, G. (73) (Leicester) 1962/3 *S, Braz, Czecho, E/Germ*; 1963/4 *W, FIFA, I, S, U, Port, US, Port, Arg*; 1964/5 *I, S, H, Y, G, Swdn*; 1965/6 *I, Sp, Pol, G, S, Y, Fin,*

Pol, Y, Mex, F, Arg, Port, G; 1966/7 *I, Czecho, W, S;* 1967/8 (Stoke) *W, I, Rus, S, Sp, G, Y, Rus*; 1968/9 *Ru* (2), *F, I, S, U, Braz*; 1969/70 *Holl, Bel, W, I, S, Co, Ec, Ru, Braz, Czecho*; 1970/1 *M, Gr, M, I, S*; 1971/2 *Switz, Gr, G* (2), *W, S.*

Banks, T. (6) (Bolton Wanderers) 1957/8 *Rus* (2), *Braz, Aust, Rus*; 1958/9 *I.*

Barlow, R. (1) (West Bromwich Albion) 1954/5 *I.*

Barnes, P. (22) (Manchester City) 1977/8 *It, G, Braz, W, S, H*; 1978/9 *D, Eire, Czecho, I, I, S, Bulg, Aust*; 1979/80 (West Bromwich Albion) *D, W;* 1980/81 *Sp, Braz, W, Switz;* 1981/2 (Leeds U.) *N, Holl.*

Barrass, M. (3) (Bolton Wanderers) 1951/2 *W, I*; 1952/3 *S.*

Baynham, R. (3) (Luton Town) 1955/6 *D, I, Sp.*

Beattie, T. K. (9) (Ipswich Town) 1974/5 *C* (2), *S*; 1975/6 *Switz, Port*; 1976/7 *Fin, It, Holl*; 1977/8 *Lux.*

Bell, C. (48) (Manchester City) 1967/8 *Swdn, G*; 1968/9 *Bulg, F, W, U, Braz*; 1969/70 *Holl, Port, Holl, I, Braz, Czecho, G*; 1971/2 *Gr, G* (2), *W, I, S*; 1972/3 *Y, W* (2), *S, I, W, S, Czecho, Pol*; 1973/4 *Pol, It, W, I, S, Arg, Aust, E/Germ, Bulg, Y*; 1974/5 *Czecho, Port, G, C* (2), *I, S*; 1975/6 *Switz, Czecho.*

Bentley, R. (12) (Chelsea) 1948/9 *Swdn*; 1949/50 *S, Port, Bel, Ch, US*; 1952/3 *W, Bel*; 1954/5 *W, G, Sp, Port.*

Berry, J. (4) (Manchester United) 1952/3 *Arg, Ch, U*; 1955/6 *Swdn.*

Birtles, G. (3) (Nottingham Forest) 1979/80 *Arg, It;* 1980/81 (Manchester U.) *Ru.*

Blockley, J. (1) (Arsenal) 1972/3 *Y.*

Blunstone, F. (5) (Chelsea) 1954/5 *W, S, F, Port*; 1956/7 *Y.*

Bonetti, P. (7) (Chelsea) 1965/6 *D*; 1966/7 *Sp, Aust*; 1967/8 *Sp*; 1969/70 *Holl, Port, G.*

Bowles, S. (5) (Queens Park Rangers) 1973/4 *Port, W, I*; 1976/7 *It, Holl.*

Boyer, P. (1) (Norwich City) 1975/6 *W.*

Brabrook, P. (3) (Chelsea) 1957/8 *Rus*; 1959/60 *I, Sp.*

Bradford, G (1) (Bristol Rovers) 1955/6 *D.*

Bradley, W. (3) (Manchester United) 1958/9 *It, Mex, US.*

Bridges, B. (4) (Chelsea) 1964/5 *S, H, Y*; 1965/6 *Aust.*

Broadbent, P. (7) (Wolverhampton Wanderers) 1957/8 *Rus*; 1958/9 *I, W, S, It, Braz*; 1959/60 *S.*

Broadis, I. (14) (Manchester City) 1951/2 *Aust, S, It*; 1952/3 *S, Arg, Ch, U, US* (Newcastle United); 1953/4 *S, Y, H, Bel, Switz, U.*

Brooking, T. (46) (West Ham United) 1973/4 *Port, Arg, E/Germ, Bulg, Y*; 1974/5 *Czecho, Port*; 1975/6 *W, Port, Braz, It, Fin*; 1976/7 *Eire, Fin, It, Hol, I, W*; 1977/8 *It, G, W, S, H*; 1978/9 *D, Eire, I, S, Bulg, Swdn, Aust*; 1979/80 *D, I, Arg, W, I, S, Bel, Sp;* 1980/81 *Switz, Sp, Ru, H;* 1981/2 *H, S, Fin, Sp.*

Brooks, J. (3) (Tottenham Hotspur) 1956/7 *W, Y, D.*

Brown, Tony (1) (West Bromwich Albion) 1970/1 *W.*

Brown, K. (1) (West Ham United) 1959/60 *I.*

Butcher, T. (8) (Ipswich T.) 1979/80 *Au;* 1980/81 *Sp;* 1981/2 *W, S, F, Czecho, G, Sp.*

Byrne, G. (2) (Liverpool) 1962/3 *S*; 1965/6 *N.*

Byrne, J. (11) (Crystal Palace) 1961/2 *I*; 1962/3 (West Ham United) *Switz*; 1963/4 *S, U, Port, Eire, Braz, Arg*; 1964/5 *W, S.*

Byrne, R. (33) (Manchester United) 1953/4 *S, Y, H, Bel, Switz, U*; 1954/5 *I, W, G, S, F, Sp, Port*; 1955/6 *D, W, I, Sp, Braz, Swdn, Fin, G*; 1956/7 *I, W, Y, D, S, Eire*; 1957/8 *W, I, F.*

Callaghan, I. (4) (Liverpool) 1965/6 *Fin, F*; 1977/8 *Switz, Lux.*
Carter, H. (7) (Derby County) 1946/7 *I, W, S, Eire, Holl, F, Switz.*
Channon, M. (46) (Southampton) 1972/3 *Y, S, I, W, S, Czecho, Rus, It;* 1973/4 *Pol, It, Port, W, I, S, Arg, Aust, E/Germ, Bulg, Y*; 1974/5 *Czecho, Port, G, C* (2), *I, W, S*; 1975/6 *Switz, Czecho, Port, W, I, S, Braz, It, Fin*; 1976/7 *Fin, It, Lux, I, W, S, Braz, Arg, U*; 1977/8 *Switz.*
Charlton, J. (35) (Leeds United) 1964/5 *S, H, Y, G, Swdn*; 1965/6 *W, Aust, I, Sp, Pol, G, S, Y, Fin, D, Pol, U, Mex, F, Arg, Port, G*; 1966/7 *I, Czecho, W, S*; 1967/8 *W, Sp*; 1968/9 *Ru, F, W*; 1969/70 *Holl, Port, Holl, Czecho.*
Charlton, R. (106) (Manchester United) 1957/8 *S, Port, Y*; 1958/9 *I, Rus, W, S, It, Braz, Per, Mex, US*; 1959/60 *W, Swdn, S, Y, Sp, H*; 1960/1 *I, Lux, Sp, W, S, Mex, Port, It, Aust*; 1961/2 *Lux, W, Port, I, Aust, S, Switz, Per, H, Arg, Bulg, Braz*; 1962/3 *F, S, Braz, Czecho, E/Germ, Switz*; 1963/4 *W, FIFA, I, S, U, Port, Eire, US, Braz, Arg*; 1964/5 *I, Holl, S*; 1965/6 *W, Aust, I, G, S, Sp, Y, Fin, N, Pol, U, Mex, F, Arg, Port, G*; 1966/7 *I, Czecho, W, S*; 1967/8 *W, I, Rus, S, Sp* (2), *Swdn, Y, Rus*; 1968/9 *Ru, Bulg, Ru, I, W, S, Mex, Braz*; 1969/70 *Holl, Port, Holl, W, I, Co, Ec, Ru, Braz, Czecho, G.*
Charnley, R. (1) (Blackpool) 1961/2 *F.*
Cherry, T. (27) (Leeds United) 1975/6 *W, S, Braz, Fin*; 1976/7 *Eire, It, Lux, I, S, Braz, Arg, U*; 1977/8 *Switz, Lux, It, Braz, W*; 1978/9 *Czecho, W, Swdn*; 1979/80 *Eire, Arg, W, I, S, Au, Sp.*
Chilton, A. (2) (Manchester United) 1950/1 *I*; 1951/2 *F.*
Chivers, M. (24) (Tottenham Hotspur) 1970/1 *M, Gr, M, I, S*; 1971/2 *Switz* (2), *Gr, G* (2), *S*; 1972/3 *W* (2), *S, I, W, S, Czecho, Pol, Rus, It*; 1973/4 *Pol, Aust.*
Clamp, E. (4) (Wolverhampton Wanderers) 1957/8 *Rus* (2), *Braz, Aust.*
Clapton, D. (1) (Arsenal) 1958/9 *W.*
Clarke, A. (19) (Leeds United) 1969/70 *Czecho*; 1970/1 *E/Germ, M, I, W, S*; 1972/3 *S, W, S, Czecho, Pol, Rus, It*; 1973/4 *Pol, It, Aust*; 1974/5 *Port*; 1975/6 *Czecho, Port.*
Clarke, H. (1) (Tottenham Hotspur) 1953/4 *S.*
Clayton, R. (35) (Blackburn Rovers) 1955/6 *I, Sp, Braz, Swdn, Fin, G*; 1956/7 *I, W, Y, D, S, Eire*; 1957/8 *W, I, F, S, Port, Y, Rus*; 1958/9 *I, Rus, W, S, It, Braz, Per, Mex, US*; 1959/60 *W, Swdn, I, S, Y.*
Clemence, R. (59) (Liverpool) 1972/3 *W* (2); 1973/4 *E/Germ, Bulg, Y*; 1974/5 *Czecho, Port, G, C, I, W, S*; 1975/6 *Switz, Czecho, Port, U* (2), *I, S, Braz, Fin*; 1976/7 *Eire, Fin, It, Holl, Lux, S, Braz, Arg, U*; 1977/8 *Switz, Lux, It, G, I, S*; 1978/9 *D, Eire, I, I, S, Bulg, Aust*; 1979/80 *D, Bulg, Eire, Arg, W, S, Bel, Sp;* 1980/81 *Ru, Sp, Braz, Switz, H;* 1981/2 (Tottenham H.) *N, I, Fin.*
Clement, D. (5) (Queens Park Rangers) 1975/6 *W* (2), *It*; 1976/7 *It, Holl.*
Clough, B. (2) (Middlesbrough) 1959/60 *W, Swdn.*
Coates, R. (4) (Burnley) 1969/70 *I*; 1970/1 *Gr,* (Tottenham Hotspur) *M, W.*
Cockburn, H. (13) (Manchester United) 1946/7 *I, W, Eire*; 1947/8 *S, It*; 1948/9 *I, S, D, Switz*; 1950/1 *Arg, Port*; 1951/2 *F.*
Cohen, G. (37) (Fulham) 1963/4 *U, Port, Eire, US, Braz*; 1964/5 *I, Bel, W, Holl, S, H, Y, G, Swdn*; 1965/6 *W, Aust, I, Sp, Pol, G, S, N, D, Pol, U, Mex, F, Arg, Port, G*; 1966/7 *I, Czecho, W, S, Sp*; 1967/8 *W, I.*
Compton, L. (2) (Arsenal) 1950/1 *W, Y.*
Connelly J. (20) (Burnley) 1959/60 *W, Swdn, I, S*; 1961/2 *W, Port, Aust, Switz*; 1962/3 *W, F*; 1964/5 (Manchester United) *H, Y, Swdn*; 1965/6 *W, Aust, I, S, N, D, U.*

Cooper, T. (20) (Leeds United) 1968/9 *F, W, S, Mex*; 1969/70 *Holl, Bel, Co, Ec, Ru, Braz, Czecho, G*; 1970/1 *E/Germ, M, I, W, S*; 1971/2 *Switz* (2); 1974/5 *Port.*
Coppell, S. (39) (Manchester United) 1977/8 *It, G, Braz, W, I, S, H*; 1978/9 *D, Eire, Czecho, I, I, S, Bulg, Aust*; 1979/80 *D, I, Eire, Sp, Arg, W, S, Bel, It;* 1980/81 *Ru, Switz, Ru, Braz, W, S, Switz, H;* 1981/2 *H, S, Fin, F, Czecho, K, G.*
Corrigan J. (9) (Manchester City) 1975/6 *It;* 1977/8 *Braz;* 1978/9 *W*; 1979/80 *I, Au;* 1980/81 *W, S;* 1981/2 *W, Ic.*
Crawford, R. (2) (Ipswich Town) 1961/2 *I, Aust.*
Crowe, C. (1) Wolverhampton Wanderers) 1962/3 *F.*
Cunningham, L. (6) (West Bromwich Albion) 1978/9 *W, Swdn, Aust*; (Real Madrid) 1979/80 *Eire, Sp;* 1980/81 *Ru.*
Currie, A. (17) (Sheffield United) 1971/2 *I*; 1972/3 *Rus, It*; 1973/4 *Pol, It, Aust*; 1975/6 *Switz*; (Leeds United) 1977/8 *Braz, W, I, S, H*; 1978/9 *Czecho, I, I, W, Swdn.*

Deeley, N. (2) (Wolverhampton Wanderers) 1958/9 *Braz, Per.*
Devonshire, A. (4) (West Ham United) 1979/80 *I, Au;* 1981/2 *Holl, Ic.*
Dickinson, J. (48) (Portsmouth) 1948/9 *N, F*; 1949/50 *W, S, Eire, Port, Bel, Ch, US, Sp*; 1950/1 *I, W, Y*; 1951/2 *W, I, Aust* (2), *S, It, Switz*; 1952/3 *I, W, Bel, S, Arg, Ch, U, US*; 1953/4 *W, FIFA, I, H* (2), *S, Y, Bel, Switz, U*; 1954/5 *Sp, Port*; 1955/6 *D, W, I, Sp, S*; 1956/7 *W, Y, D.*
Ditchburn, E. (6) (Tottenham Hotspur) 1948/9 *Switz, Swdn*; 1952/3 *US*; 1956/7 *W, Y, D.*
Dobson, M. (5) (Burnley) 1973/4 *Port, E/Germ, Bulg, Y*; 1974/5 (Everton) *Czecho.*
Douglas, B. (36) (Blackburn Rovers) 1957/8 *W, I, F, S, Port, Y, Rus* (2), *Braz, Aust*; 1958/9 *Rus, S*; 1958/9 *Rus, S*; 1959/60 *Y, H*; 1960/1 *I, Lux, Sp, W, S, Mex, Port, It, Aust*; 1961/2 *Lux, W, Port, I, S, Per, H, Arg, Bulg, Braz*; 1962/3 *S, Braz, Switz.*
Doyle, M. (5) (Manchester City) 1975/6 *W, S, Braz, It*; 1976/7 *Holl.*

Eastham, G. (19) (Arsenal) 1962/3 *Braz, Czecho, E/Germ*; 1963/4 *W, FIFA, I, S, U, Port, Eire, US, Braz, Arg*; 1964/5 *H, G, Swdn*; 1965/6 *Sp, Pol, D.*
Eckersley, W. (17) (Blackburn Rovers) 1949/50 *Sp*; 1950/1 *Y, S, Arg, Port*; 1951/2 *Aust* (2), *Switz*; 1952/3 *I, Arg, Ch, U, US*; 1953/4 *W, FIFA, I, H.*
Edwards, D. (18) (Manchester United) 1954/5 *S, F, Sp, Port*; 1955/6 *S, Braz, Swdn, Fin, G*; 1956/7 *I, D, S, Eire, D, Eire*; 1957/8 *W, I, F.*
Ellerington, W. (2) (Southampton) 1948/9 *N, F.*
Elliott, W. H. (5) (Burnley) 1951/2 *It, Aust*; 1952/3 *I, W, Bel.*

Fantham, J. (1) (Sheffield Wednesday) 1961/2 *Lux.*
Finney, T. (76) (Preston) 1946/7 *I, Eire, Holl, F, Port*; 1947/8 *W, I, S, Bel, Swdn, It*; 1948/9 *I, W, S, Swdn, N, F*; 1949/50 *W, I, S, Eire, It, Port, Bel, Ch, US, Sp*; 1950/1 *W, S, Arg, Port*; 1951/2 *F, W, I, S, It, Aust, Switz*; 1952/3 *I, W, Bel, S, Arg, Ch, U, US*; 1953/4 *D, S, Y, H, Bel, Switz, U*; 1954/5 *G;* 1955/6 *D, W, I, Sp, S*; 1956/7 *W, Y, D, S, Eire, D, Eire*; 1957/8 *W, F, S, Port, Y, Rus* (2); 1958/9 *I, Rus.*
Flowers, R. (49) (Wolverhampton Wanderers) 1954/5 *F*; 1958/9 *W, S, It, Braz, Per, Mex, US*; 1959/60 *W, S, Y, Sp, H, Swdn, I*; 1960/1 *Lux, Sp, W, S, Mex, Port, It, Aust*; 1961/2 *Lux, W, Port, I, Aust, S, Switz, Per, H, Arg, Bulg, Braz*; 1962/3 *F, I, W, F, S, Switz*; 1963/4 *Eire, US, Port*; 1964/5 *W, Holl, G*; 1965/6 *N.*
Foster, S. (3) (Brighton) 1981/2 *I, Holl, K.*

Foulkes, W. (1) (Manchester United) 1954/5 *I.*
Francis, G. (12) (Queens Park Rangers) 1974/5 *Czecho, Port, W, S*; 1975/6 *Switz, Czecho, Port, W, I, S, Braz, Fin.*
Francis, T. (32) (Birmingham City) 1976/7 *Holl, Lux, S, Braz*; 1977/8 *Switz, Lux, It, G, Braz, W, S, H*; 1978/9 *Bulg, Swdn, Aust*; (Nottingham Forest) 1979/80 *I, Bulg, Sp;* 1980/81 *Sp, Ru, S, Switz;* 1981/2 (Manchester C.) *N, I, W, S, Fin, F, Czecho, K, G, Sp.*
Franklin, N. (27) (Stoke City) 1946/7 *I, W, S, Eire, Holl, F, Switz, Port*; 1947/8 *W, I, S, Bel, Swdn, It*; 1948/9 *I, W, S, D, Switz, Swdn, N, F*; 1949/50 *W, I, S, Eire, It.*
Froggatt, J. (13) (Portsmouth) 1949/50 *I, It*; 1950/1 *S*; 1951/2 *Aust* (2), *S, It, Switz*; 1952/3 *I, W, Bel, S, US.*
Froggatt, R. (4) (Sheffield Wednesday) 1952/3 *W, Bel, S, US.*

Garrett, T. (3) (Blackpool) 1951/2 *S, It*; 1953/4 *W.*
Gates, E. (2) (Ipswich T.) 1980/81 *N, Ru.*
George, F. C. (1) (Derby County) 1976/7 *Eire.*
Gidman, J. (1) (Aston Villa) 1976/7 *Lux.*
Gillard, I. (3) (Queens Park Rangers) 1974/5 *G, W*; 1975/6 *Czecho.*
Goddard, P. (1) (West Ham U.) 1981/2 *Ic.*
Grainger, C. (7) (Sheffield United) 1955/6 *Braz, Swdn, Fin, G*; 1956/7 *I, W,* (Sunderland) *S.*
Greaves, J. (57) (Chelsea) 1958/9 *Per, Mex, US*; 1959/60 *W, Swdn, Y, Sp*; 1960/1 *I, Lux, Sp, W, S, Port, It, Aust*; 1961/2 (Tottenham Hotspur) *S, Switz, Per, H, Arg, Bulg, Braz*; 1962/3 *F, I, W, F, S, Braz, Czecho, Switz*; 1963/4 *W, FIFA, I, U, Port, Eire, Braz, Port, Arg*; 1964/5 *I, Bel, Holl, S, H, Y*; 1965/6 *W, Aust, Y, N, D, Pol, U, Mex, F*; 1966/7 *S, Sp, Aust.*
Greenhoff, B. (18) (Manchester United) 1975/6 *W, I*; 1976/7 *Eire, Fin, It, Holl, I, W, S, Braz, Arg, U*; 1977/8 *Braz, W, I, S, H*; 1979/80 *Au.*

Hagan, J. (1) (Sheffield United) 1948/9 *D.*
Haines, J. (1) (West Bromwich Albion) 1948/9 *Switz.*
Hall, J. (17) (Birmingham City) 1955/6 *D, I, W, Sp, S, Braz, Swdn, Fin, G*; 1956/7 *I, W, Y, D, S, Eire, D, Eire.*
Hancocks, J. (3) (Wolverhampton Wanderers) 1948/9 *Switz*; 1949/50 *W*; 1950/1 *Y.*
Hardwick, G. (13) (Middlesbrough) 1946/7 *I, W, S, Eire, Holl, F, Switz, Port*; 1947/8 *W, I, S, Bel, Swdn.*
Harris, G. (1) (Burnley) 1965/6 *Pol.*
Harris, P. (2) (Portsmouth) 1949/50 *Eire*; 1953/4 *H.*
Harvey, C. (1) (Everton) 1970/1 *M.*
Hassall, H. (5) (Huddersfield Town) 1950/1 *S, Arg, Port*; 1951/2 *F* (Bolton Wanderers); 1953/4 *I.*
Haynes, J. (56) (Fulham) 1954/5 *I*; 1955/6 *I, Sp, S, Swdn, Fin, G*; 1956/7 *W, Y, Eire, D, Eire*; 1957/8 *W, I, F, S, Port, Y, Rus* (2), *Braz, Aust, Rus*; 1958/9 *I, Rus, S, It, Braz, Per, Mex, US*; 1959/60 *I, Y, Sp, H*; 1960/1 *I, Lux, Sp, W, S, Mex, Port, It, Aust*; 1961/2 *W, Port, I, Aust, S, Switz, H, Per, Arg, Bulg, Braz.*
Hector, K. (2) (Derby County) 1973/4 *Pol, It.*
Hellawell, M. (2) (Birmingham City) 1962/3 *F, I.*
Henry, R. (1) (Tottenham Hotspur) 1962/3 *F.*

Hill, F. (2) (Bolton Wanderers) 1962/3 *I, W.*
Hill, G. (6)(Manchester United)1975/6 *It*; 1976/7 *Eire, Fin, Lux*; 1977/8 *Switz, Lux.*
Hinton, A. (3) (Wolverhampton Wanderers) 1962/3 *F*; 1964/5 (Nottingham Forest) *Bel, W.*
Hitchens, G. (7) (Aston Villa) 1960/1 *Mex, It, Aust* (Inter Milan); 1961/2 *Switz, Per, H; Braz.*
Hoddle, G. (13) (Tottenham Hotspur) 1979/80 *Bulg, W, Au, Sp;* 1980/81 *Sp, W, S;* 1981/2 *N, I, W, Ic, Czecho, K.*
Hodgkinson, A. (5) (Sheffield United) 1956/7 *S, Eire, D, Eire*; 1960/1 *W.*
Holden, D. (5) (Bolton Wanderers) 1958/9 *S, It, Braz, Per, Mex.*
Holliday, E. (3) (Middlesbrough) 1959/60 *W, Swdn, I.*
Hollins, J. (1) (Chelsea) 1966/7 *Sp.*
Hopkinson, E. (14) (Bolton Wanderers) 1957/8 *W, I, F, S, Port, Y*; 1958/9 *S, It, Braz, Per, Mex, US*; 1959/60 *W, Swdn.*
Howe, D. (23) (West Bromwich Albion) 1957/8 *W, I, E, F, S, Port, Y, Rus* (2), *Braz, Aust, Rus*; 1958/9 *I, Rus, W, S, It, Braz, Per, Mex, US*; 1959/60 *W, Swdn, I.*
Howe, J. (3) (Derby County) 1947/8 *It*; 1948/9 *I, S.*
Hudson, A. (2) (Stoke City) 1974/5 *G, C.*
Hughes, E. (61) (Liverpool) 1969/70 *Holl, Port, Bel, W, I, S*; 1970/1 *E/Germ, M, Gr, M, W*; 1971/2 *Switz, Gr, G* (2), *W, I, S*; 1972/3 *W* (2), *S, W, S, Pol, Rus, It*; 1973/4 *Pol, It, W, I, S, Arg, Aust, E/Germ, Bulg, Y*; 1974/5 *Czecho, Port, C, I*; 1976/7 *It, Lux, W, S, Braz, Arg, U*; 1977/8 *Switz, Lux, It, G, I, S, H*; 1978/9 *D, I, W, Swdn*; (Wolverhampton Wanderers) 1979/80 *Sp, I, S.*
Hughes, L. (3) (Liverpool) 1949/50 *Ch, US, Sp.*
Hunt, R. (34) (Liverpool) 1961/2 *Aust*; 1962/3 *E/Germ*; 1963/4 *S* (2), *US, Port*; 1964/5 *W*; 1965/6 *Sp, Pol, G, S, Fin, N, Pol, U, Mex, F, Arg, Port, G*; 1966/7 *I, Czecho, W, Sp, Aust*; 1967/8 *W, I, Rus, Sp* (2), *Swdn, Y, Rus*; 1968/9 *Ru* (2).
Hunter, N. (28) (Leeds United) 1965/6 *Sp, G, Y, Fin*; 1966/7 *Aust*; 1967/8 *Sp, Swdn, G, Y, Rus*; 1968/9 *Ru, W*; 1969/70 *Holl, G*; 1970/1 *M*; 1971/2 *G* (2), *W, I, S*; 1972/3 *W* (2), *Rus*; 1973/4 *Pol, I, S, Aust*; 1974/5 *Czecho.*
Hurst, G. (49) (West Ham United) 1965/6 *G, S, Y, Fin, D, Arg, Port, G*; 1966/7 *I, Czecho, W, S, Sp, Aust*; 1967/8 *W, I, Rus, S, Swdn, G, Rus*; 1968/9 *Ru, Bulg, Ru, F, I, S, Mex, U, Braz*; 1969/70 *Holl* (2), *Bel, W, I, S, Co, Ec, Ru, Braz, G*; 1970/1 *E/Germ, Gr, W, S*; 1971/2 *Switz* (2), *Gr, G.*

Jezzard, B. (2) (Fulham) 1953/4 *H*; 1955/6 *I.*
Johnson, D. (8) (Ipswich Town) 1974/5 *W, S*; 1975/6 *Switz*; (Liverpool) 1979/80 *Eire, Arg, I, S, Bel.*
Johnston, H. (10) (Blackpool) 1946/7 *S, Holl*; 1950/1 *S*; 1952/3 *Arg, Ch, U, US*; 1953/4 *W, I, H.*
Jones, M. (3) (Sheffield United) 1964/5 *G, Swdn* (Leeds United); 1969/70 *Holl.*
Jones, W. H. (2) (Liverpool) 1949/50 *Port, Bel.*

Kay, A. (1) (Everton) 1962/3 *Switz.*
Keegan, K. (63) (Liverpool) 1972/3 *W* (2); 1973/4 *W, I, Arg, E/Germ, Bulg, Y*; 1974/5 *Czecho, G, C* (2), *I, S*; 1975/6 *Switz, Czecho, Port, W* (2), *I, S, Braz, Fin*; 1976/7 *Eire, Fin, It, Holl, Lux,* (SV Hamburg), *W, Braz, Arg, U*; 1977/8 *Switz, It, G, Braz, H*; 1978/9 *D, Eire, Czecho, I, W, S, Bulg, Swdn, Aust*; 1979/80 *D, I, Eire, Sp,*

Arg, Bel, It, Sp; 1980/81 *Sp, Switz, H;* 1981/2 (Southampton) *N, H, I, S, Fin, Sp.*

Kennedy, R. (17) (Liverpool) 1975/6 *W* (2), *I, S*; 1976/7 *Lux, W, S, Braz, Arg*; 1977/8 *Switz, Lux*; 1979/80 *Bulg, Sp, Arg, W, Bel, It.*

Kevan, D. (14) (West Bromwich Albion) 1956/7 *S;* 1957/8 *W, I, S, Port, Y, Rus* (2), *Braz, Aust, Rus*; 1958/9 *Mex, US*; 1960/1 *Mex.*

Kidd, B. (2) (Manchester United) 1969/70 *I, Ec.*

Knowles, C. (4) (Tottenham Hotspur) 1967/8 *Rus, Sp, Swdn, G.*

Labone, B. (26) (Everton) 1962/3 *I, W, F*; 1966/7 *Sp, Aust*; 1967/8 *S, Sp, Swdn, G, Y, Rus,* 1968/9 *Ru, Bulg, I, S, Mex, U, Braz*; 1969/70 *Bel, W, S, Co, Ec, Ru, Braz, G.*

Lampard, F. (2) (West Ham United) 1972/3 *Y*; 1979/80 *Au.*

Langley, J. (3) (Fulham) 1957/8 *S, Port, Y.*

Langton, R. (11) (Blackburn Rovers) 1946/7 *I, W, Eire, Holl, F, Switz*; 1947/8 *Swdn*; 1948/9 (Preston North End) *D, Swdn*; 1949/50 (Bolton Wanderers) *S*; 1950/1 *I.*

Latchford, R. (12) (Everton) 1977/8 *It, Braz, W*; 1978/9 *D, Eire, Czecho, I, I, W, S, Bulg, Aust.*

Lawler, C. (4) (Liverpool) 1970/1 *M, W, S*; 1971/2 *Switz.*

Lawton, T. (15) (Chelsea) 1946/7 *I, W, S, Eire, Holl, F, Switz, Port*; 1947/8 *W, I* (Notts County), *S, Bel, Swdn, It*; 1948/9 *D.*

Lee, F. (27) (Manchester City) 1968/9 *Bulg, F, I, W, S, Mex, U*; 1969/70 *Holl, Port, Holl, Bel, W, Co, Ec, Ru, Braz, G*; 1970/1 *E/Germ, Gr, M, I, W, S*; 1971/2 *Switz* (2), *Gr, G.*

Lee, J. (1) (Derby County) 1950/1 *I.*

Lindsay, A. (4) (Liverpool) 1973/4 *Arg, E/Germ, Bulg, Y.*

Little, B. (1) (Aston Villa) 1974/5 *W.*

Lloyd, L. (4) (Liverpool) 1970/1 *W*; 1971/2 *Switz, I*; (Nottingham Forest) 1979/80 *W.*

Lofthouse, N. (33) (Bolton Wanderers) 1950/1 *Y*; 1951/2 *W, I, Aust* (2), *It, Switz*; 1952/3 *I, W, Bel, S, Arg, Ch, U, US*; 1953/4 *W, FIFA, I, Bel, U*; 1954/5 *I, S, F, Sp, Port*; 1955/6 *D, W, Sp, S, Fin*; 1958/9 *Rus, W.*

Lowe, E. (3) (Aston Villa) 1946/7 *F, Switz, Port.*

Macdonald, M. (14) (Newcastle United) 1971/2 *W, I, S*; 1972/3 *Rus;* 1973/4 *Port, S, Y*; 1974/5 *G, C* (2), *I,* (Arsenal) 1975/6 *Switz, Czecho, Port.*

Madeley, P. (24) (Leeds United) 1970/1 *I*; 1971/2 *Switz* (2), *Gr, G* (2), *W, S*; 1972/3 *S, Czecho, Pol, Rus, It*; 1973/4 *Pol, It, Aust*; 1974/5 *Czecho, Port, C*; 1975/6 *Czecho, Port, Fin*; 1976/7 *Eire, Holl.*

Mannion, W. (26) (Middlesbrough) 1946/7 *I, W, S, Eire, Holl, F, Switz, Port*; 1947/8 *W, I, Bel, Swdn, It*; 1948/9 *N, F*; 1949/50 *S, Eire, Port, Bel, Ch, US*; 1950/1 *I, W, Y, S*; 1951/2 *F.*

Mariner, P. (26) (Ipswich Town) 1976/7 *Lux, I*; 1977/8 *Lux, W, S*; 1979/80 *W, I, S, Au, It, Sp;* 1980/81 *N, Switz, Sp, Switz, H;* 1981/2 *N, H, Holl, S, Fin, F, Czecho, K, G, Sp.*

Marsh, R. (9) (Queens Park Ranger) 1971/2 *Switz,* (Manchester City), *G* (2), *W, I, S*; 1972/3 *Y, W* (2).

Martin, A. (4) (West Ham U.) 1980/81 *Braz, S;* 1981/2 *H, Fin.*

Matthews, R. (5) (Coventry City) 1955/6 *S, Braz, Swdn, G*; 1956/7 *I,* (Chelsea).

Matthews, S. (37) (Stoke City) 1946/7 *S* (Blackpool), *Switz, Port*; 1947/8 *W, I, S, Bel, It*; 1948/9 *I, W, S, D, Switz*; 1949/50 *Sp*; 1950/1 *I, S*; 1953/4 *FIFA, I, H, Bel, U*; 1954/5 *I, W, G, S, F, Sp, Port*; 1955/6 *W, Braz*; 1956/7 *I, W, Y, D, S, Eire, D.*
McDermott, T. (24) (Liverpool) 1977/8 *Switz, Lux*; 1978/9 *I, W, Swdn*; 1979/80 *D, I, Eire, Bel, Sp;* 1980/81 *N, Ru, Switz, Ru, Braz, Switz, H;* 1981/2 *N, H, W, Holl, S, Ic.*
McDonald, C. (8) (Burnley) 1957/8 *Rus* (2), *Braz, Aust, Rus*; 1958/9 *I, Rus, W.*
McFarland, R. (28) (Derby County) 1970/1 *M, Gr, M, I, S*; 1971/2 *Switz, Gr, G, W, S*; 1972/3 *W* (2), *I, W, S, Czecho, Pol, Rus, It*; 1973/4 *Pol, It, W, I, Aust*; 1975/6 *Czecho, S*; 1976/7 *Eire, It.*
McGarry, W. (4) (Huddersfield Town) 1953/4 *Switz, U*; 1955/6 *D, W.*
McGuinness, W. (2) (Manchester United) 1958/9 *I, Mex.*
McNab, R. (4) (Arsenal) 1968/9 *Ru, Bulg, Ru, I.*
McNeil, M. (9) (Middlesbrough) 1960/1 *I, Lux, Sp, W, Mex, Port, It*; 1961/2 *Lux.*
Meadows, J. (1) (Manchester City) 1954/5 *S.*
Medley, L. (6) (Tottenham Hotspur) 1950/1 *W, Y*; 1951/2 *F, W, I, Aust.*
Melia, J. (2) (Liverpool) 1962/3 *S, Switz.*
Merrick, G. (23) (Birmingham City) 1951/2 *I, Aust* (2), *S, It, Switz*; 1952/3 *I, W, Bel, S, Arg, Ch, U*; 1953/4 *W, FIFA, I, H* (2), *S, Y, Bel, Switz, U.*
Metcalfe, V. (2) (Huddersfield Town) 1950/1 *Arg, Port.*
Milburn, J. (13) (Newcastle United) 1948/9 *I, W, S, Switz*; 1949/50 *W, Port, Bel, Sp*; 1950/1 *W, Arg, Port*; 1951/2 *F*; 1955/6 *D.*
Miller, B. (1) (Burnley) 1960/1 *Aust.*
Mills, M. (44) (Ipswich Town) 1972/3 *Y;* 1975/6 *W* (2), *I, S, Braz, It, Fin*; 1976/7 *Fin, It, I, W, S*; 1977/8 *G, Braz, W, I, S, H*; 1978/9 *D, Eire, I, I, S, Bulg, Aust*; 1979/80 *D, I, Sp, I, S, Sp;* 1980/81 *Switz, Switz, H;* 1981/2 *N, H, S, Fin, F, Czecho, K, G, Sp.*
Milne, G. (14) (Liverpool) 1962/3 *Braz, Czecho, E/Germ*; 1963/4 *W, FIFA, I, S, U, Port, Eire, Braz, Arg*; 1964/5 *I, Bel.*
Milton, C. A. (1) (Arsenal) 1951/2 *Aust.*
Moore, I. (1) (Nottingham Forest) 1969/70 *Holl.*
Moore, R. (108) (West Ham United) 1961/2 *Per, H, Arg, Bulg, Braz*; 1962/3 *F, I, W, F, S, Braz, Czecho, E/Germ, Switz*; 1963/4 *W, FIFA, I, S, U, Port, Eire, Braz, Port, Arg*; 1964/5 *I, Bel, S, H, Y, G, Swdn*; 1965/6 *W, Aust, I, Sp, Pol, G, S, N, D, Pol, U, Mex, F, Arg, Port, G*; 1966/7 *I, Czecho, W, S, Sp, Aust*; 1967/8 *W, I, Rus, S, Sp* (2), *Swdn, G, Y, Rus*; 1968/9 *Ru, Bulg, F, I, W, S, Mex, U, Braz*; 1969/70 *Holl, Port, Bel, W, I, S, Co, Ec, Ru, Braz, Czecho, G*; 1970/1 *E/Germ, Gr, M, I, S*; 1971/2 *Switz* (2), *Gr, G* (2), *W, S*; 1972/3 *Y, W* (3), *S* (2), *I, Czecho, Pol, Rus, It*; 1973/4 *It.*
Morley, A (4) (Aston Villa) 1981/2 *H, I, W, Ic.*
Morris, J. (3) (Derby County) 1948/9 *N, F*; 1949/50 *Eire.*
Mortensen, S. (25) (Blackpool) 1946/7 *Port;* 1947/8 *W, I, S, Bel, Swdn, It*; 1948/9 *I, W, S, Swdn, N*; 1949/50 *W, I, S, It, Port, Bel, Ch, US, Sp*; 1950/1 *S, Arg*; 1953/4 *FIFA, H.*
Mozley, B. (3) (Derby County) 1949/50 *W, I, Eire.*
Mullen, J. (12) (Wolverhampton Wanderers) 1946/7 *S*; 1948/9 *N, F*; 1949/50 *Bel, Ch, US*; 1953/4 *W, FIFA, I, S, Y, Switz.*
Mullery, A. (35) (Tottenham Hotspur) 1964/5 *Holl*; 1966/7 *Sp, Aust*; 1967/8 *W, I, Rus, S, Sp* (2), *Swdn, Y*; 1968/9 *Ru, Bulg, F, I, S, Mex, U, Braz*; 1969/70 *Holl, Port, Holl, W, I, S, Co, Ec, Ru, Braz, Czecho, G*; 1970/1 *E/Germ, M, Gr*; 1971/2 *Switz.*

Neal, P. (39) (Liverpool) 1975/6 *W, It*; 1976/7 *W, S, Braz, Arg, U*; 1977/8 *Switz, It, G, I, S, H*; 1978/9 *D, Eire, I, I, S, Bulg, Aust*; 1979/80 *D, I, Sp, Arg, W, Bel, It;* 1980/81 *Ru, Switz, Sp, Braz, H;* 1981/2 *N, H, W, Holl, Ic, F, K.*
Newton, K. (27) (Blackburn Rovers) 1965/6 *G, S*; 1966/7 *Sp, Aust*; 1967/8 *W, S, Sp, Swdn, G, Y*; 1968/9 *Ru, Bulg, F, I, W, S, Mex, U, Braz*; 1969/70 (Everton) *Holl, I, S, Co, Ec, Ru, Czecho, G.*
Nicholls, J. (2) (West Bromwich Albion) 1953/4 *S, Y.*
Nicholson, W. (1) (Tottenham Hotspur) 1950/1 *Port.*
Nish, D. (5) (Derby County) 1972/3 *I;* 1973/4 *Port, W, I, S.*
Norman, M. (23) (Tottenham Hotspur) 1961/2 *Per, H, Arg, Bulg, Braz*; 1962/3 *F, S, Braz, Czecho, E/Germ*; 1963/4 *W, FIFA, I, S, U, Port, US, Braz, Port, Arg*; 1964/5 *I, Bel, Holl.*

Owen, S. (3) (Luton Town) 1953/4 *H, Bel.*
O'Grady, M. (2) (Huddersfield Town) 1962/3 *I;* 1968/9 (Leeds United) *F.*
Osgood, P. (4) (Chelsea) 1969/70 *Bel, Ru, Czecho*; 1973/4 *It.*
Osman, R. (6) (Ipswich Town) 1979/80 *Au;* 1980/81 *Sp, Ru, Switz;* 1981/2 *N, Ic.*

Paine, T. (19) (Southampton) 1962/3 *Czecho, E/Germ*; 1963/4 *W, FIFA, I, S, U, US, Port*; 1964/5 *I, H, Y, G, Swdn*; 1965/6 *W, Aust, Y, N, Mex.*
Parkes, P. (1) (Queens Park Rangers) 1973/4 *Port.*
Parry, R. (2) (Bolton Wanderers) 1959/60 *I, S.*
Peacock, A. (6) (Middlesbrough) 1961/2 *Arg, Bulg*; 1962/3 *I, W*; 1965/6 (Leeds United) *W, I.*
Pearson, Stan (8) (Manchester United) 1947/8 *S;* 1948/9 *I, S*; 1949/50 *I, It*; 1950/1 *Port*; 1951/2 *S, It.*
Pearson, Stuart (15) (Manchester United) 1975/6 *W, I, S, Braz, Fin*; 1976/7 *Eire, Holl, W, S, Braz, Arg, U*; 1977/8 *It, G, I.*
Pegg, D. (1) (Manchester United) 1956/7 *Eire.*
Pejic, M. (4) (Stoke City) 1973/4 *Port, W, I, S.*
Perry, W. (3) (Blackpool) 1955/6 *I, Sp, S.*
Perryman, S. (1) (Tottenham H.) 1981/2 *Ic.*
Peters, M. (67) (West Ham United) 1965/6 *Y, Fin, Pol, Mex, F, Arg, Port, G*; 1966/7 *I, Czecho, W, S*; 1967/8 *W, I, Rus, S, Sp* (2), *Swdn, Y, Rus*; 1968/9 *Ru, Bulg, F, I, S, Mex, U, Braz*; 1969/70 *Holl, Port, Holl, Bel,* (Tottenham Hotspur) *W, I, S, Co, Ec, Ru, Braz, Czecho, G*; 1970/1 *E/Germ, M, Gr, M, I, W, S*; 1971/2 *Switz, Gr, G* (2), *I;* 1972/3 *S, I, W, S, Czecho, Pol, Rus, It*; 1973/4 *Pol, It, Port, S, Aust.*
Phillips, L. (3) (Portsmouth) 1951/2 *I*; 1954/5 *W, G.*
Pickering, F. (3) (Everton) 1963/4 *US*; 1964/5 *I, Bel.*
Pilkington, B. (1) (Burnley) 1954/5 *I.*
Pointer, R. (3) (Burnley) 1961/2 *Lux, W, Port.*
Pye, J. (1) (Wolverhampton Wanderers) 1949/50 *Eire.*

Quixall, A. (5) (Sheffield Wednesday) 1953/4 *W, FIFA, I*; 1954/5 *Sp, Port.*

Radford, J. (2) (Arsenal) 1968/9 *Ru*; 1971/2 *Switz.*
Ramsey, A. (32) (Southampton) 1948/9 *Switz*; 1949/50 (Tottenham Hotspur) *S, It, Port, Bel, Ch, US, Sp*; 1950/1 *I, W, Y, S, Arg, Port*; 1951/2 *F, W, I, Aust* (2), *S, It,*

Switz; 1952/3 *I, W, Bel, S, Arg, Ch, U, US*; 1953/4 *FIFA, H.*
Reaney, P. (3) (Leeds United) 1968/9 *Bulg*; 1969/70 *Port*; 1970/1 *M.*
Reeves, K. (2) (Norwich City) 1979/80 *Bulg, I.*
Regis, C. (2) (W.B.A.) 1981/2 *I, Ic.*
Revie, D. (6) (Manchester City) 1954/5 *I, S, F*; 1955/6 *D, W*; 1956/7 *I.*
Richards, J. (1) (Wolverhampton Wanderers) 1972/3 *I.*
Rickaby, S. (1) (West Bromwich Albion) 1953/4 *I.*
Rimmer, J. (1) (Arsenal) 1975/6 *It.*
Rix, G. (13) (Arsenal) 1980/81 *N, Ru, Switz, Braz, W, S;* 1981/2 *Holl, Fin, F, Czecho, K, G, Sp.*
Robb, G. (1) (Tottenham Hotspur) 1953/4 *H.*
Robson, B. (23) (West Bromwich Albion) 1979/80 *Eire, Au;* 1980/81 *N, Ru, Switz, Sp, Ru, Braz, W, S, Switz, H;* 1981/2 *N,* (Manchester U.) *H, I, W, Holl, S, Fin, F, Czecho, G, Sp.*
Robson, R. (20) (West Bromwich Albion) 1957/8 *F, Rus* (2), *Braz, Aust*; 1959/60 *Sp, H*; 1960/1 *I, Lux, Sp, W, S, Mex, Port, It*; 1961/2 *Lux, W, Port, I, Switz.*
Rowley, J. (6) (Manchester United) 1948/9 *Switz, Swdn, F*; 1949/50 *I, It*; 1951/2 *S.*
Royle, J. (6) (Everton) 1970/1 *M*; 1972/3 *Y;* (Manchester City) 1975/6 *I, It*; 1976/7 *Fin, Lux.*

Sadler, D. (4) (Manchester United) 1967/8 *I, Rus*; 1969/70 *Ec*; 1970/1 *E/Germ.*
Sansom, K. (27) (Crystal Palace) 1978/9 *W;* 1979/80 *Bulg, Eire, Arg, W, I, S, Bel, It;* 1980/81 (Arsenal) *N, Ru, Switz, Sp, Ru, Braz, W, S, Switz;* 1981/2 *I, W, Holl, S, Fin, F, Czecho, G, Sp.*
Scott, L. (17) (Arsenal) 1946/7 *I, W, S, Eire, Holl, F, Switz, Port*; 1947/8 *W, I, S, Bel, Swdn, It*; 1948/9 *I, W, D.*
Sewell, J. (6) (Sheffield Wednesday) 1951/2 *I, Aust, Switz*; 1952/3 *I;* 1953/4 *H* (2).
Shackleton, L. (5) (Sunderland) 1948/9 *W, D*; 1949/50 *W;* 1954/5 *W, G.*
Shaw, G. (5) (Sheffield United) 1958/9 *Rus, W, S, It*; 1962/3 *W.*
Shellito, K. (1) (Chelsea) 1962/3 *Czecho.*
Shilton, P. (42) (Leicester City) 1970/1 *E/Germ, W*; 1971/2 *Switz, I*; 1972/3 *Y, S, I, W, S, Czecho, Pol, Rus, It*; 1973/4 *Pol, It, W, I, S, Arg, Aust*; 1974/5 (Stoke City) *C;* 1976/7 *I, W*; (Nottingham Forest) 1977/8 *W, H*; 1978/9 *Czecho, Swdn, Aust*; 1979/80 *I, Sp, It;* 1980/81 *N, Switz, Ru;* 1981/2 *H, Holl, S, F, Czecho, K, G, Sp.*
Shimwell, E. (1) (Blackpool) 1948/9 *Swdn.*
Sillett, P. (3) (Chelsea) 1954/5 *F, Sp, Port.*
Slater, W. (12) (Wolverhampton Wanderers) 1954/5 *W, G*; 1957/8 *S, Port, Y, Rus* (2), *Braz, Aust, Rus*; 1958/9 *Rus*; 1959/60 *S.*
Smith, L. (6) (Arsenal) 1950/1 *W*; 1951/2 *W, I*; 1952/3 *W, Bel, S.*
Smith, Tom (1) (Liverpool) 1970/1 *W.*
Smith, Trevor (2) (Birmingham City) 1959/60 *W, Swdn.*
Smith, R. (15) (Tottenham Hotspur) 1960/1 *I, Lux, Sp, W, S, Port*; 1961/2 *S*; 1962/3 *F, S, Braz, Czecho, E/Germ*; 1963/4 *W, FIFA, I.*
Springett, R. (33) (Sheffield Wednesday) 1959/60 *I, S, Y, Sp, H*; 1960/1 *I, Lux, Sp, Mex, Port, It, Aust*; 1961/2 *Lux, W, Port, I, Aust, S, Switz, Per, H, Arg, Bulg, Braz*; 1962/3 *F, I, W, F, Switz*; 1965/6 *W, Aust, N.*
Staniforth, R. (8) (Huddersfield Town) 1953/4 *S, Y, H, Bel, Switz, U*; 1954/5 *W, G.*
Stepney, A. (1) (Manchester United) 1967/8 *Swdn.*

Stiles, N. (28) (Manchester United) 1964/5 *S, H, Y, Swdn*; 1965/6 *W, Aust, I, Sp, Pol, G, S, N, D, Pol, U, Mex, F, Arg, Port, G*; 1966/7 *I, Czecho, W, S*; 1967/8 *Rus;* 1968/9 *Ru;* 1969/70 *I, S.*
Storey, P. (19) (Arsenal) 1970/1 *Gr, I, S*; 1971/2 *Switz, G, W, I, S*; 1972/3 *Y, W* (2), *S, I, W, S, Czecho, Pol, Rus, It.*
Streten, B. (1) (Luton Town) 1949/50 *I.*
Summerbee, M. (8) (Manchester City) 1967/8 *S, Sp, G*; 1971/2 *Switz, G, W, I*; 1972/3 *Rus.*
Sunderland, A. (1) (Arsenal) 1979/80 *Au.*
Swan, P. (19) (Sheffield Wednesday) 1959/60 *Y, Sp*; 1960/1 *I, Lux, Sp, W, S, Mex, Port, It, Aust*; 1961/2 *Lux, W, Port, I, Aust, S, Switz.*
Swift, F. (19) (Manchester City) 1946/7 *I, W, S, Eire, Holl, F, Switz, Port*; 1947/8 *W, I, S, Bel, Swdn, It*; 1948/9 *I, W, S, D, N.*

Talbot, B. (6) (Ipswich Town) 1976/7 *I, S, Braz, Arg, U*; 1979/80 *Au.*
Tambling, R. (3) (Chelsea) 1962/3 *W, F*; 1965/6 *Y.*
Taylor, E. (1) (Blackpool) 1953/4 *H.*
Taylor, J. (2) (Fulham) 1950/1 *Arg, Port.*
Taylor, P. (3) (Liverpool) 1947/8 *W, I, Swdn.*
Taylor, P. (4) (Crystal Palace) 1975/6 *W* (2), *I, S.*
Taylor, T. (19) (Manchester United) 1952/3 *Arg, Ch, U*; 1953/4 *Bel, Switz*; 1955/6 *S, Braz, Swdn, Fin, G*; 1956/7 *I, Y, D, Eire, D, Eire*; 1958/9 *W, I, F.*
Temple, D. (1) (Everton) 1964/5 *G.*
Thomas, D. (8) (Queens Park Rangers) 1974/5 *Czecho, Port, C* (2), *W, S*; 1975/6 *Czecho, Port.*
Thomson, R. (8) (Wolverhampton Wanderers) 1963/4 *I, US, Port, Arg*; 1964/5 *I, Bel, W, Hol.*
Thompson, P. (16) (Liverpool) 1963/4 *Port, Eire, US, Braz, Port, Arg*; 1964/5 *I, Bel, W, Holl, S*; 1965/6 *I;* 1967/8 *I, G*; 1969/70 *Holl.*
Thompson, P. (40) (Liverpool) 1975/6 *W* (2), *I, S, Braz, It, Fin*; 1976/7 *Fin*; 1978/9 *Eire, Czecho, I, S, Bulg, Swdn, Aust*; 1979/80 *D, I, Bulg, Eire, Sp, Arg, W, S, Bel, It, Sp;* 1980/81 *N, Ru, H;* 1981/2 *N, H, W, Holl, S, Fin, F, Czecho, K, G, Sp.*
Thompson, T. (2) (Aston Villa) 1951/2 *W* (Preston); 1956/7 *S.*
Todd, C. (27) (Derby County) 1971/2 *I;* 1973/4 *Port, W, I, S, Arg, E/Germ, Bulg, Y*; 1974/5 *Port, G, C* (2), *I, W, S*; 1975/6 *Switz, Czecho, Port, I, S, Braz, Fin*; 1976/7 *Eire, Fin, Holl, I.*
Towers, T. (2) (Sunderland) 1975/6 *W, It.*
Tueart, D. (6) (Manchester City) 1974/5 *C, I*; 1976/7 *Fin, I, W, S.*

Ufton, D. (1) (Charlton Athletic) 1953/4 *FIFA.*

Venables, T. (2) (Chelsea) 1964/5 *Bel, Holl.*
Viljoen, C. (2) (Ipswich Town) 1974/5 *I, W.*
Viollet, D. (2) (Manchester United) 1959/60 *H*; 1961/2 *Lux.*

Waiters, A. (5) (Blackpool) 1963/4 *Eire, Braz*; 1964/5 *Bel, W, Holl.*
Ward, P. (1) (Brighton) 1979/80 *Au.*

Ward, T. (2) (Derby County) 1947/8 *Bel;* 1948/9 *W.*
Watson, D. (65) (Sunderland) 1973/4 *Port, S, Arg, E/Germ, Bulg, Y*; 1974/5 *Czecho, Port, G, C* (2), *I, W, S*; 1975/6 (Manchester City) *Switz, Czecho, Port*; 1976/7 *Holl, Lux, I, W, S, Braz, Arg, U*; 1977/8 *Switz, Lux, It, G, Braz, W, I, S, H*; (Southampton) 1978/9 *D, Eire, Czecho, I, I, W, S, Bulg, Swdn, Aust*; 1979/80 *D, I, Bulg, Eire, Sp, Arg, I, S, Bel, It, Sp;* 1980/81 *N, Ru, Switz, Ru, W, S, Switz, H;* 1981/2 (Stoke C.) *I, Ic.*
Watson, W. (4) (Sunderland) 1949/50 *I, It*; 1950/1 *W, Y.*
Weller, K. (4) (Leicester City) 1973/4 *W, I, S, Arg.*
West, G. (3) (Everton) 1968/9 *Bulg, W, Mex.*
Wheeler, J. (1) (Bolton Wanderers) 1954/5 *I.*
Whitworth, S. (7) (Leicester City) 1974/5 *G, C, I, W, S*; 1975/6 *Switz, Port.*
Whymark, T. (1) (Ipswich Town) 1977/8 *Lux.*
Wignall, F. (2) (Nottingham Forest) 1964/5 *W, Holl.*
Wilkins, R. (52) (Chelsea) 1975/6 *It*; 1976/7 *Eire, Fin, I, Braz, Arg, U*; 1977/8 *Switz, Lux, It, G, W, I, S, H*; 1978/9 *D, Eire, Czecho, I, W, S, Bulg, Swdn, Aust*; (Manchester United) 1979/80 *D, I, Bulg, Sp, Arg, W, I, S, Bel, It, Sp;* 1980/81 *Sp, Ru, Braz, W, S, Switz, H;* 1981/2 *I, W, Holl, S, Fin, F, Czecho, K, G, Sp.*
Williams, B. (24) (Wolverhampton Wanderers) 1948/9 *F*; 1949/50 *W, S, Eire, It, Port, Bel, Ch, US, Sp*; 1950/1 *I, W, Y, S, Arg, Port*; 1951/2 *F, W*; 1954/5 *G, S, F, Sp, Port*; 1955/6 *W.*
Willis, A. (1) (Tottenham Hotspur) 1951/2 *F.*
Wilshaw, D. (12) (Wolverhampton Wanderers) 1953/4 *W, Switz, U*; 1954/5 *S, F, Sp, Port*; 1955/6 *W, I, Fin, G*; 1956/7 *I.*
Wilson, R. (63) (Huddersfield Town) 1959/60 *S, Y, Sp, H*; 1961/2 *W, Port, I, Aust, S, Switz, Per, H, Aust, Bulg, Braz*; 1962/3 *F, I, Braz, Czecho, E/Germ, Switz*; 1963/4 *W, FIFA, S, U, Port, Eire, Braz, Port, Arg*; 1964/5 (Everton) *S, H, Y, G, Swdn*; 1965/6 *W, Aust, I, Sp, Pol, G, Y, Fin, D, Pol, U, Mex, F, Arg, Port, G*; 1966/7 *I, Czecho, W, S, Aust*; 1967/8 *I, Rus, S, Sp* (2), *Y, Rus.*
Withe, P. (6) (Aston Villa) 1980/81 *Braz, W, S;* 1981/2 *N, W, Ic.*
Wood, R. (3) (Manchester United) 1954/5 *I, W*; 1955/6 *Fin.*
Woodcock, A. (24) (Nottingham Forest) 1977/8 *I;* 1978/9 *Eire, Czecho, Bulg, Swdn*; (FC Cologne) 1979/80 *I, Bulg, Eire, Sp, Arg, Bel, It, Sp;* 1980/81 *N, Ru, Switz, Ru, W, S;* 1981/2 *I, Holl, Fin,* (Arsenal) *G, Sp.*
Worthington, F. (8) (Leicester City) 1973/4 *I, S, Arg, E/Germ, Bulg, Y*; 1974/5 *Czecho, Port.*
Wright, T. (11) (Everton) 1967/8 *Rus*; 1968/9 *Ru* (2), *Mex, U, Braz*; 1969/70 *Holl, Bel, W, Ru, Braz.*
Wright, W. (105) (Wolverhampton Wanderers) 1946/7 *I, W, S, Eire, Holl, Switz, Port*; 1947/8 *W, I, S, Bel, Swdn, It*; 1948/9 *I, W, S, D, Switz, Swdn, N, F*; 1949/50 *W, I, S, Eire, It, Port, Bel, Ch, US, Sp*; 1950/1 *I, S, Arg*; 1951/2 *F, W, I, Aust* (2), *S, It, Switz*; 1952/3 *I, W, Bel, S, Arg, Ch, U, US*; 1953/4 *W, FIFA, I, H* (2), *S, Y, Bel, Switz, Y*; 1954/5 *I, W, G, S, F, Sp, Port*; 1955/6 *D, W, I, Sp, Braz, Swdn, Fin, G*; 1956/7 *I, W, Y, D, S, Eire, D, Eire*; 1957/8 *W, I, F, S, Port, Y, Rus* (2), *Braz, Aust, Rus*; 1958/9 *Rus, W, S, It, Braz, Per, Mex, US.*

Young, G. (1) (Sheffield Wednesday) 1964/5 *W.*

NORTHERN IRELAND

Aherne, T. (4) (Belfast Celtic) 1946/7 *E*; 1947/8 *S*; 1948/9 *W*; 1949/50 (Luton Town) *W*.

Anderson, T. (22) (Manchester United) 1972/3 *C, E, S, W*; 1973/4 *Bulg, Port*; 1974/5 (Swindon Town) *S*; 1975/6 *Isr*; 1976/7 *Holl, G, Bel, E, S, W, Ic*; 1977/8 *Ic, Holl, Bel, S, E, W*; 1978/9 *D*.

Armstrong, G. (42) (Tottenham Hotspur) 1976/7 *G, E, W, Ic*; 1977/8 *Bel, S, E, W*; 1978/9 *Eire, D, Bulg, E, Bulg, E, S, W, D*; 1979/80 *E, Eire, Isr, S, E, W, Au, Au, Au;* 1980/81 *Swdn* (Watford), *Port, S, Port, S, Swdn;* 1981/2 *S, Isr, F, E, W, Y, Hon, Sp, Aust, F*.

Barr, H. (Linfield) 1961/2 *E*; 1962/3 (Coventry City) *Pol, E*.

Best, G. (37) (Manchester United) 1963/4 *W, U*; 1964/5 *E, Switz* (2), *S, Holl* (2), *A*; 1965/6 *S, E, A*; 1966/7 *E*; 1967/8 *S*; 1968/9 *T, E, S, W*; 1969/70 *Rus, S, E, W*; 1970/1 *Sp, C* (2), *E, S, W*; 1971/2 *Rus, Sp*; 1972/3 *Bulg*; 1973/4 *Port*; 1976/7 *Holl, G, Bel*; (Fulham) 1977/8 *Ic, Holl*.

Bingham, W. (56) (Sunderland) 1950/1 *F*; 1951/2 *S, E, W*; 1952/3 *E, S, F, W*; 1953/4 *S, E, W*; 1954/5 *E, S, W*; 1955/6 *S, E, W*; 1956/7 *E, S, W, It, Port* (2); 1957/8 *S, E, It, W, Czecho, Arg, G, It, Czecho, F*; 1958/9 (Luton Town) *E, S, W, Sp*; 1959/60 *S, E, W*; 1960/1 (Everton) *E, G, S, It, Gr, G*; 1961/2 *Gr, E*; 1962/3 *Pol, E, S, Pol, Sp*; 1963/4 (Port Vale) *S, Sp, E*.

Blair, R. (5) (Oldham Athletic) 1974/5 *Swdn, S, W*; 1975/6 *Swdn, Isr*.

Blanchflower, D. (54) (Barnsley) 1949/50 *S, W*; 1950/1 *E, S, F*; 1951/2 (Aston Villa) *W*; 1952/3 *E, S, F, W*; 1953/4 *S, E, W*; 1954/5 *E, S* (Tottenham Hotspur), *W;* 1955/6 *S, E, W*; 1956/7 *E, S, W, It, Port*; 1957/8 *S, E, It* (2); *W, Czecho, Arg, Czecho, F*; 1958/9 *E, S, W, Sp*; 1959/60 *S, E, W*; 1960/1 *F, G, S, W, G*; 1961/2 *S, Gr, E, W, Holl*; 1962/3 *Pol, E, S, Pol*.

Blanchflower, J. (11) (Manchester United) 1953/4 *W*; 1954/5 *E, S*; 1955/6 *S.W*; 1956/7 *E, S*; 1957/8 *S, E, It* (2).

Bowler, G. (4) (Hull City) 1949/50 *S, E, W, G*.

Braithwaite, R. (10) (Linfield) 1961/2 *W*; 1962/3 *Pol, Sp* (Middlesbrough) 1963/4 *W, U*; 1964/5 *E, Switz* (2), *S, Holl*.

Brennan, R. (5) (Luton Town) 1948/9 *W*; 1949/50 (Birmingham City) *S, E, W*, (Fulham); 1950/1 *E*.

Briggs, R. (2) (Manchester United) 1961/2 *W*; 1964/5 (Swansea) *Holl*.

Brotherston, N. (16) (Blackburn Rovers) 1979/80 *S, E, W, Au, Au, Au;* 1980/81 *Swdn, Port;* 1981/2 *S, Isr, F, E, S, W, Hon, Aust*.

Bruce, W. (2) (Glentoran) 1960/1 *S*; 1966/7 *W*.

Campbell, J. (2) (Fulham) 1950/1 *E, S*.

Campbell, R. (2) (Crusaders) 1962/3 *W*; 1964/5 *Switz*.

Cambell, R.M. (2) (Bradford C) 1981/2 *S, W*.

Campbell, W. (6) (Dundee) 1967/8 *S, E*; 1968/9 *T*; 1969/70 *Rus, S, W*.

Carey, J. (7) (Manchester United) 1946/7 *E, S, W*; 1947/8 *E*; 1948/9 *E, S, W*.

Casey, T. (11) (Newcastle United) 1954/5 *W*; 1955/6 *W*; 1956/7 *E, S, W, It, Port*; 1957/8 *G, F*; 1958/9 (Portsmouth) *E, Sp*.

Caskey, A. (6) (Derby County) 1978/9 *Bulg, E, Bulg, E*; 1979/80 *E;* 1981/2 (Tulsa Roughnecks) F.

Cassidy, T. (25) (Newcastle United) 1970/1 *E*; 1971/2 *Rus*; 1973/4 *Bulg, S, E, W*; 1974/5 *N*; 1975/6 *S, E, W*; 1976/7 *G*; 1979/80 *E, Eire, Isr, S, E, W, Au, Au, Au;* 1980/81 *Swdn, Port;* 1981/2 (Burnley) *Isr, Sp.*
Cleary, J. (2) (Glentoran) 1981/2 *S, W.*
Clements, D. (48) (Coventry City) 1964/5 *Holl, W*; 1965/6 *Mex*; 1966/7 *S, W*; 1967/8 *S, E;* 1968/9 *T* (2), *S, W;* 1969/70 *Rus* (2), *S, E, W;* 1970/1 *Sp, C, E, S, W;* 1971/2 (Sheffield Wednesday) *Rus* (2), *Sp, S, E, W*; 1972/3 *Bulg, C, Port, C, E, S, W*; (Everton) 1973/4 *Bulg, Port, S, E, W*; 1974/5 *N, Y, E, S, W*; 1975/6 *Swdn, Y, E, W.*
Cochrane, A. (20) (Coleraine) 1975/6 *S;* (Burnley) 1978/9 *Eire, D, Bulg, E, Bulg,* (Middlesbrough) *E*; 1979/80 *Isr, E, W, Au, Au, Au;* 1980/81 *Swdn, Port, S, Port, S, Swdn;* 1981/2 *F, E.*
Cochrane, D. (10) (Leeds United) 1946/7 *E, S, W*; 1947/8 *S, E, W*; 1948/9 *S, W*; 1949/50 *S, E.*
Cowan, J. (1) (Newcastle United) 1969/70 *E.*
Coyle, F. (3) (Coleraine) 1955/6 *S, E*; 1957/8 (Nottingham Forest) *Arg.*
Coyle, R. (3) (Sheffield Wednesday) 1972/3 *Port, W*; 1973/4 *Bulg.*
Craig, D. (25) (Newcastle United) 1966/7 *W*; 1967/8 *W*; 1968/9 *T* (2), *E, S, W*; 1969/70 *Rus, S, E, W*; 1970/1 *Sp, C* (2), *S*; 1971/2 *Rus, S*; 1972/3 *C* (2), *E, S, W*; 1973/4 *Bulg, Port*; 1974/5 *N.*
Crossan, E. (3) (Blackburn Rovers) 1949/50 *S*; 1950/1 *E*; 1954/5 *W.*
Crossan, J. (23) (Rotterdam Sparta) 1959/60 *E*; 1962/3 (Sunderland) *Pol, W, Sp*; 1963/4 *S, Sp, E, W, U*; 1964/5 *E, Switz* (2), *S, Holl* (2), *W*; 1965/6 (Manchester City) *S, E, A, G*; 1966/7 *E, S*; 1967/8 (Middlesbrough) *S.*
Cunningham, W. (29) (St Mirren) 1950/1 *W*; 1952/3 *E*; 1953/4 *S*; 1954/5 *S*; 1955/6 *S, E, W*; 1956/7 (Leicester City) *E, S, W, It, Port*; 1957/8 *S, It, W, Czecho, Arg, G, Czecho, F*; 1958/9 *E, S, W*; 1959/60 *S, E, W*; 1960/1 (Dunfermline Athletic) *W, Holl.*
Cush, W. (25) (Glentoran) 1950/1 *E, S*; 1953/4 *S, E*; 1956/7 *W, It, Port*; 1957/8 *It* (Leeds United), *W, Czecho, Arg, F, Czecho, It, F*; 1958/9 *E, S, W, Sp*; 1959/60 *S, E, W*; 1960/1 (Portadown) *Gr, G*; 1961/2 *Gr.*

D'Arcy, S. (5) (Chelsea) 1951/2 *W*; 1952/3 *E,* (Brentford), *S, F, W.*
Dickson, D. (2) (Coleraine) 1972/3 *C, Port.*
Dickson, T. (1) (Linfield) 1956/7 *S.*
Dickson, W. (12) (Chelsea) 1950/1 *W, F*; 1951/2 *S, E, W*; 1952/3 *E, S, F, W*; (Arsenal) 1953/4 *E, W*; 1954/5 *E.*
Dixon, D. (2) (Coleraine) 1969/70 *S, W.*
Doherty, P. (6) (Derby County) 1946/7 *E* (Huddersfield Town), *W*; 1947/8 *E, W*; 1948/9 *S*; 1950/1 *S.*
Donaghy, M. (16) (Luton Town) 1979/80 *S, E, W;* 1980/81 *Swdn, Port, S;* 1981/2 *S, Isr, F, E, S, W, Y, Hon, Sp, F.*
Dougan, D. (41) (Portsmouth) 1957/8 *Czecho*; 1959/60 (Blackburn Rovers) *S*; 1960/1 *W, It, Gr*; 1962/3 (Aston Villa) *Pol, S, Pol*; 1965/6 (Leicester City) *S, E, A, W, G, Mex*; 1966/7 *E* (Wolverhampton Wanderers), *W*; 1967/8 *S, W*; 1968/9 *Isr, T, T, E, S, W*; 1969/70 *Rus* (2), *S, E*; 1970/1 *Sp, C* (2), *E, S, W*; 1971/2 *Rus* (2), *S, E, W*; 1972/3 *Bulg, C.*
Douglas, S. (1) (Belfast Celtic) 1946/7 *E.*
Dowd, D. (3) (Glentoran) 1972/3 *W*; 1974/5 (Sheffield Wednesday) *N, Swdn.*

Eglington, T. (6) (Everton) 1946/7 *S, W*; 1947/8 *S, E, W*; 1948/9 *E*.
Elder, A. (39) (Burnley) 1959/60 *W*; 1960/1 *E, G, S, W, Gr*; 1961/2 *S, Gr, E*; 1962/3 *Pol, E, S, Pol, W, Sp*; 1963/4 *W, U*; 1964/5 *W, Switz* (2), *S, Holl* (2), *W*; 1965/6 *S, E, A, W, Mex*; 1966/7 *E, S, W*; (Stoke City) 1967/8 *E, W*; 1968/9 *E, S, W*; 1969/70 *Rus*.

Farrell, P. (7) (Everton) 1946/7 *S, W*; 1947/8 *S, E, W*; 1948/9 *E, W*.
Feeney, A. (1) (Glentoran) 1975/6 *Isr*.
Feeney, J. (2) (Linfield) 1946/7 *S* (Swansea City); 1949/50 *E*.
Ferguson, W. (2) (Linfield) 1965/6 *Mex*; 1966/7 *E*.
Ferris, R. (3) (Birmingham City) 1949/50 *S*; 1950/1 *F*; 1951/2 *S*.
Finney, T. (14) (Sunderland) 1974/5 *N, E, S, W*; 1975/6 *N, Y, S*; (Cambridge United) 1979/80 *E, Isr, S, E, W, Au, Au*.
Forde, T. (4) (Ards) 1958/9 *Sp*; 1960/1 *E, G, S*.

Gaston, R. (1) (Coleraine) 1968/9 *Isr*.
Gallogly, C. (2) (Huddersfield Town) 1950/1 *E, S*.
Gorman, W. (4) (Brentford) 1946/7 *E, S, W*; 1947/8 *W*.
Graham, R. (13) (Doncaster Rovers) 1950/1 *W, F*; 1951/2 *S, E, W*; 1952/3 *S, F*; 1953/4 *E, W*; 1954/5 *S, W*; 1955/6 *E*; 1958/9 *E*.
Gregg, H. (24) (Doncaster Rovers) 1953/4 *W*; 1956/7 *E, S, W, It, Port*; 1957/8 *E* (Manchester United) *W, Czecho, Arg, G, F, It*; 1958/9 *E, W*; 1959/60 *S, E, W*; 1960/1 *E, S*; 1961/2 *S, Gr*; 1963/4 *S, E*.

Hamilton, B. (50) (Linfield) 1968/9 *T*; 1970/1 *C* (2), *E, S, W*; 1971/2 (Ipswich Town) *Rus* (2), *Sp*; 1972/3 *Bulg, C, Port, C, E, S, W*; 1973/4 *Bulg, S, E, W*; 1974/5 *N, Swdn, Y, E*; 1975/6 *Swdn, N, Y*, (Everton) *Isr, S, E, W*; 1976/7 *Holl, G, Bel, E, S, W, Ic*; 1977/8 *S, E, W*; (Millwall) 1978/9 *Eire, Bulg, Bulg*, (Swindon) *S, E, W, D, Au, Au*.
Hamilton, W. (21) (Queens Park Rangers) 1977/8 *S*; 1979/80 (Burnley) *S, E, W, Au, Au;* 1980/81 *Swdn, Port, S, Port, S, Swdn;* 1981/2 *S, Isr, E, W, Y, Hon, Sp, Aust, F*.
Harkin, T. (5) (Southport) 1967/8 *W*; 1968/9 *T, W*; 1969/70 *Rus*; 1970/1 *Sp*.
Harvey, M. (34) (Sunderland) 1960/1 *It*; 1961/2 *Holl*; 1962/3 *W, Sp*; 1963/4 *S, Sp, E, W, U*; 1964/5 *W, Switz* (2), *E, S, Holl* (2), *A*; 1965/6 *S, E, A, W, G, Mex*; 1966/7 *E, S*; 1967/8 *E, W*; 1968/9 *Isr, T, T, E*; 1969/70 *Rus*; 1970/1 *C, W*.
Hatton, S. (2) (Linfield) 1962/3 *Pol, S*.
Healy, P. (3) (Coleraine) 1981/2 *S, W, Hon*.
Hegan, D. (7) (West Bromwich Albion) 1969/70 *Rus*; 1971/2 (Wolverhampton Wanderers) *Rus, S, E, W*; 1972/3 *Bulg, C*.
Hill, J. (6) (Norwich City) 1958/9 *W*; 1959/60 *W*; 1960/1 *G* (Everton); 1963/4 *S, Sp, E*.
Hinton, E. (7) (Fulham) 1946/7 *S, W*; 1947/8 *S, E, W* (Millwall); 1950/1 *W, F*.
Hughes, W. (1) (Bolton Wanderers) 1950/1 *W*.
Humphries, W. (13) (Ards) 1961/2 *W* (Coventry City) *Holl*; 1962/3 *Pol, E, S, W, Sp*; 1963/4 *S, Sp, E*; 1964/5 *S, Holl, W*.
Hunter, A. (53) (Blackburn Rovers) 1969/70 *Rus*; 1970/1 *C* (2), *E, S, W*; 1971/2

(Ipswich Town) *Rus* (2), *Sp, S, E, W*; 1972/3 *Bulg, C, Port, C, E, S, W*; 1973/4 *Bulg, S, E, W*; 1974/5 *N, Swdn, Y, E, S; W*; 1975/6 *Swdn, N, Y, Isr, S, E, W*; 1976/7 *Holl, G, Bel, E, S, W, Ic*; 1977/8 *Ic, Holl, Bel*; 1978/9 *Eire, D, S, W, D*; 1979/80 *E, Eire*.

Irvine, R. (8) (Linfield) 1961/2 *Holl*; 1962/3 *Pol, E, S, Pol, W, Sp*; (Stoke City) 1964/5 *W*.

Irvine, W. (22) (Burnley) 1962/3 *W, Sp*; 1964/5 *Switz, S, Holl* (2), *W*; 1965/6 *S, E, A, W, Mex*; 1966/7 *E, S*; 1967/8 *E, W*; 1968/9 (Preston North End) *Isr, T, E*; (Brighton & Hove Albion) 1971/2 *S, E, W*.

Jackson, T. (35) (Everton) 1968/9 *Isr, E, S, W;* 1969/70 *Rus* (2); 1970/1 (Nottingham Forest) *Sp;* 1971/2 *S, E, W;* 1972/3 *C, E, S, W;* 1973/4 *Bulg, Port, S, E, W;* 1974/5 *N, Swdn, Y, E, S, W*; 1975/6 *Swdn, N, Y*; 1976/7 *Holl, G, Bel, E, S, W, Ic*.

Jamison, A. (1) (Glentoran) 1975/6 *N*.

Jennings, P. (95) (Watford) 1963/4 *W, U*; 1964/5 (Tottenham Hotspur) *E, Switz* (2), *S, Holl, A*; 1965/6 *S, E, A, W, G*; 1966/7 *E, S*; 1967/8 *S, E, W*; 1968/9 *Isr, T* (2), *E, S, W*; 1969/70 *Rus* (2), *S, E*; 1970/1 *C* (2), *E, S, W*; 1971/2 *Rus, Sp, S, E, W*; 1972/3 *Bulg, C, Port, E, S, W*; 1973/4 *Port, S, E, W*; 1974/5 *N, Swdn, Y, E, S, W*; 1975/6 *Swdn, N, Y, Isr, S, E, W*; 1976/7 *Holl, G, Bel, E, S, W, Ic*; (Arsenal) 1977/8 *Ic, Holl, Bel*; 1978/9 *Eire, D, Bulg, E, Bulg, E, S, W, D*; 1979/80 *E, Eire, Isr;* 1980/81 *S, Port, S, Swdn;* 1981/2 *S, Isr, E, W, Y, Hon, Sp, F*.

Johnston, W. (1) (Glentoran) 1961/2 *W*.

Johnston, W. (1) (Oldham Athletic) 1965/6 *Mex*.

Jones, J. (4) (Glenavon) 1955/6 *W*; 1956/7 *E, S, W*.

Keane, T. (1) (Swansea City) 1948/9 *S*.

Keith, R. (23) (Newcastle United) 1957/8 *E, W, Czecho, Arg, G, Czecho, F*; 1958/9 *It, E, S, W, Sp*; 1959/60 *S, E*; 1960/1 *E, G, S, W, It, Gr, G*; 1961/2 *W, Holl*.

Kelly, H. (4) (Fulham) 1949/50 *E, W* (Southampton); 1950/1 *E, S*.

Kelly, P. (1) (Barnsley) 1949/50 *S*.

Lawther, I. (4) (Sunderland) 1959/60 *W*; 1960/1 *It*; 1961/2 (Blackburn Rovers) *S, Holl*.

Lockhart, N. (8) (Linfield) 1946/7 *E*; 1949/50 (Coventry City) *W*; 1950/1 *W*; 1951/2 *W*; 1953/4 (Aston Villa) *S, E*; 1954/5 *W*; 1955/6 *W*.

Lutton, B. (5) (Wolverhampton Wanderers) 1969/70 *S, E*; 1972/3 (West Ham United) *S, W*; 1973/4 *Port*.

Magill, E. (25) (Arsenal) 1961/2 *S, Gr, E*; 1962/3 *Pol, E, S, Pol, W, Sp*; 1963/4 *S, Sp, E, W, U*; 1964/5 *E, Switz* (2), *S, Holl*; 1965/6 *S, E*, (Brighton & Hove Albion) *A, W, G, Mex*.

Martin, C. (6) (Glentoran) 1946/7 *S*; 1947/8 (Leeds United) *S, E, W*; 1948/9 (Aston Villa) *E*; 1949/50 *W*.

McAdams, W. (16) (Manchester City) 1953/4 *W*; 1954/5 *S*; 1956/7 *E, S*; 1957/8 *S, It*; 1960/1 (Bolton Wanderers) *E, G, S, W, It, Gr, G*; 1961/2 (Leeds United) *Gr, E, Holl*.

McAlinden, J. (2) (Portsmouth) 1946/7 *E*; 1948/9 (Southend United) *E*.

McCabe, J. (6) (Leeds United) 1948/9 *S, W*; 1949/50 *E*; 1950/1 *W*; 1952/3 *W*; 1953/4 *S*.

McCavana, T. (3) (Coleraine) 1954/5 *S*; 1955/6 *S, E*.

McCleary, J. W. (1) (Cliftonville) 1954/5 *W.*
McClelland, J. (6) (Arsenal) 1960/1 *G, W, It, Gr, G*; 1965/6 (Fulham) *Mex.*
McClelland, J. (15) (Mansfield Town) 1979/80 *S, Au, Au, Au;* 1980/81 *Swdn, S, S, Swdn;* 1981/2 (Rangers) *S, W, Y, Hon, Sp, Aust, F.*
McCourt, F. (6) (Manchester City) 1951/2 *E, W*; 1952/3 *E, S, F, W.*
McCreery, D. (44) (Manchester United) 1975/6 *S, E, W*; 1976/7 *Holl, G, Bel, E, S, W, Ic*; 1977/8 *Ic, Holl, Bel, S, E, W*; 1978/9 *Eire, D, Bulg, E, Bulg, W, D*; 1979/80 (Q.P.R.) *E, Eire, S, E, W, Au, Au;* 1980/81 *Swdn, Port, S, Port* (Tulsa Roughnecks), *Swdn;* 1981/2 *S, Isr, F, E, Y, Hon, Sp, Aust, F.*
McCrory, S. (1) (Southend United) 1957/8 *E.*
McCullough, W. (10) (Arsenal) 1960/1 *It*; 1962/3 *Sp*; 1963/4 *S, Sp, E, W, U*; 1964/5 *E, Switz*; 1966/7 (Millwall) *E.*
McCurdy, C. (1) (Linfield) 1979/80 *Au.*
McFaul, I. (6) (Linfield) 1966/7 *E*; 1969/70 (Newcastle United) *W*; 1970/1 *Sp*; 1971/2 *Rus*; 1972/3 *C*; 1973/4 *Bulg.*
McGarry, J. K. (3) (Cliftonville) 1950/1 *S, W, E.*
McGrath, R. (21) (Tottenham Hotspur) 1973/4 *S, E, W*; 1974/5 *N*; 1975/6 *Isr;* (Manchester United) 1976/7 *Holl, G, Bel, E, S, W, Ic*; 1977/8 *Ic, Holl, Bel, S, E, W*; 1978/9 *Bulg, E, E.*
McIlroy, J. (53) (Burnley) 1951/2 *S, E, W*; 1952/3 *E, S, W*; 1953/4 *S, E, W*; 1954/5 *E, S, W*; 1955/6 *S, E, W*; 1956/7 *E, S, W, It, Port*; 1957/8 *S, E, It, W, Czecho, Arg, Czecho, F, It*; 1958/9 *E, S, W, Sp*; 1959/60 *S, W, E*; 1960/1 *E, G, W, Gr, G*; 1961/2 *S, Gr, E, Holl*; 1962/3 *Pol, E, S, Pol, W*; 1965/6 (Stoke City) *S, E, A.*
McIlroy, S. (61) (Manchester United) 1971/2 *Sp, S*; 1973/4 *S, E, W*; 1974/5 *N, Swdn, Y, E, S, W*; 1975/6 *Swdn, N, Y, S, E, W*; 1976/7 *Hol, Bel, E, S, W, Ic*; 1977/8 *Ic, Holl, Bel, S, E, W*; 1978/9 *Eire, D, Bulg, E, Bulg, E, S, W, D*; 1979/80 *E, Eire, Isr, S, E, W;* 1980/81 *Swdn, Port, S, Port, S, Swdn;* 1981/2 (Stoke C.) *F, E, S, W, Y, Hon, Sp, Aust, F.*
McKeag, W. (2) (Glentoran) 1967/8 *S, W.*
McKenna, J. (7) (Huddersfield Town) 1949/50 *S, E, W*; 1950/1 *E, S, F*; 1951/2 *E.*
McKenzie, R. (1) (Airdrieonians) 1966/7 *W.*
McKinney, W. (1) (Falkirk) 1965/6 *G.*
McLaughlin, J. (12) (Shrewsbury Town) 1961/2 *S, Gr, E, W*; 1962/3 *W*, (Swansea City); 1963/4 *W, U*; 1964/5 *E, Switz* (2); 1965/6 *W.*
McMichael, A. (39) (Newcastle United) 1949/50 *S, E*; 1950/1 *E, S, F*; 1951/2 *S, E, W*; 1952/3 *E, S, F, W*; 1953/4 *S, E, W*; 1954/5 *E, W*; 1955/6 *W*; 1956/7 *E, S, W, It, Port*; 1957/8 *E, S, It, W, Czecho, Arg, G, Czecho, F, It*; 1958/9 *S, W, Sp*; 1959/60 *S, E, W.*
McMillan, S. (2) (Manchester United) 1962/3 *E, S.*
McMordie, E. (21) (Middlesbrough) 1968/9 *Isr, T, T, E, S, W*; 1969/70 *Rus, S, E, W*; 1970/1 *C* (2) *E, S, W*; 1971/2 *Rus, Sp, S, E, W*; 1972/3 *Bulg.*
McMorran, E. (15) (Belfast Celtic) 1946/7 *E* (Barnsley); 1950/1 *E, S, W*; 1951/2 *E, S, W*; 1952/3 *E, S, F* (Doncaster Rovers), *W*; 1953/4 *E*; 1955/6 *W*; 1956/7 *It, Port.*
McParland, P. (34) (Aston Villa) 1953/4 *W*; 1954/5 *E, S*; 1955/6 *S, E*; 1956/7 *E, S, W, Port*; 1957/8 *S, E, It, W, Czecho, Arg, G, Czecho, F, It*; 1958/9 *E, S, W, Sp*; 1959/60 *S, F, W*; 1960/1 *E, G, S, W, It, Gr, G*; 1961/2 (Wolverhampton Wanderers) *Holl.*

Montgomery, F. (1) (Coleraine) 1954/5 *E.*
Moore, C. (1) (Glentoran) 1948/9 *W.*
Moreland, A. (5) (Derby County) 1978/9 *Bulg, E, S*; 1979/80 *E, Eire.*
Morgan, S. (18) (Port Vale) 1971/2 *Sp*; 1972/3 *Bulg, Port, C, E, S, W*; 1973/4 (Aston Villa) *Bulg, Port, S, E*; 1974/5 *Swdn*; 1975/6 *Swdn, N, Y* (Brighton & Hove Albion), *S, W*; 1978/9 *D.*

Napier, R. (1) (Bolton Wanderers) 1965/6 *G.*
Neill, T. (58) (Arsenal) 1960/1 *It, Gr, G*; 1961/2 *S, Gr, E, W*; 1962/3 *E, Pol, W, Sp*; 1963/4 *S, Sp, E, W, U*; 1964/5 *E, Switz, S, Holl* (2), *W*; 1965/6 *S, E, A, W, G, Mex*; 1966/7 *S, W*; 1967/8 *S, E*; 1968/9 *Isr, T, T, E, S, W*; 1969/70 *Rus* (2), *S, E, W*; 1970/1 *Sp, C*; 1971/2 (Hull City) *Rus* (2), *Sp, S, E, W*; 1972/3 *Bulg, C, Port, C, E, S, W.*
Nelson, S. (51) (Arsenal), 1969/70 *E, W*; 1970/1 *Sp, C, E, S, W*; 1971/2 *Rus* (2), *Sp, S, E, W*; 1972/3 *Bulg, C, Port*; 1973/4 *S, E*; 1974/5 *Swdn, Y*; 1975/6 *Swdn, N, Isr, E*; 1976/7 *G, Bel, W, Ic*; 1977/8 *Ic, Holl, Bel*; 1978/9 *Eire, D, Bulg, E, Bulg, E, S, W, D*; 1979/80 *E, Eire, Isr;* 1980/81 *S, Port, S, Swdn;* 1981/2 (Brighton) *E, S, Sp, Aust.*
Nicholl, C. (47) (Aston Villa) 1974/5 *Swdn, Y, E, S, W*; 1975/6 *Swdn, N, Y, S, E, W*; 1976/7 *W*; 1977/8 *Bel, S, E, W* (Southampton); 1978/9 *Eire, Bulg, E, Bulg, E, W*; 1979/80 *E, Eire, Isr, S, E, W, Au, Au, Au* 1980/81 *Swdn, Port, S, Port, S, Swdn;* 1981/2 *S, Isr, F, E, W, Y, Hon, Sp, Aust, F.*
Nicholl, J. (47) (Manchester United) 1975/6 *Isr, W*; 1976/7 *Holl, Bel, E, S, W, Ic*; 1977/8 *Ic, Holl, Bel, S, E, W*; 1978/9 *Eire, D, Bulg, E, Bulg, E, S, W, D*; 1979/80 *Eire, Isr, S, E, W, Au, Au, Au;* 1980/81 *Swdn, Port, S, Port, S, Swdn;* 1981/2 *S, Isr, F, E,* (Toronto Blizzards) *W, Y, Hon, Sp, Aust, F.*
Nicholson, J. (40) (Manchester United) 1960/1 *S, W*; 1961/2 *Gr, E, W, Holl*; 1962/3 *Pol, E, S, Pol*; 1964/5 (Huddersfield Town) *Holl* (2), *W*; 1965/6 *S, E, A, W, Mex*; 1966/7 *S, W*; 1967/8 *S, E, W*; 1968/9 *T, T, E, S, W*; 1969/70 *Rus* (2), *S, E, W*; 1970/1 *C* (2), *E, S, W*; 1971/2 *Rus* (2).

O'Doherty, A. (3) (Coleraine) 1969/70 *S, E, W.*
O'Driscoll, J. (3) (Swansea City) 1948/9 *E, S, W.*
O'Kane, L. (20) (Nottingham Forest) 1969/70 *E, W, S*; 1970/1 *Sp, E, S, W*; 1971/2 *Rus* (2); 1972/3 *Port, C*; 1973/4 *Bulg, Port, S, E, W*; 1974/5 *N, Swdn, E, S.*
O'Neill, J. (1) (Sunderland) 1961/2 *W.*
O'Neill, J. (18) (Leicester City) 1979/80 *Isr, S, E, W, Au, Au, Au;* 1980/81 *Port, S, Port, S, Swdn;* 1981/2 *S, Isr, F, E, S, F.*
O'Neill, M. (49) (Distillery) 1971/2 *Rus,* (Nottingham Forest), *Sp, W*; 1972/3 *Port, C, E, S, W*; 1973/4 *Bulg, Port, E, W*; 1974/5 *Swdn, Y, E, S*; 1975/6 *Y*; 1976/7 *E, S*; 1977/8 *Ic, Holl, S, E, W*; 1978/9 *Eire, D, Bulg, E, Bulg, D*; 1979/80 *Eire, Isr, Au, Au, Au;* 1980/81 *Swdn, Port,* (Norwich C.) *Port, S, Swdn;* 1981/2 (Manchester C.) *S,* (Norwich C.) *F, E, S, Y, Hon, Sp, Aust, F.*

Parke, J. (13) (Hibernian) 1963/4 *S, Sp, E*; 1964/5 (Sunderland) *Switz, S, Holl* (2), *W*; 1965/6 *G*; 1966/7 *E, S*; 1967/8 *S, E.*
Peacock, R. (31) (Glasgow Celtic) 1951/2 *S*; 1952/3 *F*; 1953/4 *W*; 1954/5 *E, S*; 1955/6 *S, E*; 1956/7 *W, It, Port*; 1957/8 *S, E, It, W, Czecho, Arg, G, Czecho, It*; 1958/9 *E, S, W*; 1959/60 *S, E*; 1960/1 *E, G, S, It, Gr, G*; 1961/2 *S.*
Platt, J. (15) (Middlesbrough) 1975/6 *Isr*; 1977/8 *S, E, W*; 1979/80 *S, E, W, Au, Au, Au;* 1980/81 *Swdn, Port;* 1981/2 *F, S, Aust.*

Rafferty, W. (1) (Wolverhampton Wanderers) 1979/80 *E.*
Rice, P. (49) (Arsenal) 1968/9 *Isr*; 1969/70 *Rus*; 1970/1 *E, S, W*; 1971/2 *Rus, Sp, S, E, W*; 1972/3 *Bulg, C, E, S, W*; 1973/4 *Bulg, Port, S, E, W*; 1974/5 *N, Y, E, S, W*; 1975/6 *Swdn, N, Y, Isr, S, E, W*; 1976/7 *Holl, G, Bel, E, S, Ic*; 1977/8 *Ic, Holl, Bel*; 1978/9 *Eire, D, E, E, S, W, D*; 1979/80 *E.*
Ross, E. (1) (Newcastle United) 1968/9 *Isr.*
Russell, A. (1) (Linfield) 1946/7 *E.*
Ryan, R. (1) (West Bromwich Albion) 1949/50 *W.*

Scott, J. (2) (Grimsby Town) 1957/8 *Czecho, F.*
Scott, P. (8) (Everton) 1974/5 *W*; 1975/6 (York City) *Y, Isr, S, W*; 1977/8 *S, E, W.*
Sharkey, P. (1) (Ipswich Town) 1975/6 *S.*
Shields, J. (1) (Southampton) 1956/7 *S.*
Simpson, W. (12) (Glasgow Rangers) 1950/1 *W, F*; 1953/4 *S, E*; 1954/5 *E*; 1956/7 *It, Port*; 1957/8 *S, E, It, W*; 1958/9 *S.*
Sloan, A. (1) (Manchester United) 1978/9 *S.*
Sloan, D. (2) (Oxford) 1968/9 *Isr*; 1970/1 *Sp.*
Sloan, W. (1) (Arsenal) 1946/7 *W.*
Smyth, S. (9) (Wolverhampton Wanderers) 1947/8 *S, E, W*; 1948/9 *S, W*; 1949/50 *S, E, W* (Stoke City); 1951/2 *E.*
Smyth, W. (4) (Distillery) 1948/9 *E, S*; 1953/4 *S, E.*
Spence, D. (27) (Bury) 1974/5 *Y, E, S, W*; 1975/6 *Swdn, Isr, E, W, S*; (Blackpool) 1976/7 *Holl, G, E, S, W, Ic*; 1978/9 *Eire, D, E, E, S, W, D*; 1979/80 *Eire, Isr, Au;* 1980/81 (Southend U.) *Swdn;* 1981/82 *F.*
Stevenson, A. (3) (Everton) 1946/7 *S, W*; 1947/8 *S.*
Stewart, A. (6) (Glentoran) 1966/7 *W*; 1967/8 *S, E,* (Derby) *W*; 1968/9 *Isr. T.*
Stewart, I. (1) (Q.P.R.) 1981/2 *F.*
Stewart, P. (1) (Linfield) 1960/1 *W.*
Stewart, D. (1) (Hull City) 1977/8 *Bel.*

Todd, S. (9) (Burnley) 1966/7 *E*; 1967/8 *W*; 1968/9 *E, S, W*; 1969/70 *Rus, S*; 1970/1 *Sp* (Sheffield Wednesday), *C* (2).
Trainor, D. (1) (Crusaders) 1966/7 *W.*
Tulley, C. (10) (Glasgow Celtic) 1948/9 *E*; 1949/50 *E*; 1951/2 *S*; 1952/3 *E, S, F, W*; 1953/4 *S*; 1955/6 *E*; 1958/9 *Sp.*

Uprichard, N. (18) (Swindon Town) 1951/2 *S, E, W*; 1952/3 *E, S,* (Portsmouth) *F, W*; 1954/5 *E, S, W*; 1955/6 *S, E, W*; 1957/8 *S, It, Czecho*; 1958/9 *S, Sp.*

Whiteside, N. (5) (Manchester U.) 1981/2 *Y, Hon, Sp, Aust, F.*

SCOTLAND

Aird, J. (4) (Burnley) 1953/4 *N* (2), *Aust, U.*
Aitken, G. (8) (East Fife) 1948/9 *E, F;* 1949/50 *I, W, Switz;* 1952/3 (Sunderland) *W, I;* 1953/4 *E.*
Aitken, R. (5) (Celtic) 1979/80 *Per, Bel, W, E, Pol.*
Albiston, A. (1) (Manchester U.) 1981/2 *I.*
Allan, T. (2) (Dundee) 1973/4 *G, N.*
Anderson, J. (1) (Leicester City) 1953/4 *Fin.*
Archibald, S. (16) (Aberdeen) 1979/80 *Port, I, Pol, H;* 1980/81 (Tottenham H.) *Isr, I, Isr, I, E;* 1981/2 *I, Port, Holl, Sp, NZ, Braz, Rus.*
Auld, B. (3) (Celtic) 1958/9 *Holl, Port;* 1959/60 *W.*

Baird, H. (1) (Airdrieonians) 1955/6 *Aust.*
Baird, S. (7) (Rangers) 1956/7 *Y, Sp, Switz, G, Sp;* 1957/8 *I, F.*
Bannon, E. (1) (Heart of Midlothian) 1979/80 *Bel.*
Bauld, W. (3) (Heart of Midlothian) 1949/50 *E, Switz, Port.*
Baxter, J. (34) (Rangers) 1960/1 *I, Eire* (2), *Czecho;* 1961/2 *Czecho, I, W, Czecho, E, U;* 1962/3 *W, I, E, Aust, N, Eire, Sp;* 1963/4 *N, W, E, G;* 1964/5 *W, Fin, I* (Sunderland); 1965/6 *I, It, W, E, Port, Braz;* 1966/7 *W, E, Rus;* 1967/8 *W.*
Bell, W. (2) (Leeds United) 1965/6 *Port, Braz.*
Bett, J. (1) (Rangers) 1981/2 *Holl.*
Black, I. (1) (Southampton) 1947/8 *E.*
Blacklaw, A. (3) (Burnley) 1962/3 *N, Sp;* 1965/6 *It.*
Blackley, J. (7) (Hibernian) 1973/4 *Czecho, E, Bel, Z;* 1975/6 *Switz;* 1976/7 *W, Swdn.*
Blair, J. (1) (Blackpool) 1946/7 *W.*
Blyth, J. (2) (Coventry City) 1977/8 *Bulg, W.*
Bone, J. (1) (Norwich City) 1972/3 *D.*
Brand, R. (8) (Rangers) 1960/1 *I, Eire* (2), *Czecho;* 1961/2 *I, W, Czecho, U.*
Brazil, A. (9) (Ipswich Town) 1979/80 *Pol, H;* 1981/2 *Holl, Sp, I, W, E, NZ, Rus.*
Bremner, D. (1) (Hibernian) 1975/6 *Switz.*
Bremner, W. (54) (Leeds United) 1964/5 *Sp;* 1965/6 *Pol, It* (2), *E, Port, Braz;* 1966/7 *W, I, E;* 1967/8 *W, E;* 1968/9 *D, C, Aust, G, W, I, E, C;* 1969/70 *Eire, G, Aust;* 1970/1 *W, E;* 1971/2 *Port, Bel, Holl, I, W, E, Y, Czecho, Braz;* 1972/3 *D* (2), *E, I, E, Switz, Braz;* 1973/4 *Czecho, G, I, W, E, Bel, N, Z, Braz, Y;* 1974/5 *Sp* (2); 1975/6 *D.*
Brennan, F. (7) (Newcastle United) 1946/7 *W, I;* 1952/3 *W, I, E;* 1963/4 *I, E.*
Brogan, J. (4) (Celtic) 1970/1 *Port, W, I, E.*
Brown, A. (14) (East Fife) 1949/50 *Switz, Port, F;* (Blackpool) 1951/2 *US, D, Swdn;* 1952/3 *W;* 1953/4 *W, E, N* (2), *Fin, Aust, U.*
Brown, H. (3) (Partick Thistle) 1946/7 *W, Bel, Lux.*
Brown, J. (1) (Sheffield United) 1974/5 *Rus.*
Brown, R. (3) (Rangers) 1946/7 *I;* 1948/9 *I;* 1951/2 *E.*
Brown, W. (28) (Dundee) 1957/8 *F;* 1958/9 *W, I, E;* 1959/60 (Tottenham Hotspur) *I, N, Pol, Aust, H, T;* 1961/2 *Czecho, I, W, E;* 1962/3 *W, I, E, Aust;* 1963/4 *I, N, W;* 1964/5 *E, Sp, Pol, Fin;* 1965/6 *I, Pol, It.*
Brownlie, J. (7) (Hibernian) 1970/1 *Rus;* 1971/2 *Per, I, E;* 1972/3 *D* (2); 1975/6 *Ru.*

Buchan, M. (34) (Aberdeen) 1971/2 *Bel* (Manchester United) *W, Y, Port, Czecho, Braz;* 1972/3 *D (2), E;* 1973/4 *G, I, W, N, Braz, Y;* 1974/5 *E/Germ, Sp, Port;* 1975/6 *D, Ru;* 1976/7 *Fin, Czecho, Ch, Arg, Braz;* 1977/8 *E/Germ, W, I;* 1978/9 *Per, Ir, Holl, Aust, N, Port.*

Buckley, P. (3) (Aberdeen) 1953/4 *N;* 1954/5 *W, I.*

Burley, G. (11) (Ipswich Town) 1978/9 *W, I, E, N, Arg;* 1979/80 *Port, I, E, Pol;* 1981/2 *W, E.*

Burns, F. (1) (Manchester United) 1969/70 *Aust.*

Burns, K. (20) (Birmingham City) 1973/4 *G;* 1974/5 *E/Germ, Sp* (2); 1976/7 *Czecho, W, Swdn, W;* (Nottingham Forest) 1977/8 *I, W, E;* 1978/9 *Per, Ir, N;* 1979/80 *Per, Aust, Bel;* 1980/81 *Isr, I, W.*

Burns, T. (3) (Celtic) 1980/81 *I;* 1981/2 *Holl, W.*

Caldow, E. (40) (Rangers) 1956/7 *E, Sp, Switz, G, Sp;* 1957/8 *I, Switz, W, H, Pol, Y, Per, F;* 1958/9 *W, I, E, G, Holl, Port;* 1959/60 *I, W, E, Aust, H, T;* 1960/1 *W, I, E, Eire* (2), *Czecho;* 1961/2 *Czecho, I, W, Czecho, E, U;* 1962/3 *W, I, E.*

Callaghan, T. (2) (Dunfermline) 1969/70 *Eire, W.*

Campbell, R. (3) (Chelsea) 1949/50 *Switz, Port, F.*

Campbell, W. (7) (Morton) 1946/7 *I, Bel, Lux;* 1947/8 *E, Bel, Switz, F.*

Carr, W. (6) (Coventry City) 1969/70 *I, W, E;* 1970/1 *D;* 1971/2 *Per;* 1972/3 *D.*

Chalmers, S. (5) (Celtic) 1964/5 *W, Fin;* 1965/6 *Port, Braz;* 1966/7 *I.*

Clark, J. (4) (Celtic) 1965/6 *Braz;* 1966/7 *W, I, Rus.*

Clark, R. (16) (Aberdeen), 1967/8 *W, Holl;* 1969/70 *I;* 1970/1 *Port, W, I, E, D, Rus;* 1971/2 *Bel, I, W, E, Czecho, Braz;* 1972/3 *D, E.*

Collins, R. (31) (Celtic) 1950/1 *W, I, Aust;* 1954/5 *Y, Aust, H;* 1955/6 *I, W;* 1956/7 *W, E, Sp, Switz, G, Sp;* 1957/8 *I, Switz, W, H, Pol, Y, Par, F;* 1958/9 (Everton) *W, I, E, G, Holl, Port;* 1964/5 (Leeds United) *E, Sp, Pol.*

Colquhoun, E. (9) (Sheffield United) 1971/2 *Port, Holl, Per, Y, Czecho, Braz;* 1972/3 *D (2), E.*

Combe, R. (3) (Hibernian) 1947/8 *E, Bel, Switz.*

Conn, A. (1) (Heart of Midlothian) 1955/6 *Aust.*

Conn, A. (2) (Tottenham Hotspur) 1974/5 *I, E.*

Connachan, E. (2) (Dunfermline Athletic) 1961/2 *Czecho, U.*

Connelly, G. (2) (Celtic) 1973/4 *Czecho, G.*

Connolly, J. (1) (Everton) 1972/3 *Switz.*

Cooke, C. (16) (Dundee) 1965/6 *W, It, Port, Braz* (Chelsea); 1967/8 *E, Holl;* 1968/9 *C, Aust, G, W, I, C;* 1969/70 *Aust;* 1970/1 *Bel;* 1974/5 *Sp, Port.*

Cooper, D. (2) (Rangers) 1979/80 *Per, Aust.*

Cormack, P. (9) (Hibernian) 1965/6 *Braz;* 1969/70 *Eire, G, Aust;* (Nottingham Forest) 1970/1 *D, Port, W, E;* 1971/2 *Holl.*

Cowan, J. (25) (Morton) 1947/8 *Bel, Switz, F;* 1948/9 *W, E, F;* 1949/50 *I, W, E, Switz, Port, F;* 1950/1 *W, I, Aust* (2), *E, D, F, Bel;* 1951/2 *I, W, US, D, Swdn.*

Cowie, D. (20) (Dundee) 1952/3 *E, Swdn;* 1953/4 *I, W, N, Fin, Aust, U;* 1954/5 *W, I, Aust, H;* 1955/6 *W, Aust;* 1956/7 *I, W;* 1957/8 *H, Pol, Y, Par.*

Cox, S. (25) (Rangers) 1947/8 *F;* 1948/9 *E, F;* 1949/50 *I, W, E, Switz, Port, F;* 1950/1 *E* (2), *F, Bel, Aust;* 1951/2 *I, W, US, D, Swdn;* 1952/3 *W, I, E;* 1953/4 *I, W, E.*

Craig, J. (1) (Celtic) 1967/8 *W.*

Craig, J. (1) (Celtic) 1976/7 *Swdn.*

Craig, T. (1) (Newcastle United) 1975/6 *Switz.*
Crerand, P. (16) (Celtic) 1960/1 *Eire* (2), *Czecho;* 1961/2 *Czecho, I, W, Czecho, E, W;* 1962/3 *W, I;* 1963/4 *I;* 1964/5 (Manchester United) *E, Pol, Fin;* 1965/6 *Pol.*
Cropley, A. (2) (Hibernian) 1971/2 *Port, Bel.*
Cruickshank, J. (6) (Heart of Midlothian) 1963/4 *G;* 1969/70 *W, E;* 1970/1 *D, Bel;* 1975/6 *Ru.*
Cullen, M. (1) (Luton Town) 1955/6 *Aust.*
Cumming, J. (9) (Heart of Midlothian) 1954/5 *H, E, Port, Y;* 1959/60 *E, Pol, Aust, H, T.*
Cunningham, W. (8) (Preston North End) 1953/4 *N (2), Fin, Aust, U;* 1954/5 *W, H, E.*
Curran, H. (5) (Wolverhampton Wanderers) 1969/70 *Aust;* 1970/1 *I, E, D, Rus.*

Dalglish, K. (87) (Celtic) 1971/2 *Bel, Holl;* 1972/3 *D* (2), *E, W, I, E, Switz, Braz;* 1973/4 *Czecho* (2), *G (2), I, W, E, Bel, N, Z, Braz, Y;* 1974/5 *E/Germ, Sp* (2), *Swdn, Port, W, I, E, Ru;* 1975/6 *D* (2), *Ru, Switz, I, E;* 1976/7 *Fin, Czecho, W, Swdn, W, I, E, Ch, Arg, Braz;* (Liverpool) 1977/8 *E/Germ, Czecho, W* (2), *Bulg, I, E;* 1978/9 *Per, Ir, Holl, Aust, N, Port, W, I, E, N, Arg;* 1979/80 *Per, Aust, Bel, Bel, Port, I, W, E, Pol, H;* 1980/81 *Swdn, Port, Isr;* 1981/2 *Swdn, I, Holl, Sp, I, W, E, NZ, Braz.*
Davidson, J. (8) (Partick Thistle) 1953/4 *N (2), Aust, U;* 1954/5 *W, I, H, E.*
Dawson, A. (2) (Rangers) 1979/80 *Pol, H.*
Deans, D. (2) (Celtic) 1974/5 *E/Germ, Sp.*
Delaney, J. (4) (Manchester United) 1946/7 *E;* 1947/8 *I, W, E.*
Dick, J. (1) (West Ham United) 1958/9 *E.*
Dickson, A. (5) (Kilmarnock) 1969/70 *I, W, E;* 1970/1 *D, Rus.*
Docherty, T. (25) (Preston North End) 1951/2 *W;* 1952/3 *E, Swdn;* 1953/4 *N (2), Aust, U;* 1954/5 *W, H (2), F, Aust;* 1956/7 *E, Sp, Switz, G, Sp;* 1957/8 *I, Switz, W, E;* 1958/9 (Arsenal) *W, I, E.*
Donachie, W. (35) (Manchester City) 1971/2 *Per, I, E, Y, Czecho, Braz;* 1972/3 *D, E, W, I;* 1973/4 *I;* 1975/6 *Ru, I, W, E;* 1976/7 *Fin, Czecho, W, Swdn, W, I, E, Ch, Arg, Braz;* 1977/8 *E/Germ, W* (2), *Bulg, E;* 1978/9 *Ir, Holl, Aust, N, Port.*
Dougall, C. (1) (Birmingham City) 1946/7 *W.*
Dougan, R. (1) (Heart of Midlothian) 1949/50 *Switz.*
Doyle, J. (1) (Ayr United) 1975/6 *Ru.*
Duncan, A. (6) (Hibernian) 1974/5 *Port, W, I, E, Ru;* 1975/6 *D.*
Duncan, D. (3) (East Fife) 1947/8 *Bel, Switz, F.*
Duncanson, J. (1) (Rangers) 1946/7 *I.*

Evans, A. (4) (Aston Villa) 1981/2 *Holl, I, E, NZ.*
Evans, R. (48) (Celtic) 1948/9 *W, I, E, F;* 1949/50 *I, W, Switz, Port;* 1950/1 *Aust, E;* 1951/2 *I;* 1952/3 *Swdn;* 1953/4 *I, W, E, N, Fin;* 1954/5 *I, Port, Y, Aust, H;* 1955/6 *I, W, E, Aust;* 1956/7 *G, Sp;* 1957/8 *I, Switz, W, E, H, Pol, Y, Par, F;* 1958/9 *E, G, Holl, Port;* 1959/60 *I, W, E,* (Chelsea) *Pol, Aust, H, T.*
Ewing, T. (2) (Partick Thistle) 1957/8 *W, E.*

Farm, G. (10) (Blackpool) 1952/3 *W, I, E, Swdn;* 1953/4 *I, W, E;* 1958/9 *G, Holl, Port.*
Ferguson, R. (7) (Kilmarnock) 1965/6 *W, E, Holl, Port, Braz;* 1966/7 *W, I.*

Fernie, W. (11) (Celtic) 1953/4 *Fin, Aust, U;* 1954/5 *W, I;* 1956/7 *Y, W, E;* 1957/8 *Switz, W, Per.*
Flavell, R. (2) (Airdrieonians) 1946/7 *Bel, Lux.*
Fleming, C. (1) (East Fife) 1953/4 *I.*
Forbes, A. (14) (Sheffield United) 1946/7 *E, Bel, Lux;* 1947/8 *I, W,* (Arsenal); 1949/50 *E, Port, F;* 1950/51 *W, I, Aust;* 1951/52 *W, D, Swdn.*
Ford, D. (3) (Heart of Midlothian) 1973/4 *Czecho, G, W.*
Forrest, J. (1) (Motherwell) 1957/8 *E.*
Forrest, J. (2) (Rangers) 1965/6 *W, It.*
Forrest, J. (3) (Aberdeen) 1970/1 *Bel, D, Rus.*
Forsyth, A. (18) (Partick Thistle) 1971/2 *Y, Czecho, Braz;* 1972/3 *D,* (Manchester United), *E;* 1974/5 *E/Germ, Sp, I, Ru;* 1975/6 *D;* 1977/8 *Czecho, W* (2), *I, E;* 1978/9 *Per, Ir, Holl.*
Forsyth, C. (3) (Kilmarnock) 1963/4 *E;* 1964/5 *W, Fin.*
Forsyth, T. (14) (Motherwell) 1970/1 *D* (Rangers); 1973/4 *Czecho;* 1975/6 *Switz, I, W, E;* 1976/7 *Fin, Swdn, W, I, E, Ch, Arg, Braz.*
Fraser, D. (2) (West Bromwich Albion) 1967/8 *Holl;* 1968/9 *C.*
Fraser, W. (2) (Sunderland) 1954/5 *D, I.*

Gabriel, J. (1) (Everton) 1960/1 *W.*
Gardiner, W. (1) (Motherwell) 1957/8 *W.*
Gemmell, T. (2) (St Mirren) 1954/5 *Port, Y.*
Gemmell, T. (18) (Celtic) 1965/6 *E;* 1966/7 *W, I, E, Rus;* 1967/8 *I, E;* 1968/9 *Aust, D, G, W, I, E, C;* 1969/70 *Eire, G, E;* 1970/1 *Bel.*
Gemmill, A. (43) (Derby County) 1970/1 *Bel;* 1971/2 *Port, Holl, Per, I, W, E;* 1975/6 *D, Ru, I, W, E,* 1976/7 *Fin, Czecho, W* (2), *I, E, Ch, Arg, Braz;* (Nottingham Forest) 1977/8 *E/Germ, Bulg, I, W, E;* 1978/9 *Per, Ir, Holl, Aust, N, Port, N;* (Birmingham City) 1979/80 *Aust, Port, I, W, E;* 1980/81 *Swdn, Port, Isr, I.*
Gibson, D. (7) (Leicester City) 1962/3 *Aust, N, Eire, Sp;* 1963/4 *I;* 1964/5 *W, Fin, H.*
Gilzean, A. (22) (Dundee) 1963/4 *N, W, E, G;* 1964/5 *I* (Tottenham Hotspur), *Sp;* 1965/6 *I, Pol, It, W;* 1967/8 *W;* 1968/9 *C, Aust, G, W, E, C;* 1969/70 *G, Aust, I, E;* 1970/1 *Port.*
Glavin, R. (1) (Celtic) 1976/7 *Swdn.*
Glen, A. (2) (Aberdeen) 1955/6 *I, E.*
Govan, J. (6) (Hibernian) 1947/8 *W, E, Bel, Switz, F;* 1948/9 *I.*
Graham, G. (11) (Arsenal) 1971/2 *Port, Holl, I, Y, Czecho, Braz;* 1972/3 *D* (2), (Manchester United) *E, W, I.*
Graham, A. (10) (Leeds United) 1977/8 *E/Germ;* 1978/9 *Aust, N, W, I, E, N, Arg;* 1979/80 *Aust;* 1980/81 *W.*
Gray, A. (14) (Aston Villa) 1975/6 *Ru, Switz;* 1976/7 *Fin, Czecho;* 1978/9 *Aust, N, Arg;* (Wolverhampton Wanderers) 1979/80 *Port, E;* 1980/81 *Swdn, Port, Isr, I;* 1981/2 *Swdn.*
Gray, E. (12) (Leeds United) 1968/9 *E, C;* 1969/70 *G, Aust;* 1970/1 *W, I;* 1971/2 *Bel, Holl;* 1975/6 *W, E;* 1976/7 *Fin, W.*
Gray, F. (24) (Leeds United) 1975/6 *Switz;* 1978/9 *N, Port, W, I, E;* 1979/80 (Nottingham F.) *Bel;* 1980/81 *Swdn, Port, Isr, I, Isr* (Leeds U.) *W, I, E;* 1981/2 *Swdn, I, Port, Holl, Sp, W, NZ, Braz, Rus.*
Grant, J. (2) (Hibernian) 1958/9 *W, I.*

Green, A. (16) (Blackpool) 1970/1 *Bel, Port, I, E;* (Newcastle United) 1971/2 *W, E.*
Greig, J. (44) (Rangers) 1963/4 *E, G;* 1964/5 *W, Fin, I, E, Sp, Pol, Fin;* 1965/6 *I, Pol, It, W, It, E, Holl, Port, Braz;* 1966/7 *W, I, E;* 1967/8 *I, W, E, Holl;* 1968/9 *D, C, Aust, G, W, I, E, C;* 1969/70 *Eire, G, Aust, W, E;* 1970/1 *D, Bel, W, I, E;* 1975/6 *D.*

Haddock, H. (6) (Clydebank) 1954/5 *H* (2), *E, Port, Y;* 1957/8 *E.*
Haffey, H. (2) (Celtic) 1959/60 *E;* 1960/1 *E.*
Hamilton, A. (24) (Dundee) 1961/2 *W, Czecho, E, U;* 1962/3 *W, I, E, Aust, N, I, Eire;* 1963/4 *I, N, W, E, G;* 1964/5 *W, Fin, I, E, Sp, Pol, Fin;* 1965/6 *I, Pol.*
Hamilton, G. (5) (Aberdeen) 1946/7 *I;* 1950/1 *Bel, Aust;* 1953/4 *N* (2).
Hamilton, W. (1) (Hibernian) 1964/5 *Fin.*
Hansen, A. (17) (Liverpool) 1978/9 *W, Arg;* 1979/80 *Bel, Port;* 1980/81 *Swdn, Port, Isr;* 1981/2 *Swdn, I, Port, Sp, I, W, E, NZ, Braz, Rus.*
Hansen, J. (1) (Partick Thistle) 1971/2 *Bel.*
Harper, J. (4) (Aberdeen) 1972/3 *D* (2); 1975/6 *D;* 1978/9 *Ir.*
Hartford, A. (49) (West Bromwich Albion) 1971/2 *Per, W, E, Y, Czecho, Braz;* 1975/6 (Manchester City) *D, Ru, I;* 1976/7 *Czecho, W, Swdn, W, I, E, Ch, Arg, Braz;* 1977/8 *E/Germ, Czecho, W* (2), *Bulg, E;* 1978/9 *Per, Ir, Holl, Aust, N, Port, W, I, E, N, Arg;* 1979/80 (Everton) *Per, Bel;* 1980/81 *Isr, W, I, E;* 1981/2 *Swdn,* (Manchester C.) *I, Port, Sp, I, W, E, Braz.*
Harvey, D. (16) (Leeds United) 1972/3 *D;* 1973/4 *Czecho, G, I, W, E, Bel, Z, Braz, Y;* 1974/5 *E/Germ, Sp* (2); 1975/6 *D* (2); 1976/7 *Fin.*
Haughney, M. (1) (Celtic) 1953/4 *E.*
Hay, D. (27) (Celtic) 1969/70 *I, W, E;* 1970/1 *D, Bel, Port, W;* 1971/2 *Port, Bel, Holl;* 1972/3 *W, I, E, Switz, Braz;* 1973/4 *Czecho* (2), *G, I, W, E, Bel, N, Z, Braz, Y.*
Hegarty, P. (6) (Dundee United) 1978/9 *W, I, E, Arg;* 1979/80 *W, E.*
Henderson, J. (7) (Portsmouth) 1952/3 *Swdn;* 1953/4 *I, E, N;* 1955/6 *W;* 1958/9 (Arsenal) *W, I.*
Henderson, W. (29) (Rangers) 1962/3 *W, I, E, Aust, N, Eire, Sp;* 1963/4 *I, N, W, E, G;* 1964/5 *E, Sp, Pol, Fin;* 1965/6 *I, Pol, It, W, Holl;* 1966/7 *W, I;* 1967/8 *Holl;* 1968/9 *I, E, C;* 1969/70 *Eire, Czecho.*
Herd, D. (5) (Arsenal) 1958/9 *W, I, E;* 1960/1 *Eire*; 1970/1 *Port.*
Herd, G. (5) (Clydebank) 1957/8 *E;* 1959/60 *H, T;* 1960/1 *W, I.*
Herriot, J. (8) (Birmingham City) 1968/9 *D, C, W, I, E, C;* 1969/70 *Eire, G.*
Hewie, J. (19) (Charlton Athletic) 1955/6 *E, Aust;* 1956/7 *Y, I, W, E, Sp, Switz, G, Sp;* 1957/8 *W, Pol, Y, F;* 1958/9 *Holl, Port;* 1959/60 *I, W, Pol.*
Holt, D. (4) (Heart of Midlothian) 1962/3 *Aust, N, Eire, Sp.*
Holton, J. (15) (Manchester United) 1972/3 *W, I, E, Switz, Braz;* 1973/4 *Czecho, G, I, W, E, N, Z, Braz, Y;* 1974/5 *E/Germ.*
Hope, R. (2) (West Bromwich Albion) 1967/8 *Hol;* 1968/9 *D.*
Houliston, W. (3) (Queen of the South) 1948/9 *I, E, F.*
Houston, S. (1) (Manchester United) 1975/6 *D.*
Howie, H. (1) (Hibernian) 1948/9 *W.*
Hughes, J. (8) (Celtic) 1964/5 *Sp, Pol;* 1965/6 *I, It* (2); 1967/8 *E;* 1968/9 *Aust;* 1969/70 *Eire.*
Hughes, W. (1) (Sunderland) 1974/5 *Swdn.*
Humphries, W. (1) (Motherwell) 1951/2 *Swdn.*
Hunter, A. (3) (Kilmarnock) 1971/2 *Per;* 1972/3 (Celtic) *E;* 1973/4 *Czecho.*

Hunter, N. (3) (Motherwell) 1959/60 *H, T;* 1960/1 *W.*
Husband, J. (1) (Partick Thistle) 1946/7 *W.*
Hutchison, T. (17) (Coventry City) 1973/4 *Czecho* (2), *G* (2), *I, W, Bel, N, Z, Y;* 1974/5 *E/Germ, Sp* (2), *Port, E, Ru;* 1975/6 *D.*

Imlach, S. (4) (Nottingham Forest) 1957/8 *H, Pol, Y, F.*

Jackson, C. (8) (Rangers) 1974/5 *Swdn, Port, W;* 1975/6 *D, Ru, I, W, E.*
Jardine, A. (37) (Rangers) 1970/1 *D;* 1971/2 *Port, Bel, Holl;* 1972/3 *E, Switz, Braz;* 1973/4 *Czecho* (2), *G* (2), *I, W, E, Bel, N, Z, Braz, Y;* 1974/5 *E/Germ, Sp* (2), *Swdn, Port, W, I, E;* 1976/7 *Swdn, Ch;* 1977/8 *Czecho, W, I;* 1978/9 *Ir;* 1979/80 *Per, Aust, Bel* (2).
Jarvie, A. (3) (Airdrieonians) 1970/1 *Port, I, E.*
Johnston, W. (21) (Rangers) 1965/6 *Pol, W, E, Holl;* 1967/8 *W, E;* 1968/9 *I;* 1969/70 *I;* 1970/1 *D;* (West Bromwich Albion) 1976/7 *Swdn, W, I, Ch, Arg, Braz;* 1977/8 *E/Germ, Czecho, W* (2), *E.*
Johnstone, D. (15) (Rangers) 1972/3 *W, I, E, Switz, Braz;* 1974/5 *E/Germ, Swdn;* 1975/6 *Switz, I, E;* 1977/8 *Bulg, I, W;* 1978/9 *Per;* 1979/80 *Bel.*
Johnstone, J. (23) (Celtic) 1964/5 *W, Fin;* 1965/6 *E;* 1966/7 *W, Rus;* 1967/8 *W;* 1968/9 *Aust, G;* 1969/70 *G, E;* 1970/1 *D, E;* 1971/2 *Port, Bel, Holl, I, E;* 1973/4 *W, E, Bel, N;* 1974/5 *E/Germ, Sp.*
Johnstone, L. (2) (Clydebank) 1947/8 *Bel, Switz.*
Johnstone, R. (17) (Hibernian) 1950/1 *E, D, F;* 1951/2 *I, E;* 1952/3 *E, Swdn;* 1953/4 *W, E, N, Fin;* 1954/5 *I, H,* (Manchester City), *E;* 1955/6 *I, W, E.*
Jordan, J. (52) (Leeds United) 1972/3 *E, Switz, Braz;* 1973/4 *Czecho* (2), *G, I, W, E, Bel, N, Z, Braz, Y;* 1974/5 *E/Germ, Sp* (2); 1975/6 *I, W, E;* 1976/7 *Czecho, W, I, E;* (Manchester United) 1977/8 *E/Germ, Czecho, W, Bulg, I, E;* 1978/9 *Per, Ir, Holl, Aust, Port, W, I, E, N;* 1979/80 *Bel, I, W, E, Pol;* 1980/81 *Isr, W, E;* 1981/2 (AC Milan) *Swdn, Holl, W, E, Rus.*

Kelly, H. (1) (Blackpool) 1951/2 *US.*
Kelly, J. (2) (Barnsley) 1948/9 *W, I.*
Kennedy, J. (6) (Celtic) 1963/4 *W, E, G;* 1964/5 *W, Fin, I.*
Kennedy, S. (12) (Rangers) 1974/5 *Swdn, Port, W, I, E;* 1977/8 *Bulg, W, E;* 1978/9 *Per, Holl, Aust, Port.*
Kerr, A. (2) (Partick Thistle) 1954/5 *Aust, H.*

Law, D. (55) (Huddersfield Town) 1958/9 *W, I, Holl, Port;* 1959/60 *I, W,* (Manchester City) *E, Pol, Aust;* 1960/1 *I, E;* 1961/2 (Torino) *Czecho* (2), *E;* 1962/3 (Manchester United) *W, I, E, Aust, N, Eire, Sp;* 1963/4 *N, W, E, G;* 1964/5 *W, Fin, I, E, Sp, Pol, Fin;* 1965/6 *I, Pol, E;* 1966/7 *W, E, Rus;* 1967/8 *I;* 1968/9 *Aust, G, I;* 1971/2 *Per, I, W, E, Y, Czecho, Braz;* 1973/4 (Manchester City) *Czecho* (2), *G* (2), *I, Z.*
Lawrence, T. (3) (Liverpool) 1962/3 *Eire;* 1968/9 *G, W.*
Leggat, G. (18) (Aberdeen) 1955/6 *E;* 1956/7 *W;* 1957/8 *I, H, Pol, Y, Par;* 1958/9 (Fulham) *W, I, E, G, Holl;* 1959/60 *I, W, E, Pol, Aust, H.*
Lennox, R. (10) (Celtic) 1966/7 *I, E, Rus;* 1967/8 *W, E;* 1968/9 *D, W, Aust, G, C.*
Leslie, L. (5) (Airdrieonians) 1960/1 *W, I, Eire* (2), *Czecho.*
Liddell, W. (28) (Liverpool) 1946/7 *W, I;* 1947/8 *I, W, E;* 1949/50 *W, E, Port, F;*

1950/1 *W, I, Aust, E;* 1951/2 *I, W, E, US, D, Swdn;* 1952/3 *W, I, E;* 1953/4 *W;* 1954/5 *Port, Y, Aust, H;* 1955/6 *I.*

Linwood, A. (1) (Clydebank) 1949/50 *W.*

Little, A. (1) (Rangers) 1952/3 *Swdn.*

Logie, J. (1) (Arsenal) 1952/3 *I.*

Long, H. (1) (Clyde) 1946/7 *I.*

Lorimer, P. (21) (Leeds United) 1969/70 *Aust;* 1970/1 *W, I;* 1971/2 *I, W, E;* 1972/3 *D* (2), *E* (2); 1973/4 *G, E, Bel, N, Z, Braz, Y;* 1974/5 *Sp;* 1975/6 *D* (2), *Ru.*

Macari, L. (24) (Celtic) 1971/2 *W, E, Y, Czecho, Braz;* 1972/3 *D,* (Manchester United) *F, W, I, E;* 1974/5 *Swdn, Port, W, E, Ru;* 1976/7 *I, E, Ch, Arg;* 1977/8 *E/Germ, W, Bulg;* 1978/9 *Per, Ir.*

Macaulay, A. (7) (Brentford) 1946/7 *E* (Arsenal); 1947/8 *I, W, E, Bel, Switz, F.*

Macdougall, E. (7) (Norwich City) 1974/5 *Swdn, Port, W, I, E;* 1975/6 *D, Ru.*

Mackay, D. (22) (Heart of Midlothian) 1956/7 *Sp;* 1957/8 *F;* 1958/9 *W, I,* (Tottenham Hotspur) *E, G;* 1959/60 *I, W, Pol, Aust, H, T;* 1960/1 *W, I, E;* 1962/3 *E, Aust, N;* 1963/4 *I, N, W;* 1965/6 *I.*

Martin, F. (7) (Aberdeen) 1953/4 *N* (2), *Aust, U;* 1954/5 *N, E, N.*

Martin, N. (3) (Hibernian) 1964/5 *Pol, Fin;* 1965/6 (Sunderland) *It.*

Martis, J. (1) (Motherwell) 1960/1 *W.*

Mason, J. (7) (Third Lanark) 1948/9 *W, I, E;* 1949/50 *I;* 1950/1 *I, Bel, Aust.*

Masson, D. (17) (Queens Park Rangers) 1975/6 *I, W, E;* 1976/7 *Fin, Czecho, W, I, E, Ch, Arg, Braz;* (Derby County) 1977/8 *E/Germ, Czecho, W, I, E;* 1978/9 *Per.*

Mathers, D. (1) (Partick Thistle) 1953/4 *Fin.*

McBride, J. (2) (Celtic) 1966/7 *W, I.*

McCalliog, J. (5) (Sheffield Wednesday) 1966/7 *E, Rus;* 1967/8 *I;* 1968/9 *D;* 1970/1 (Wolverhampton Wanderers) *Port.*

McCann, A. (5) (Motherwell) 1958/9 *G;* 1959/60 *I, W, E;* 1960/1 *E.*

McCloy, P. (4) (Rangers) 1972/3 *Switz, Braz, W, I.*

McColl, I. (14) (Rangers) 1949/50 *E, F;* 1950/1 *W, I, Bel;* 1956/7 *Y, I, W, E, Sp, Switz, G;* 1957/8 *I, E.*

McCreadie, E. (23) (Chelsea) 1964/5 *E, Sp, Pol, Fin;* 1965/6 *I, Pol, W, It, Port;* 1966/7 *E, Rus;* 1967/8 *I, W, E, Holl;* 1968/9 *D, C, Aust, G, W, I, E, C.*

MacDonald, A. (1) (Rangers) 1975/6 *Switz.*

MacDonald, J. (2) (Sunderland) 1955/6 *I, W.*

McFarlane, W. (1) (Heart of Midlothian) 1946/7 *Lux.*

McGarr, E. (2) (Aberdeen) 1969/70 *Eire, Aust.*

McGarvey, A. (1) (St Mirren) 1978/9 *Arg.*

McGrain, D. (62) (Celtic) 1972/3 *W, I, E, Switz, Braz;* 1973/4 *Czecho* (2); *G, W, E, Bel, N, Z, Braz, Y;* 1974/5 *Sp, Swdn, Port, W, I, E, Ru;* 1975/6 *D* (2), *Switz, I, W, E;* 1976/7 *Fin, Czecho, W, Swdn, W, I, E, Ch, Arg, Braz;* 1977/8 *E/Germ, Czecho;* 1979/80 *Bel, Port, I, W, E, Pol, H;* 1980/81 *Swdn, Port, Isr, I, Isr, W, I, E;* 1981/2 *Swdn, Holl, Sp, I, E, NZ, Rus.*

McGrory, J. (3) (Kilmarnock) 1964/5 *Fin, I;* 1965/6 *Port, Pol, H.*

McKay, D. (13) (Celtic) 1958/9 *E, G, Holl, Port;* 1959/60 *E, Pol, Aust, H, T;* 1960/1 *W, I;* 1961/2 *Czecho, I.*

McKean, R. (1) (Rangers) 1975/6 *Switz.*

McKenzie, J. (9) (Partick Thistle) 1953/4 *W, E, N, Fin, Aust, U;* 1954/5 *H, E;* 1955/6 *Aust.*

McKinnon, R. (28) (Rangers) 1965/6 *It, W, It, E, Holl, Braz;* 1966/7 *W, I, E;* 1967/8 *I, W, E, Holl;* 1968/9 *D, C, Aust, G;* 1969/70 *Eire, G, Aust, I, W, E;* 1970/1 *D, Bel, Port, D, Rus.*
McLaren, A. (4) (Preston North End) 1946/7 *E, Bel, Lux;* 1947/8 *W.*
McLean, G. (1) (Dundee) 1967/8 *Holl.*
McLean, T. (5) (Kilmarnock) 1968/9 *D, W;* 1969/70 *I, W;* 1970/1 (Rangers) *D.*
McLeish, A. (16) (Aberdeen) 1979/80 *Port, I, W, E, Pol, H;* 1980/81 *Swdn, Isr, I, Isr, I, E;* 1981/2 *Swdn, Sp, I, Braz.*
McLeod, J. (4) (Hibernian) 1960/1 *E, Eire* (2), *Czecho.*
McLintock, F. (8) (Leicester City) 1962/3 *Eire, Sp;* 1964/5 (Arsenal) *I;* 1966/7 *Rus;* 1969/70 *I;* 1970/1 *W, I, E.*
McMillan, I. (6) (Airdrieonians and Rangers) 1951/2 *E, US, D;* 1954/5 *E;* 1955/6 *E;* 1960/1 *Czecho.*
McNaught, W. (5) (Raith Rovers) 1950/1 *W, I, Aust;* 1951/2 *E;* 1954/5 *I.*
McNeill, W. (28) (Celtic) 1960/1 *E, Eire* (2), *Czecho;* 1961/2 *Czecho, I, E, U;* 1962/3 *Eire, Sp;* 1963/4 *W, E, G;* 1964/5 *E, Sp, Pol, Fin;* 1965/6 *I, Pol;* 1966/7 *Rus;* 1967/8 *E;* 1968/9 *W, E, C;* 1969/70 *G;* 1971/2 *I, W, E.*
McPhail, J. (5) (Celtic) 1949/50 *W;* 1950/1 *W, I, Aust;* 1953/4 *I.*
McQueen, G. (30) (Leeds United) 1973/4 *Bel;* 1974/5 *Sp* (2), *Port, W, I, E, Ru;* 1975/6 *D;* 1976/7 *Czecho, W* (2), *I, E;* (Manchester United) 1977/8 *E/Germ, Czecho, W* (2), *Bulg, I;* 1978/9 *Aust, N, Port, I, E, N;* 1979/80 *Per, Aust, Bel;* 1980/81 *W.*
Millar, W. (6) (Celtic) 1946/7 *W, E, Bel, Lux;* 1947/8 *I, W.*
Miller, J. (2) (Rangers) 1962/3 *Aust, Eire.*
Miller, W. (19) (Aberdeen) 1974/5 *Ru;* 1977/8 *Bulg;* 1979/80 *Bel, W, E, Pol, H;* 1980/81 *Swdn, Port, Isr, I, W, I, E;* 1981/2 *I, Port, Holl, Braz, Rus.*
Mitchell, R. (2) (Newcastle United) 1950/1 *F, D.*
Mochan, H. (3) (Celtic) 1953/4 *N, Aust, U.*
Moir, W. (1) (Bolton Wanderers) 1949/50 *E.*
Moncur, R. (16) (Newcastle United) 1967/8 *Hol;* 1969/70 *Eire, I, W, E;* 1970/1 *D, Bel, Port, W, I, E, D;* 1971/2 *Per, I, W, E.*
Morgan, W. (21) (Burnley) 1967/8 *I;* (Manchester United) 1971/2 *Per, Y, Czecho, Braz;* 1972/3 *D* (2), *E, W, I, E, Switz, Braz;* 1973/4 *Czecho* (2), *G* (2), *I, Bel, Braz, Y.*
Morris, H. (1) (East Fife) 1949/50 *I.*
Mudie, J. (17) (Blackpool) 1956/7 *Y, I, W, E, Sp, Switz, G, Sp*; 1957/8 *I, Switz, W, E, H, Pol, Y, Par, F.*
Mulhall, G. (3) (Aberdeen) 1959/60 *I*; 1962/3 (Sunderland) *I*; 1963/4 *I.*
Munro, F. (9) (Wolverhampton Wanderers) 1970/1 *I, E, D, Rus*; 1974/5 *Swdn, W, I, E, Ru.*
Munro, J. (7) (St Mirren) 1978/9 *N, Arg*; 1979/80 *Per, Aust, Bel, W, E.*
Murdoch, R. (12) (Celtic) 1965/6 *It, W, It, E*; 1966/7 *I*; 1967/8 *I*; 1968/9 *C, G, W, I, E*; 1969/70 *Aust.*
Murray, J. (5) (Heart of Midlothian) 1957/8 *E, H, Pol, Y, F.*
Murray, S. (1) (Aberdeen) 1971/2 *Bel.*

Narey, D. (15) (Dundee United) 1976/7 *Swdn*; 1978/9 *Port, Arg*; 1979/80 *Port, I, Pol, H;* 1980/81 *W, E;* 1981/2 *Holl, W, E, NZ, Braz, Rus.*

…are, J. (13) (Derby County) 1969/70 *I, W, E*; 1970/1 *D, Bel, W, I*; 1971/2 *Port, …el, Holl, Per, I, W.*
Ormond, W. (6) (Hibernian) 1953/4 *E, N, Fin, Aust, U*; 1958/9 *E.*
Orr, T. (2) (Morton) 1951/2 *I, W.*

Parker, A. (15) (Falkirk) 1954/5 *Port, Y, Aust*; 1955/6 *I, W, E, Aust*; 1956/7 *Y, I, W*; 1957/8 *I, Switz, W, E, Par.*
Parlane, D. (13) (Rangers) 1972/3 *W, Switz, Braz*; 1974/5 *Sp, Swdn, Port, W, I, E, Ru*; 1975/6 *D*; 1976/7 *W, Braz.*
Paton, A. (2) (Motherwell) 1951/2 *D, Swdn.*
Pearson, T. (2) (Newcastle United) 1946/7 *E, Bel.*
Penman, A. (1) (Dundee) 1965/6 *Holl.*
Pettigrew, W. (5) (Motherwell) 1975/6 *Switz, I, W*; 1976/7 *W, Swdn.*
Plenderleith, J. (1) (Manchester City) 1960/1 *I.*
Provan, D. (5) (Rangers) 1963/4 *I, N*; 1965/6 *It* (2), *Holl.*
Provan, D. (10) (Celtic) 1979/80 *Bel, Bel, Port, I;* 1980/81 *Isr, W, E;* 1981/2 *Swdn, Port, I.*

Quinn, P. (4) (Motherwell) 1960/1 *E, Eire* (2); 1961/2 *U.*

Redpath, W. (9) (Motherwell) 1948/9 *W, I*; 1950/1 *E, D, F, Bel, Aust*; 1951/2 *I, E.*
Reilly, L. (38) (Hibernian) 1948/9 *W, E, F*; 1949/50 *I, W, Switz, F*; 1950/1 *W, E, D, F, Bel, Aust*; 1951/2 *I, W, E, US, D, Swdn*; 1952/3 *W, I, E, Swdn*; 1953/4 *W*; 1954/5 *H* (2), *E, Port, Y, Aust*; 1955/6 *I, W, E, Aust*; 1956/7 *Y, I, W, E.*
Ring, T. (12) (Clydebank) 1952/3 *Swdn*; 1954/5 *W, I, H, E*; 1956/7 *E, Sp, Switz, G, Sp*; 1957/8 *I, Switz.*
Rioch, B. (24) (Derby County) 1974/5 *Port, W, I, E, Ru*; 1975/6 *D* (2), *Ru, I, W, E*; 1976/7 *Fin, Czecho, W,* (Everton) *W, I, E, Ch, Braz*; (Derby County) 1977/8 *Czecho, I, E*; 1978/9 *Per, Holl.*
Robb, D. (5) (Aberdeen) 1970/1 *Port, W, E, D, Rus.*
Robertson, A. (5) (Clydebank) 1954/5 *Port, Aust, H*; 1957/8 *Switz, Par.*
Robertson, H. (1) (Dundee) 1961/2 *Czecho.*
Robertson, J. (1) (Tottenham Hotspur) 1964/5 *W.*
Robertson, J. (23) (Nottingham Forest) 1977/8 *I*; 1978/9 *Ir, Port, N*; 1979/80 *Per, Aust, Bel, Bel, Port;* 1980/81 *Swdn, Port, Isr, I, Isr, I, E;* 1981/2 *Swdn, I, I, E, NZ, Braz, Rus.*
Robinson, B. (4) (Dundee) 1973/4 *G*;1974/5 *Swdn, I, Ru.*
Rough, A. (51) (Partick Thistle) 1975/6 *Switz, I, W, E*; 1976/7 *Fin, Czecho, W, Swdn, W, I, E, Ch, Arg, Braz*; 1977/8 *Czecho, W, I, E*; 1978/9 *Per, Ir, Holl, Aust, Port, W, N, Arg*; 1979/80 *Per, Aust, Bel, Bel, Port, W, E, Pol, H;* 1980/81 *Swdn, Port, Isr, I, Isr, W, E;* 1981/2 *Swdn, I, Holl, Sp, W, E, NZ, Braz, Rus.*
Rutherford, E. (1) (Rangers) 1947/8 *F.*

Schaedler, E. (1) (Hibernian) 1973/4 *G.*
Scott, A. (16) (Rangers) 1956/7 *Y, I, G*; 1957/8 *Switz, W*; 1958/9 *Port*; 1961/2 *Czecho, I, W, E, W* (Everton); 1963/4 *N, W*; 1964/5 *Fin*; 1965/6 *Port, Braz.*
Scott, A. (1) (Hibernian) 1965/6 *Holl.*

Scott, J. (2) (Dundee) 1970/1 *D, Rus.*
Scoular, J. (9) (Portsmouth) 1950/1 *D, I, Aust*; 1951/2 *E, US, D, Swdn*; 1952/3 *W, I.*
Shaw, D. (8) (Hibernian) 1946/7 *W, I*; 1947/8 *E, Bel, Switz, F*; 1948/9 *W, I.*
Shaw, J. (4) (Rangers) 1946/7 *E, Bel, Lux*; 1947/8 *I.*
Shearer, R. (4) (Rangers) 1960/1 *Eire* (2), *E, Czecho.*
Simpson, R. (5) (Celtic) 1966/7 *E, Rus*; 1967/8 *I, E*; 1968/9 *Aust.*
Sinclair, J. (1) (Leicester City) 1965/6 *Port.*
Smith, D. (2) (Aberdeen) 1965/6 *Holl*; 1967/8 (Rangers) *Holl.*
Smith, E. (2) (Celtic) 1958/9 *Holl, Port.*
Smith, G. (19) (Hibernian) 1946/7 *I, E*; 1947/8 *W, Bel, Switz, F*; 1951/2 *E, US*; 1954/5 *Port, Y, Aust, H*; 1955/6 *I, E, W*; 1956/7 *E, Sp, Switz, Sp.*
Smith, J. (4) (Aberdeen) 1967/8 *Holl*; 1973/4 (Newcastle United) *G, I, W.*
Souness, G. (26) (Middlesbrough) 1974/5 *E/Germ, Sp, Swdn*; (Liverpool) 1977/8 *Bulg, W, E*; 1978/9 *Holl, Aust, N, W, I, E*; 1979/80 *Per, Aust, Bel, Port, I;* 1980/81 *Port, Isr, Isr;* 1981/2 *I, Port, Sp, W, E, NZ, Braz, Rus.*
Stanton, P. (16) (Hibernian) 1965/6 *Holl*; 1968/9 *I*; 1969/70 *Eire, Aust*; 1970/1 *D, Bel, Port, D, Rus*; 1971/2 *Port, Bel, Holl, W*; 1972/3 *W, I*; 1973/4 *G.*
Steel, W. (30) (Morton) 1946/7 *E, Bel, Lux*; 1947/8 (Derby County) *I, W, E, F*; 1948/9 *W, I, E, F*; 1949/50 *I, W, E, Switz, Port, F* (Dundee); 1950/1 *W, I, Aust* (2), *E, D, F, Bel*; 1951/2 *W*; 1952/3 *W, I, E, Swdn.*
Stein, C. (20) (Rangers) 1968/9 *D, C, W, I, E, C*; 1969/70 *Eire, G, I, W, E*; 1970/1 *D, Bel, D, Rus*; 1971/2 *Czecho*; (Coventry City), *E, W, I, E.*
Stephen, J. (2) (Bradford City) 1946/7 *W*; 1947/8 *W.*
Stewart, D. (2) (Leeds United) 1977/8 *E/Germ*; 1978/9 *N.*
Stewart, J. (1) (Kilmarnock) 1976/7 *Ch.*
Stewart, R. (6) (West Ham U.) 1980/81 *W, I, E;* 1981/2 *I, Port, W.*
Sturrock, P. (7) (Dundee U.) 1980/81 *W, I, E;* 1981/2 *Port, I, W, E.*
St John, I. (31) (Motherwell) 1958/9 *G*; 1959/60 *I, W, E, Pol, Aust*; 1960/1 *E*; 1961/2 (Liverpool) *Czecho, I, W, Czecho, E, W*; 1962/3 *W, I, E, N, Eire, Sp*; 1963/4 *I*; 1964/5 *E.*
Strachan, G. (14) (Aberdeen) 1979/80 *I, W, E, Pol, H;* 1980/81 *Swdn, Port;* 1981/2 *I, Port, Holl, Sp, NZ, Braz, Rus.*

Telfer, W. (1) (St Mirren) 1953/4 *W.*
Thomson, W. (3) (St Mirren) 1979/80 *I;* 1980/81 *I;* 1981/2 *Port.*
Thornton, W. (7) (Rangers) 1946/7 *W*; 1947/8 *I, E*; 1948/9 *F*; 1951/2 *D, Swdn.*
Toner, W. (2) (Kilmarnock) 1958/9 *W, I.*
Turnbull, E. (8) (Hibernian) 1957/8 *Bel, Switz*; 1950/1 *Aust*; 1957/8 *H, Pol, Y, Par, F.*

Ure, I. (11) (Dundee) 1961/2 *W, Czecho*; 1962/3 *W, I, E, Aust, N, Sp,* (Arsenal); 1963/4 *I, N*; 1967/8 *I.*

Waddell, W. (17) (Rangers) 1946/7 *W*; 1948/9 *W, I, E, F*; 1949/50 *I, E*; 1950/1 *E, D, F, Bel, Aust*; 1951/2 *I, W*; 1953/4 *I*; 1954/5 *W, I.*
Wallace, I. (3) (Coventry City) 1977/8 *Bulg*; 1978/9 *Port, W.*
Wallace, W. (7) (Heart of Midlothian) 1964/5 *I*; 1965/6 *E, Holl*; 1966/7 (Celtic) *E, Rus*; 1967/8 *I*; 1968/9 *E.*

ardhaugh, J. (2) (Heart of Midlothian) 1954/5 *H*; 1956/7 *I.*
Wark, J. (17) (Ipswich Town) 1978/9 *W, I, E, Arg*; 1979/80 *Per, Aust, Bel, Bel;* 1980/81 *Isr, I;* 1981/2 *Swdn, Holl, Sp, I, NZ, Braz, Rus.*
Watson, J. (2) (Motherwell) 1947/8 *I*; 1953/4 *I.*
Watson, R. (1) (Motherwell) 1970/1 *Rus.*
Weir, A. (5) (Motherwell) 1959/60 *E, Pol, Aust, H, T.*
Weir, P. (4) (St Mirren) 1979/80 *I, W, Pol, H.*
White, J. (22) (Falkirk) 1958/9 *G, Holl, Port*; 1959/60 *I,* (Tottenham Hotspur) *W, Pol, Aust, T*; 1960/1
W; 1961/2 *Czecho, I, W, Czecho, E*; 1962/3 *W, I, E*; 1963/4 *I, N, W, E, G.*
Wilson, A. (1) (Portsmouth) 1953/4 *Fin.*
Wilson, D. (22) (Rangers) 1960/1 *W, I, E, Eire* (2), *Czecho;* 1961/2 *Czecho, I, W, E, U*; 1962/3 *W, E, Aust, N, Eire, Sp*; 1963/4 *E, G*; 1964/5 *I, E, Fin.*
Wilson, P. (1) (Celtic) 1974/5 *Sp.*
Wilson, R. (2) (Arsenal) 1971/2 *Port, Holl.*
Wood, G. (4) (Everton) 1978/9 *I, E, Arg;* 1981/2 (Arsenal) *I.*
Woodburn, W. (24) (Rangers) 1946/7 *E, Bel, Lux*; 1947/8 *I, W*; 1948/9 *Y, E, F*; 1949/50 *I, W, E, Port, F*; 1950/1 *W, I, Aust* (2), *E, D, F, Bel*; 1951/2 *I, W, E, US.*
Wright, T. (2) (Sunderland) 1952/3 *W, I, E.*

Yeats, R. (2) (Liverpool) 1964/5 *W*; 1965/6 *It.*
Yorston, H. (1) (Aberdeen) 1954/5 *W.*
Young, A. (9) (Heart of Midlothian) 1959/60 *F, Aust, H, E, T*; 1960/1 (Everton) *W, Eire*; 1965/6 *Port.*
Young, G. (53) (Rangers) 1946/7 *I, E, Bel, Lux*; 1947/8 *I, E, Bel, Switz, F*; 1948/9 *W, I, E, F*; 1949/50 *I, W, E, Switz, Port, F*; 1950/1 *W, I, Aust* (2), *E, D, F, Bel*; 1951/2 *I, W, E, US, D, Swdn*; 1952/3 *W, I, E, Swdn*; 1953/4 *I, W*; 1954/5 *W, I, Port, Y*; 1955/6 *I, W, E, Aust*; 1956/7 *Y, I, W, E, Sp, Switz.*
Younger, T. (24) (Hibernian) 1954/5 *Port, Y, Aust, H*; 1955/6 *I, W, E, Aust*; 1956/7 (Liverpool) *Y, I, N, E, Sp, Switz, G, Sp*; 1957/8 *I, Switz, W, E, H, Pol, W, Par.*

WALES

Allchurch, I. (68) (Swansea City) 1950/1 *E, I, Port, Switz*; 1951/2 *E, S, UK, I*; 1952/3 *S, E, I, F, Y*; 1953/4 *E, S, I, Aust*; 1954/5 *Y, S, E, I*; 1955/6 *E, S, Aust, I*; 1956/7 *S, E*; 1957/8 *Isr* (2), *I, H, Mex, Swdn, H, Braz*; 1958/9 (Newcastle United) *S, E, I*; 1959/60 *E, S*; 1960/1 *T, Sp* (2), *H*; 1961/2 *E, S, Braz* (2), *Mex*; 1962/3 (Cardiff City) *S, H, E, H, I*; 1963/4 *E*; 1964/5 *S, E, Gr, I, It, Rus*; 1965/6 (Swansea City) *E, Rus, S, D, Braz, Braz 'B', Ch.*

Allchurch, L. (11) (Swansea City) 1954/5 *I*; 1955/6 *Aust*; 1957/8 *E/Germ, S, Isr, I*; 1958/9 *S*; 1961/2 (Sheffield United) *S, I, Braz*; 1963/4 *E.*

Allen, B. (2) (Coventry City) 1950/1 *S, E.*

Baker, C. (7) (Cardiff City) 1957/8 *Mex*; 1959/60 *S, I*; 1960/1 *Eire, S, E*; 1961/2 *S.*

Baker, W. (1) (Cardiff City) 1947/8 *I.*

Barnes, W. (22) (Arsenal) 1947/8 *E, S, I*; 1948/9 *S, E, I*; 1949/50 *E, S, Bel, I*; 1950/1 *S, E, I, Port*; 1951/2 *E, S, UK, I*; 1953/4 *E, S*; 1954/5 *Y. S.*

Berry, G. (4) (Wolverhampton Wanderers) 1978/9 *G*; 1979/80 *Eire, G, T.*

Bowen, D. (19) (Arsenal) 1954/5 *Y, S*; 1956/7 *I, Czecho, E/Germ*; 1957/8 *E/Germ, E, S, Isr* (2), *I, H, Mex, Swdn, H, Braz*; 1958/9 *S, E, I.*

Boyle, T. (2) (Crystal Palace) 1980/81 *Eire, S.*

Burgess, R. (32) (Tottenham Hotspur) 1946/7 *S, E, I*; 1947/8 *E, S*; 1948/9 *S, E, I, Port, Bel, Switz*; 1949/50 *E, S, Bel, I*; 1950/1 *S, I, Port, Switz*; 1951/2 *E, S, UK, I*; 1952/3 *S, E, I, F, Y*; 1953/4 *E, S, I, Aust.*

Burton, O. (9) (Norwich City) 1962/3 *H, I*, (Newcastle United); 1963/4 *E*; 1968/9 *It, E/Germ, S, E, I*; 1971/2 *Czecho.*

Cartwright, L. (6) (Coventry City) 1973/4 *E, S, I*; 1975/6 *S*; 1976/7 *G*; (Wrexham) 1978/9 *M.*

Charles, J. (38) (Leeds United) 1949/50 *I*; 1950/1 *Switz*; 1952/3 *I, F, Y*; 1953/4 *E, S, I, Aust*; 1954/5 *Y, S, E, I*; 1955/6 *E, S, Aust, I*; 1956/7 *S, E, I*, (Juventus Turin) *Czecho, E/Germ, Czecho*; 1957/8 *Isr* (2), *H, Mex, Swdn, H*; 1959/60 *S*; 1961/2 *E, Braz* (2), *Mex*; 1962/3 (Leeds United) *S*, (Cardiff City); 1963/4 *S*; 1964/5 *S, Rus.*

Charles, J. (5) (Swansea C.) 1980/81 *Czecho, T, S, USSR;* 1981/2 *Ic.*

Charles, M. (31) (Swansea City) 1954/5 *I*; 1955/6 *E, S, Aust*; 1956/7 *E, I, Czecho, E/Germ, Czecho*; 1957/8 *E/Germ, E, S, Isr (2), H, Mex, Swdn, H, Braz*; 1958/9 *S, E*, (Arsenal) 1960/1 *I, Sp* (2), *H*; 1961/2 *E, S*, (Cardiff City) *I, Braz*; 1962/3 *S, H.*

Clarke, R. (22) (Manchester City) 1948/9 *E*; 1949/50 *S, Bel, I*; 1950/1 *S, E, I, Port, Switz*; 1951/2 *E, S, UK, I*; 1952/3 *S, E*; 1953/4 *E, S, I*; 1954/5 *Y, S, E*; 1955/6 *I.*

Crowe, V. (16) (Aston Villa) 1958/9 *E*; 1959/60 *E, I*; 1960/1 *Eire, S, E, I, Sp* (2), *H*; 1961/2 *E, S, Braz, Mex*; 1962/3 *H.*

Curtis, A. (27) (Swansea City) 1975/6 *E* (2), *S, I, Y* (2); 1976/7 *G, S, I*; 1977/8 *G, E, S*; 1978/9 *G, S, E, I, M*; 1979/80 *Eire, G, T;* 1981/2 *Czecho, Ic, Rus, Sp, E, S, I.*

Daniel, R. (21) (Arsenal) 1950/1 *E, I, Port*; 1951/2 *E, S, UK, I*; 1952/3 *S, E, I, F, Y*; 1953/4 (Sunderland) *E, S, I*; 1954/5 *E, I*; 1956/7 *S, E, I. Czecho.*

Davies, D. (55) (Everton) 1974/5 *H, Lux, S, E, I*; 1975/6 *Y* (2), *E, I*; 1976/7 *G, S, Czecho, E, I*; 1977/8 *K, S* (2), *Czecho, G, E, I*; (Wrexham) 1978/9 *M, T, G, S, E, I, M*; 1979/80 *Eire, G, T, E, S, I, Ic;* 1980/81 *T, Czecho, Eire, T, S, E, USSR;* 1981/2

Davies, G. (2) (Fulham) 1981/2 *Sp, F.*
Davies, Reg (6) (Newcastle United) 1952/3 *S, E*; 1953/4 *E, S*; 1957/8 *E/Germ, E.*
Davies, Ron (29) (Norwich City) 1963/4 *I*; 1964/5 *E*; 1965/6 *Braz, Braz 'B', Ch*; 1966/7 (Southampton) *S, E, I*; 1967/8 *I, G*; 1968/9 *It, G, S, E, I*; 1969/70 *UK, E, S, I*; 1970/1 *Czecho, S, E, I*; 1971/2 *Ru, E, S, I*; 1973/4 (Portsmouth) *E.*
Davies, R. Wyn (34) (Bolton Wanderers) 1963/4 *E*; 1964/5 *S, D, E, Gr, I, Rus*; 1965/6 *E, Rus, S, D, I, Braz, Braz 'B', Ch*; 1966/7 *S* (Newcastle United) *E*; 1967/8 *S, I, G*; 1968/9 *It, S, E, I*; 1969/70 *E/Germ*; 1970/1 *Ru, Czecho*; 1971/2 (Manchester City) *E, S, I*; 1972/3 (Manchester United) *E, S, I*; 1973/4 *Pol.*
Davis, G. (4) (Wrexham) 1977/8 *I, E*; 1979/80 *T, Ic.*
Deacy, T. (11) (PSV Eindhoven) 1976/7 *Czecho, S, E, I*; 1977/8 *K, S* (2), *Czecho, G, I*; 1978/9 *T.*
Derrett, S. (4) (Cardiff City) 1968/9 *G, S*; 1969/70 *It*; 1970/1 *Fin.*
Durban, A. (26) (Derby County) 1966/7 *I*; 1967/8 *E, S, I, G*; 1968/9 *G, E/Germ, S, E, I*; 1969/70 *E/Germ, It, E, S, I*; 1970/1 *Ru, Czecho, S, E, I, Fin*; 1971/2 *Fin, Czecho, E, S, I.*
Dwyer, A. (8) (Wrexham) 1977/8 *E, S, I*; 1978/9 *T, S, E, I*; 1979/80 *G.*

Edwards, I. (4) (Chester) 1977/8 *K*; 1978/9 *M, G*; 1979/80 *T.*
Edwards, G. (12) (Birmingham City) 1946/7 *S, E, I*; 1947/8 *E, S, I*(Cardiff City); 1948/9 *I, Port, Bel, Switz*; 1949/50 *E, S.*
Edwards, T. (2) (Charlton Athletic) 1956/7 *I, E/Germ.*
Emanuel, J. (2) (Bristol City) 1972/3 *E, I.*
England, M. (44) (Blackburn Rovers) 1961/2 *I, Braz, Mex*; 1962/3 *H, I*; 1963/4 *E, S, I*; 1964/5 *D, E, Gr* (2), *I, It, Rus*; 1965/6 *E, Rus, S, D, I*; 1966/7 (Tottenham Hotspur) *S, E*; 1967/8 *E, I, G*; 1968/9 *E/Germ*; 1969/70 *UK, E/Germ, It, E, S, I*; 1970/1 *Ru*; 1971/2 *Fin, E, S, I*; 1972/3 *E* (2), *S, E*; 1973/4 *Pol*; 1974/5 *H, Lux.*
Evans, I. (13) (Crystal Palace) 1975/6 *Aust, E, Y* (2), *E, I*; 1976/7 *G, S* (2), *Czecho, E, I*; 1977/8 *K.*
Evans, R. (1) (Swansea City) 1963/4 *I.*

Flynn, B. (51) (Burnley) 1974/5 *Lux* (2), *H, S, E, I*; 1975/6 *Aust, E* (2), *Y* (2), *I*; 1976/7 *G, S, Czecho, S, E, I*; 1977/8 *K* (2), *S* (2), *Czecho, G, E, I*; (Leeds United) 1978/9 *M, T, S, E, I, M*; 1979/80 *Eire, G, E, S, I, Ic;* 1980/81 *T, Czecho, Eire, T, S, E, USSR;* 1981/2 *Czecho, Rus, E, S, I, F.*
Ford, T. (38) (Swansea City) 1946/7 *S,* (Aston Villa) *I*; 1947/8 *S, I*; 1948/9 *S, E, I, Port, Bel, Switz;* 1949/50 *E, S, Bel, I*; 1950/1 *S,* (Sunderland), *E, I, Port, Switz*; 1951/2 *E, S, UK, I*; 1952/3 *S, E, I, F, Y* (Cardiff City); 1953/4 *Aust*; 1954/5 *Y, S, E, I*; 1955/6 *E, S, Aust, I, I*; 1956/7 *S.*
Foulkes, W. (11) (Newcastle United) 1951/2 *E, S, UK, I*; 1952/3 *S, E, F, Y*; 1953/4 *E, S, I.*

Giles, D. (10) (Wrexham) 1979/80 *E, S, I, Ic;* 1980/81 (Swansea City) *T, Czecho, T, E, USSR;* 1981/2 (Crystal Palace) *Sp.*
Godfrey, B. (3) (Preston North End) 1963/4 *I*; 1964/5 *D, It.*
Green, C. (15) (Birmingham City) 1964/5 *It, Rus*; 1965/6 *E, Rus, S, Braz, Braz 'B'*; 1966/7 *E*; 1967/8 *E, S, I, G*; 1968/9 *It, S, I.*

Griffiths, A. (17) (Wrexham) 1970/1 *Czecho*; 1974/5 *Aust, H* (2), *Lux* (2), *E, I*; 1975/6 *Aust, E* (2), *Y* (2), *S, I*; 1976/7 *G, S*.
Griffiths, H. (1) (Swansea City) 1952/3 *I*.
Griffiths, M. (11) (Leicester City) 1946/7 *I*; 1948/9 *Port, Bel*; 1949/50 *E, S, Bel*; 1950/1 *E, I, Port, Switz*; 1953/4 *Aust*.

Harrington, A. (11) (Cardiff City) 1955/6 *I*; 1956/7 *S, E*; 1957/8 *S, Isr* (2), *I*; 1960/1 *S, E*; 1961/2 *E, S*.
Harris, C. (19) (Leeds United) 1975/6 *S, E*; 1977/8 *G, E, S, I*; 1978/9 *M, T, G, M*; 1979/80 *I*; 1980/81 *T, Czecho, Eire, T, S, E, USSR*; 1981/2 *Czecho, Ic*.
Harris, W. (6) (Middlesbrough) 1953/4 *Aust*; 1956/7 *E/Germ, Czecho*; 1957/8 *E/Germ, E, S*.
Hennessey, T. (39) (Birmingham City) 1961/2 *I, Braz* (2); 1962/3 *S, H, E, H*; 1963/4 *E, S*; 1964/5 *S, D, E, Gr, Rus*; 1965/6 *E, Rus*, (Nottingham Forest), *S, D, I, Braz, Braz 'B', Ch*; 1966/7 *S, E*; 1967/8 *E, S, I*; 1968/9 *G, E/Germ*; 1969/70 *UK, E/Germ* (Derby County), *E, S, I*; 1971/2 *Fin, Czecho, E, S*; 1972/3 *E*.
Hewitt, R. (5) (Cardiff City) 1957/8 *Isr, I, Swdn, H, Braz*.
Hill, M. (2) (Ipswich Town) 1971/2 *Czecho, Ru*.
Hockey, T. (9) (Sheffield United) 1971/2 *Fin, Ru*; 1972/3 *E* (1), (Norwich City), *Pol, S, E, I*; 1973/4 (Aston Villa) *Pol*.
Hole, B. (30) (Cardiff City) 1962/3 *I*; 1963/4 *I*; 1964/5 *S, D, E, Gr* (2), *I, It, Rus*; 1965/6 *E, Rus, S, D, I, Braz 'B', Ch*; 1966/7 (Blackburn Rovers) *S, E, I*; 1967/8 *E, S, I, G*; 1968/9 (Aston Villa) *It, G, E/Germ*; 1969/70 *It*; (Swansea City) 1970/1 *Ru*.
Hollins, D. (11) (Newcastle United) 1961/2 *Braz, Mex*; 1962/3 *H, I*; 1963/4 *E*; 1964/5 *Gr, I, It*; 1965/6 *S, D, Braz*.
Hopkins, M. (34) (Tottenham Hotspur) 1955/6 *I*; 1956/7 *S, E, I, Czecho, E/Germ, Czecho*; 1957/8 *E/Germ, E, S, Isr* (2), *I, H, Mex, Swdn, H, Braz*; 1958/9 *S, E, I*; 1959/60 *E, S*; 1960/1 *I, Sp* (2), *H*; 1961/2 *I, Braz* (2), *Mex*; 1962/3 *S, H, I*.
Howells, R. (2) (Cardiff City) 1953/4 *E, S*.
Hughes, I. (4) (Luton Town) 1950/1 *E, I, Port, Switz*.
Hughes, W. (3) (Birmingham City) 1946/7 *S, E, I*.
Hughes, W. A. (5) (Blackburn Rovers) 1948/9 *E, I, Port, Bel, Switz*.
Humphreys, J. (1) (Everton) 1946/7 *I*.

James, G. (9) (Blackpool) 1965/6 *Braz, Braz 'B', Ch*; 1966/7 *I*; 1967/8 *S*; 1970/1 *Czecho, S, E, I*.
James, L. (59) (Burnley) 1971/2 *Czecho, Rus, S*; 1972/3 *E* (2), *Pol, S, E, I*; 1973/4 *Pol, E, S, I*; 1974/5 *Aust, H* (2), *Lux* (2), *S, E, I*; 1975/6 *Aust, E, S, Y* (2), *I*; (Derby County) 1976/7 *G, S, Czecho, S, E, I*; 1977/8 *K* (2) *G* (Swansea City); 1978/9 *M, T, S, E, I, M*; 1979/80 *G, E, S, I, Ic*; 1980/81 *T, Eire, T, S, E*; 1981/2 *Czecho, Ic, Rus, E, S, I, F*.
James, R. (7) (Swansea C.) 1981/2 *Czecho, Ic, Sp, E, S, I, F*.
Jarvis, A. (3) (Hull City) 1966/7 *S, E, I*.
Johnson, M. (1) (Swansea City) 1963/4 *I*.
Jones, Barrie (14) (Swansea City) 1962/3 *S, H, E, I*; 1963/4 *S, I*; 1964/5 (Plymouth Argyle) *D*; 1968/9 (Cardiff City) *G, E/Germ, S, E, I*; 1969/70 *UK*.
Jones, Bryn (4) (Arsenal) 1946/7 *S, I*; 1947/8 *E*; 1948/9 *S*.
Jones, C. (59) (Swansea City) 1953/4 *Aust*; 1955/6 *E, S, Aust, I*; 1956/7 *S, E, J*,

Czecho, E/Germ, Czecho; 1957/8 *E/Germ, E, S, Isr* (2), (Tottenham Hotspur), *I, H, Mex, Swdn, H, Braz*; 1958/9 *I*; 1959/60 *E, S, I*; 1960/1 *Eire, S, E, I, Sp, H*; 1961/2 *E, S, I, Braz* (2), *Mex*; 1962/3 *S, H, I*; 1963/4 *E, S, I*; 1964/5 *S, D, E, Gr* (2), *I, It, Rus*; 1966/7 *S, E*; 1967/8 *E, S, G*; 1968/9 (Fulham) *It*; 1969/70 *UK*.

Jones, D. (11) (Norwich City) 1975/6 *E, S*; 1977/8 *S, Czecho, G, E*; 1979/80 *Eire, G, T, E, I, Ic*.

Jones, E. (4) (Swansea City) 1947/8 *S, E* (Tottenham Hotspur); 1948/9 *S, E*.

Jones, J. (39) (Liverpool) 1975/6 *Aust, E, S*; 1976/7 *G, S* (2), *Czecho, E, I*; 1977/8 *K* (2), *S* (2), *Czecho, G, E, I*; (Wrexham) 1978/9 *M, T, G, S, E, M*; 1979/80 *E, S*; 1980/81 *T, Eire, T, S, E, USSR*; 1981/2 *Czecho, Ic, Rus, Sp, E, S, I, F*.

Jones, K. (1) (Aston Villa) 1949/50 *S*.

Jones, T. G. (13) (Everton) 1946/7 *S, E*; 1947/8 *E, S, I*; 1948/9 *E, I, Port, Bel, Switz*; 1949/50 *E, S, Bel*.

Jones, W. (1) (Bristol Rovers) 1970/1 *Fin*.

Kelsey, J. (41) (Arsenal) 1953/4 *I, Aust*; 1954/5 *Y, S, I*; 1955/6 *E, S, Aust, I*; 1956/7 *S, E, I, Czecho, E/Germ, Czecho*; 1957/8 *E, S, Isr* (2), *I, H, Mex, Swdn, H, Braz*; 1958/9 *S, E*; 1959/60 *E, S, I*; 1960/1 *S, E, I, Sp* (2), *H*; 1961/2 *E, S, I, Braz* (2).

King, J. (1) (Swansea City) 1954/5 *E*.

Kinsey, N. (7) (Norwich City) 1950/1 *I, Port, Switz*; 1951/2 *E*; 1953/4 (Birmingham City) *I*; 1955/6 *E, S*.

Krzywicki, R. (8) (West Bromwich Albion) 1969/70 *E/Germ, It*, (Huddersfield Town) *E, S, I*; 1970/1 *Ru, Fin*; 1971/2 *Czecho*.

Lambert, R. (5) (Liverpool) 1946/7 *S*; 1947/8 *E*; 1948/9 *Port, Bel, Switz*.

Lea, C. (2) (Ipswich Town) 1964/5 *I, It*.

Leek, L. (13) (Leicester City) 1960/1 *S, E, I, Sp* (2), *H*; 1961/2 (Newcastle United) *S*, (Birmingham City) *Braz, Mex*; 1962/3 *E*; 1964/5 *S, Gr* (2).

Lever, A. (1) (Leicester City) 1952/3 *S*.

Lloyd, B. (3) (Wrexham) 1975/6 *Aust, S, E*.

Lovell, S. (1) (Crystal Palace) 1981/2 *Rus*.

Lowrie, G. (4) (Coventry City) 1947/8 *E, S, I*; 1948/9 (Newcastle United) *Port*.

Lucas, M. (4) (Leyton Orient) 1961/2 *I, Mex*; 1962/3 *S, E*.

Lucas, W. (7) (Swansea City) 1948/9 *S, I, Port, Bel, Switz*; 1949/50 *E*; 1950/1 *E*.

Mahoney, J. (48) (Stoke City) 1967/8 *E*; 1968/9 *E/Germ*; 1970/1 *Czecho*; 1972/3 *E* (2), *Pol, S, E, I*; 1973/4 *Pol, E, S, I*; 1974/5 *Aust, H* (2), *Lux* (2), *S, E, I*; 1975/6 *Aust, Y* (2), *E, I*; 1976/7 *G, Czecho, S, E, I*; 1977/8 *K* (2), *S*(2), *Czecho, E, I*; (Middlesbrough) 1978/9 *G, S, E, I, M*; 1979/80 *Eire, G, T*; 1981/2 (Swansea C.) *Ic Rus*.

Marustik, C. (5) (Swansea C.) 1981/2 *Sp, E, S, I, F*.

Medwin, T. (30) (Swansea City) 1952/3 *I, F, Y*; 1956/7 (Tottenham Hotspur) *S, E, I, Czecho, E/Germ, Czecho*; 1957/8 *E, S, Isr* (2), *I, H, Mex, H, Braz*; 1958/9 *S, E, I*; 1959/60 *E, S, I*; 1960/1 *Eire, S, E, Sp*; 1962/3 *H, E*.

Mielczarek, R. (1) (Rotherham United) 1970/1 *Fin*.

Millington, A. (21) (West Bromwich Albion) 1962/3 *S, H, E*; 1964/5 (Crystal Palace) *E, Rus*; 1965/6 (Peterborough United) *Braz 'B', Ch*; 1966/7 *E, I*; 1967/8 *I, G*; 1968/9 *It, E/Germ*; 1969/70 (Swansea City) *E, S, I*; 1970/1 *Czecho, Fin*; 1971/2 *Fin, Czecho, Ru*.

Moore, G. (21) (Cardiff City) 1959/60 *E, S, I*; 1960/1 *Eire, Sp*; 1961/2 (Chelsea) *Braz*; 1962/3 *H, I*; (Manchester United) 1963/4 *S, I*; (Northampton Town) 1965/6 *I, Ch*; 1968/9 (Charlton Athletic) *S, E, I*; 1969/70 *UK, It, E, S, I*; 1970/1 *Ru.*
Morris, W. (5) (Burnley) 1946/7 *I*; 1948/9 *E*; 1951/2 *S, UK, I.*

Nardiello, D. (2) (Coventry City) 1977/8 *Czecho, G.*
Nicholas, P. (23) (Crystal Palace) 1978/9 *M*; 1979/80 *Eire, G, T, E, S, I, Ic;* 1980/81 *T, Czecho, Eire,* (Arsenal) *T, S, E, USSR;* 1981/2 *Czecho, Ic, Rus, Sp, E, S, I, F.*
Nurse, M. (12) (Swansea City) 1959/60 *E, I*; 1960/1 *Eire, S, E, I, Sp* (2), *H*; 1962/3 (Middlesbrough) *H, E*; 1963/4 *S.*

O'Sullivan, P. (3) (Brighton & Hove Albion) 1972/3 *S*; 1975/6 *S*; 1978/9 *M.*

Page, M. (27) (Birmingham City) 1970/1 *Fin*; 1971/2 *S, I*; 1972/3 *E* (2), *I*; 1973/4 *S, I*; 1974/5 *H, Lux, S, E, I*; 1975/6 *E* (2), *Y* (2), *I*; 1976/7 *G, S*; 1977/8 *K* (2), *G, E, S*; 1978/9 *M, G.*
Palmer, D. (3) (Swansea City) 1956/7 *Czecho*; 1957/8 *E/Germ, E.*
Parry, J. (1) (Swansea City) 1950/1 *S.*
Paul, R. (33) (Swansea City) 1948/9 *S, E, I, Port, Switz*; 1949/50 *E, S, Bel, I*; (Manchester City) 1950/1 *S, E, I, Port, Switz*; 1951/2 *E, S, UK, I*; 1952/3 *S, E, I, F, Y*; 1953/4 *E, S, I*; 1954/5 *Y, S, E*; 1955/6 *E, S, Aust, I.*
Phillips, J. (4) (Chelsea) 1972/3 *E*; 1973/4 *E*; 1974/5 *H*; 1977/8 *K.*
Phillips, L. (58) (Cardiff City) 1970/1 *Czecho, S, E, I*; 1971/2 *Czecho, Ru, S, I*; 1972/3 *E*; 1973/4 *Pol, I*; 1974/5 *Aust,* (Aston Villa) *H* (2), *Lux* (2), *S, E, I*; 1975/6 *Aust, E* (2), *Y* (2), *I*; 1976/7 *G, S, Czecho, S, E*; 1977/8 *K* (2), *S* (2), *Czecho, G, E*; 1978/9 *M, T, G,* (Swansea City) *S, E, I, M*; 1979/80 *Eire, G, T, S, I, Ic;* 1980/81 *T, Czecho, T, S, E, USSR;* 1981/2 (Charlton Ath.) *Czecho, Rus.*
Pontin, K. (2) (Cardiff City) 1979/80 *E, S.*
Powell, A. (8) (Leeds United) 1946/7 *S, E*; 1947/8 *E, S, I*; 1948/9 (Everton) *E*; 1949/50 *Bel*; 1950/1 (Birmingham City) *S.*
Powell, D. (11) (Wrexham) 1967/8 *G*; 1968/9 (Sheffield United) *It, G, S, E, I*; 1969/70 *E/Germ, E, S, I*; 1970/1 *Ru.*
Powell, J. (8) (Queen's Park Rangers) 1946/7 *E*; 1947/8 *E, S*; 1948/9 (Aston Villa) *Bel*; 1949/50 *S, Bel*; 1950/1 *S.*
Price, P. (14) (Luton Town) 1979/80 *E, S, I, Ic;* 1980/81 *T, Czecho, Eire, T, S, E, USSR;* 1981/2 (Tottenham H.) *Rus, Sp, F.*
Pring, K. (3) (Rotherham United) 1965/6 *D, Ch*; 1966/7 *I.*

Rankmore, F. (1) (Peterborough United) 1965/6 *Ch.*
Ratcliffe, K. (11) (Everton) 1980/81 *Czecho, Eire, T, S, E, USSR;* 1981/2 *Czecho, Ic, Rus, Sp, E.*
Reece, G. (29) (Sheffield United) 1965/6 *E, Rus, S, I*; 1966/7 *S*; 1969/70 *UK, It*; 1970/1 *S, E, I, Fin*; 1971/2 *Fin, Ru, E, S, I*; (Cardiff City) 1972/3 *E, I*; 1973/4 *Pol, E, S, I*; 1974/5 *Aust, H* (2), *Lux* (2), *S, I.*
Reed, W. (2) (Ipswich Town) 1954/5 *Y, S.*
Rees, R. (37) (Coventry City) 1964/5 *S, D, E, Gr* (2), *I, It, Rus*; 1965/6 *E, Rus, S, D, I, Braz, Braz 'B', Ch*; 1966/7 *E, I*; 1967/8 *E, S, I* (West Bromwich Albion), *G*; 1968/9 *It,* (Nottingham Forest) *G, E/Germ, S*; 1969/70 *UK, E/Germ, It, E, S, I*; 1970/1 *Ru,*

Czecho, Fin; 1971/2 *Czecho, Ru.*
Rees, W. (4) (Cardiff City) 1948/9 *I, Bel, Switz,* (Tottenham Hotspur); 1949/50 *I.*
Richards, S. (1) (Cardiff City) 1946/7 *E.*
Roberts, D. (17) (Oxford United) 1972/3 *Pol, E, I*; 1973/4 *E, S*; 1974/5 *Aust,* (Hull City) *Lux, I*; 1975/6 *Y, S, I*; 1976/7 *E, I*; 1977/8 *K* (2), *S, I.*
Roberts, J. (21) (Arsenal) 1970/1 *S, E, I, Fin*; 1971/2 *Fin, E, I*; 1972/3 (Birmingham City) *E, Pol, S, E, I*; 1973/4 *Pol, E, S, I*; 1974/5 *Aust, H, S, E*; 1975/6 *S.*
Roberts, J. (1) (Bolton Wanderers) 1948/9 *Bel.*
Roberts, P. (4) (Portsmouth) 1973/4 *E*; 1974/5 *Aust, H, Lux.*
Rodrigues, P. (40) (Cardiff City) 1964/5 *Gr* (2), *I*; 1965/6 *E, Rus, S, D,* (Leicester City), *I, Braz, Braz 'B', Ch*; 1966/7 *S*; 1967/8 *E, S, I*; 1968/9 *E/Germ, E, I*; 1969/70 *UK, E/Germ, E, S, I*; (Sheffield Wednesday) 1970/1 *Ru, Czecho, S, E, I*; 1971/2 *Fin, Czecho, Ru, E, I*; 1972/3 *E* (2), *Pol, S, E, I*; 1973/4 *Pol.*
Rouse, V. (1) (Crystal Palace) 1958/9 *I.*
Rowley, T. (1) (Tranmere Rovers) 1958/9 *I.*
Rush, I. (8) (Liverpool) 1979/80 *S, I;* 1980/81 *E;* 1981/2 *Rus, E, S, I, F.*

Sayer, P. (7) (Cardiff City) 1976/7 *Czecho, S, E, I*; 1977/8 *K* (2), *S.*
Scrine, F. (2) (Swansea City) 1949/50 *E, I.*
Sear, C. (1) (Manchester City) 1962/3 *E.*
Sherwood, A. (41) (Cardiff City) 1946/7 *E*; 1947/8 *S, I*; 1948/9 *S, E, I, Port, Switz*; 1949/50 *E, S, Bel, I*; 1950/1 *S, E, I, Port, Switz*; 1951/2 *E, S, UK, I*; 1952/3 *S, E, I, F, Y*; 1953/4 *E, S, I, Aust*; 1954/5 *Y, S, E, I*; 1955/6 *S, E, Aust, I*; 1955/6 *S, E, Aust, I*; 1956/7 (Newport County) *S, E.*
Shortt, W. (12) (Plymouth Argyle) 1946/7 *I*; 1949/50 *Bel, I*; 1951/2 *E, S, UK, I*; 1952/3 *S, E, I, F, Y.*
Showers, D. (2) (Cardiff City) 1974/5 *E, I.*
Sidlow, C. (7) (Liverpool) 1946/7 *S, E*; 1947/8 *E, S, I*; 1948/9 *S*; 1949/50 *E.*
Smallman, D. (7) (Wrexham) 1973/4 *E, S, I*; 1974/5 *H, E, I*; 1975/6 (Everton) *Aust.*
Southall, N. (1) (Everton) 1981/2 *I.*
Sprake, G. (37) (Leeds United) 1963/4 *S, I*; 1964/5 *S, D, Gr*; 1965/6 *E, Rus, I*; 1966/7 *S*; 1967/8 *E, S*; 1968/9 *G, S, E, I*; 1969/70 *UK, E/Germ, It*; 1970/1 *Ru, S, E, I*; 1971/2 *Fin, E, S, I*; 1972/3 *E* (2), *Pol, S, I*; 1973/4 (Birmingham City) *Pol, S, I*; 1974/5 *Aust, H, Lux.*
Stansfield, G. (1) (Cardiff City) 1948/9 *S.*
Stevenson, B. (15) (Leeds United) 1977/8 *I*; 1978/9 *M, T, S, E, I, M*; 1979/80 *G, T, Ic;* 1981/2 *Czecho,* (Birmingham C.) *Sp, S, I, F.*
Stevenson, N. (3) (Swansea C.) 1981/2 *E, S, I.*
Stitfall, R. (2) (Cardiff City) 1952/3 *E*; 1956/7 *Czecho.*
Sullivan, D. (17) (Cardiff City) 1952/3 *I, F, Y*; 1953/4 *I*; 1954/5 *E, S*; 1956/7 *S, E*; 1957/8 *I, H, Swdn, H, Braz*; 1958/9 *S, I*; 1959/60 *E, I.*

Tapscott, D. (14) (Arsenal) 1953/4 *Aust*; 1954/5 *Y, S, E, I*; 1955/6 *E, S, Aust, I*; 1956/7 *I, Czecho, E/Germ*; 1958/9 (Cardiff City) *E, I.*
Thomas, D. (2) (Swansea City) 1956/7 *Czecho*; 1957/8 *E/Germ.*
Thomas, M. (27) (Wrexham) 1976/7 *G, S* (2), *I*; 1977/8 *K, S, Czecho, E*; 1978/9 *M, T, G*; (Manchester United) 1979/80 *Eire, G, T, E, S, I;* 1980/81 *Czecho, S, E, USSR;* 1981/2 (Everton) *Czecho,* (Brighton) *Rus, Sp, E, S, I.*

Thomas, R. (50) (Swindon Town) 1966/7 *I*; 1967/8 *G*; 1968/9 *It, G, E, I*; 1969/70 *UK, E/Germ, It, E, S, I*; 1970/1 *Ru, Czecho, S, E, I*; 1971/2 *Fin, Czecho, Ru, E, S, I*; 1972/3 *E* (2), *Pol, S, E, I*; 1973/4 (Derby County) *Pol, E, S, I*; 1974/5 *H* (2), *Lux* (2), *S, E, I*; 1975/6 *Aust, Y, E*; 1976/7 *S, Czecho, E, I*; 1977/8 *K, S, Czecho.*
Thomas, S. (4) (Fulham) 1947/8 *E, S, I*; 1948/9 *S.*
Toshack, J. (39) (Cardiff City) 1968/9 *G, E/Germ, S, E, I*; 1969/70 *UK, E/Germ, It*; 1970/1 *S, E, I, Fin*; 1971/2 (Liverpool) *Fin, E*; 1972/3 *E* (2), *Pol, S, E*; 1974/5 *Aust, H* (2), *Lux* (2), *S, E*; 1975/6 *Y* (2), *E*; 1976/7 *S*; 1977/8 *K* (2), *S, Czecho*; (Swansea City) 1978/9 *S, E, I, M*; 1979/80 *G.*

Vearncombe, G. (2) (Cardiff City) 1957/8 *E/Germ*; 1960/1 *Eire.*
Vernon, R. (32) (Blackburn Rovers) 1956/7 *I, Czecho, E/Germ, Czecho;* 1957/8 *E/Germ, E, S, Swdn*; 1958/9 *S*; 1959/60 (Everton) *I*; 1960/1 *Eire, S, E*; 1961/2 *I, Braz* (2), *Mex*; 1962/3 *S, H, E*; 1963/4 *E, S*; 1964/5 (Stoke City) *Gr, I, It*; 1965/6 *E, Rus, S, D, I*; 1966/7 *I*; 1967/8 *E.*
Villars, A. (2) (Cardiff City) 1973/4 *E, S.*

Walley, T. (1) (Watford) 1970/1 *Czecho.*
Walsh, I. (18) (Crystal Palace) 1979/80 *Eire, T, E, S, Ic;* 1980/81 *T, Czecho, Eire, T, S, E, USSR;* 1981/2 *Czecho, Ic,* (Swansea C.) *Sp, S, I, F.*
Ward, D. (2) (Bristol Rovers) 1958/9 *E*; 1961/2 (Cardiff City) *E.*
Webster, C. (4) (Manchester United) 1956/7 *Czecho*; 1957/8 *H, Mex, Braz.*
Williams, G. (1) (Cardiff City) 1950/1 *Switz.*
Williams, G. E. (26) (West Bromwich Albion) 1959/60 *I*; 1960/1 *Eire, S, E*; 1962/3 *I*; 1963/4 *H, E, S, I*; 1964/5 *S, D, E, Gr* (2), *I, It, Rus*; 1965/6 *I, Braz, Braz 'B', Ch*; 1966/7 *S, E, I*; 1967/8 *I*; 1968/9 *It.*
Williams, G. G. (5) (Swansea City) 1960/1 *I, Sp* (2), *H*; 1961/2 *E.*
Williams, H. (4) (Newport County) 1948/9 *I, Switz* (Leeds United); 1949/50 *I*; 1950/1 *S.*
Williams, Herbert (3) (Swansea City) 1964/5 *Gr* (2); 1970/1 *Ru.*
Williams, S. (43) (West Bromwich Albion) 1953/4 *Aust*; 1954/5 *E, I*; 1955/6 *E, S, Aust*; 1957/8 *E, S, Isr* (2), *I, H, Mex, Swdn, H, Braz*; 1958/9 *S, E, I*; 1959/60 *E, S, I*; 1960/1 *Eire, I, Sp* (2), *H*; 1961/2 *E, S, I, Braz* (2), *Mex*; 1962/3 (Southampton) *S, H, E, H*; 1963/4 *E, S*; 1964/5 *S, D, E*; 1965/6 *D.*
Witcombe, D. (3) (West Bromwich Albion) 1946/7 *S, E,* Sheffield Wednesday) *I.*
Woosnam, P. (17) (Leyton Orient) 1958/9 *S,* (West Ham United), *E*; 1959/60 *E, S, I*; 1960/1 *Eire, S, E, I, Sp, H*; 1961/2 *E, S, I, Braz*; 1962/3 (Aston Villa) *H, I.*

Yorath, T. (58) (Leeds United) 1969/70 *It*; 1970/1 *S, E, I*; 1971/2 *Czecho, E, S, I*; 1972/3 *E, Pol, S*; 1973/4 *Pol, E, S, I*; 1974/5 *Aust, H* (2), *Lux* (2), *S*; 1975/6 *Aust, E* (2), *Y* (2), *S, I*; (Coventry City) 1976/7 *G, S, Czecho, S, E, I*; 1977/8 *K* (2), *S* (2), *Czecho, G, E, I*; 1978/9 *T, G, S, E, I*; (Tottenham Hotspur) 1979/80 *Eire, T, E, S, I, Ic;* 1980/81 *T, Czecho, Eire, T, USSR.*

THE FIFA WORLD CUP 1982

The Qualifying Competition

The qualifying competition was a regional affair, with the world divided into five areas for the purpose. These areas were Europe, South America, Asia/Oceania, Africa and CONCACAF (The Confederation of Northern and Central American and Caribbean Football Associations). Spain qualified automatically as host nation for the 1982 Final Tournament, and Argentina qualified automatically as reigning Champions.

EUROPE

There were six groups of five teams each, and one group of three teams in the European Zone. After a straightforward league competition within each group, the two top teams from groups 1-6 qualified, plus the winner of group 7.

Group 1 (West Germany, Austria, Bulgaria, Albania, Finland)

Finland (0) 0, Bulgaria (1) 2	4 June 1980
Albania (2) 2, Finland (0) 0	3 September 1980
Finland (0) 0, Austria (1) 2	24 September 1980
Bulgaria (1) 2, Albania (0) 1	19 October 1980
Austria (3) 5, Albania (0) 0	15 November 1980
Bulgaria (0) 1, West Germany (2) 3	3 December 1980
Albania (0) 0, Austria (1) 1	6 December 1980
Albania (0) 0, West Germany (1) 2	1 April 1981
West Germany (2) 2, Austria (0) 0	29 April 1981
Bulgaria (1) 4, Finland (0) 0	13 May 1981
Finland (0) 0, West Germany (3) 4	24 May 1981
Austria (1) 2, Bulgaria (0) 0	28 May 1981
Austria (2) 5, Finland (0) 1	17 June 1981
Finland (0) 2, Albania (0) 1	2 September 1981
West Germany (2) 7, Finland (1) 1	23 September 1981
Austria (1) 1, West Germany (2) 3	14 October 1981
Albania (0) 0, Bulgaria (0) 2	14 October 1981
Bulgaria (0) 0, Austria (0) 0	11 November 1981
West Germany (5) 8, Albania (0) 0	18 November 1981
West Germany (1) 4, Bulgaria (0) 0	22 November 1981

FINAL TABLE	P	W	D	L	F	A	Pts
WEST GERMANY	8	8	0	0	33	3	16
AUSTRIA	8	5	1	2	16	86	11
Bulgaria	8	4	1	3	11	10	9
Albania	8	1	0	7	4	22	2
£uFinland	8	1	0	7	4	27	2

Group 2 (Belgium, France, Eire, Netherlands, Cyprus)

Cyprus (1) 2, Eire (3) 3 — 26 March 1980
Cyprus: Fanos; Papacostas, Fitas, Papadorolous, Stefanos, Pantziaras, Filipos (Tsingis), Mavroudis, Kaiafas, Kossongergis, Kanaris (Theophanus).
Eire: Peyton; Grealish, O'Leary, D., Lawrenson, Grimes, Daly, Brady, Murphy (O'Brien, F.), Heighway (Ryan), McGee, Stapleton.
Scorers: Cyprus – Pantziaras, Kaiafas (pen); Eire – McGee, Lawrenson, Stefanos og.

Eire (0) 2, Netherlands (0) 1 — 10 September 1980
Eire: Peyton; Langan, Hughton, O'Leary, P., O'Leary, D., Brady, Daly, Lawrenson, Stapleton, Grealish, Givens.

Netherlands: Hiele; Wijnstekers, Spelbos, Van de Korput (Metgod), Brandts, van Mierlo, Thijssen, Schoenmaker (van der Kerkhof, W.), Peters, van Diensen, Tahamata.
Scorers: Eire – Daly, Lawrenson; Netherlands – Tahamata.

Cyprus (0) 0, France (4) 7 — 11 October 1980
Eire (1) 1, Belgium (1) 1 — 15 October 1980
Eire: Peyton; Hughton, Langan, Moran, Lawrenson, Daly, Grealish, Brady, Stapleton, Heighway, Givens (McGee).
Belgium: Pfaff; Gerets, Millecamps (De Wolfe), Meeuws, Renquin, Cluytens, Van der Eycken, Van Moer (Heyligan), Vandenburg, Coeck, Cuelemans.
Scorers: Eire – Grealish; Belgium – Cluytens.

France (1) 2, Eire (0) 0 — 28 October 1980
France: Dropsy; Battison, Specht, Lopes, Bobsis, Larios, Tigana, Platini (Pettit), Rocheteau, Lacombe (Zimako), Six.
Eire: Peyton; Langan, Lawrenson, Moran, Hughton, Martin (Ryan), Brady, Grealish, Heighway, Stapleton, Robinson.
Scorers: France – Platini, Zimako.

Belgium (0) 1, Netherlands (0) 0 — 19 November 1980
Eire (4) 6, Cyprus (0) 0 — 19 November 1980
Eire: Peyton; Hughton, Langan, Lawrenson, Moran, Daly, Grealish, Brady, Stapleton, Robinson (Givens), Heighway.
Cyprus: Constantino; Kalotheou, Loucia, Lysandrou, Pantziaris, Erotokiou, Theofamous, Ylagoudakis, Kalafas (Kouis), Tsingis, Miamiliotis (Maroudis).
Scorers: Eire – Daly 2 (1 pen), Grealish, Robinson, Stapleton, Hughton.

Cyprus (0) 0, Belgium (1) 2 — 21 December 1980
Belgium (2) 3, Cyprus (1) 2 — 18 February 1981
Netherlands (1) 3, Cyprus (0) 0 — 22 February 1981
Netherlands (0) 0, France (0) 0 — 25 March 1981

Belgium (0) 1, Eire (0) 0 — 25 March 1981
Belgium: Preud Homme; Cerets, Millecamps, Meeuws, Renquin, Mommens (Vercauteren), Van der Eycken, Cluytens, Vandenburg, Coeck (Wellens), Ceulemans.
Eire: McDonagh; Langan, Martin, Moran, Hughton, Daly, Grealish, Brady, Stapleton (Walsh), Robinson, Heighway.
Scorer: Belgium – Ceulemans.

France (3) 3, Belgium (1) 2 — 29 April 1981
Cyprus (0) 0, Netherlands (1) 1 — 29 April 1981

Netherlands (1) 2, Eire (1) 2 — 9 September 1981
Netherlands: Schrijvers; Van de Korput, Krol, Brandts, Wijnstekers, Muhren, Thijssen, van Kooten, La Ling, Rep, Geels.
Eire: McDonagh; Langan, O'Leary, Lawrenson, Devine, Martin, Grealish, Brady, Stapleton, Robinson, Heighway.
Scorers: Netherlands – Thijssen, Muhren (pen); Eire – Robinson, Stapleton.

Belgium (1) 2, France (0) 0 — 9 September 1981
Netherlands (2) 3, Belgium (0) 0 — 14 October 1981

Eire (3) 3, France (1) 2 — 14 October 1981
Eire: McDonagh; Langan, O'Leary, Moran, Hughton, Whelan, Martin, Lawrenson, Brady, Stapleton, Robinson.
France: Castaneda; Janvion, Mahut (Bracci), Lopez, Bossis. Christophe, Giard, Larios, Platini, Couriol, Bellone (Six).
Scorers: Eire – Mahut (og), Stapleton, Robinson; France – Bellone, Platini.

France (0) 2, Netherlands (0) 0 — 18 November 1981
France (2) 4, Cyprus (0) 0 — 5 December 1981

FINAL TABLE	P	W	D	L	F	A	Pts
BELGIUM	8	5	1	2	12	9	11
FRANCE	8	5	0	3	20	8	10
Eire	8	4	2	2	17	11	10
Netherlands	8	4	1	3	11	7	9
Cyprus	8	0	0	8	4	29	0

Group 3 (USSR, Czechoslovakia, Wales, Iceland, Turkey)

Iceland (0) 0, Wales (1) 4 — 2 June 1980
Iceland: Olafsson; Haraldsson, Jonsson, Halldorsson, Geirsson, Thordarson, Edvaldsson, Gudlaugsson, Thorbjorsson, Petursson, Gudjohnson.
Wales: Davies; Nicholas, Price, Phillips, Jones, J., Yorath (Stevenson), Flynn, Giles, James, L., Walsh, Davies, G. (Harris).
Scorers: Wales – Walsh 2, Giles, Flynn (pen).

Iceland (0) 1, USSR (1) 2 — 3 September 1980
Turkey (0) 1, Iceland (1) 3 — 24 September 1980

Wales (2) 4, Turkey (0) 0 — 15 October 1980
Wales: Davies; Nicholas, Jones, Philips, Price, Yorath, Flynn, Giles, Harris, Walsh, James, L.
Turkey: Senol; Tungay, Cem, Husnu, Fatih, Erham, Necdet (Serrdar), Gungor, Tuncay, Sedat, Halil.
Scorers: Wales – Flynn, James, L. 2 (1 pen), Walsh.

USSR (2) 5, Iceland (0) 0 — 15 October 1980

Wales (1) 1, Czechoslovakia (0) 0 — 19 November 1980
Wales: Davies; Price, Ratcliffe, Nicholas, Yorath, Phillips, Thomas, Flynn, Walsh, Giles (Harris, C.), Charles.
Czechoslovakia: Hruska; Barmos, Vojacek, Jurkemik, Macela, Radimec, Kozak, Panenka, Vizek, Masny, Nehoda.
Scorer: Wales – Giles.

Czechoslovakia (2) 2, Turkey (0) 0 — 3 December 1980

Turkey (0) 0, Wales (0) 1 — 25 March 1981
Turkey: Senol; Onur, Necati, Husnu, Gelik-Sedat, Gungor, Sedat, Volkan, Necdet, Tuncay, Halil (Sinan).
Wales: Davies; Jones, Price, Phillips, Ratcliffe, Flynn, Nicholas, Yorath, James, Harris (Giles), Walsh (Charles).
Scorer: Wales – Harris.

Turkey (0) 0, Czechoslovakia (0) 3 — 15 April 1981
Czechoslovakia (2) 6, Iceland (0) 1 — 27 May 1981

Wales (0) 0, USSR (0) 0 — 30 May 1981
Wales: Davies; Jones, Price, Phillips, Ratcliffe, Flynn, Yorath, Nicholas, Thomas, Walsh (Charles), Harris (Giles).
USSR: Dasaev; Sulakvelidze, Chivadze, Blatcha, Burovsky, Buriak, Bessonov, Oganvsian, Andreev, Kipiani (Gavrilov), Blokhin.

Iceland (1) 2, Turkey (0) 0 — 9 September 1981

Czechoslovakia (1) 2, Wales (0) 0 — 9 September 1981
Czechoslovakia: Seman; Bocovsky, Vojacek, Jurkemik, Barmos, Radimec, Kozak, Berger, Nehoda, Panenka, Vizek (Licka).

Wales: Davies; Stevenson, Jones, Phillips (Walsh), Ratcliffe, Flynn, Nicholas, Thomas (James, R.), Harris, Curtis, James, L.
Scorers: Czechoslovakia – Davies (og), Licka.

Iceland (1) 1, Czechoslovakia (0) 1 — 23 September 1981
USSR (3) 4, Turkey (0) 0 — 23 September 1981
Turkey (0) 0, USSR (2) 3 — 7 October 1981

Wales (1) 2, Iceland (0) 2 — 14 October 1981
Wales: Davies; Ratcliffe, Jones, Nicholas, Mahoney, Curtis, James, R., Walsh, Charles, Harris, James, L.
Iceland: Baldursson; Halldorsson, Oskarsson, Ormslev, Geirsson, Jonsson, Gudlaugsson, Sigurvinsson, Edvaldsson, Gudjohnsen, Bergs.
Scorers: Wales – James, R., Curtis; Iceland – Sigurvinsson 2.

USSR (1) 2, Czechoslovakia (0) 0 — 28 October 1981

USSR (2) 3, Wales (0) 0 — 18 November 1981
USSR: Dasaev; Borovsky, Susloparov, Demianenko, Baltacha, Daraselia, Shangelia, Sulakvelidze, Gavrilov (Gutseav), Burjak, Blokhin.
Wales: Davies; Ratcliffe, Jones (Lovell), Nicholas, Phillips, Price, Curtis, Flynn, Rush, Mahoney (Thomas), James, L.
Scorers: USSR – Daraselia, Blokhin, Shengelia.

Czechoslovakia (1) 1, USSR (1) 1 — 29 November 1981

FINAL TABLE	P	W	D	L	F	A	Pts
USSR	8	6	2	0	20	2	14
CZECHOSLOVAKIA	8	4	2	2	15	6	10
Wales	8	4	2	2	12	7	10
Iceland	8	2	2	4	10	21	6
Turkey	8	0	0	8	1	22	0

Group 4 (Hungary, England, Rumania, Switzerland, Norway)
England (1) 4, Norway (0) 0 — 10 September 1980
England: Shilton; Anderson, Sansom, Thompson, Watson, Robson, Gates, McDermott, Mariner, Woodcock, Rix.
Norway: Jacobsen, O.; Berntsen, Kordahl, Aas, Grondalen, Albertsen, Hareide, Dokken, Larsen-Okland, Jacobsen, P., Erlandsen (Ottesen).
Scorers: England – McDermott 2 (1 pen), Woodcock, Mariner.

Norway (1) 1, Rumania (1) 1 — 24 September 1980

Rumania (1) 2, England (0) 1 — 15 October 1980
Rumania : Iordache; Negrila, Munteanu, Sames, Stefanescu, Beldaenu, Crisan, Iordanescu, Camataru, Ticleanu, Raducanu.
England: Clemence; Neal, Sansom, Thompson, Watson, Robson, Rix, McDermott, Birtles (Cunningham), Woodcock, Gates (Coppell).
Scorers: Rumania – Raducanu, Iordanescu (pen); England – Woodcock.

Switzerland (0) 1, Norway (1) 2 — 29 October 1980

England (2) 2, Switzerland (0) 1 — 19 November 1980
England: Shilton; Neal, Sansom, Robson, Watson, Mills, Coppell, McDermott, Mariner, Brooking (Rix), Woodcock.
Switzerland: Burgener; Wehrli, Hermann, Ludi, Geiger, Barberis, Pfister, Tanner (Egli), Schonenberger (Marti), Elsener, Botteron.
Scorers: England – Tanner og, Mariner; Switzerland – Pfister.

Switzerland (1) 2, Hungary (1) 2 — 28 April 1981

England (0) 0, Rumania (0) 0 — 29 April 1981
England: Shilton, Anderson, Sansom, Robson, Watson, Osman, Wilkins, Brooking (McDermott), Coppell, Francis, Woodcock.
Rumania: Iordache; Negrila, Munteanu, Sames, Stefanescu, Beldeanu, Crisan, Iordanescu, Camataru, Stoica, Balaci.

Hungary (1) 1, Rumania (0) 0 — 13 May 1981
Norway (0) 1, Hungary (0) 2 — 20 May 1981
Switzerland (2) 2, England (0) 1 — 30 May 1981
Switzerland: Burgener; Ludi, Zappa, Egli, Hermann (Weber), Wehrli, Barberis, Botteron, Scheiwiler, Sulser, Elsener (Maissen).
England: Clemence; Mills, Osman, Watson (Barnes), Sansom, Coppell, Wilkins, Robson, Keegan, Mariner, Francis (McDermott).
Scorers: Switzerland – Scheiwiler, Sulser; England – McDermott.

Rumania (0) 1, Norway (0) 0 — 3 June 1981
Hungary (1) 1, England (1) 3 — 6 June 1981
Hungary: Ketzirz; Martos, Balint, Varga, Mueller (Komjati), Garaba, Fazekas (Bodonyi), Nyilasi, Kiss, Mucha, Torocsik.
England: Clemence; Neal, Mills, Thompson, Watson, Robson, Keegan, Coppell, Mariner, Brooking (Wilkins), McDermott.
Scorers: Hungary – Garaba; England – Brooking 2, Keegan (pen).

Norway (0) 1, Switzerland (0) 1 — 17 June 1981

Norway (2) 2, England (1) 1 — 9 September 1981
Norway: Antonsen; Berntsen, Hareide, Aas, Grondalen, Albertsen, Giske, Thoresen, Okland, Jacobsen, Lund.
England: Clemence; Neal, Mills, Thompson, Osman, Robson, Keegan, Francis, Mariner (Withe), Hoddle (Barnes), McDermott.
Scorers: Norway – Albertsen, Thoresen; England – Robson.

Rumania (0) 0, Hungary (0) 0 — 23 September 1981
Rumania (0) 1, Switzerland (0) 2 — 10 October 1981
Hungary (1) 3, Switzerland (0) 0 — 14 October 1981
Hungary (1) 4, Norway (1) 1 — 31 October 1981
Switzerland (0) 0, Rumania (0) 0 — 11 November 1981

England (1) 1, Hungary (0) 0 — 18 November 1981
England: Shilton; Neal, Mills, Thompson, Martin, Robson, Keegan, Coppell (Morley), Mariner, Brooking, McDermott.
Hungary: Meszaros; Martos, Balint, Toth, Muller, Caraba, Fazekas, Csapo (Szanto), Torocsik, Kiss, Sallai.
Scorer: England – Mariner.

FINAL TABLE	P	W	D	L	F	A	Pts
HUNGARY	8	4	2	2	13	8	10
ENGLAND	8	4	1	3	13	8	9
Rumania	8	2	4	2	5	5	8
Switzerland	8	2	3	3	9	12	7
Norway	8	2	2	4	8	15	6

Group 5 (Yugoslavia, Italy, Denmark, Greece, Luxembourg)
Luxembourg (0) 0, Yugoslavia (0) 5 — 10 September 1980
Yugoslavia (2) 2, Denmark (1) 1 — 27 September 1980
Luxembourg (0) 0, Italy (1) 2 — 11 October 1980
Denmark (0) 0, Greece (0) 1, — 15 October 1980
Italy (1) 2, Denmark (0) 0 — 1 November 1980

Italy (1) 2, Yugoslavia (0) 0	15 November 1980
Denmark (2) 4, Luxembourg (0) 0	19 November 1980
Greece (0) 0, Italy (1) 2	6 December 1980
Greece (2) 2, Luxembourg (0) 0	28 January 1981
Luxembourg (0) 0, Greece (1) 2	11 March 1981
Yugoslavia (3) 5, Greece (0) 1	29 April 1981
Luxembourg (1) 1, Denmark (0) 2	1 May 1981
Denmark (0) 3, Italy (0) 1	3 June 1981
Denmark (0) 1, Yugoslavia (0) 2	9 September 1981
Greece (0) 2, Denmark (2) 3	14 October 1981
Yugoslavia (1) 1, Italy (1) 1	17 October 1981
Italy (0) 1, Greece (0) 1	14 November 1981
Yugoslavia (2) 5, Luxembourg (0) 0	21 November 1981
Greece (1) 1, Yugoslavia (2) 2	29 November 1981
Italy (1) 1, Luxembourg (0) 0	5 December 1981

FINAL TABLE	P	W	D	L	F	A	Pts
YUGOSLAVIA	8	6	1	1	22	7	13
ITALY	8	5	2	1	12	5	12
Denmark	8	4	0	4	14	11	8
Greece	8	3	1	4	10	13	7
Luxembourg	8	0	0	8	1	23	0

Group 6 (Scotland, Northern Ireland, Sweden, Portugal, Israel)

Israel (0) 0, N. Ireland (0) 0 — 26 March 1980
Israel: Haviv; Mahness, G., Shum, Barr, Cohen, A., Spiegel, Rifat, Cohen, J., Gariani (Mahness, O.), Damti, Peretz.
N. Ireland: Jennings; Nicholl, J., Nelson, Nicholl, C., O'Neill, J., O'Neill, M., McIlroy, Cassidy, Finney (Spence), Armstrong, Cochrane.

Sweden (1) 1, Israel (0) 1 — 18 June 1980

Sweden (0) 0, Scotland (0) 1 — 10 September 1980
Sweden: Hellstroem; Gustavsson, Borg, Bild, Arvidsson, Erlandsson, Ramberg, Nordgren, Nilsson, Sjoberg, Ohlsson.
Scotland: Rough; McGrain, Gray, F., Miller, McLeish, Hansen, Dalglish, Strachan, Gray, A., Gemmill, Robertson.
Scorer: Scotland – Strachan.

N. Ireland (3) 3, Sweden (0) 0 — 15 October 1980
N. Ireland: Platt; Nicholl, J., Nicholl, C., McClelland, Donaghy, Brotherston, O'Neill, Cassidy (McCreery), McIlroy, Hamilton (Cochrane), Armstrong.
Sweden: Moller; Borg, Borgesson, Arvidsson, Larsson, Ramberg (Erlandsson), Nilsson, P., Halmgren, Nilsson, T., Edstroem, Ohlsson (Sjoeberg).
Scorers: N. Ireland – Brotherston, McIlroy, Nicholl, C.

Scotland (0) 0, Portugal (0) 0 — 15 October 1980
Scotland: Rough; McGrain, Gray, F., Souness, Hansen, Miller, Strachan, Dalglish, Gray, A., Gemmill, Robertson.
Portugal: Bento; Gabriel, Pietra, Simoes, Larangeira, Fernandes, Eurico, Costa, Chalana, Dos Santos, Jordao (Nene).

Israel (0) 0, Sweden (0) 0 — 12 November 1980

Portugal (0) 1, N. Ireland (0) 0 — 19 November 1980
Portugal: Bento; Gabriel, Simoes, Larangeira, Pietra, Sheu, Carlos Manuel (Nene) Alves (Texeira), Chalana, Jordao, Costa.
N. Ireland: Platt; Nicholl, J., O'Neill, J., Nicholl, C., Donaghy, O'Neill, M., Cassidy

(McCreery), McIlroy, Brotherston, Armstrong, Hamilton (Cochrane).
Scorer: Portugal – Jordao.

Portugal (2) 3, Israel (0) 0 — 17 December 1980

Israel (0) 0, Scotland (0) 1 — 24 February 1981
Israel: Mizrahi; Mahness, Cohen, J., Ejhois, Cohen, A., Barr, Shum, Cohen, N., Sinai, Damti, Tabak.
Scotland: Rough: McGrain, Gray, F., Souness, McLeish, Burns, Wark (Miller), Dalglish (Gray, A.), Archibald, Gemmill, Robertson.
Scorer: Scotland – Dalglish.

Scotland (0) 1, N. Ireland (0) 1 — 25 March 1981
Scotland: Rough; McGrain, Gray, F., Burns, McLeish, Miller, Wark, Archibald, Gray, A., Gemmill, Robertson.
N. Ireland: Jennings; Nicholl, J., Nicholl, C., O'Neill, J., Nelson, McCreery, McIlroy, McClelland, Cochrane, Armstrong, Hamilton.
Scorers: Scotland – Wark; N. Ireland – Hamilton.

Scotland (2) 3, Israel (0) 1 — 28 April 1981
Scotland: Rough; McGrain, Gray, F., Souness, McLeish, Hansen, Provan, Archibald, Jordan, Hartford, Robertson.
Israel: Mizrahi; Mahness, Cohen, J., Ekhois, Cohen, A., Barr, Shum, Zeituni, Sinai, Damti, Tabak.
Scorers: Scotland – Robertson (2 pens), Provan; Israel – Sinai.

N. Ireland (0) 1, Portugal (0) 0 — 29 April 1981
N. Ireland: Jennings; Nicholl, J., Nicholl, C., O'Neill, J., Nelson, O'Neill, M., McCreery, McIlroy, Cochrane, Armstrong, Hamilton.
Portugal: Bento; Gabriel, Humberto, Simoes, Pietra, Sheu, Manuel, Alves, Jordao, Oliveria (Nene), Costa.
Scorer: N. Ireland – Armstrong.

Sweden (0) 1, N. Ireland (0) 0 — 3 June 1981
Sweden: Ravelli; Fredriksson, Hysen, Borjesson, Erlandsson, Persson, Borg, Nilsson P., Nilsson T., Sjoberg, Svensson.
N. Ireland: Jennings; Nicholl J. (Spence), Nicholl C., O'Neill J., Nelson, O'Neill M., McCreery (McClelland), McIlroy, Cochrane, Hamilton, Armstrong.
Scorer: Sweden – Sjoberg.

Sweden (1) 3, Portugal (0) 0 — 24 June 1981

Scotland (1) 2, Sweden (0) 0 — 9 September 1981
Scotland: Rough; McGrain, Gray, F., Wark, McLeish, Hansen, Provan, Dalglish (Gray, A.), Jordan, Hartford, Robertson.
Sweden: Ravelli, T.; Erlandsson, Hysen, Oergesson, B.B., Fredriksson, Borg, Ravelli, A., Bjorklund, Larsson, Sjoberg, Svensson.
Scorers: Scotland – Jordan, Robertson (pen).

Portugal (0) 1, Sweden (1) 2 — 14 October 1981

N. Ireland (0) 0, Scotland (0) 0 — 14 October 1981
N. Ireland: Jennings; Nicholl, J., Nicholl, C., O'Neill, J., Donaghy, O'Neill, M., McIlroy, McCreery, Brotherston, Armstrong, Hamilton.
Scotland: Rough; Stewart, Hansen, Miller, Gray, F., Strachan, Souness, Hartford, Robertson, Dalglish, Archibald.

Israel (4) 4, Portugal (1) 1 — 28 October 1981

N. Ireland (1) 1, Israel (0) 0 — 18 November 1981
N. Ireland: Jennings; Nicholl, J., Donaghy, McCreery, Nicholl, C., O'Neill, J.,

Brotherston, Cassidy, Armstrong, McIlroy, Hamilton.
Israel: Haviv; Machness, Cohen, J., Bar, Cohen, A., Schum, Ekhois, Malmilian, Iam (Sinai), Damti, Tabak.
Scorer: N. Ireland – Armstrong.

Portugal (1) 2, Scotland (1) 1 — 18 November 1981
Portugal: Bento; Frixo, Simoes, Teixeira, Eurico, Dito, Jaime, Romeu, Fernandes, Oliveria, Costa.
Scotland: Thompson; Stewart, Gray, F., Souness, Hansen, Miller, Provan, Strachan, Archibald, Hartford, Sturrock.
Scorers: Portugal – Fernandes 2; Scotland – Sturrock.

FINAL TABLE	P	W	D	L	F	A	Pts
SCOTLAND	8	4	3	1	9	4	11
N. IRELAND	8	3	3	2	6	3	9
Sweden	8	3	2	3	7	8	8
Portugal	8	3	1	4	8	11	7
Israel	8	1	3	4	6	10	5

Group 7 (Poland, East Germany, Malta)

Malta (0) 0, Poland (0) 2	7 December 1980
Malta (1) 1, East Germany (2) 2	4 April 1981
Poland (0) 1, East Germany (0) 0	2 May 1981
East Germany (0) 2, Poland (2) 3	10 October 1981
East Germany (2) 5, Malta (1) 1	11 November 1981
Poland (1) 6, Malta (0) 0	15 November 1981

FINAL TABLE	P	W	D	L	F	A	Pts
POLAND	4	4	0	0	12	2	8
East Germany	4	2	0	2	9	6	4
Malta	4	0	0	4	2	15	0

CONCACAF

This federation was split into three zones for the qualifying competition. The top two teams from each zone went through to the play-off, and the top two teams from the play-off qualified for the final tournament in Spain.

Northern Zone (Canada, USA, Mexico)

Canada (1) 1, Mexico (0) 1	18 October 1980
USA (0) 0, Canada (0) 0	25 October 1980
Canada (2) 2, USA (0) 1	1 November 1980
Mexico (4) 5, USA (0) 1	9 November 1980
Mexico (0) 1, Canada (0) 1	16 November 1980
USA (1) 2, Mexico (1) 1	23 November 1980

FINAL TABLE	P	W	D	L	F	A	Pts
CANADA	4	1	3	0	4	3	5
MEXICO	4	1	2	1	8	5	4
USA	4	1	1	2	4	8	3

Canada and Mexico qualify for the play-off.

Central Zone (Panama, Costa Rica, El Salvador, Guatemala, Honduras)

Panama (0) 0, Guatemala (1) 2	2 July 1980
Panama (0) 0, Honduras (1) 2	30 July 1980
Panama (1) 1, Costa Rica (0) 1	10 August 1980
Panama (0) 1, El Salvador (1) 3	24 August 1980
Costa Rica (0) 2, Honduras (2) 3	1 October 1980

El Salvador (2) 4, Panama (1) 1 — 5 October 1980
Guatemala (0) 0, Costa Rica (0) 0 — 12 October 1980
Honduras (0) 0, Guatemala (0) 0 — 26 October 1980
El Salvador v Costa Rica *Match not played – result by forfeit 2-0* -
Costa Rica (1) 2, Panama (0) 0 — 5 November 1980
Guatemala (0) 0, El Salvador (0) 0 — 9 November 1980
Guatemala (2) 5, Panama (0) 0 — 16 November 1980
Honduras (0) 1, Costa Rica (1) 1 — 16 November 1980
El Salvador (1) 2, Honduras (0) 1 — 23 November 1980
Costa Rica (0) 0, Guatemala (1) 3 — 26 November 1980
Honduras (1) 2, El Salvador (0) 0 — 30 November 1980
Guatemala (0) 0, Honduras (0) 1 — 7 December 1980
Costa Rica (0) 0, El Salvador (0) 0 — 10 December 1980
Honduras (3) 5, Panama (0) 0 — 14 December 1980
El Salvador (0) 1, Guatemala (0) 0 — 21 December 1980

FINAL TABLE	P	W	D	L	F	A	Pts
HONDURAS	8	5	2	1	15	5	12
EL SALVADOR	8	5	2	1	12	5	12
Guatemala	8	3	3	2	10	2	9
Costa Rica	8	1	4	3	6	10	6
Panama	8	0	1	7	3	24	1

Honduras and El Salvador qualify for the play-off.

Caribbean Zone

Extra Preliminary Round

Guyana (2) 5, Grenada (2) 2 — 30 March 1980
Grenada (0) 2, Guyana (2) 3 — 13 April 1980

Group A (Cuba, Surinam, Guyana)

Cuba (0) 3, Surinam (0) 0 — 17 August 1980
Surinam (0) 0, Cuba (0) 0 — 7 September 1980
Guyana (0) 0, Surinam (1) 1 — 28 September 1980
Surinam (2) 4, Guyana (0) 0 — 12 October 1980
Cuba (1) 1, Guyana (0) 0 — 9 November 1980
Guyana (0) 0, Cuba (3) 3 — 30 November 1980

FINAL TABLE	P	W	D	L	F	A	Pts
CUBA	4	3	1	0	7	0	7
Surinam	4	2	1	1	5	3	5
Guyana	4	0	0	4	0	9	0

Cuba qualifies for the play-off.

Group B (Haiti, Trinidad & Tobago, Netherlands Antilles)

Haiti (0) 2, Trinidad & Tobago (0) 0 — 1 August 1980
Trinidad & Tobago (0) 1, Haiti (0) 0 — 17 August 1980
Haiti (0) 1, Netherlands Antilles (0) 0 — 12 September 1980
Trinidad & Tobago (0) 0, Netherlands Antilles (0) 0 — 9 November 1980
Netherlands Antilles (0) 0, Trinidad & Tobago (0) 0 — 29 November 1980
Netherlands Antilles (0) 1, Haiti (1) 1 — 12 December 1980

FINAL TABLE	P	W	D	L	F	A	Pts
HAITI	4	2	1	1	4	2	5
Trinidad & Tobago	4	1	2	1	1	2	4
Netherlands Antilles	4	0	3	1	1	2	3

Haiti qualifies for the play-off.

Play-Off

(All matches played in Tegucigalpa, Honduras)

Mexico (2) 4, Cuba (0) 0	1 November 1981
Canada (0) 1, El Salvador (0) 0	2 November 1981
Honduras (2) 4, Haiti (0) 0	3 November 1981
Haiti (1) 1, Canada (0) 1	6 November 1981
Mexico (0) 0, El Salvador (0) 1	6 November 1981
Honduras (1) 2, Cuba (0) 0	8 November 1981
El Salvador (0) 0, Cuba (0) 0	11 November 1981
Mexico (0) 1, Haiti (0) 1	11 November 1981
Honduras (2) 2, Canada (1) 1	12 November 1981
Haiti (0) 0, Cuba (0) 2	15 November 1981
Mexico (1) 1, Canada (0) 1	15 November 1981
Honduras (0) 0, El Salvador (0) 0	16 November 1981
Haiti (0) 0, El Salvador (1) 1	19 November 1981
Cuba (1) 2, Canada (0) 2	21 November 1981
Honduras (0) 0, Mexico (0) 0	22 November 1981

FINAL TABLE	P	W	D	L	F	A	Pts
HONDURAS	5	3	2	0	8	1	8
EL SALVADOR	5	2	2	1	2	1	6
Mexico	5	1	3	1	6	3	5
Canada	5	1	3	1	6	6	5
Cuba	5	1	2	2	4	8	4
Haiti	5	0	2	3	2	9	2

SOUTH AMERICA (Conmebol)

Argentina were joined in the finals by the winners of each of the following three groups.

Group 1 (Brazil, Bolivia, Venezuela)

Venezuela (0) 0, Brazil (0) 1	8 February 1981
Bolivia (1) 3, Venezuela (0) 0	15 February 1981
Bolivia (1) 1, Brazil (1) 2	22 February 1981
Venezuela (1) 1, Bolivia (0) 0	15 March 1981
Brazil (1) 3, Bolivia (0) 1	22 March 1981
Brazil (1) 5, Venezuela (0) 0	29 March 1981

FINAL TABLE	P	W	D	L	F	A	Pts
BRAZIL	4	4	0	0	11	2	8
Bolivia	4	1	0	3	5	6	2
Venezuela	4	1	0	3	1	9	2

Group 2 (Peru, Uruguay, Colombia)

Colombia (0) 1, Peru (0) 1	26 July 1981
Uruguay (1) 3, Colombia (1) 2	9 August 1981
Peru (1) 2, Colombia (0) 0	16 August 1981
Uruguay (0) 1, Peru (2) 2	23 August 1981
Peru (0) 0, Uruguay (0) 0	6 September 1981
Colombia (1) 1, Uruguay (1) 1	13 September 1981

FINAL TABLE	P	W	D	L	F	A	Pts
PERU	4	2	2	0	5	2	6
Uruguay	4	1	2	1	5	5	4
Colombia	4	0	2	2	4	7	2

Group 3 (Chile, Ecuador, Paraguay)

Ecuador (0) 1, Paraguay (0) 0 — 17 May 1981
Ecuador (0) 0, Chile (0) 0 — 24 May 1981
Paraguay (0) 3, Ecuador (0) 1 — 31 May 1981
Paraguay (0) 0, Chile (0) 1 — 7 June 1981
Chile (1) 2, Ecuador (0) 0 — 14 June 1981
Chile (3) 3, Paraguay (0) 0 — 21 June 1981

FINAL TABLE	P	W	D	L	F	A	Pts
CHILE	4	3	1	0	6	0	7
Ecuador	4	1	1	2	2	5	3
Paraguay	4	1	0	3	3	6	2

AFRICA

First Round

Qualified by draw for Second Round: Zimbabwe, Sudan, Liberia, Togo.

Senegal (0) 0, Morocco (1) 1 — 22 June 1980
Morocco (0) 0, Senegal (0) 0 — 6 July 1980
Zaire (1) 5, Mozambique (1) 2 — 13 July 1980
Mozambique (0) 1, Zaire (2) 2 — 27 July 1980
Cameroon (1) 3, Malawi (0) 0 — 29 June 1980
Malawi (0) 1, Cameroon (0) 1 — 20 July 1980
Guinea (1) 3, Lesotho (1) 1 — 22 June 1980
Lesotho (0) 1, Guinea (1) 1 — 6 July 1980
Tunisia (1) 2, Nigeria (0) 0 — 29 June 1980
Nigeria (1) 2, Tunisia (0) 0 — 12 July 1980
Nigeria won 4-3 on penalties
Libya (1) 2, Gambia (0) 1 — 8 May 1980
Gambia (0) 0, Libya (0) 0 — 6 July 1980
Ethiopia (0) 0, Zambia (0) 0 — 18 May 1980
Zambia (2) 4, Ethiopia (0) 0 — 1 June 1980
Niger (0) 0, Somalia (0) 0 — 16 July 1980
Somalia (0) 1, Niger (1) 1 — 27 July 1980
Sierra Leone (0) 2, Algeria (0) 2 — 31 May 1980
Algeria (1) 3, Sierra Leone (0) 1 — 13 June 1980
Ghana v Egypt – *Ghana withdrew, 11.6.80: Egypt qualify for Second Round.*
Kenya (1) 3, Tanzania (1) 1 — 5 July 1980
Tanzania (1) 5, Kenya (0) 0 — 19 July 1980
Uganda v Madagascar – *Uganda withdrew, 26.6.80: Madagascar qualify for Second Round.*

Second Round

Libya v Egypt – *Libya withdrew, 22.12.80: Egypt qualify for Third Round.*
Algeria (2) 2, Sudan (0) 0 — 12 December 1980
Sudan (0) 1, Algeria (0) 1 — 28 December 1980
Niger (0) 0, Togo (0) 1 — 14 December 1980
Togo (0) 1, Niger (0) 2 — 28 December 1980
Liberia (0) 0, Guinea (0) 0 — 7 December 1980
Guinea (1) 1, Liberia (0) 0 — 21 December 1980
Cameroon (0) 2, Zimbabwe (0) 0 — 12 October 1980
Zimbabwe (1) 1, Cameroon (0) 0 — 16 November 1980
Morocco (2) 2, Zambia (0) 0 — 16 November 1980
Zambia (0) 2, Morocco (0) 0 — 30 November 1980
Morocco won 4-5 on penalties
Nigeria (1) 1, Tanzania (0) 1 — 6 December 1980
Tanzania (0) 0, Nigeria (1) 2 — 20 December 1980

Madagascar (1) 1, Zaire (0) 1	16 November 1980
Zaire (2) 3, Madagascar (2) 2	21 December 1980

Third Round

Algeria (1) 4, Niger (0) 0	1 May 1981
Niger (0) 0, Algeria (0) 0	31 May 1981
Guinea (0) 1, Nigeria (1) 1	12 April 1981
Nigeria (0) 1, Guinea (0) 0	25 April 1981
Morocco (1) 1, Egypt (0) 0	26 April 1981
Egypt (0) 0, Morocco (0) 0	8 May 1981
Zaire (1) 1, Cameroon (0) 0	12 April 1981
Cameroon (3) 6, Zaire (0) 1	26 April 1981

Fourth Round

Nigeria (0) 0, Algeria (2) 2	10 October 1981
Algeria (1) 2, Nigeria (1) 1	30 October 1981

ALGERIA qualified.

Morocco (0) 0, Cameroon (2) 2	15 November 1981
Cameroon (1) 2, Morocco (1) 1	29 November 1981

CAMEROON qualified.

ASIA/OCEANIA

The winning team from each group qualified for the play-off, and the top two teams from the play-off qualified for Spain.

Group 1 (New Zealand, Australia, Indonesia, Taiwan, Fiji)

New Zealand (2) 3, Australia (3) 3	25 April 1981
Fiji (0) 0, New Zealand (3) 4	3 May 1981
Taiwan (0) 0, New Zealand (0) 0	7 May 1981
Indonesia (0) 0, New Zealand (1) 2	11 May 1981
Australia (0) 0, New Zealand (1) 2	16 May 1981
Australia (2) 2, Indonesia (0) 0	20 May 1981
New Zealand (2) 5, Indonesia (0) 0	23 May 1981
New Zealand (1) 2, Taiwan (0) 0	30 May 1981
Fiji (0) 0, Indonesia (0) 0	31 May 1981
Fiji (1) 2, Taiwan (0) 1	6 June 1981
Australia (1) 3, Taiwan (0) 2	10 June 1981
Indonesia (0) 1, Taiwan (0) 0	15 June 1981
Taiwan (2) 2, Indonesia (0) 0	28 June 1981
Fiji (0) 1, Australia (4) 4	26 July 1981
Taiwan (0) 0, Fiji (0) 0	4 August 1981
Indonesia (3) 3, Fiji (1) 3	10 August 1981
Australia (3) 10, Fiji (0) 0	14 August 1981
New Zealand (7) 13, Fiji (0) 0	16 August 1981
Indonesia (0) 1, Australia (0) 0	30 August 1981
Taiwan (0) 0, Australia (0) 0	6 September 1981

FINAL TABLE	P	W	D	L	F	A	Pts
NEW ZEALAND	8	6	2	0	31	3	14
Australia	8	4	2	2	22	9	10
Indonesia	8	2	2	4	5	14	6
Taiwan	8	1	3	4	5	8	5
Fiji	8	1	3	4	6	35	5

Group 2 (Iraq, Syria, Bahrain, Qatar, Saudi Arabia)
Tournament staged in Riyadh, Saudi Arabia.

Qatar (0) 0, Iraq (0) 1	18 March 1981
Syria (0) 0, Bahrain (0) 1	19 March 1981
Iraq (0) 0, Saudi Arabia (0) 1	21 March 1981
Qatar (2) 3, Bahrain (0) 0	22 March 1981
Syria (0) 0, Saudi Arabia (0) 2	24 March 1981
Iraq (1) 2, Bahrain (0) 0	25 March 1981
Qatar (1) 2, Syria (1) 1	27 March 1981
Bahrain (0) 0, Saudi Arabia (0) 1	28 March 1981
Iraq (1) 2, Syria (0) 1	30 March 1981
Qatar (0) 0, Saudi Arabia (0) 1	31 March 1981

FINAL TABLE	P	W	D	L	F	A	Pts
SAUDI ARABIA	4	4	0	0	5	0	8
Iraq	4	3	0	1	5	2	6
Qatar	4	2	0	2	5	3	4
Bahrain	4	1	0	3	1	6	2
Syria	4	0	0	4	2	7	0

Group 3 (Kuwait, South Korea, Malaysia, Thailand, Iran)
Note: Iran officially withdrew from the tournament 17.3.81.

Malaysia (1) 1, South Korea (1) 2	21 April 1981
Kuwait (4) 6, Thailand (0) 0	22 April 1981
South Korea (2) 5, Thailand (1) 1	24 April 1981
Kuwait (2) 4, Malaysia (0) 0	25 April 1981
Malaysia (0) 2, Thailand (0) 2	27 April 1981
Kuwait (0) 2, South Korea (0) 0	29 April 1981

FINAL TABLE	P	W	D	L	F	A	Pts
KUWAIT	3	3	0	0	12	0	6
South Korea	3	2	0	1	7	4	4
Malaysia	3	0	1	2	3	8	1
Thailand	3	0	1	2	3	13	1

Group 4 (Hong Kong, Macao, China, North Korea, Japan, Singapore)

Play-off matches	
Hong Kong (0) 0, China (0) 1	21 December 1980
North Korea (2) 3, Macao (0) 0	22 December 1980
Singapore (0) 0, Japan (1) 1	22 December 1980
Group matches	
China (2) 3, Macao (0) 0	24 December 1980
Hong Kong (0) 1, Singapore (0) 1	24 December 1980
China (1) 1, Japan (0) 0	26 December 1980
Singapore (0) 0, North Korea (1) 1	26 December 1980
Hong Kong (1) 2, North Korea (2) 2	28 December 1980
Japan (0) 3, Macao (0) 0	28 December 1980
Semi-finals	
North Korea (0) 1, Japan (0) 0	30 December 1980
China (0) 0, Hong Kong (0) 0	31 December 1980
China won 5-4 on penalties	
Final:	
North Korea (1) 2, China (1) 2	4 January 1981
China won 4-2 after extra time	

Final Round

China (0) 0, New Zealand (0) 0	24 September 1981
New Zealand (1) 1, China (0) 0	3 October 1981
New Zealand (1) 1, Kuwait (0) 2	10 October 1981
China (2) 3, Kuwait (0) 0	18 October 1981
Saudi Arabia (0) 0, Kuwait (0) 1	4 November 1981
Saudi Arabia (2) 2, China (0) 4	12 November 1981
China (2) 2, Saudi Arabia (0) 0	19 November 1981
New Zealand (2) 2, Saudi Arabia (1) 2	28 November 1981
Kuwait (1) 1, China (0) 0	30 November 1981
Kuwait (1) 2, Saudi Arabia (0) 0	7 December 1981
Kuwait (1) 2, New Zealand (0) 2	14 December 1981
Saudi Arabia (0) 0, New Zealand (5) 5	19 December 1981

FINAL TABLE	P	W	D	L	F	A	Pts
KUWAIT	6	4	1	1	8	6	9
CHINA	6	3	1	2	9	4	7
NEW ZEALAND	6	2	3	1	11	6	7
Saudi Arabia	6	0	1	5	4	16	1

Play-off for second place: China (0) 1, New Zealand (1) 2 — 10 January 1982

WORLD CUP – 1982 FINAL TOURNAMENT

FIRST PHASE
Group 1 (Poland, Italy, Cameroon, Peru)
Italy (0) 0, Poland (0) 0
Vigo, June 14 1982, 27,000
Italy: Zoff; Gentile, Collovati, Scirea, Cabrini, Marini, Tardelli, Antognoni, Conti, Rossi, Graziani.
Poland: Mlynarczyk; Majewski, Zmuda, Janas, Jalocha, Matysik, Boniek, Buncol, Lato, Iwan (Kusto), Smolarek.

Peru (0) 0, Cameroon (0) 0
La Coruna, June 15 1982, 11,000
Peru: Quiroga; Duarte, Gonsales, Diaz, Olaechea, Uribe, Cueto, Velasquez, Leguia (La Rosa), Cubillas (Barbadillo), Oblitas.
Cameroon: Nkono; Mbom, Aoudou, Onana, Kaham, Abega, Mbida, Kunde, Milla (Tokoto), Ndjeya, Nguea (Bahoken).

Italy (1) 1, Peru (0) 1
Vigo, June 18 1982, 31,000
Italy: Zoff; Cabrini, Collovati, Gentile, Scirea, Antognoni, Marini, Tardelli, Conti, Graziani, Rossi (Causio).
Peru: Quiroga; Duarte, Diaze, Salguero, Olaechea, Cueto, Velasquez (La Rosa), Cubillas, Uribe, Oblitas, Barbadillo (Leguia).
Scorers: Italy – Conti; Peru – Diaz.

Poland (0) 0, Cameroon (0) 0
La Coruna, June 19 1982, 25,000
Poland: Mlynarczyk; Majewski, Janas, Zmuda, Jalocha, Buncol, Boniek, Palasz (Kusto), Lato, Iwan (Szarmach), Smolarek.
Cameroon: Nkono; Kaham, Onana, Ndjeya, Mbom, Aoudou, Abega, Kunde, Mbida, Milla, Nguea (Tokoto).

Poland (0) 5, Peru (0) 1
La Rosa, June 22 1982, 25,000
Poland: Mlynarczyk; Majewski, Janas, Zmuda, Jalocha (Dziuba), Buncol, Matysik, Kupcewicz, Łato, Boniek, Smolarek (Ciolek).
Peru: Quiroga; Duarte, Diaz, Salguero, Olaechea, Cubillas (Barbadillo), Velasquez, Cueto, Leguia, La Rosa, Oblitas (Uribe).
Scorers: Poland – Smolarek, Lato, Boneik, Buncol, Ciolek; Peru – La Rosa.

Italy (0) 1, Cameroon (0) 1
Vigo, June 23 1982, 31,000
Italy: Zoff; Gentile, Collovati, Scirea, Cabrini, Oriali, Tardelli, Antognoni, Conti, Rossi, Graziani.
Cameroon: Nkono; Kaham, Ndjeya, Onana, Mbom, Aoudou, Kunde, Mbida, Abega, Milla, Tokoto.
Scorers: Italy – Graziani; Cameroon – Mbida.

Final Table	*P*	*W*	*D*	*L*	*F*	*A*	*Pts*
POLAND	3	1	2	0	5	1	4
ITALY	3	0	3	0	2	2	3
Cameroon	3	0	3	0	1	1	3
Peru	3	0	2	1	2	6	2

Group 2 (West Germany, Austria, Algeria, Chile)
Algeria (0) 2, West Germany (0) 1
Gijon, June 16 1982, 42,000
Algeria: Cerbah; Guendouz, Kourichi, Merzekane, Mansouri, Belloumi, Dahleb, Fergani, Madjer (Larbes), Zidane (Bensaoula), Assad.
West Germany: Schumacher; Kaltz, Stielike, K-H. Forster, Briegel, Breitner, Magath (Fischer), Dremmler, Rummenigge, Hrubesch, Littbarski.
Scorers: Algeria – Madjer, Belloumi: West Germany – Rummenigge.

Austria (1) 1, Chile (0) 0
Oviedo, June 17 1982, 22,500
Austria: Koncilia; Krauss, Obermayer, Pezzey, Degeorgi (Baumeister), Hattenberger, Hintermaier, Weber (Jurtin), Prohaska, Krankl, Schachner.
Chile: Osben; Garrido, Figueroa, Valenzuela, Bigorra, Bonvallet, Dubo, Neira, (Manuel Rojas), Moscoso (Gamboa), Yanez, Caszely.
Scorer: Austria – Schachner.

West Germany (1) 4, Chile (0) 1
Gijon, June 20 1982, 30,000
West Germany: Schumacher; Kaltz, Stielike, K-H. Forster, Briegel, Dremmler, Breitner (Matthaus), Magath, Littbarski (Reinders), Hrubesch, Rummenigge.
Chile: Osben; Garrido, Figueroa, Valenzuela, Bigorra, Dubo, Bonvallet, Soto (Letelier), Moscoso, Yanez, Gamboa (Neira).
Scorers: West Germany – Rummenigge 3, Reinders; Chile – Moscoso.

Algeria (0) 0, Austria (0) 2
Oviedo, June 21 1982, 22,000
Algeria: Cerbah; Guendouz, Kourichi, Merzekane, Mansouri, Belloumi (Bensoula), Dahleb, (Tlemcani), Fergani, Madjer, Zidane, Assad.
Austria: Koncilia; Krauss, Obermayer, Degeorgi, Pezzey, Hattenberger, Hintermaier, Baumeister (Welzl), Prohaska (Weber), Krankl, Schachner.
Scorers: Austria – Schachner, Krankl.

Algeria (3) 3, Chile (0) 2
Oviedo, June 24 1982, 18,500
Algeria: Cerbah; Kourichi, Merzekane, Guendouz, Larbes, Mansouri (Dahleb), Fergani, Assad, Bensoula, Bourebbon (Yahi), Madjer.
Chile: Osben; Gallindo, Valenzuela, Figueros, Bigorra, Bonvallet (Soto), Dubo, Neira, Yanez, Caszely (Letelier), Moscoso.
Scorers: Algeria – Assad 2, Bensoula; Chile – Neira (pen), Letelier.

West Germany (1) 1, Austria (0) 0
Gijon, June 25 1982, 41,000
West Germany: Schumacher; Kaltz, Stielike, K-H. Forster, Briegel, Dremmler, Breitner, Magath, Littbarski, Hrubesch (Fischer), Rummenigge (Matthaus).
Austria: Koncilia; Krauss, Pezzey, Obermayer, Degeorgi, Hattenberger, Prohaska, Hintermaier, Weber, Schachner, Krankl.
Scorer: West Germany – Hrubesch.

Final Table	*P*	*W*	*D*	*L*	*F*	*A*	*Pts*
WEST GERMANY	3	2	0	1	6	3	4
AUSTRIA	3	2	0	1	3	1	4
Algeria	3	2	0	1	5	5	4
Chile	3	0	0	3	3	8	0

Group 3 (Belgium, Argentina, Hungary, El Salvador)
Argentina (0) 0, Belgium (0) 1
Barcelona, June 13 1982, 85,000
Argentina: Fillol; Olguin, Galvan, Passarella, Tarantini, Ardiles, Gallego, Maradona, Bertoni, Diaz (Valdano), Kempes.
Belgium: Pfaff; Gerets, Millecamps, De Schrijver, Baecke, Coeck, Vercauteren, Vandermissen, Czerniatynski, Vandenbergh, Ceulemans.
Scorer: Belgium – Vandenbergh.

Hungary (3) 10, El Salvador (0) 1
Elche, June 15 1982, 19,750
Hungary: Meszaros; Martos, Balint, Toth, Muller (Szentes), Garaba, Nyilasi, Sallai, Fazekas, Torocsik (Kiss), Poloskei.
El Salvador: Mora; Castillo, Jovel, Rodriguez, Recinos, Rugamas, Portillo (Zapata), Ventura, Huezo, Hernandez, Gonzalez, Rivas.
Scorers: Hungary – Nyilasi 2, Poloskei, Fazekas 2, Toth, Kiss 3, Szentes; El Salvador – Zapata.

Argentina (2) 4, Hungary (0) 1
Alicante, June 18 1982, 32,000
Argentina: Fillol; Galvan, Tarantini (Barbas), Passarella, Olguin, Ardiles, Gallego, Maradona, Bertoni, Kempes, Valdano (Calderon).
Hungary: Meszaros; Martos (Fazekas), Balint, Toth, Varga, Garaba, Nyilasi, Rab, Sallai, Kiss (Szentes), Poloskei.
Scorers: Argentina – Bertoni, Maradona 2, Ardiles: Hungary – Poloskei.

Belgium (1) 1, El Salvador (0) 0
Elche, June 19 1982, 10,000
Belgium: Pfaff; Gerets, Millecamps, Meeuws, Baecke, De Schrijver, Vandermissen, Vandenbergh (Van der Elst), Coeck, Vercauteren, Ceulemans (Van Moer).
El Salvador: Mora; Osorto (Diaz), Jovel, Rodriguex, Recinos, Fagoaga, Ventura, Huezo, Zapata, Gonzalez, Rivas.
Scorer: Belgium – Coeck.

Belgium (0) 1, Hungary (1) 1
Elche, June 22 1982, 30,000
Belgium: Pfaff; Gerets (Plessers), Millecamps, Meeuws, Baecke, Coeck, Vercauteren, Vandermissen (Van Moer), Czerniatynski, Vandenbergh, Ceulemans.
Hungary: Meszaros; Martos, Kerekes (Sallai), Fazekas, Torocsik, Kiss (Csongradi), Poloskei, Balint, Toth, Nyilasi, Varga.
Scorers: Belgium – Czerniatynski; Hungary – Varga.

Argentina (1) 2, El Salvador (0) 0
Alicante, June 23 1982, 28,000
Argentina: Fillol; Olguin, Passarella, Tarantini, Galvan, Ardiles, Gallego, Maradona, Bertoni (Diaz), Kempes, Calderon (Santamaria).
El Salvador: Mora; Osorto (Diaz), Jovel, Rodriguez, Ortiz, Fagoaga, Ventura (Alfaro), Huezo, Ramirez, Rivas, Gonzalez.
Scorers: Argentina – Passarella (pen), Bertoni.

Final Table	*P*	*W*	*D*	*L*	*F*	*A*	*Pts*
BELGIUM	3	2	1	0	3	1	5
ARGENTINA	3	2	0	1	6	2	4
Hungary	3	1	1	1	12	6	3
El Salvador	3	0	0	3	1	13	0

Group 4 (England, France, Czechoslovakia, Kuwait)
England (1) 3, France (1) 1
Bilbao, June 16 1982, 45,000
England: Shilton; Butcher, Mills, Sansom (Neal), Thompson, Coppell, Robson, Wilkins, Francis, Mariner, Rix.
France: Ettori; Battiston, Bossis, Tresor, Lopez, Larios (Tigana), Girard, Giresse, Rocheteau (Six), Platini, Soler.
Scorers: England – Robson 2, Mariner; France – Soler.

Czechoslovakia (1) 1, Kuwait (0) 1
Valladolid, June 17 1982, 25,000
Czechoslovakia: Hruska; Barmos, Jurkemik, Fiala, Kukucka, Panenka, Berger, Kriz (Bicovski), Janecka (Petrzela), Nehoda, Vizek.
Kuwait: Al-Tarabulsi; Naiim Saed, Ma'yoof, Mahboub, Waleed-Jasem, Al-Buloushi, Saed Al-Houti, Karem (Fajthi-Kaleem), Faisal Al-Dakheel, Jasem Yacoub, Al-Anbari.
Scorers: Czechoslovakia – Panenka (pen); Kuwait – Al-Dakheel.

England (0) 2, Czechoslovakia (0) 0
Bilbao, June 20 1982, 42,000
England: Shilton; Mills, Thompson, Butcher, Sansom, Coppell, Robson (Hoddle), Wilkins, Francis, Mariner, Rix.
Czechoslovakia: Seman (Stromsik); Barmos, Fiala, Radimec, Vojacek, Jurkemik, Chalonka, Vizek, Berger, Janecka (Masny), Nehoda.
Scorers: England – Francis, Barmos (own goal).

France (2) 4, Kuwait (0) 1
Valladolid, June 21 1982, 18,000
France: Ettori; Amoros, Tresor, Janvion, Bossis, Giresse, Platini (Girard), Genghini, Soler, Lacombe, Six.
Kuwait: Al-Tarabulsi; Saad, Ma'yoof, Mubarak, Jasem (Al-Shemmaro), Al-Buloushi, Al-Houti, Karem (Kameel), Al-Dakhil, Yacoub, Al-Anbari.
Scorers: France – Genghini, Platini, Six, Bossis; Kuwait – Al-Buloushi.

France (0) 1, Czechoslovakia (0) 1
Valladolid, June 24 1982, 25,000
France: Ettori; Amoros, Tresor, Janvion, Bossis, Giresse, Platini, Genghini, Soler (Girard), Lacombe (Couriol), Six.
Czechoslovakia: Stromsik; Barmos, Fiala, Stambacher, Vojacek, Jurkemik, Kriz (Masny), Bicovsky, Vizek, Janecka (Panenka), Nehoda.
Scorers: France – Six; Czechoslovakia – Panenka (pen).

England (1) 1, Kuwait (0) 0
Bilbao, June 25 1982, 39,700
England: Shilton; Neal Thompson, Foster, Mills, Coppell, Hoddle, Wilkins, Rix, Mariner, Francis.
Kuwait: Al-Tarabulsi; N. Mubarak, M. Mubarak, Al-Mubarak, (Al-Shammari), Ma'yoof, Al-Houti, Al-Buloushi, Al-Suwaayed, Kamil, Al-Dakhil, Al-Anbari.
Scorer: England – Francis.

Final Table	*P*	*W*	*D*	*L*	*F*	*A*	*Pts*
ENGLAND	3	3	0	0	6	1	6
FRANCE	3	1	1	1	6	5	3
Czechoslovakia	3	0	2	1	2	4	2
Kuwait	3	0	1	2	2	6	1

Group 5 (Northern Ireland, Spain, Yugoslavia, Honduras)
Honduras (1) 1, Spain (0) 1
Valencia, June 16 1982, 47,000
Honduras: Arvu; Guttierrez, Costly, Villegas, Bulnez, Toledo, Yearwood, Maradiaga, Morales (Caballero), Betancourt, Figueroa (Zelaya).
Spain: Arconada; Gordillo, Meceda, Alesanco, Camacho, Zamora, M. Alonso, J. Alfonso (Sanchez), Gonzalez (Saura), Satrustegui, Ufarte.
Scorers: Honduras – Zelaya; Spain – Ufarte (pen).

Northern Ireland (0) 0, Yugoslavia (0) 0
Zaragoza, June 17 1982, 25,000
Northern Ireland: Jennings; J. Nicholl, C. Nicholl, McClelland, Donaghy, McIlroy, M. O'Neill, McCreery, Armstrong, Hamilton, Whiteside.
Yugoslavia: Pantelic; Gudelj, Zajec, Stojkovic, Petrovic, Slijvo, Zlatko (Vujovic), Susic, Jovanovic, Hrstic, Surjak.

Spain (1) 2, Yugoslavia (1) 1
Valencia, June 20 1982, 47,500
Spain: Arconada; Camacho, Tendillo, Alesanco, Gordillo, Alonso, Sanchez, (Saura), Zamora, Juanito, Satrustegui (Quini), Ufarte.
Yugoslavia: Pantelic; Krmpotic, Zajec, Stojkovic, Jovanovic (Halilhodzic), Gudelj, Petrovic, Slijvo, Vujovic (Sestic), Surjak, Susic.
Scorers: Spain – Juanito (pen), Saura; Yugoslavia – Gudelj.

Honduras (0) 1, Northern Ireland (1) 1
Zaragoza, June 21 1982, 20,000
Honduras: Arzu; Guttierrez, Villegas, Cruz, Costly, Maradiaga, Gilberto, Zelaya, Morales (Laing), Betancourt, Figueroa.
Northern Ireland: Jennings; J. Nicholl, C. Nicholl, McClelland (Healy), Donaghy, M. O'Neill, McCreery, McIlroy, Armstrong, Hamilton, Whiteside (Brotherston).
Scorers: Honduras – Laing; Northern Ireland – Armstrong.

Honduras (0) 0, Yugoslavia (0) 1
Zaragoza, June 24 1982, 12,000
Honduras: Arzu; Droumond, Villegas, Costly, Bulnes, Zelaya, Yearwood, Maradiaga, Murillo (Laing), Betancourt, Figueroa.
Yugoslavia: Pantelic; Krmpotic, Stojkovic, Zajec, Jovanovic (Halilhodzic), Slijvo, Gudelj, Surjak, Vujovic (Sestic), Susic, Petrovic.
Scorer: Yugoslavia – Petrovic.

Northern Ireland (0) 1, Spain (0) 0
Valencia, June 25 1982, 49,562
Northern Ireland: Jennings; J. Nicholl, C. Nicholl, McClelland, Donaghy, M. O'Neill, McCreery, McIlroy (Cassidy), Armstrong, Hamilton, Whiteside (Nelson).
Spain: Arconada; Camacho, Tendillo, Alesanco, Gordillo, Sanchez, Alonso, Saura, Juanito, Satrustegui (Quini), Ufarte (Gallega).
Scorer: Northern Ireland – Armstrong.

Final Table	*P*	*W*	*D*	*L*	*F*	*A*	*Pts*
NORTHERN IRELAND	3	1	2	0	2	1	4
SPAIN	3	1	1	1	3	3	3
Yugoslavia	3	1	1	1	2	2	3
Honduras	3	0	2	1	2	3	2

Group 6 (Brazil, USSR, Scotland, New Zealand)
Brazil (0) 2, USSR (1) 1
Seville, June 15 1982, 50,000
Brazil: Waldir Peres; Leandro, Oscar, Luizinho, Junior, Socrates, Serginho, Zico, Eder, Falcao, Dirceu (Isidoro).
USSR: Dasaev; Sulakvelidze, Chivadze, Baltacha, Demianenko, Shengelia (Andreev), Bessonov, Gavrilov (Susloparov), Blokhin, Bal, Daraselia.
Scorers: Brazil – Socrates, Eder; USSR – Bal.

Scotland (3) 5, New Zealand (0) 2
Malaga, June 15 1982, 30,000
Scotland: Rough; McGrain, F. Gray, Souness, Hansen, Evans, Strachan (Narey), Dalglish, Brazil (Archibald), Wark, Robertson.
New Zealand: Van Hattum; Hill, Elrick, Mackay, Malcolmson (Cole), Almond (Herbert), Rufer, Boath, Wooddin, Sumner, Cresswell.
Scorers: Scotland – Dalglish, Wark 2, Robertson, Archibald; New Zealand – Sumner, Wooddin.

Brazil (1) 4, Scotland (1) 1
Seville, June 18 1982, 47,000
Brazil: Waldir Peres; Leandro, Oscar, Luizinho, Junior, Cerezo, Falcao, Socrates, Serginho (Isidoro), Zico, Eder.
Scotland: Rough; Narey, F. Gray, Souness, Hansen, Miller, Strachan (Dalglish), Hartford (McLeish), Archibald, Wark, Robertson.
Scorers: Brazil – Zico, Oscar, Eder, Falcao; Scotland – Narey.

USSR (1) 3, New Zealand (0) 0
Malaga, June 19 1982, 20,000
USSR: Dasaev; Sulakvelidze, Chivadze, Baltacha, Demianenko, Bessonov, Bal, Daraselia (Oganessian), Shengelia, Gavrilov (Radianov), Blokhin.
New Zealand: Van Hattum; Dods, Herbert, Elrick, Boath, Cole, Sumner, McKay, Cresswell, Rufer, Wooddin.
Scorers: USSR – Gavrilov, Blokhin, Baltacha.

Scotland (1) 2, USSR (0) 2
Malaga, June 22 1982, 38,000
Scotland: Rough; Narey, F. Gray, Souness, Hansen, Miller, Strachan (McGrain), Archibald, Jordan (Brazil), Wark, Robertson.
USSR: Dasaev; Sulakvelidze, Chivadze, Baltacha, Demianenko, Borovsky, Shengelia, Bessonov, Gavrilov, Bal, Blokhin.
Scorers: Scotland – Jordan, Souness; USSR – Chivadze, Shengelia.

Brazil (2) 4, New Zealand (0) 0
Seville, June 23 1982, 40,000
Brazil: Waldir Peres; Leandro, Oscar (Edinho), Luizinho, Junior, Cerezo, Socrates, Zico, Falcao, Serginho (Isidoro), Eder.
New Zealand: Van Hattum; Dods, Herbert, Elrick, Boath, Sumner, Mackay, Cresswell, (Turner), Almond, Rufer (Cole), Wooddin.
Scorers: Brazil – Zico 2, Falcao, Serginho.

Final Table	*P*	*W*	*D*	*L*	*F*	*A*	*Pts*
BRAZIL	3	3	0	0	10	2	6
USSR	3	1	1	1	6	4	3
Scotland	3	1	1	1	8	8	3
New Zealand	3	0	0	3	2	12	0

SECOND PHASE

Group A (Poland, USSR, Belgium)

Poland (2) 3, Belgium (0) 0
Nou Camp, Barcelona, June 28 1982, 20,000
Poland: Młynarczyk; Dziuba, Zmuda, Janas, Majewski, Kupcewicz (Ciolek), Buncol, Matysik, Lato, Boniek, Smolarek.
Belgium: Custers; Renquin, Millecamps, Meeuws, Plessers (Baecke), Van Moer, Coeck, Vercauteren, Czerniatynski (Van der Elst), Vandenbergh, Ceulemans.
Scorer: Poland – Boniek 3

Belgium (0) 0, USSR (0) 1
Nou Camp, Barcelona, July 1 1982, 25,000
Belgium: Munaron; Renquin, Millecamps, Meeuws, De Schrijver (M. Millecamps), Verheyen, Coeck, Vercauteren, Vandermissen (Czerniatynski), Vandenbergh, Ceulemans.
USSR: Dasaev; Borovsky, Chivadze, Baltacha, Demianenko, Bal, (Daraselia), Oganessian, Bessonov, Shengelia, (Rodionov), Gavrilov, Blokhin.
Scorer: USSR – Oganessian.

USSR (0) 0, Poland (0) 0
Nou Camp, Barcelona, July 4 1982, 40,000
USSR: Dasaev; Sulakvelidze, Chivadze, Baltacha, Demianenko, Borovsky, Oganessian, Bessonov, Shengelia (Andreev), Gavrilov (Daraselia), Blokhin.
Poland: Mlynarczyk; Dziuba, Zmuda, Janas, Majewski, Kupcewicz (Ciolek), Buncol, Matysik, Lato, Boniek, Smolarek.

Final Table	*P*	*W*	*D*	*L*	*F*	*A*	*Pts*
POLAND	2	1	1	0	3	0	3
USSR	2	1	1	0	1	0	3
Belgium	2	0	0	2	0	4	0

Group B
(West Germany, England, Spain)

West Germany (0) 0, England (0) 0
Bernabeu, Madrid, June 29 1982, 75,000
West Germany: Schumacher; Kaltz, K-H. Forster, Stielike, B. Forster, Muller (Fischer), Breitner, Dremmler, Briegel, Rummenigge, Reinders (Littbarski).
England: Shilton; Mills, Thompson, Butcher, Sansom, Coppell, Wilkins, Robson, Rix, Francis (Woodcock), Mariner.

Spain (0) 1, West Germany (0) 2
Bernabeu, Madrid, July 2 1982, 98,000
Spain: Arconada; Camacho, Gordillo, Alonso, Tendillo, Alesanco, Juanito (Ufarte), Zamora, Urquiaga, Santillana, Quini (Sanchez).
West Germany: Schumacher; Kaltz, K-H. Forster, Stielike, B. Forster, Breitner, Briegel, Dremmler, Littbarski, Fischer, Rummenigge, (Reinders).
Scorers: Spain – Zamora; West Germany – Littbarski, Fischer.

England (0) 0, Spain (0) 0
Bernabeu, Madrid, July 5 1982, 75,000
England: Shilton; Mills, Thompson, Butcher, Sansom, Wilkins, Robson, Rix (Brooking), Francis, Mariner, Woodcock (Keegan).
Spain: Arconada; Camacho, Gordillo, Alonso, Tendillo, (Macedo), Alesanco, Satrustegui, Zamora, Urquiaga, Saura (Uraldi), Santillana.

Final Table

	P	W	D	L	F	A	Pts
WEST GERMANY	2	1	1	0	2	1	3
England	2	0	2	0	0	0	2
Spain	2	0	1	1	1	2	1

Group C (Italy, Brazil, Argentina)
Italy (0) 2, Argentina (0) 1
Sarria, Barcelona, June 29 1982, 39,150
Italy: Zoff; Gentile, Collovati, Scirea, Cabrini, Oriali (Marini), Tardelli, Antognoni, Conti, Rossi (Altobelli), Graziani.
Argentina: Fillol; Olguin, Passarella, Galvan, Tarantini, Ardiles, Gallego, Maradona, Bertoni, Diaz (Calderon), Kempes (Valencia).
Scorers: Italy – Tardelli, Cabrini; Argentina – Passarella.

Brazil (1) 3, Argentina (0) 1
Sarria, Barcelona, July 2 1982, 44,000
Brazil: Waldir Peres; Leandro (Edevaldo), Oscar, Luizinho, Junior, Cerezo, Falcao, Socrates, Serginho, Zico (Batista), Eder.
Argentina: Fillol; Olguin, Barbas, Passarella, Tarantini, Ardiles, Galvan, Maradona, Bertoni (Santamaria), Calderon, Kempes (Diaz).
Scorers: Brazil – Zico, Serginho, Junior; Argentina – Diaz.

Italy (2) 3, Brazil (1) 2
Sarria, Barcelona, July 5 1982, 44,000
Italy: Zoff; Collovati (Bergomi), Gentile, Scirea, Cabrini, Oriali, Antognoni, Tardelli (Marini), Conti, Graziani, Rossi.
Brazil: Waldir Peres; Leandro, Oscar, Luizinho, Junior, Cerezo, Falcao, Socrates, Zico, Serginho (Isidoro), Eder.
Scorers: Italy – Rossi 3; Brazil – Socrates, Falcao.

Final Table

	P	W	D	L	F	A	Pts
ITALY	2	2	0	0	5	3	4
Brazil	2	1	0	1	5	4	2
Argentina	2	0	0	2	2	5	0

Group D (France, Austria, Northern Ireland)
France (1) 1, Austria (0) 0
Vicente Calderon, Madrid, June 28 1982, 37,000
France: Ettori; Battiston, Janvion, Tresor, Bossis, Giresse, Genghini (Girard), Tigana, Soler, Lacombe (Rocheteau), Six.
Austria: Koncilia; Krauss, Obermayer, Pezzey, Degeorgi, (Baumeister), Hattenberger, Hintermaier, Jara (Welzl), Schachner, Prohaska, Krankl.
Scorer: France – Genghini.

Northern Ireland (1) 2, Austria (0) 2
Vicente Calderson, Madrid, July 1 1982, 24,000
Northern Ireland: Platt; J. Nicholl, C. Nicholl, McClelland, Nelson, McCreery, M. O'Neill, McIlroy, Armstrong, Hamilton, Whiteside (Brotherston).
Austria: Koncilia; Krauss, Obermayer, Pezzey, Schachner, Prohaska, Pichler, Hagmayr (Welzl), Baumeister, Pregesbauer (Hintermaier), Jurtin.
Scorers: Northern Ireland – Hamilton 2; Austria – Pezzey, Hintermaier.

Northern Ireland (0) 1, France (1) 4
Vicente Calderon, Madrid, July 4 1982, 26,000
Northern Ireland: Jennings; J. Nicholl, McClelland, Donaghy, McIlroy, McCreery (J. O'Neill), M. O'Neill, Armstrong, Hamilton, Whiteside.

France: Ettori; Amoros, Janvion, Tresor, Bossis, Giresse, Genghini, Tigana, Platini, Soler (Six), Rocheteau (Couriol).
Scorers: Northern Ireland – Armstrong; France – Giresse 2, Rocheteau 2.

Final Table	*P*	*W*	*D*	*L*	*F*	*A*	*Pts*
FRANCE	2	2	0	0	5	1	4
Austria	2	0	1	1	2	3	1
Northern Ireland	2	0	1	1	3	6	1

Semi-finals
Poland (0) 0, Italy (1) 2
Nou Camp, Barcelona, July 8 1982, 75,000
Poland: Mlynarczyk; Dziuba, Zmuda, Janas, Majewski, Kupcewicz, Buncol, Matysik, Lato, Ciolek, (Palasz), Smolarek, (Kusto).
Italy: Zoff; Bergomi, Collovati, Scirea, Cabrini, Oriali, Antognoni (Marini), Tardelli, Conti, Rossi, Graziani (Altobelli).
Scorer: Italy – Rossi 2.

West Germany (1) 3, France (1) 3,
Sanchez Pizjuan, Seville, July 8 1982, 70,500
West Germany won 5-4 on penalties.
West Germany: Schumacher; Kaltz, K-H. Forster, Stielike, B. Forster, Briegel (Rummenigge), Dremmler, Breitner, Littbarski, Fischer, Magath (Hrubesch).
France: Ettori; Amoros, Janvion, Tresor, Bossis, Genghini (Battiston) (Lopez), Tigana, Platini, Giresse, Rocheteau, Six.
Scorers: West Germany – Littbarski, Rummenigge, Fischer; France – Platini (pen), Tresor, Giresse.

Third Place Play-off
Poland (2) 3, France (1) 2
Alicante, July 10 1982, 25,000
Poland: Mlynarczyk; Dziuba, Zmuda, Janas, Majewski, Kupcewicz, Buncol, Matysik (Wojcicki), Lato, Boniek, Szarmach.
France: Castenada; Amoros, Mahut, Tresor, Janvion, (Lopez), Girard, Larios, Tigana (Six), Couriol, Soler, Bellone.
Scorers: Poland – Szarmach, Majewski, Kupcewicz; France – Girard, Couriol.

Final
Italy (0) 3, West Germany (0) 1
Bernabeu, Madrid, July 11 1982, 90,089
Italy: Zoff; Bergomi, Cabrini, Collovati, Scirea, Gentile, Oriali, Tardelli, Conti, Graziani (Altobelli) (Causio), Rossi.
West Germany: Schumacher; Kaltz, K-H. Forster, Stielike, B. Forster, Breitner, Dremmler (Hrubesch), Littbarski, Briegel, Fischer, Rummenigge (Muller).
Scorers: Italy – Rossi, Tardelli, Altobelli; West Germany – Breitner.

WORLD CUP STATISTICS

Total goals: 146 in 52 games (average 2.8 per game)
Leading scorer: Paulo Rossi (Italy) – 6
Highest team aggregate: France – 16
Highest match aggregate: 11 (Hungary 10, El Salvador 1)
Best goalkeeping: Peter Shilton (England) 426 minutes without conceding a goal
Fastest goal: Bryan Robson (England) v France 27 seconds.

THE WORLD CUP FINALS

URUGUAY 1930

Uruguay 4, Argentina 2 (1–2)
Uruguay: Ballesteros; Nasazzi (capt), Mascheroni, Andrade, Fernandez, Gestido, Dorado, Scarone, Castro, Cea, Iriarte.
Argentina: Botasso; Della Torre, Paternoster, Evaristo, J., Monti, Suarez, Peucelle, Varallo, Stabile, Ferreira (capt), Evaristo, M.
Scorers: Dorado, Cea, Iriarte, Castro for Uruguay; Peucelle, Stabile for Argentina.
Leading scorers: Stabile (Argentina) 8.

ITALY 1934

Italy 2, Czechoslovakia 1 (0–0) (1–1) after extra time. *Rome*
Italy: Combi (capt), Monzeglio, Allemandi, Ferraris IV, Monti, Bertolini, Guaita, Meazza, Schiavio, Ferrari, Orsi.
Czechoslovakia: Planicka (capt), Zenisek, Ctyroky, Kostalek, Cambal, Krcil, Junek, Svoboda, Sobotka, Nejedly, Puc.
Scorers: Orsi, Schiavio for Italy, Puc for Czechoslovakia.
Leading scorers: Schiavio (Italy), Nejedly (Czechoslovakia), Conen (Germany) each 4.

FRANCE 1938

Italy 4, Hungary 2 (3–1). *Paris*
Italy: Olivieri; Foni, Rava, Serantoni, Andreolo, Locatelli, Biavati, Meazza (capt), Piola, Ferrari, Colaussi.
Hungary: Szabo; Polgar, Biro, Szalay, Szucs, Luzar, Sas, Vincze, Sarosi, (capt), Szengeller, Titkos.
Scorers: Colaussi (2), Piola (2) for Italy, Titkos, Sarosi for Hungary.
Leading scorer: Leonidas (Brazil) 8.

BRAZIL 1950

Final pool replaced knock-out system.
Final pool
Uruguay 2, Spain 2
Brazil 7, Sweden 1
Uruguay 3, Sweden 2
Brazil 6, Spain 1
Sweden 3, Spain 1
Uruguay 2, Brazil 1

Final positions

	P	W	D	L	F	A	Pts
Uruguay	3	2	1	0	7	5	5
Brazil	3	2	0	1	14	4	4
Sweden	3	1	0	2	6	11	2
Spain	3	0	1	2	4	11	1

Leading scorers: Ademir (Brazil) 7, Schiaffino (Uruguay), Basora (Spain) 5.

SWITZERLAND 1954

West Germany 3, Hungary 2.
West Germany: Turek; Posipal, Kohlmeyer, Eckel, Liebrich, Mai, Rahn, Morlock, Walter, O., Walter, F. (capt), Schaefer.
Hungary: Grosics; Buzansky, Lantos, Boszik, Lorant, Zakarias, Czibor, Kocsis, Hidegkuti, Puskas (capt), Toth, J.
Scorers: Morlock, Rahn (2) for Germany, Puskas, Czibor for Hungary.
Leading scorer: Kocsis (Hungary) 11.

SWEDEN 1958

Brazil 5, Sweden 2 (2–1). *Stockholm.*
Brazil: Gilmar; Santos, D., Santos, N., Zito, Bellini, Orlando, Garrincha, Didi, Vava, Pele, Zagalo.
Sweden: Svensson; Bergmark, Axbom, Boerjesson, Gustavsson, Parling, Hamrin, Gren, Simonsson, Liedholm, Skoglund.
Scorers: Vava (2), Pele (2), Zagalo for Brazil, Liedholm, Simonsson for Sweden.
Leading scorer: Fontaine 13 (present record total).

CHILE 1962

Brazil 3, Czechoslovakia 1 (1–1). *Santiago.*
Brazil; Gilmar; Santos, D., Mauro, Zozimo, Santos, N., Zito, Didi, Garrincha, Vava, Amarildo, Zagalo.
Czechoslovakia: Schroiff; Tichy, Novak, Pluskal, Popluhar, Masopust, Pospichal, Scherer, Kvasniak, Kadraba, Jelinek.
Scorers: Amarildo, Zito, Vava for Brazil, Masopust for Czechoslovakia.
Leading scorers: Albert (Hungary), Ivanov (Russia), Sanchez, L. (Chile), Garrincha, Vava (Brazil), Jerkovic (Yugoslavia) each 4.

ENGLAND 1966

England 4, West Germany 2 (1–1) (2–2) after extra time. *Wembley.*
England: Banks; Cohen, Wilson, Stiles, Charlton, J., Moore, Ball, Hurst, Hunt, Charlton, R., Peters.
West Germany: Tilkowski; Hottges, Schulz, Weber, Schnellinger, Haller, Beckenbauer, Overath, Seller, Held, Emmerich.
Scorers: Hurst 3, Peters for England, Haller, Weber for Germany.
Leading scorer: Eusebio (Portugal) 9.

MEXICO 1970

Brazil 4, Italy 1. *Mexico City.*
Brazil: Felix; Carlos Alberto, Brito, Piazza, Everaldo, Gerson, Clodoaldo, Jairzinho, Pele, Tostao, Rivelino. No subs.
Italy: Albertosi, Burgnich, Cera, Rosato, Facchetti, Bertini, Riva, Domenghini, Mazzola, De Sisti, Boninsegna. Subs: Juliano for Bertini, Rivera for Boninsegna.
Scorers: Pele, Gerson, Jairzinho, Carlos Alberto for Brazil, Boninsegna for Italy.

WEST GERMANY 1974

West Germany 2, Netherlands 1 (2–1). *Munich.*
West Germany: Maier; Vogts, Schwarzenbeck, Beckenbauer, Breitner, Bonhof, Hoeness, Overath, Grabowski, Muller, Holzenbein.
Netherlands: Jongbloed; Suurbier, Rijsbergen (De Jong), Haan, Krol, Jansen, Van Hanegem, Neeskens, Rep, Cruyff, Rensenbrink (Van der Kerkhof, R.).
Scorers: Breitner (*pen*), Muller for West Germany, Neeskens (*pen*) for Netherlands.

ARGENTINA 1978

Argentina 3, Netherlands 1 (after extra time). *Buenos Aires.*
Argentina: Fillol; Olguin, Passarella, Galvan, Tarantini, Ardiles (Larossa), Gallego, Ortiz (Houseman), Bertoni, Luque, Kempes.
Netherlands: Jongbloed; Poortvliet, Brandts, Krol, Jansen (Suurbier), Neeskens, W. Van der Kerkhof, R. Van der Kerkhof, Haan, Rep (Nanninga), Rensenbrink.
Scorers: Kempes 2, Bertoni for Argentina, Nanninga for Netherlands.

UEFA UNDER-21 COMPETITION 1980-82

In the eight qualifying groups, each team plays each other team twice, and points are awarded on the basis of two for a win and one for a draw. The eight group winners then go forward to the quarter-finals, and thereafter the competition is decided on a knock-out basis. The final of this competition will be held in two legs, the first in England on September 21, 1982 and the second in West Germany on October 12, 1982.

Group 1	*P*	*W*	*D*	*L*	*F*	*A*	*Pts*
West Germany	6	5	0	1	15	5	10
Bulgaria	6	5	0	1	7	5	10
Austria	6	1	1	4	3	9	3
Finland	6	0	1	5	4	10	1

Group 2	*P*	*W*	*D*	*L*	*F*	*A*	*Pts*
France	4	3	0	1	7	4	6
Belgium	4	2	0	2	4	4	4
Cyprus	4	1	0	3	4	7	2

Group 3	*P*	*W*	*D*	*L*	*F*	*A*	*Pts*
USSR	4	1	3	0	1	0	5
Czechoslovakia	4	1	2	1	4	2	4
Turkey	4	1	1	2	2	5	3

Group 4	*P*	*W*	*D*	*L*	*F*	*A*	*Pts*
England	6	4	1	1	12	5	9
Hungary	6	3	0	3	12	9	6
Rumania	6	2	1	3	9	12	5
Switzerland	6	1	2	3	5	12	4

Group 5	*P*	*W*	*D*	*L*	*F*	*A*	*Pts*
Italy	4	3	0	1	5	2	6
Yugoslavia	4	2	1	1	4	2	5
Greece	4	0	1	3	2	7	1

Group 6	*P*	*W*	*D*	*L*	*F*	*A*	*Pts*
Scotland	4	2	1	1	7	4	5
Denmark	4	1	2	1	4	4	4
Sweden	4	1	1	2	3	6	3

Group 7	*P*	*W*	*D*	*L*	*F*	*A*	*Pts*
Poland	4	4	0	0	11	3	8
Norway	4	1	1	2	5	6	3
East Germany	4	0	1	3	4	11	1

Group 8

	P	W	D	L	F	A	Pts
Spain	4	4	0	0	13	3	8
Netherlands	4	2	0	2	4	4	4
Luxembourg	4	0	0	4	2	12	0

Quarter-finals

France (0) 0, USSR (0) 0 — 10 March 1982
USSR (1) 4, France (0) 2 — 24 March 1982

Spain (1) 1, West Germany (0) 0 — 24 February 1982
West Germany (0) 2, Spain (0) 0 — 6 April 1982

Poland (0) 1, England (1) 2 — 17 March 1982
England (2) 2, Poland (0) 2 — 7 April 1982

Italy (0) 0, Scotland (1) 1 — 23 February 1982
Scotland (0) 0, Italy (0) 0 — 24 March 1982

Semi-finals

Scotland (0) 0, England (1) 1 — 19 April 1982
England (1) 1, Scotland (1) 1 — 28 April 1982

USSR (2) 3, West Germany (2) 4 — 21 April 1982
West Germany (2) 5, USSR (0) 0 — 30 April 1982

OTHER LEAGUE TABLES

Alliance Premier League

	P	*W*	*D*	*L*	*F*	*A*	*Pts*
Runcorn	42	28	9	5	75	37	93
Enfield	42	26	8	8	90	46	86
Telford United	42	23	8	11	70	51	77
Worcester City	42	21	8	13	70	60	71
Dagenham	42	19	12	11	69	51	69
Northwich Victoria	42	20	9	13	56	46	69
Scarborough	42	19	11	12	65	52	68
Barrow	42	18	11	13	59	50	65
Weymouth	42	18	9	15	56	47	63
Boston United	42	17	11	14	61	57	62
Altrincham	42	14	13	15	66	56	55
Bath City	42	15	10	17	50	57	55
Yeovil Town	42	14	11	17	56	68	53
Stafford Rangers	42	12	16	14	48	47	52
Frickley Athletic	42	14	10	18	47	60	52
Maidstone United	42	11	15	16	55	59	48
Trowbridge Town	42	12	11	19	38	54	47
Barnet	42	9	14	19	36	52	41
Kettering Town	42	9	13	20	64	76	40
Gravesend & Northfleet	42	10	10	22	51	69	40
Dartford	42	10	9	23	47	69	39
AP Leamington	42	4	10	28	40	105	22

Northern Premier League

	P	*W*	*D*	*L*	*F*	*A*	*Pts*
Bangor City	42	27	8	7	108	60	62
Mossley	42	27	11	7	76	43	59
Witton Albion	42	22	10	10	75	44	54
Gateshead	42	19	14	9	65	49	52
King's Lynn	42	19	12	11	61	36	50
Grantham	42	18	13	11	65	53	49
Burton Albion	42	19	9	14	71	62	47
Southport	42	16	14	12	63	55	46
Marine	42	17	12	13	64	57	46
Macclesfield Town	42	17	9	16	67	58	43
Workington	42	18	7	17	62	60	43
Worksop Town	42	15	13	14	52	60	43
South Liverpool	42	13	13	16	55	57	39
Goole Town	42	13	13	16	56	60	39
Oswestry Town	42	14	11	17	55	59	39
Buxton	42	14	11	17	48	56	39
Lancaster City	42	13	12	17	47	50	38
Gainsborough Trinity	42	10	13	19	60	69	33
Tamworth	42	10	9	23	31	56	29
Morecambe	42	9	11	22	43	86	29
Matlock Town	42	7	12	23	38	72	26
Netherfield	42	5	9	28	31	91	19

Southern League – Midland Division

	P	W	D	L	F	A	Pts
Nuneaton Borough	42	27	11	4	88	32	65
Alvechurch	42	26	10	6	79	34	62
Kidderminster Harriers	42	22	12	8	71	40	56
Stourbridge	42	21	10	11	69	47	52
Gloucester City	42	21	9	12	64	48	51
Bedworth United	42	20	10	12	59	40	50
Enderby Town	42	20	10	12	79	66	50
Witney Town	42	19	8	15	71	49	46
Barry Town	42	16	14	12	59	46	46
Corby Town	42	19	8	15	70	59	46
Merthyr Tydfil	42	16	12	14	63	54	44
Wellingborough Town	42	15	12	15	50	45	42
Bridgend Town	42	13	13	16	50	62	39
Bromsgrove Rovers	42	15	8	19	57	63	38
Bedford Town	42	12	13	17	45	54	37
Cheltenham Town	42	11	14	17	65	68	36
Taunton Town	42	12	8	22	46	76	32
Banbury United	42	11	8	23	63	91	30
Minehead	42	12	6	24	38	69	30
Cambridge City	42	10	8	24	38	80	28
Milton Keynes City	42	6	11	25	34	70	23
Redditch United	42	8	5	29	37	103	21

Southern League – Southern Division

	P	W	D	L	F	A	Pts
Wealdstone	46	32	8	6	100	32	72
Hastings United	46	31	9	6	79	34	71
Dorchester Town	46	21	18	7	76	41	60
Gosport Borough	46	26	8	12	76	45	60
Fareham Town	46	20	14	12	58	48	54
Poole Town	46	19	15	12	92	63	53
Waterlooville	46	22	9	15	75	53	53
Welling United	46	19	13	14	70	48	51
Addlestone & Weybridge Town	46	17	17	12	71	53	51
Chelmsford City	46	20	11	15	64	53	51
Aylesbury United	46	19	12	15	79	61	50
Basingstoke Town	46	18	12	16	75	61	48
Dover	46	19	8	19	61	63	46
Ashford Town	46	16	14	16	52	56	46
Tonbridge AFC	46	19	7	20	62	70	45
Dunstable	46	18	8	20	63	68	44
Salisbury	46	16	10	20	64	81	42
Hounslow	46	15	11	20	59	83	41
Hillingdon Borough	46	14	10	22	46	58	38
Canterbury City	46	10	16	20	49	78	36
Crawley Town	46	9	12	25	46	81	30
Folkestone	46	10	6	30	49	101	26
Andover	46	4	11	31	39	100	19
Thanet United	46	5	7	34	37	110	17

The Football Combination

	P	W	D	L	F	A	Pts
Queens Park Rangers	38	27	5	6	90	40	59
Southampton	38	26	6	6	88	36	58
Ispwich Town	38	25	6	7	84	37	56
Watford	38	20	9	9	57	46	49
Fulham	38	16	15	7	58	30	47
Norwich City	38	18	9	11	67	52	45
West Ham United	38	18	7	13	74	48	43
Tottenham Hotspur	38	16	10	12	56	46	42
Birmingham City	38	16	10	12	48	40	42
Luton Town	38	13	11	14	52	52	37
Arsenal	38	10	12	16	47	51	32
Orient	38	11	9	18	53	59	31
Swindon Town	38	11	9	18	52	66	31
Chelsea	38	11	9	18	42	58	31
Leicester City	38	10	10	18	47	64	30
Plymouth Argyle	38	10	9	19	41	64	29
Crystal Palace	38	12	2	24	46	78	26
Bristol Rovers	38	10	6	22	35	80	26
Oxford United	38	8	7	23	38	68	23
Reading	38	7	9	22	39	99	23

United Counties – Premier Division

	P	W	D	L	F	A	Pts
Stamford	36	25	5	6	71	28	55
Irthlingborough Diamonds	36	23	8	5	73	34	54
Rushden Town	36	19	7	10	61	32	45
Buckingham Town	36	19	7	10	63	43	45
Bourne Town	36	18	7	11	64	44	43
Potton United	36	14	11	10	41	30	41
Ampthill Town	36	14	11	11	73	67	39
Long Buckby	36	14	10	12	57	60	38
Holbeach United	36	14	9	13	53	46	37
Wooton Blue Cross	36	14	9	13	57	58	37
Kempston Rovers	36	13	10	13	63	62	36
Stevenage Borough	36	12	9	15	50	49	33
Desborough Town	36	10	13	13	49	55	33
S & L Corby	36	10	12	14	46	57	32
Rothwell Town	36	12	6	18	48	60	30
Brit Timken Duston	36	11	8	17	46	67	30
Eynesbury Rovers	36	8	9	19	35	58	25
Wolverton Town	36	8	4	24	36	68	20
St Neots Town	36	2	7	27	25	91	11

West Midlands (Regional) League – Premier Division

	P	*W*	*D*	*L*	*F*	*A*	*Pts*
Shifnal Town	42	26	11	5	82	36	63
Sutton Coldfield Town	42	26	9	7	80	43	61
Halesowen Town	42	24	8	10	84	45	56
Bilston	42	23	8	11	70	49	54
Ledbury Town	42	19	14	9	83	58	52
Rushall Olympic	42	16	18	8	72	54	50
Willenhall Town	42	18	11	13	64	46	47
VS Rugby	42	20	7	15	67	51	47
Blakenall	42	20	7	15	59	53	47
Dudley Town	42	17	12	13	61	52	46
Wednesfield Social	42	15	13	14	43	42	43
Lye Town	42	15	12	15	59	49	42
Hednesford Town	42	17	8	17	61	57	42
Coventry Sporting	42	13	11	18	43	54	37
Gresley Rovers	42	13	9	20	50	59	35
Hinckley Athletic	42	12	10	20	43	66	34
Tividale	42	13	6	23	56	82	32
Malvern Town	42	11	10	21	49	78	32
Armitage	42	10	11	21	43	69	31
Oldswinford	42	9	11	22	48	74	29
Brereton Social	42	7	10	25	47	100	24
Darlaston	42	6	8	28	37	84	20

Welsh Football League – Premier Division

	P	*W*	*D*	*L*	*F*	*A*	*Pts*
Ton Pentre	34	21	7	6	84	46	70
Cardiff Corinthians	34	20	5	9	67	44	65
Caerleon	34	20	3	11	59	46	63
Haverfordwest County	34	19	3	12	60	42	60
Milford United	34	17	8	9	56	39	59
Sully	34	14	12	8	55	41	54
Ammanford Town	34	16	5	13	38	39	53
Maesteg Park	34	15	5	14	56	43	50
Methyr Tydfil	34	14	6	14	43	42	48
Pembroke Boro'	34	12	10	12	54	52	46
Pontllanfraith	34	13	7	14	49	56	46
Newport YMCA	34	12	9	13	43	52	45
Barry Town	34	13	5	16	67	60	44
Lake United	34	12	6	16	47	51	42
Llanelli	34	11	6	17	38	54	39
Bridgend Town	34	7	10	17	44	60	31
Briton Ferry Athletic	34	7	6	21	34	62	27
Pontlottyn	34	4	5	25	31	96	17

South-East Counties – Senior League

	P	*W*	*D*	*L*	*F*	*A*	*Pts*
Queens Park Rangers	30	22	7	1	80	23	51
West Ham United	30	20	5	5	94	31	45
Tottenham Hotspur	30	16	7	7	63	42	39
Norwich City	30	13	12	5	47	29	38
Ipswich Town	30	12	11	7	50	35	35
Charlton Athletic	30	13	9	8	38	28	35
Gillingham	30	10	10	10	38	43	31
Arsenal	30	14	2	14	45	44	30
Watford	30	11	5	14	56	63	27
Crystal Palace	30	10	6	14	40	54	26
Millwall	30	8	10	12	32	47	26
Chelsea	30	11	4	15	30	47	26
Portsmouth	30	10	5	15	40	51	25
Fulham	30	9	5	17	44	74	21
Southend United	30	5	5	20	26	67	15
Orient	30	4	3	23	47	92	11

Central League

	P	*W*	*D*	*L*	*F*	*A*	*Pts*
Liverpool	42	29	9	4	87	30	67
Everton	42	30	3	9	98	32	63
Aston Villa	42	25	7	10	94	45	57
Nottingham Forest	42	23	10	9	102	37	56
Newcastle United	42	19	10	13	61	57	48
Wolverhampton Wanderers	42	19	10	13	79	69	48
West Bromwich Albion	42	17	13	12	57	44	47
Sheffield United	42	16	14	12	51	43	46
Manchester United	42	18	8	16	58	44	44
Derby County	42	18	8	16	60	54	44
Leeds United	42	18	5	19	60	53	41
Sheffield Wednesday	42	18	5	19	75	76	41
Coventry City	42	15	11	16	49	59	41
Stoke City	42	11	15	16	50	61	37
Bury	42	13	9	20	48	74	35
Blackpool	42	14	7	21	56	85	35
Blackburn Rovers	42	10	14	18	58	81	34
Manchester City	42	12	9	21	43	73	33
Preston North End	42	12	8	22	60	86	32
Huddersfield Town	42	12	5	25	45	87	29
Burnley	42	7	11	24	42	88	25
Bolton Wanderers	42	6	9	27	54	109	21

Isthmian League – Division One

	P	*W*	*D*	*L*	*F*	*A*	*Pts*
Wokingham Town	40	29	5	6	86	30	92
Bognor Regis Town	40	23	10	7	65	34	79
Metropolitan Police	40	22	11	7	75	48	77
Oxford City	40	21	11	8	82	47	74
Feltham	40	20	8	12	65	49	68
Lewes	40	19	7	14	73	66	64
Hertford Town	40	16	10	14	62	54	58
Wembley	40	14	15	11	69	55	57
Farnborough Town	40	15	11	14	71	57	56
Epsom & Ewell	40	16	8	16	53	44	56
Kingstonian	40	16	7	17	57	56	55
Hampton	40	15	9	16	52	52	54
Hornchurch	40	13	15	12	42	50	54
Aveley	40	14	10	16	46	58	52
St Albans City	40	14	9	17	55	55	51
Maidenhead United	40	11	10	19	49	70	43
Tilbury	40	9	15	16	49	67	42
Walton & Hersham	40	10	11	19	43	65	41
Chesham United	40	9	9	22	39	71	36
Clapton	40	9	7	24	44	73	34
Ware	40	5	2	33	29	105	17

Cheshire County League – Division One

	P	*W*	*D*	*L*	*F*	*A*	*Pts*
Hyde United	38	27	8	3	91	34	62
Chorley	38	23	9	6	70	34	55
Burscough	38	21	10	7	70	39	52
Winsford United	38	21	9	8	68	43	51
Rossendale United	38	18	10	10	62	44	46
Glossop	38	13	19	6	52	30	45
Darwen*	38	16	10	12	63	62	40
Curzon Ashton	38	12	15	11	57	50	39
Prescot Cables*	38	16	8	14	51	45	38
Stalybridge Celtic	38	14	9	15	71	66	37
Fleetwood Town	38	12	13	13	42	55	37
Formby	38	12	11	15	42	55	35
Accrington Stanley	38	11	11	16	40	57	33
Nantwich Town*	38	10	13	15	48	49	31
Leek Town	38	10	11	17	39	45	31
Horwich RMI	38	12	7	19	58	72	31
Bootle	38	11	12	15	49	47	30
St Helens Town	38	7	11	20	34	71	25
Ashton United	38	8	6	24	38	77	22
Droylsden	38	3	4	31	26	96	10

*2 points deducted for fielding ineligible players.

Northern Football League

	P	W	D	L	F	A	Pts
Blyth Spartans	38	25	8	5	77	31	83
Whitby Town	38	23	11	4	64	21	80
South Bank	38	20	7	11	72	44	67
Tow Law Town	38	18	8	12	76	58	62
Spennymoor United	38	16	13	9	59	37	61
Billingham Synthonia	38	17	9	12	57	46	60
Bishop Auckland	38	17	8	13	63	51	59
Durham City	38	17	5	16	75	67	56
Shildon	38	16	8	14	57	53	56
North Shields	38	14	13	11	67	61	55
Ferryhill Athletic	38	16	6	16	57	59	54
Horden Colliery Welfare	38	15	6	17	55	58	51
Crook Town	38	15	6	17	60	69	51
Evenwood Town	38	13	9	16	57	66	48
Penrith*	38	13	10	15	63	66	46
Consett	38	10	10	18	46	64	40
West Auckland Town	38	9	10	19	42	67	37
Ashington	38	9	8	21	50	87	35
Whitley Bay	38	8	7	23	47	83	31
Willington	38	3	10	25	46	102	19

*3 points deducted

Western League – Premier Division

	P	W	D	L	F	A	Pts
Bideford	38	26	10	2	88	20	62
Barnstaple Town*	38	26	8	4	78	31	59
Bridgwater Town	38	16	16	6	70	46	48
Clandown	38	17	12	9	49	37	46
Melksham Town	38	17	11	10	58	50	45
Frome Town	38	16	9	13	67	58	41
Weston-super-Mare	38	15	11	12	47	42	41
Saltash United	38	15	7	16	47	53	37
Devizes Town	38	14	7	17	53	60	35
Dawlish	38	11	13	14	45	53	35
Liskeard Athletic	38	11	12	15	39	48	34
Bridport	38	12	10	16	43	54	34
Clevedon Town*	38	11	12	15	58	60	33
Chippenham Town	38	12	9	17	33	39	33
Falmouth Town	38	12	9	17	46	55	33
Portway-Bristol	38	9	13	16	40	47	31
Wellington	38	10	11	17	50	62	31
Keynsham Town	38	9	13	16	39	55	31
Mangotsfield United	38	11	6	21	30	59	28
Welton Rovers	38	7	7	24	37	88	21

*1 point deducted for fielding an ineligible player.

Yorkshire League – Division One

	P	W	D	L	F	A	Pts
Emley	30	16	9	5	57	27	41
Guiseley	30	17	5	8	52	33	39
Leeds Ashley Road	30	15	9	6	44	30	39
Scarborough	30	15	7	8	51	38	37
Bentley VW	30	13	9	8	46	37	35
Lincoln United	30	13	8	9	47	35	34
Winterton Rangers	30	13	8	9	37	30	34
Thackley	30	13	7	10	51	35	33
Ossett Albion	30	10	11	9	28	26	31
North Ferriby United	30	10	7	13	46	46	27
Sheffield	30	10	7	13	33	46	27
Hallam	30	10	6	14	46	53	26
Frecheville CA	30	11	3	16	39	48	25
Farsley Celtic	30	10	2	18	38	54	22
Liversedge	30	6	5	19	24	52	17
York RI	30	5	3	22	28	77	13

Lancashire Combination

	P	W	D	L	F	A	Pts
Caernarfon Town	34	23	8	3	71	27	54
Colne Dynamoes	34	24	4	6	72	33	52
Nelson	34	19	7	8	66	44	45
Wren Rovers	34	18	7	9	67	47	43
Clitheroe	34	13	16	5	67	40	42
Great Harwood Town	34	16	8	10	61	47	40
Chadderton	34	17	5	12	62	43	39
Blackpool Mechanics	34	14	9	11	47	34	37
Vulcan Newton	34	13	8	13	61	46	34
Padiham	34	14	6	14	47	47	34
Lytham	34	11	11	12	74	66	33
Oldham Dew	34	12	6	16	48	61	30
Wigan Rovers	34	11	7	16	44	53	29
Bacup Borough	34	9	8	17	47	77	26
Whitworth Valley	34	5	12	17	42	68	22
Daisy Hill	34	5	9	20	31	64	19
Bolton ST	34	7	4	23	40	86	18
Ashton Athletic	34	4	7	23	22	76	15

ENFIELD WIN FA CHALLENGE TROPHY

First round	Second round	Third round	Fourth round	Semi-finals	Final
Telford U. 1	Telford U. 0, 3	Telford U. 0	Enfield 4	Enfield 0, 1	**ENFIELD 1** *Taylor* 15 May, Wembley
Burton Albion 0					
Bedford T. *1, 3	Bedford T. 0, 0				
Staines T. 1, 2					
Merthyr Tydfil 2	Merthyr Tydfil 1	Enfield 1			
Dorchester T. 1					
Weymouth 0	Enfield 6				
Enfield 1					
Dulwich Hamlet .1, 3	St. Albans C. 0	Scarborough 1, 2	Scarborough 2		
St. Albans C. 1, 4					
Marine 0	Scarborough 1				
Scarborough 1					
Slough T. 4	Slough T. 1	Slough T. 1, 1			
Bath C. 2					
Buxton 1	Rossendale U. 0				
Rossendale U. 2					
Dartford 2	Dartford 0	Northwich Victoria .3	Northwich Victoria .2	Northwich Victoria .0, 0 (at home in first leg)	
Leatherhead 1					
Northwich Victoria .3	Northwich Victoria .2				
Bangor C. 2					
Runcorn 2	Runcorn 4	Runcorn 0			
Stafford Rangers ...0					
Lancaster C. 2	Lancaster C. 0				
Spennymoor U. 0					
Tooting & Mit. U. .0, 1	Harlow T. 0	Sutton U. 1, 2	Worcester C. 1		
Harlow T. 0, 2					
Aylesbury U. 2	Sutton U. 1				
Sutton U. 4					
Minehead 1, 2	Worcester C. 4	Worcester C. ...1, 5*			
Worcester C. 1, 5					
Alvechurch 1	Croydon 1				
Croydon 3					

ALTRINCHAM 0

score after 90 minutes 0-0

Attendance: 17,500

Cheltenham T. 2	Epsom & Ewell 0	Altrincham 2	Altrincham 2, 3	Altrincham 1, 3	ALTRINCHAM 0
Epsom & Ewell 3					
Altrincham 1	Altrincham 1				
Nuneaton Borough .0					
Woking 2	Woking 0, 0	Mossley 0			
Barking 1					
Kettering T. 0	Mossley 0, 5				
Mossley 1					
Yeovil T. 2	Bishop's Stortford ..3	Bishop's Stortford ..6	Bishop's Stortford 2, 1		
Bishop's Stortford ..3					
Maidstone U. ...1, 2	Maidstone 0				
Hastings U. 1, 0					
Horden CW. ..1, 2, 1	Witton Albion 1	Witton Albion 1			
Witton Albion .1, 2, 2					
Hendon X5	Hendon 0				
Taunton T. 1					
Kidderminster H. 0, 2, 2	Kidderminster H. ..2	Kidderminster H. ..4	Kidderminster H. ..0	Wycombe W. 1, 0	
Barrow 0, 2, 1					
Ashington 1	Blythe Spartans 1				
Blythe Spartans 2					
Wealdstone 3	Wealdstone 1	Dagenham 3			
Gloucester C. 1					
Dagenham 1	Dagenham 2				
Hitchin T. 0					
Boston U. 0	Hyde U. 0, 2	Wycombe W. 4	Wycombe W. 1		
Hyde U. 1					
W'stow A. 1, 1, 1	Wycombe W. 0, 3				
Wycombe W. .1, 1, 5					
Stalybridge Celtic ..0	Chorley 0	Bishop Auckland ..1			
Chorley 1					
Frickley Ath. 0	Bishop Auckland ..1				
Bishop Auckland ..1					

** after extra time*

X at Queens Park Rangers

FOREST GREEN ROVERS WIN FA CHALLENGE VASE

Third round	Fourth round	Fifth round	Sixth round	Semi-finals	Final
Bedlington Terr. ...1	Seaham CW RS ...0	Guisborough T. 0	Blue Star 1, 1	Blue Star ....1, 1 (at home in first leg)	**FOREST GREEN ROVERS 3** *Leitch 2, Norman* 8 May Wembley
Seaham CW RS ...3					
Peterlee Newton ...3	Guisborough T. 1				
Guisborough T. 4					
Blue Star 3	Blue Star 2	Blue Star 1			
Eppleton C. W. 0					
Padiham 0, 1, 1	Osset Albion 1				
Osset Albion ..0, 1, 3					
Hemel Hempstead *3	Hemel Hempstead *2	Hemel Hempstead .1	Cheshunt 1, 0		
Rainham T. 2					
Redhill 1	Redhill 1				
Whitstable T. 0					
Marlow 3	Windsor & Eton ...0	Cheshunt 3			
Windsor & Eton ...4					
Cheshunt 1	Cheshunt 1				
Tiptree U. 0					
Wednesfield Social ‖0	Willenhall T. ...0, 1	Willenhall T. 1	Willenhall T. 1	Forest GR 4, 0	
Willenhall T. 2					
Shifnal T. *5	Shifnal T. 0, 0				
Hinckley Ath. 3					
Irlam T. *5	Irlam T 2	Irlam T. 0			
Maghull 0					
Hallam 3	Hallam 1				
Wren Rovers 1					
Shortwood U. 3	Shortwood U. 2	Shortwood U. 0	Forest GR *2		
Devizes T. 1					
Whyteleafe 0	Sholing Sports 0				
Sholing Sports 1					
Forest GR *2	Forest GR 3	Forest Green Rovers 1			
Almondsbury G ...1					
Paulton Rovers 1	Odd Down 1				
Odd Down 3					

RAINWORTH MINERS WELFARE 0

Attendance: 12,500

I'borough Dmds . . .2	I'borough Dmds . . .2	I'borough Dmds . . .2	I'borough Dmds .1, 0	Barton Rovers . . .0, 1 (at home in first leg)
Ampthill T. 1				
Harwich & P. 0	Gorleston 0			
Gorleston 1				
Buckingham T. 2	Buckingham T. 3	Buckingham T. 1		
Wivenhoe T. 1				
Grays Ath. 2	Grays Ath. 1			
Arlesey T. 1				
Leyton Wingate . . .8	Leyton Wingate . . .0	Barton Rovers 2	Barton Rovers . . .1, 1	
Horsham 0				
Ford U. 2, 1	Barton Rovers 2			
Barton Rovers . . .2, 4				
Knowle 3	Knowle 4	Knowle 1		
Halesowen T. 1				
Middlewich Ath. .□ 3	Middlewich Ath. . . .1			
Walsall Sportsco . . .2				
Newbury T. 0	Brockenhurst 1, 0	Molesey 2	Molesey 0	Rainworth MW . .0, 2
Brockenhurst 1				
Molesey 4	Molesey 1, 1			
Melksham T. 1				
Southall 4	Southall 1	Three Bridges 1		
Ruislip Manor 0				
Three Bridges . . . .◇ 3	Three Bridges 2			
Eastbourne U. 1				
Rainworth MW . . .*4	Rainworth MW 1	Rainworth MW 1	Rainworth MW 1	
Appleby F 1				
Frecheville C 2	Frecheville C 0			
Waterloo Dock 1				
WM Police . . . .‡4	WM Police 1	Skegness T. 0		
Long Eaton Grange 3				
Staveley Works . . .† 0	Skegness T. 3			
Skegness T. 1				

* after extra time X at Seaham † at Eastwood T. □ at Winsford U. ‖ at Willenhall ‡ at Burton Albion ◇ at Eastbourne U.

WATFORD WIN FA YOUTH CHALLENGE CUP

Third round	Fourth round	Fifth round	Semi-finals	Final
Loughton BC 0	Watford 3	Watford 5	Watford ....2, 5 (at home in first leg)	**Watford** **3, 4**
Watford 4				
Arsenal 0	Southampton 0			
Southampton 1				
Bury 2	Bury 4	Middlesbrough 0		
Sheffield W. 0				
Leicester C. 0	Middlesbrough 7			
Middlesbrough 3				
QPR 10	QPR 3	QPR 3, 1	Wolverhampton W. 1, 1	
Portsmouth 0				
Coventry C. 0, 1	Burnley 0			
Burnley 0, 2				
Stoke C. 1, 1	Wolverhampton W. ..1	Wolverhampton W. 3, 2		
Wolverhampton W. 1, 4				
Haringey Bor. 0	Charlton Ath. 0			
Charlton Ath. 3				
Birmingham C. 2	Birmingham C. 3	Birmingham C. 0, 0	Manchester U. .....1, 2 (at home in first leg)	**Manchester U.** .....**2, 4** (at home in first leg)
West Ham U. 1				
Cambridge U. 3	Cambridge U. 0			
Millwall 1				
Newcastle U. 2, 2	Leeds U. 0, 0	Manchester U. 0, 2		
Leeds U. 2, 3				
Manchester U. 0, 1	Manchester U. 0, 1			
Liverpool 0, 0				
Everton 0	Aston Villa 3, 5	Aston Villa 1	Sunderland 0, 1	
Aston Villa 2				
Chelsea 1, 0	Cardiff C. 3, 2			
Cardiff C. 1, 2				
Tottenham H. 1, 2	Tottenham H. 0, 0	Sunderland 2		
Fulham 1, 1				
Sunderland 1, 1	Sunderland 0, 1			
Chester 1, 0				

DINGLE RAIL WIN FA SUNDAY CUP

Third round	Fourth round	Fifth round	Semi-finals	Final
Dingle Rail 3	Dingle Rail 1			
Hartlepool LH 1		Dingle Rail 1		
Newbiggin SC 1, 1	Aireville 0			
Aireville 1, 2			Dingle Rail 2 (played at Formby)	
Highgate 1	Eagle 4			
Eagle 3		Eagle 0		
Fantail 0	Marklynn Motors 3			
Marklynn Motors 1				**Dingle Rail** 2 (played at Hitchin Town)
Road Sea 1, 2, 0	Byron & Counts XI 0			
By. & Cts. XI 1, 2, 4		Olympic Star 0		
Olympic Star 2	Olympic Star 1			
Quality Carpets 0			Crox. & G'moss RBL 1	
Club Layfayette 2	Cobblers 1			
Cobblers 7		Crox. & G'moss RBL 2		
AD Bulwell 1	Crox. & G'moss RBL 3			
Crox. & G'moss RBLK 2				
Clifda 1, 0	Two-Seven-Nine 1			
Two-Seven-Nine 1, 3		Lee Chapel Nth. 0		
Lakeside 0	Lee Chapel Nth. 2			
Lee Chapel Nth. 3			Twin Foxes 3 (played at Letchworth Garden City)	
Sheffield HR 2	Sheffield HR 0			
Laverstoke PA 0		Twin Foxes 1		
Evergreen 0	Twin Foxes 3			
Twin Foxes 2				**Twin Foxes** 1
Ely Crusaders 0	Oxford RS 1			
Oxford Road Social 2		Arras 2		
Sun 2, 0	Arras 4			
Arras 2, 4			Arras 1	
Hallen Sunday 2, 3	Hallen Sunday 4			
Pk Rngrs (W'field) 2, 1		Hallen Sunday 1		
Lion Rangers 1	Lion Rangers 0			
Allis TC 0				

ALLIANCE PREMIER LEAGUE — 1981-82 RESULTS

	Altrincham	Automotive Products Leamington	Barnet	Barrow	Bath City	Boston United	Dagenham
Altrincham		2–3	2–0	1–1	1–0	1–1	1–1
Automotive Products Leamington	0–1		0–2	1–1	0–1	2–2	0–4
Barnet	0–0	0–0		1–2	0–1	0–0	1–2
Barrow	1–0	4–2	2–1		0–1	1–0	2–2
Bath City	1–1	7–0	2–1	0–0		1–2	0–3
Boston United	1–1	2–0	1–1	2–1	4–0		3–4
Dagenham	2–0	0–0	1–1	1–0	0–1	2–0	
Dartford	0–1	2–2	2–1	0–2	1–1	2–1	0–3
Enfield	1–1	6–1	0–0	7–2	5–1	4–0	3–2
Frickley Athletic	1–1	4–0	0–1	2–1	1–3	4–1	3–1
Gravesend and Northfleet	1–1	4–1	2–3	3–1	2–0	3–1	1–2
Kettering Town	5–4	1–2	5–2	0–2	1–3	1–1	3–1
Maidstone United	0–0	4–0	0–0	1–0	1–0	0–2	2–2
Northwich Victoria	2–0	3–0	1–1	2–0	2–1	1–0	3–0
Runcorn	5–4	3–0	1–0	0–0	5–1	4–0	1–0
Scarborough	1–3	6–1	1–0	2–0	1–1	1–1	1–1
Stafford Rangers	2–0	3–1	1–0	1–1	2–0	0–0	0–0
Telford United	4–3	2–0	3–0	0–0	0–2	4–1	0–2
Trowbridge Town	0–2	2–1	1–1	2–0	1–1	1–0	0–1
Weymouth	1–0	1–2	0–2	3–0	2–0	2–1	1–1
Worcester City	4–3	2–1	3–1	4–0	2–0	0–0	2–1
Yeovil Town	2–1	3–2	4–1	0–0	2–0	0–1	1–4

Dartford	Enfield	Frickley Athletic	Gravesend and Northfleet	Kettering Town	Maidstone United	Northwich Victoria	Runcorn	Scarborough	Stafford Rangers	Telford United	Trowbridge Town	Weymouth	Worcester City	Yeovil Town
2–0	1–0	1–1	3–1	2–1	1–2	0–2	2–2	2–0	0–1	3–0	1–2	0–0	6–3	7–1
0–2	2–3	1–0	3–3	3–3	1–1	0–2	1–1	1–2	1–5	0–2	0–1	2–2	0–1	2–5
2–0	4–1	0–0	2–0	2–1	1–1	0–1	1–3	1–1	0–2	1–0	0–0	0–3	1–2	0–0
2–0	0–2	2–0	3–1	7–2	2–0	6–1	1–1	3–2	1–1	2–0	1–0	2–0	0–0	3–1
1–1	0–1	1–3	1–0	3–2	1–1	1–1	0–2	2–0	1–1	1–2	1–1	2–1	2–3	2–0
3–2	1–0	3–1	2–2	4–2	6–0	2–0	0–1	2–0	2–1	4–2	1–0	0–0	3–2	0–0
2–1	2–4	2–0	1–1	2–1	1–1	2–1	0–1	2–2	2–2	3–2	1–2	2–1	1–2	3–0
	0–2	1–0	0–1	2–2	2–1	0–1	1–2	0–1	2–2	2–0	1–0	0–0	0–2	5–0
1–1		3–0	4–0	1–1	3–2	1–0	2–0	1–4	2–0	3–4	2–1	3–0	1–2	2–0
3–0	1–1		1–1	3–2	0–3	1–0	2–0	2–3	2–0	0–0	2–0	0–1	1–2	2–1
1–0	1–2	4–1		1–3	2–2	0–1	2–4	3–0	1–1	0–2	1–1	2–1	1–1	1–1
4–4	0–1	0–0	2–1		2–2	0–0	0–0	1–2	3–0	1–3	4–0	1–2	0–1	1–1
5–1	1–4	0–0	0–1	2–0		6–1	1–2	0–2	3–1	2–2	3–0	0–1	2–2	0–1
3–4	2–1	0–0	1–0	2–0	3–1		1–1	2–1	1–2	2–2	0–0	0–2	3–0	1–1
4–2	2–0	1–0	1–0	3–2	1–1	0–1		2–0	1–0	2–3	2–0	3–1	5–2	2–1
2–0	1–4	0–1	5–0	1–0	0–0	0–4	3–0		1–0	0–0	3–1	2–1	1–0	2–2
0–3	0–1	0–0	1–0	1–1	1–1	2–2	0–1	1–1		1–2	0–2	3–0	0–2	3–1
2–0	0–0	7–1	1–0	1–0	1–2	2–1	1–1	1–1	0–3		2–0	2–0	3–2	2–1
2–1	2–2	2–0	2–1	0–1	3–0	1–0	0–0	1–3	1–1	1–2		1–1	1–1	2–4
2–1	2–2	5–0	1–2	2–3	1–0	1–0	0–1	3–1	1–1	0–1	1–0		3–2	1–1
2–0	1–2	3–2	2–1	1–1	4–1	0–1	0–1	2–4	1–1	2–1	3–1	0–0		0–1
1–1	1–2	1–2	2–1	1–1	1–0	4–1	1–3	0–0	2–1	1–2	2–0	1–4	3–0	

NORTHERN PREMIER LEAGUE – 1981-82 RESULTS

	Bangor City	Burton Albion	Buxton	Gainsborough Trinity	Gateshead	Goole Town	Grantham	King's Lynn	Lancaster City
Bangor City		3–2	3–1	2–1	3–1	3–0	3–1	2–0	2–1
Burton Albion	2–2		1–0	2–0	1–1	3–1	1–1	1–0	0–0
Buxton	1–0	5–1		2–1	0–0	1–0	2–3	1–0	2–1
Gainsborough Trinity	4–5	4–3	0–0		1–1	2–2	4–1	1–3	1–2
Gateshead	3–3	2–4	2–0	3–2		0–0	1–1	2–0	0–0
Goole Town	0–1	4–1	2–1	2–2	3–0		0–2	0–4	3–1
Grantham	2–2	1–2	2–0	3–0	2–1	1–1		2–2	1–0
King's Lynn (T)	2–0	3–0	4–1	3–0	1–0	2–0	3–0		2–1
Lancaster City	0–3	1–0	2–1	1–1	2–3	0–0	1–2	1–2	
Macclesfield Town	4–0	1–2	3–1	1–1	0–1	1–1	2–0	2–1	4–2
Marine	2–1	1–1	2–1	2–2	3–1	2–0	2–0	1–0	0–0
Matlock Town	2–7	0–1	0–0	1–1	1–5	1–0	0–4	1–3	2–1
Morecambe	0–9	1–2	0–0	0–2	2–3	2–2	3–1	0–0	1–4
Mossley	6–1	1–0	3–0	5–2	1–1	2–1	3–1	1–3	0–0
Netherfield	1–5	0–5	0–0	1–1	2–3	0–2	2–2	0–2	1–3
Oswestry Town	1–2	2–1	5–2	2–1	3–0	2–0	0–4	2–3	0–0
South Liverpool	3–3	3–1	0–1	3–0	1–1	3–1	0–3	0–0	0–0
Southport	2–1	2–1	0–1	1–1	2–0	2–0	2–1	1–1	2–3
Tamworth	1–4	2–3	0–0	2–1	0–1	0–0	1–2	0–2	1–0
Witton Albion	1–0	1–2	0–0	0–0	0–1	2–3	1–1	1–0	1–1
Workington	0–1	1–0	0–1	1–0	3–4	2–4	1–1	2–1	3–2
Worksop Town	1–6	0–0	1–2	1–0	1–1	3–3	0–1	2–1	1–0

T *Transferred from Southern League – Midland Division*

	Macclesfield Town	Marine	Matlock Town	Morecambe	Mossley	Netherfield	Oswestry Town	South Liverpool	Southport	Tamworth	Witton Albion	Workington	Worksop Town
	4–4	2–1	2–1	5–2	2–1	2–0	0–0	3–1	4–2	0–0	1–1	4–1	2–1
	4–1	1–1	2–2	3–1	0–2	5–1	3–1	4–2	0–2	0–3	2–1	2–2	2–0
	0–4	1–2	0–0	1–2	1–2	1–1	1–0	1–2	3–1	1–1	3–3	2–1	6–1
	1–4	2–2	2–1	2–0	0–1	3–1	1–2	2–0	4–0	0–0	0–1	4–2	3–0
	2–1	3–2	1–0	4–0	0–1	4–0	0–0	2–1	0–0	2–0	1–1	4–1	0–0
	2–2	1–1	3–2	4–0	1–1	0–1	4–1	2–0	2–2	0–1	1–0	1–0	0–3
	1–0	2–1	2–0	2–0	1–2	0–0	2–2	1–1	2–1	0–2	1–1	4–2	1–1
	1–1	1–2	2–2	1–1	0–0	0–1	0–0	2–2	0–0	1–0	1–0	3–1	1–1
	1–0	3–2	2–0	1–1	1–1	2–0	1–1	1–2	1–0	1–2	2–1	0–1	1–0
		1–1	0–1	2–1	3–0	3–0	3–2	2–1	1–1	3–1	0–2	0–3	4–2
	3–0		1–1	2–0	2–0	2–2	0–1	3–1	1–4	2–1	2–3	1–0	1–1
	0–1	3–0		1–1	2–2	1–0	0–1	0–2	1–4	2–0	1–2	1–2	0–1
	1–2	3–2	0–3		1–2	2–1	2–1	0–0	0–0	1–0	1–3	0–0	0–0
	1–0	3–1	1–1	3–2		4–2	2–0	4–1	4–2	4–0	2–2	1–3	1–0
	1–1	0–1	3–0	1–5	2–2		0–1	1–0	1–3	0–1	0–2	1–2	1–3
	2–0	2–2	4–0	1–2	1–1	1–1		2–3	2–0	2–1	0–2	3–2	0–2
	1–0	0–3	3–0	0–0	1–1	4–0	2–0		0–1	0–0	1–2	3–2	0–1
	2–2	1–0	1–1	2–1	1–0	0–2	2–2	1–1		1–1	2–1	0–0	4–1
	0–2	0–1	2–1	0–1	0–2	3–0	2–0	0–2	0–3		1–2	0–0	1–1
	3–0	5–2	0–0	5–1	1–0	6–0	2–1	2–1	4–3	5–1		2–1	3–0
	1–0	1–0	2–1	7–1	0–1	1–0	1–1	2–2	3–2	1–0	1–0		2–0
	3–2	2–2	1–1	2–1	0–2	3–0	2–1	2–2	1–1	2–0	3–0	2–1	

SOUTHERN LEAGUE MIDLAND DIVISION – 1981-82 RESULTS

	Alvechurch	Banbury United	Barry Town	Bedford Town	Bedworth United	Bridgend Town	Bromsgrove Rovers	Cambridge City	Cheltenham Town
Alvechurch		1–1	2–2	5–0	1–0	3–1	4–0	5–1	1–1
Banbury United	0–3		1–3	2–0	2–1	1–3	1–1	2–2	2–3
Barry Town	3–0	5–2		1–0	1–0	0–0	1–1	6–1	2–0
Bedford Town	0–2	1–0	1–1		1–2	2–1	5–1	4–1	0–0
Bedworth United	1–0	2–2	0–1	0–0		1–1	1–1	3–0	3–1
Bridgend Town	2–2	3–1	0–0	5–1	3–1		2–1	1–0	1–2
Bromsgrove Rovers	1–2	3–2	3–2	0–1	0–1	1–0		4–0	1–3
Cambridge City	1–1	1–0	2–0	1–1	3–0	2–2	1–1		1–0
Cheltenham Town	1–1	6–0	1–0	1–0	2–2	2–0	1–2	3–1	
Corby Town	0–3	4–2	1–2	0–4	1–1	1–1	1–3	3–1	6–2
Enderby Town	2–3	2–1	2–0	1–1	0–1	2–1	1–0	1–2	0–4
Gloucester City	0–1	3–0	2–2	2–1	0–0	6–0	1–0	3–0	2–1
Kidderminster Harriers	0–1	3–0	1–0	2–0	1–0	3–0	4–2	4–0	3–1
Merthyr Tydfil	0–0	3–0	4–0	3–1	0–0	0–0	2–3	3–0	2–2
Milton Keynes City	0–3	0–3	1–1	1–3	1–3	0–1	0–2	2–1	4–1
Minehead	1–0	1–5	1–1	0–0	0–1	1–0	1–0	2–2	2–1
Nuneaton Bor.	0–0	2–3	1–1	1–0	2–1	5–1	0–1	4–1	1–1
Redditch United (R)	0–1	2–1	1–7	1–3	0–2	0–1	3–2	3–1	0–0
Stourbridge	1–3	1–1	1–0	3–0	0–3	0–1	0–2	2–0	3–1
Taunton Town	1–3	3–5	2–1	0–3	0–1	2–0	0–3	2–0	3–2
Wellingborough Town	0–1	2–0	0–0	1–1	0–0	0–1	2–1	2–0	1–1
Witney Town	1–2	3–0	1–1	0–1	1–2	4–1	6–2	0–1	2–2

R *Relegated from Alliance Premier League*

Corby Town	Enderby Town	Gloucester City	Kidderminster Harriers	Merthyr Tydfil	Milton Keynes City	Minehead	Nuneaton Bor.	Redditch United	Stourbridge	Taunton Town	Wellingborough Town	Witney Town
1–0	3–1	3–0	0–0	3–1	1–0	5–1	0–3	5–2	0–2	3–0	1–1	0–2
2–1	1–1	0–4	1–3	1–0	2–0	3–1	2–2	8–3	0–3	0–0	3–4	0–2
1–0	0–2	3–0	2–1	1–0	0–0	2–1	0–2	2–0	1–1	2–2	1–3	0–2
0–0	1–3	0–0	1–3	0–2	1–1	0–2	0–2	2–0	3–1	1–1	1–1	0–0
3–0	3–2	0–1	0–2	3–3	2–0	4–0	1–0	5–1	1–4	3–1	0–1	1–0
0–4	1–1	0–0	1–1	0–0	3–0	2–1	1–1	2–2	1–3	4–1	1–2	1–2
0–2	0–1	1–1	1–2	0–0	1–0	2–4	0–0	2–0	2–1	3–0	1–2	2–2
0–1	2–0	0–1	0–4	1–0	2–1	0–1	2–3	1–1	0–1	2–2	2–0	0–1
1–3	2–3	1–3	0–0	0–1	1–1	2–0	2–3	1–1	1–1	1–2	5–2	2–2
	2–2	2–1	1–3	2–4	1–0	2–0	2–4	5–0	1–1	2–0	1–0	3–2
1–1		5–1	1–3	2–1	0–0	5–0	3–3	5–3	5–2	1–0	1–5	0–3
2–0	3–3		1–0	2–0	3–2	2–0	0–2	1–0	1–1	2–4	2–2	2–0
3–3	2–3	1–0		2–2	2–1	0–1	1–0	3–1	2–2	3–0	1–1	1–1
0–1	1–2	1–3	0–0		3–2	1–0	2–2	3–0	1–0	3–3	3–1	1–3
2–1	0–2	1–1	1–1	2–1		1–1	0–3	2–1	0–4	0–1	2–0	1–2
3–0	3–2	0–2	2–2	0–1	1–0		1–3	0–1	1–2	0–1	2–0	0–2
3–1	1–1	3–0	3–0	4–1	3–0	1–0		2–0	2–1	2–0	1–0	3–1
0–1	0–3	2–1	1–2	0–2	1–1	1–0	0–5		0–1	2–1	2–1	1–4
1–5	4–1	2–0	1–1	4–2	1–1	1–0	0–0	4–0		1–3	0–0	2–0
0–4	0–2	1–3	1–0	0–1	2–2	2–2	0–2	3–0	0–3		2–0	0–0
0–0	0–0	2–0	3–0	1–1	2–0	3–0	0–3	3–1	0–1	2–0		0–1
0–1	2–4	1–2	0–1	3–4	2–1	4–1	1–1	4–0	1–2	2–0	1–0	

SOUTHERN LEAGUE SOUTHERN DIVISION – 1981-82 RESULTS

	Addlestone and Weybridge Town (formerly Addlestone)	Andover	Ashford Town	Aylesbury United	Basingstoke Town	Canterbury City	Chelmsford City	Crawley Town	Dorchester Town
Addlestone and Weybridge Town (formerly Addlestone)		2–0	2–3	0–0	1–1	3–3	1–2	0–0	2–3
Andover	0–1		0–1	2–2	1–5	0–0	0–2	1–1	2–2
Ashford Town	1–1	5–1		3–1	0–0	4–2	2–3	1–0	1–0
Aylesbury United	0–0	4–1	5–1		2–2	2–0	1–2	3–1	1–1
Basingstoke Town	1–4	3–0	2–0	3–2		1–2	2–1	1–1	0–1
Canterbury City	0–1	3–1	1–2	2–2	0–0		0–1	2–0	1–2
Chelmsford City	2–2	3–0	1–0	1–1	1–1	1–0		2–0	0–1
Crawley Town	0–6	2–1	1–1	1–3	1–0	3–2	1–1		1–1
Dorchester Town	1–1	5–0	2–1	4–2	1–1	4–0	0–0	3–3	
Dover	3–3	2–2	2–1	1–4	0–4	2–3	1–2	2–0	1–0
Dunstable (formerly Dunstable Town)	1–4	1–0	1–0	0–2	0–1	4–1	3–0	3–1	1–0
Fareham Town	1–1	3–1	2–0	2–0	1–0	3–1	3–0	1–1	1–2
Folkestone (formerly Folkestone & Shepway)	2–0	4–3	1–2	2–3	1–4	0–3	0–2	2–1	2–0
Gosport Borough	3–2	6–0	1–0	0–3	3–1	2–1	2–0	2–1	0–3
Hastings United	2–1	2–1	0–0	1–1	1–0	4–0	2–1	2–3	1–0
Hillingdon Borough	2–0	0–1	5–1	0–0	1–2	0–0	1–3	0–0	0–1
Hounslow	0–2	1–1	1–1	1–0	1–3	1–1	1–1	2–0	0–0
Poole Town	2–2	1–0	1–1	2–1	3–4	1–1	2–2	2–1	0–0
Salisbury	2–6	0–2	2–0	1–1	1–3	3–1	0–0	3–0	0–0
Thanet United	1–3	3–4	2–3	2–4	2–1	1–1	2–1	0–0	0–2
Tonbridge AFC (formerly Tonbridge)	4–2	3–2	2–4	2–1	1–2	0–1	4–2	1–1	0–1
Waterlooville	2–1	2–0	3–1	2–1	2–3	4–0	2–0	1–0	2–2
Wealdstone	0–0	4–0	3–0	6–1	1–0	2–0	1–0	4–1	1–2
Welling United	2–0	2–0	0–2	3–0	6–0	0–0	3–0	2–3	1–2

Dover	Dunstable (formerly Dunstable Town)	Fareham Town	Folkestone (formerly Folkestone & Shepway)	Gosport Borough	Hastings United	Hillingdon Borough	Hounslow	Poole Town	Salisbury	Thanet United	Tonbridge AFC (formerly Tonbridge)	Waterlooville	Wealdstone	Welling United
0–1	2–0	1–0	2–1	1–1	0–0	1–3	0–0	2–1	2–1	3–0	1–0	1–1	1–0	0–0
2–1	0–1	1–1	2–2	0–1	1–1	0–1	1–2	0–4	1–2	1–1	0–2	1–1	0–1	2–4
1–1	0–0	0–0	2–1	0–0	0–0	1–0	0–0	2–2	2–1	2–0	0–1	0–1	0–0	0–1
0 1	0–1	1–1	3–2	1–0	1–2	2–0	1–2	4–0	2–1	3–0	3–1	0–0	3–0	2–1
2–3	1–3	0–2	5–0	0–3	1–1	4–1	5–0	1–0	0–1	1–1	1–1	0–0	2–3	0–0
0–2	2–2	0–0	0–1	1–0	4–2	2–2	1–6	1–1	1–1	0–0	3–1	2–1	0–5	0–0
3–1	0–0	2–0	2–0	3–3	0–1	3–0	3–1	2–1	1–2	4–0	0–0	3–1	0–2	1–2
1–3	2–2	1–2	2–0	1–2	0–2	2–0	0–1	2–1	1–3	3–0	0–2	1–5	1–2	0–1
0–0	1–0	5–1	3–3	0–0	0–1	0–0	2–0	2–2	2–1	6–0	5–1	0–2	2–2	2–2
	1–0	2–3	3–0	0–2	0–1	0–1	1–2	1–2	3–1	2–0	1–0	2–1	0–0	4–1
5–2		0–2	2–0	0–2	0–0	1–2	3–4	1–1	2–0	5–0	1–0	3–1	1–2	1–2
1–1	0–0		2–1	1–3	0–3	1–0	1–0	2–1	0–0	5–1	0–1	1–0	0–1	2–2
1–0	1–2	0–0		0–3	1–4	0–1	1–3	1–6	1–3	3–0	2–0	1–2	2–1	4–2
0–1	4–0	1–1	3–0		0–2	1–0	2–1	2–1	1–1	3–1	4–2	0–2	1–3	3–0
2–0	4–1	1–2	2–1	1–0		0–1	3–0	2–2	2–0	2–1	2–0	0–2	0–0	1–0
0–1	1–0	0–0	4–2	0–3	0–2		5–0	1–4	1–2	2–1	0–1	0–0	1–1	1–1
0–4	1–2	0–3	1–1	1–2	2–3	1–0		0–3	0–0	4–2	3–2	4–1	3–5	1–1
2–2	3–1	3–1	1–1	3–1	2–4	2–2	1–1		2–0	4–1	0–1	3–0	1–2	2–1
3–0	4–2	1–1	3–0	1–0	0–5	4–3	2–4	0–4		2–0	1–1	2–1	2–4	1–1
1–2	1–1	3–2	3–0	0–0	0–1	1–2	0–2	0–3	2–1		1–2	0–4	0–2	1–3
2–1	4–2	0–2	1–1	2–4	0–1	1–0	4–0	0–5	5–3	2–1		0–1	0–2	1–0
3–0	3–1	0–1	2–0	1–1	2–4	1–2	4–1	3–3	3–0	1–0	1–1		0–1	0–2
1–0	4–0	4–0	6–0	0–1	2–0	1–0	3–0	4–1	4–1	6–1	1–2	2–1		1–1
0–0	2–3	2–0	2–0	2–0	1–2	3–0	2–0	0–1	4–1	2–0	1–1	2–3	0–0	

FOOTBALL LEAGUE DIVISION ONE FIXTURES

	Arsenal	Aston Villa	Birmingham City	Brighton & Hove Albion	Coventry City	Everton	Ipswich Town	Liverpool	Luton Town
Arsenal	—	11-12	30-10	5-2	9-4	13.11	19-2	4-9	19-3
Aston Villa	14-5	—	4-4	13-11	19-3	12-2	28-12	18-12	8-9
Birmingham City	12-3	27-12	—	2-5	18-9	23-4	23-10	31-8	9-10
Brighton & Hove Albion	7-9	26-3	25-9	—	23-4	9-4	28-8	12-3	22-1
Coventry City	11-9	6-11	16-4	4-12	—	25-9	3-1	26-3	20-11
Everton	26-3	31-8	4-12	2-10	2-5	—	14-5	6-11	18-12
Ipswich Town	9-10	2-4	5-3	15-1	4-9	11-12	—	2-10	26-2
Liverpool	3-1	7-5	22-1	30-10	13-11	19-3	12-2	—	11-9
Luton Town	6-11	9-4	19-2	18-9	1-1	7-5	16-10	5-2	—
Manchester City	4-12	18-9	20-11	18-12	2-10	19-2	26-3	4-4	14-5
Manchester United	25-9	1-1	28-8	19-3	2-4	8-9	11-9	26-2	12-2
Norwich City	16-4	23-10	8-9	14-5	12-3	22-1	4-4	4-12	28-12
Nottingham Forest	23-10	5-2	16-10	4-9	27-12	2-4	6-11	2-5	12-3
Notts County	22-1	9-10	13-11	30-4	26-2	11-9	25-9	20-11	16-4
Southampton	28-12	4-9	14-5	5-4	15-1	30-10	20-11	16-4	30-4
Stoke City	28-8	27-11	3-1	16-10	7-5	27-12	22-1	23-10	25-9
Sunderland	18-12	15-1	30-4	16-4	5-2	5-3	4-12	28-12	13-11
Swansea City	20-11	2-5	28-12	19-2	31-8	16-10	30-4	18-9	4-12
Tottenham Hotspur	4-4	12-3	18-12	28-12	9-10	3-1	16-4	30-4	28-8
Watford	30-4	26-2	12-2	20-11	23-10	28-8	18-12	14-5	1-4
West Bromwich Albion	26-2	2-10	19-3	1-9	27-11	1-1	12-3	15-1	23-10
West Ham United	12-2	23-4	11-9	5-3	11-12	27-11	7-9	9-10	3-1

1982-83

Manchester City	Manchester United	Norwich City	Nottingham Forest	Notts County	Southampton	Stoke City	Sunderland	Swansea City	Tottenham Hotspur	Watford	West Bromwich Albion	West Ham United
23-4	2-5	31-8	5-3	18-9	2-4	15-1	7-5	1-1	27-12	27-11	16-10	2-10
22-1	20-11	5-3	11-9	19-2	3-1	30-4	28-8	25-9	30-10	16-10	16-4	4-12
1-1	15-1	9-4	26-2	26-3	11-12	4-9	27-11	2-4	7-5	2-10	6-11	5-2
7-5	6-11	11-12	3-1	27-11	27-12	26-2	11-9	9-10	2-4	1-1	12-2	23-10
12-2	28-12	30-10	5-4	16-10	28-8	18-12	7-9	22-1	19-2	5-3	30-4	14-5
9-10	16-4	18-9	28-12	5-2	12-3	4-4	23-10	26-2	4-9	15-1	20-11	30-4
13-11	5-2	27-12	19-3	9-4	1-1	18-9	23-4	27-11	31-8	7-5	30-10	2-5
27-12	16-10	23-4	7-9	1-1	25-9	5-3	2-4	9-4	27-11	11-12	28-8	19-2
11-12	2-10	2-4	30-10	4-9	27-11	2-5	26-3	23-4	15-1	27-12	5-3	31-8
—	5-3	15-1	30-4	2-5	6-11	1-9	16-10	30-10	5-2	4-9	28-12	16-4
23-10	—	27-11	22-1	11-12	9-4	9-10	27-12	7-5	13-11	23-4	3-1	12-3
28-8	30-4	—	18-12	6-11	11-9	20-11	12-2	3-1	16-10	19-2	25-9	26-3
27-11	1-9	7-5	—	23-4	26-3	2-10	1-1	11-12	9-4	18-9	19-2	15-1
7-9	14-5	19-3	4-12	—	12-2	28-12	3-1	28-8	5-3	30-10	4-4	18-12
19-3	18-9	5-2	13-11	2-10	—	4-12	19-2	5-3	2-5	31-8	18-12	16-10
9-4	19-2	1-1	12-2	2-4	23-4	—	12-3	11-9	11-12	26-3	8-9	6-11
26-2	1-4	2-10	20-11	1-9	9-10	30-10	—	19-3	18-9	2-5	14-5	4-9
12-3	18-12	4-9	14-5	15-1	23-10	16-4	6-11	—	2-10	5-2	26-3	5-4
11-9	26-3	26-2	25-9	23-10	8-9	14-5	22-1	12-2	—	6-11	4-12	20-11
3-1	4-12	9-10	16-4	12-3	22-1	13-11	25-9	7-9	19-3	—	11-9	28-12
2-4	4-9	2-5	9-10	27-12	7-5	5-2	11-12	13-11	23-4	9-4	—	18-9
25-9	30-10	13-11	28-8	7-5	26-2	19-3	9-4	27-12	1-1	2-4	22-1	—

permission. Subject to alteration.

FOOTBALL LEAGUE DIVISION TWO FIXTURES

	Barnsley	Blackburn Rovers	Bolton Wanderers	Burnley	Cambridge United	Carlisle United	Charlton Athletic	Chelsea	Crystal Palace
Barnsley	—	23-4	5-3	18-9	9-4	11-12	7-5	13-11	15-1
Blackburn Rovers	4-12	—	20-11	4-4	4-9	6-11	12-3	16-10	16-4
Bolton Wanderers	23-10	1-1	—	15-1	23-4	27-12	11-12	7-5	2-10
Burnley	22-1	27-12	28-8	—	13-11	7-9	26-2	23-4	9-10
Cambridge United	7-9	3-1	4-12	26-3	—	25-9	11-9	28-8	28-12
Carlisle United	14-5	19-3	5-4	16-4	2-5	—	9-10	30-10	18-9
Charlton Athletic	18-12	30-10	14-5	16-10	5-2	19-2	—	5-3	1-4
Chelsea	26-3	26-2	18-12	4-12	15-1	12-3	23-10	—	6-11
Crystal Palace	28-8	11-9	12-2	19-2	2-4	9-4	27-12	19-3	—
Derby County	16-4	25-9	13-11	30-4	9-10	28-8	12-2	8-9	18-12
Fulham	12-2	9-10	11-9	23-10	27-12	7-5	9-4	2-4	12-3
Grimsby Town	20-11	7-9	25-9	18-12	30-10	3-1	22-1	12-2	4-12
Leeds United	30-4	5-3	28-12	20-10	2-10	16-10	6-11	19-2	26-3
Leicester City	28-12	22-1	30-4	14-5	19-3	11-9	28-8	3-1	20-11
Middlesbrough	6-11	27-11	16-10	4-9	7-5	2-4	26-3	11-12	2-5
Newcastle United	25-9	9-4	3-1	6-11	27-11	1-1	23-4	11-9	23-10
Oldham Athletic	3-1	2-4	22-1	12-3	11-12	23-10	25-9	9-4	26-2
Queen's Park Rangers	19-2	13-11	30-10	2-10	1-1	27-11	2-4	27-12	29-9
Rotherham United	16-10	7-5	19-2	5-2	18-9	26-3	1-1	27-11	4-9
Sheffield Wednesday	4-4	12-2	7-9	20-11	26-2	22-1	3-1	25-9	14-5
Shrewsbury Town	12-3	11-12	19-3	2-5	29-9	23-4	27-11	1-1	5-2
Wolverhampton Wanderers	11-9	28-8	16-4	28-12	5-3	12-2	7-9	22-1	30-4

1982-83

Derby County	Fulham	Grimsby Town	Leeds United	Leicester City	Middlesbrough	Newcastle United	Oldham Athletic	Queen's Park Rangers	Rotherham United	Sheffield Wednesday	Shrewsbury Town	Wolverhampton Wanderers
29-9	2-10	1-1	27-11	2-4	19-3	2-5	4-9	9-10	26-2	27-12	30-10	5-2
2-5	19-2	5-2	23-10	18-9	30-4	1-9	28-12	26-3	18-12	2-10	14-5	15-1
26-3	5-2	2-5	2-4	27-11	26-2	4-9	29-9	12-3	9-10	9-4	6-11	18-9
27-11	5-3	7-5	9-4	11-12	3-1	19-3	30-10	12-2	11-9	1-1	25-9	2-4
19-2	5-4	12-3	12-2	6-11	18-12	30-4	14-5	20-11	22-1	16-10	16-4	23-10
15-1	18-12	4-9	26-2	5-2	28-12	20-11	5-3	30-4	13-11	28-9	4-12	2-10
2-10	29-9	18-9	19-3	15-1	13-11	4-12	16-4	28-12	20-11	4-9	30-4	2-5
5-2	28-12	2-10	9-10	4-9	14-5	16-4	18-9	4-4	30-4	2-5	20-11	31-8
7-5	30-10	23-4	13-11	1-1	25-9	5-3	16-10	22-1	3-1	11-12	7-9	27-11
—	14-5	26-2	22-1	23-10	11-9	4-4	20-11	3-1	4-12	19-3	28-12	12-3
11-12	—	26-3	25-9	23-4	22-1	26-2	6-11	7-9	28-8	27-11	3-1	1-1
16-10	13-11	—	28-8	19-2	16-4	28-12	30-4	14-5	4-4	5-3	11-9	19-3
18-9	16-4	15-1	—	2-5	20-11	30-10	5-4	4-12	14-5	5-2	18-12	4-9
5-3	4-12	9-10	8-9	—	5-4	13-11	18-12	25-9	16-4	30-10	12-2	26-2
9-4	18-9	29-9	1-1	27-12	—	5-2	2-10	23-10	12-3	15-1	19-2	23-4
27-12	16-10	2-4	12-3	26-3	8-9	—	19-2	28-8	12-2	7-5	22-1	11-12
1-1	19-3	27-11	27-12	7-5	12-2	9-10	—	11-9	7-9	23-4	28-8	13-11
4-9	2-5	11-12	23-4	9-4	5-3	15-1	5-2	—	19-3	18-9	16-10	7-5
23-4	15-1	27-12	11-12	31-8	30-10	2-10	2-5	6-11	—	2-4	5-3	9-4
6-11	30-4	23-10	11-9	12-3	28-8	18-12	4-12	16-4	28-12	—	26-3	9-10
2-4	4-9	9-4	7-5	2-10	9-10	18-9	15-1	26-2	23-10	13-11	—	27-12
30-10	20-11	6-11	3-1	16-10	4-12	14-5	26-3	18-12	25-9	19-2	4-4	—

permission. Subject to alteration.

FOOTBALL LEAGUE DIVISION THREE FIXTURES

	Bournemouth	Bradford City	Brentford	Bristol Rovers	Cardiff City	Chesterfield	Doncaster Rovers	Exeter City	Gillingham	Huddersfield Town
Bournemouth	—	27-11	1-1	2-11	9-10	9-4	2-5	25-9	23-10	6-11
Bradford City	30-4	—	19-3	12-2	16-2	26-2	23-10	13-11	3-1	14-5
Brentford	14-5	6-11	—	28-8	3-1	9-10	26-2	18-12	28-12	26-3
Bristol Rovers	1-3	2-10	15-1	—	14-5	29-1	4-9	28-12	7-9	30-4
Cardiff City	19-2	20-10	2-5	1-1	—	27-11	9-4	29-9	16-10	5-3
Chesterfield	4-12	16-10	19-2	11-9	30-4	—	12-3	16-4	2-11	4-4
Doncaster Rovers	3-1	5-3	16-10	8-1	4-12	30-10	—	11-9	26-3	1-3
Exeter City	5-2	26-3	23-4	2-4	29-1	2-10	7-5	—	4-9	15-1
Gillingham	5-3	2-5	2-4	7-5	26-2	15-2	13-11	8-1	—	30-10
Huddersfield Town	19-3	1-1	13-11	27-11	23-10	27-12	2-11	28-8	12-3	—
Lincoln City	18-12	30-10	5-3	22-1	13-11	19-3	9-10	20-10	14-5	28-12
Millwall	7-9	18-9	7-5	15-2	4-9	1-1	23-4	26-2	29-1	2-10
Newport County	13-11	29-1	5-2	9-10	4-4	4-9	15-1	14-5	4-12	18-9
Orient	28-12	4-9	18-9	23-10	7-9	15-1	2-10	30-4	1-3	16-4
Oxford United	4-9	2-3	20-10	27-12	2-10	7-5	8-9	30-10	15-1	5-2
Plymouth Argyle	19-10	19-2	30-10	28-9	28-12	5-3	19-3	1-4	18-12	4-12
Portsmouth	16-10	9-4	27-12	26-3	12-3	23-4	27-11	12-2	6-11	19-2
Preston North End	30-10	27-12	1-3	25-9	19-3	13-11	2-4	22-1	19-2	16-10
Reading	4-4	15-1	8-9	12-3	3-11	18-9	5-2	4-12	16-4	18-12
Sheffield United	29-1	23-4	27-11	2-5	5-2	2-4	27-12	5-3	2-10	7-9
Southend United	16-4	5-2	29-1	6-11	18-12	6-9	18-9	3-1	1-4	18-10
Walsall	15-1	7-5	2-10	9-4	18-9	19-10	1-1	19-3	5-2	29-1
Wigan Athletic	18-9	7-9	4-9	26-2	16-4	5-2	29-1	15-2	30-4	3-1
Wrexham	2-10	2-4	9-4	23-4	15-1	2-5	15-2	9-10	18-9	4-9

1982-83

Lincoln City	Millwall	Newport County	Orient	Oxford United	Plymouth Argyle	Portsmouth	Preston North End	Reading	Sheffield United	Southend United	Walsall	Wigan Athletic	Wrexham
23-4	22-1	26-3	2-4	8-1	15-2	26-2	12-3	27-12	11-9	28-9	28-8	7-5	12-2
12-3	16-4	11-9	8-1	3-11	9-10	4-12	4-4	28-8	18-12	25-9	29-9	22-1	28-12
23-10	25-9	28-9	22-1	15-2	12-3	1-4	2-11	12-2	30-4	11-9	16-4	8-1	4-12
18-9	19-10	19-2	5-3	1-4	5-2	13-11	16-4	30-10	3-1	19-3	4-12	16-10	18-12
26-3	8-1	27-12	7-5	12-2	2-4	30-10	6-11	2-3	25-9	23-4	22-1	11-9	28-8
6-11	14-5	8-1	28-8	28-9	23-10	18-12	26-3	22-1	28-12	12-2	1-3	25-9	3-1
19-2	18-12	28-8	12-2	16-4	6-11	30-4	28-12	25-9	5-4	22-1	14-5	28-9	19-10
2-3	16-10	1-1	27-11	12-3	27-12	8-9	18-9	9-4	23-10	2-5	6-11	3-11	19-2
1-1	11-9	9-4	19-10	28-8	23-4	19-3	9-10	28-9	12-2	27-12	25-9	27-11	22-1
2-4	12-2	7-5	28-9	25-9	9-4	9-10	26-2	23-4	22-1	15-2	11-9	2-5	8-1
—	4-12	12-2	25-9	30-4	26-2	16-2	3-1	11-9	29-9	8-1	4-4	28-8	16-4
9-4	—	2-5	27-12	9-10	2-11	5-2	15-1	27-11	12-3	2-4	23-10	26-3	6-11
2-10	3-1	—	26-2	28-12	7-9	16-4	15-2	19-3	2-11	23-10	18-12	12-3	30-4
5-2	4-4	16-10	—	4-12	29-1	3-1	18-12	19-2	14-5	12-3	2-11	6-11	26-3
27-11	19-2	2-4	9-4	—	26-3	18-9	29-1	2-5	6-11	1-1	16-10	23-4	5-3
16-10	1-3	22-1	11-9	13-11	—	14-5	30-4	8-1	16-4	28-8	3-1	12-2	25-9
2-11	28-9	25-9	2-5	22-1	1-1	—	23-10	2-4	28-8	7-5	8-1	1-3	11-9
2-5	28-8	19-10	23-4	11-9	27-11	5-3	—	7-5	8-1	9-4	12-2	1-1	28-9
29-1	30-4	6-11	9-10	3-1	4-9	28-12	2-10	—	16-2	26-2	26-3	23-10	14-5
7-5	30-10	1-3	1-1	19-3	18-9	15-1	4-9	19-10	—	13-11	19-2	9-4	16-10
4-9	28-12	5-3	30-10	14-5	15-1	2-10	4-12	16-10	26-3	—	30-4	19-2	28-2
27-12	5-3	23-4	15-2	26-2	2-5	4-9	7-9	13-11	9-10	27-11	—	2-4	30-10
15-1	13-11	30-10	19-3	18-12	2-10	19-10	14-5	5-3	4-12	9-10	28-12	—	4-4
7-9	19-3	27-11	13-11	23-10	7-5	29-1	5-2	1-1	26-2	2-11	12-3	27-12	—

permission. Subject to alteration.

FOOTBALL LEAGUE DIVISION FOUR FIXTURES

	Aldershot	Blackpool	Bristol City	Bury	Chester	Colchester	Crewe Alexandra	Darlington	Halifax Town	Hartlepool United
Aldershot	—	27-11	30-10	9-4	13-11	2-4	19-10	1-3	7-5	5-3
Blackpool	30-4	—	16-4	7-9	29-1	5-2	6-11	2-10	9-10	14-5
Bristol City	12-3	11-9	—	23-4	2-11	27-11	7-5	2-5	15-2	26-2
Bury	4-12	22-1	18-12	—	19-3	30-10	11-9	5-3	25-9	28-12
Chester	26-3	29-9	2-3	6-11	—	5-3	28-8	19-2	12-2	4-12
Colchester	28-12	25-9	30-4	12-3	23-10	—	22-1	16-10	28-8	3-1
Crewe Alexandra	15-2	19-3	7-9	29-1	15-1	18-9	—	4-9	12-3	16-4
Darlington	2-11	12-2	3-1	23-10	9-10	26-2	8-1	—	22-1	4-4
Halifax Town	18-9	19-2	19-10	5-2	2-10	15-1	30-10	7-9	—	30-4
Hartlepool United	23-10	1-1	16-10	2-4	9-4	2-5	29-9	27-12	27-11	—
Hereford United	3-1	5-3	28-12	15-1	5-2	4-9	16-10	29-1	19-3	13-11
Hull City	5-2	9-4	15-1	2-11	27-11	7-5	23-4	2-4	27-12	18-9
Mansfield Town	14-5	28-8	13-11	9-10	26-2	19-3	12-2	30-10	8-1	14-2
Northampton Town	2-10	13-11	18-9	2-5	7-9	19-10	27-12	27-11	9-4	29-1
Peterborough United	29-1	2-5	2-10	28-9	16-2	27-12	2-4	23-4	3-11	4-9
Port Vale	16-4	30-10	4-4	4-9	18-9	6-9	5-3	5-2	26-2	18-10
Rochdale	18-12	16-10	4-12	2-10	4-9	29-1	19-2	15-1	23-10	7-9
Scunthorpe United	4-9	23-4	5-2	27-11	1-1	2-10	26-3	7-5	2-4	15-1
Stockport County	26-2	27-12	19-3	14-2	2-4	23-4	2-5	13-11	1-1	9-10
Swindon Town	4-4	8-1	14-5	26-2	12-3	9-10	25-9	19-3	11-9	18-12
Torquay United	8-9	2-3	29-1	26-3	7-5	1-1	9-4	18-9	2-5	2-10
Tranmere Rovers	15-1	2-4	4-9	7-5	27-12	13-11	1-1	18-10	23-4	5-2
Wimbledon	9-10	7-5	5-3	1-1	2-5	15-2	27-11	9-4	13-11	19-3
York City	6-11	19-10	19-2	27-12	23-4	9-4	1-3	1-1	28-9	30-10

1982-83

	Hereford United	Hull City	Mansfield Town	Northampton Town	Peterborough United	Port Vale	Rochdale	Scunthorpe United	Stockport County	Swindon Town	Torquay United	Tranmere Rovers	Wimbledon	York City
	2-5	25-9	1-1	12-2	11-9	28-9	23-4	8-1	16-10	27-12	22-1	28-8	19-2	19-3
	23-10	4-12	15-1	26-3	3-1	12-3	26-2	18-12	1-4	4-9	2-11	28-12	18-9	15-2
	2-4	28-8	26-3	22-1	12-2	27-12	9-4	25-9	6-11	1-1	28-9	8-1	23-10	9-10
	28-8	1-3	19-2	3-1	16-4	8-1	12-2	30-4	19-10	16-10	13-11	28-9	14-5	4-4
	25-9	30-4	16-10	16-4	20-10	22-1	8-1	14-5	28-12	30-10	11-9	4-4	3-1	18-12
	8-1	28-9	6-11	1-3	1-4	12-2	11-9	16-4	18-12	19-2	14-5	26-3	2-11	4-12
	26-2	18-11	2-10	4-4	28-12	23-10	9-10	13-11	3-1	5-2	4-12	14-5	30-4	2-11
	11-9	28-12	12-3	30-4	18-12	25-9	28-8	28-9	26-3	6-11	16-4	15-2	4-12	14-5
	6-11	4-4	4-9	4-12	1-3	16-10	5-3	28-12	14-5	29-1	3-1	18-12	26-3	16-4
	26-3	22-1	3-11	11-9	8-1	2-3	7-5	28-8	19-2	23-4	12-2	25-9	6-11	12-3
	—	20-10	18-9	18-12	14-5	19-2	30-10	4-12	2-3	8-9	5-4	30-4	16-4	2-10
	15-2	—	2-5	23-10	6-11	26-3	1-1	26-2	29-1	2-10	9-10	12-3	4-9	7-9
	22-1	3-1	—	28-12	27-9	11-9	25-9	18-10	4-12	5-3	18-12	16-4	5-4	30-4
	23-4	5-3	2-4	—	30-10	1-1	15-2	19-3	5-2	7-5	26-2	9-10	15-1	4-9
	1-1	19-3	7-5	12-3	—	27-11	13-11	9-10	15-1	9-4	23-10	26-2	8-9	5-2
	9-10	13-11	29-1	14-5	30-4	—	19-3	14-2	2-10	15-1	28-12	4-12	18-12	3-1
	12-3	14-5	5-2	2-11	26-3	6-11	—	4-4	16-4	18-9	30-4	3-1	1-3	28-12
	9-4	16-10	1-3	6-11	19-2	2-11	27-12	—	7-9	2-5	12-3	23-10	29-1	18-9
	1-11	11-9	9-4	25-9	28-8	7-5	27-9	12-2	—	27-11	8-1	22-1	12-3	23-10
	12-2	16-4	23-10	28-9	4-12	28-8	22-1	3-1	30-4	—	15-2	2-11	28-12	13-11
	27-12	19-2	23-4	16-10	5-3	2-4	27-11	30-10	4-9	20-10	—	6-11	5-2	15-1
	27-11	30-10	6-9	19-2	16-10	9-4	2-5	5-3	18-9	28-2	19-3	—	2-10	29-1
	28-9	8-1	27-12	28-8	22-1	23-4	19-10	11-9	30-10	2-4	25-9	12-2	—	26-2
	7-5	12-2	27-11	8-1	25-9	2-5	2-4	22-1	5-3	26-3	28-8	11-9	16-10	—

permission Subject to alteration.

THE ALLIANCE PREMIER FOOTBALL LEAGUE FIXTURES 1982-83

14 August 1982
Altrincham v Wealdstone
Bangor City v Barnet
Bath City v Telford United
Boston United v Dagenham
Enfield v Runcorn
Kettering Town v Trowbridge Town
Nuneaton Borough v Yeovil Town
Scarborough v Maidstone United
Stafford Rangers v Frickley Athletic
Weymouth v Barrow
Worcester City v Northwich Victoria

16 August 1982
Dagenham v Wealdstone
Northwich Victoria v Frickley Athletic
Worcester City v Altrincham

17 August 1982
Barnet v Nuneaton Borough
Barrow v Stafford Rangers
Enfield v Maidstone United
Runcorn v Bangor City
Telford United v Kettering Town
Trowbridge Town v Weymouth

18 August 1982
Scarborough v Boston United
Yeovil Town v Bath City

21 August 1982
Barnet v Stafford Rangers
Barrow v Enfield
Dagenham v Altrincham
Frickley Athletic v Weymouth
Maidstone United v Bangor City
Northwich Victoria v Bath City
Runcorn v Worcester City
Telford United v Scarborough
Trowbridge Town v Nuneaton Borough
Wealdstone v Boston United
Yeovil Town v Kettering Town

28 August 1982
Altrincham v Trowbridge Town
Bangor City v Dagenham
Bath City v Frickley Athletic
Boston United v Yeovil Town
Enfield v Telford United
Kettering Town v Northwich Victoria
Nuneaton Borough v Runcorn
Scarborough v Wealdstone
Stafford Rangers v Maidstone United
Weymouth v Barnet
Worcester City v Barrow

4 September 1982
Barnet v Maidstone United
Barrow v Bangor City
Dagenham v Stafford Rangers
Enfield v Altrincham
Frickley Athletic v Nuneaton Borough
Kettering Town v Boston United
Northwich Victoria v Weymouth
Runcorn v Telford United
Trowbridge Town v Wealdstone
Worcester City v Bath City
Yeovil Town v Scarborough

6 September 1982
Altrincham v Worcester City
Nuneaton Borough v Barnet

7 September 1982
Bangor City v Runcorn
Stafford Rangers v Barrow
Wealdstone v Dagenham

8 September 1982
Bath City v Yeovil Town
Boston United v Scarborough
Frickley Athletic v Northwich Victoria
Kettering Town v Telford United
Maidstone United v Enfield
Weymouth v Trowbridge Town

11 September 1982
Altrincham v Maidstone United
Barrow v Yeovil Town
Enfield v Bangor City
Frickley Athletic v Worcester City

Kettering Town v Bath City
Runcorn v Dagenham
Scarborough v Stafford Rangers
Telford United v Boston United
Trowbridge Town v Barnet
Wealdstone v Northwich Victoria
Weymouth v Nuneaton Borough

18 September 1982
Bangor City v Scarborough
Barnet v Frickley Athletic
Boston United v Barrow
Dagenham v Northwich Victoria
Maidstone United v Nuneaton Borough
Runcorn v Kettering Town
Stafford Rangers v Telford United
Wealdstone v Bath City
Weymouth v Altrincham
Yeovil Town v Enfield

25 September 1982
Altrincham v Yeovil Town
Barrow v Maidstone United
Bath City v Runcorn
Enfield v Stafford Rangers
Frickley Athletic v Trowbridge Town
Kettering Town v Bangor City
Northwich Victoria v Barnet
Nuneaton Borough v Dagenham
Scarborough v Weymouth
Telford United v Wealdstone
Worcester City v Boston United

27 September 1982
Bangor City v Nuneaton Borough
Dagenham v Kettering Town

28 September 1982
Barnet v Bath City
Barrow v Altrincham
Runcorn v Boston United
Trowbridge Town v Stafford Rangers

29 September 1982
Scarborough v Northwich Victoria

2 October 1982
Barnet v Yeovil Town
Barrow v Trowbridge Town
Dagenham v Scarborough
Frickley Athletic v Telford United
Maidstone United** v Runcorn
Northwich Victoria v Stafford Rangers
Nuneaton Borough v Altrincham
Weymouth v Boston United
Worcester City v Enfield
Kettering Town** v Wealdstone

9 October 1982
Altrincham v Barrow
Bath City v Barnet
Boston United v Bangor City
Enfield v Nuneaton Borough
Northwich Victoria v Runcorn
Scarborough v Kettering Town

Stafford Rangers v Weymouth
Telford United v Dagenham
Trowbridge Town v Maidstone United
Wealdstone v Worcester City
Yeovil Town v Frickley Athletic

11 October 1982
Nuneaton Borough v Weymouth

12 October 1982
Barrow v Northwich Victoria
Stafford Rangers v Enfield
Trowbridge Town v Dagenham

13 October 1982
Kettering Town v Worcester City
Yeovil Town v Barnet

16 October 1982
Altrincham v Scarborough
Barnet v Telford United
Boston United v Runcorn
Dagenham v Bath City
Frickley Athletic v Enfield
Maidstone United v Northwich Victoria
Nuneaton Borough v Wealdstone
Stafford Rangers v Yeovil Town
Trowbridge Town v Barrow
Weymouth v Bangor City
Worcester City v Kettering Town

18 October 1982
Northwich Victoria v Enfield

23 October 1982
Bath City v Barrow
Boston United v Barnet
Enfield v Frickley Athletic
Kettering Town v Altrincham
Northwich Victoria v Nuneaton Borough
Runcorn v Weymouth
Scarborough v Worcester City
Telford United v Maidstone United
Trowbridge Town v Dagenham
Wealdstone v Stafford Rangers
Yeovil Town v Bangor City

30 October 1982
Altrincham v Bath City
Bangor City v Trowbridge Town
Barnet v Enfield
Wealdstone v Nuneaton Borough

6 November 1982
Bath v Boston United
Enfield v Barnet
Frickley Athletic v Wealdstone
Maidstone United v Yeovil Town
Nuneaton Borough v Bangor City
Runcorn v Scarborough
Stafford Rangers v Altrincham
Telford United v Barrow
Trowbridge Town v Northwich Victoria
Weymouth v Kettering Town
Worcester City v Dagenham

13 November 1982
Altrincham v Enfield
Bangor City v Stafford Rangers
Barnet v Runcorn
Barrow v Frickley Athletic
Boston United v Maidstone United
Dagenham v Worcester City
Kettering Town v Nuneaton Borough
Northwich Victoria v Trowbridge Town
Scarborough v Bath City
Wealdstone v Weymouth
Yeovil Town v Telford United

20 November 1982
Bath City v Worcester City
Frickley Athletic v Bangor City
Maidstone United v Kettering Town
Nuneaton Borough v Barrow
Runcorn v Wealdstone
Stafford Rangers v Boston United
Telford United v Yeovil Town
Trowbridge Town v Scarborough
Weymouth v Dagenham

27 November 1982
Altrincham v Frickley Athletic
Bangor City v Telford United
Boston United v Trowbridge Town
Dagenham v Weymouth
Kettering Town v Maidstone United
Northwich Victoria v Barrow
Nuneaton Borough v Bath City
Scarborough v Enfield
Wealdstone v Runcorn
Worcester City v Barnet
Yeovil Town v Stafford Rangers

4 December 1982
Bangor City v Yeovil Town
Barnet v Altrincham
Bath City v Dagenham
Enfield v Worcester City
Kettering Town v Barrow
Maidstone United v Boston United
Runcorn v Northwich Victoria
Telford United v Nuneaton Borough
Trowbridge Town v Stafford Rangers
Wealdstone v Frickley Athletic
Weymouth v Scarborough

11 December 1982
Altrincham v Nuneaton Borough
Bangor City v Bath City
Barrow v Telford United
Boston United v Worcester City
Dagenham v Barnet
Frickley Athletic v Runcorn
Northwich Victoria v Wealdstone
Trowbridge Town v Enfield
Weymouth v Stafford Rangers
Yeovil Town v Maidstone United

18 December 1982
Barnet v Altrincham
Dagenham v Telford United
Enfield v Trowbridge Town
Maidstone United v Frickley Athletic
Nuneaton Borough v Weymouth
Runcorn v Yeovil Town
Worcester City v Scarborough

27 December 1982
Bangor City v Northwich Victoria
Barnet v Wealdstone
Bath City v Trowbridge Town
Boston United v Frickley Athletic
Enfield v Kettering Town
Maidstone United v Dagenham
Runcorn v Altrincham
Scarborough v Barrow
Stafford Rangers v Nuneaton Borough
Telford United v Worcester City
Yeovil Town v Weymouth

1 January 1983
Bangor City v Barrow
Barnet v Dagenham
Bath City v Kettering Town
Boston United v Northwich Victoria
Enfield v Wealdstone
Maidstone United v Weymouth
Runcorn v Frickley Athletic
Scarborough v Nuneaton Borough
Stafford Rangers v Trowbridge Town
Telford United v Altrincham
Yeovil Town v Worcester City

3 January 1983
Altrincham v Bangor City
Barrow v Runcorn
Dagenham v Enfield
Frickley Athletic v Scarborough
Kettering Town v Barnet
Northwich Victoria v Telford United
Nuneaton Borough v Boston United
Trowbridge Town v Yeovil Town
Wealdstone v Maidstone United
Weymouth v Bath City
Worcester City v Stafford Rangers

8 January 1983
Boston United v Kettering Town
Enfield v Northwich Victoria
Frickley Athletic v Altrincham
Maidstone United v Barnet
Scarborough v Runcorn
Stafford Rangers v Bath City
Telford United v Bangor City
Wealdstone v Barrow
Worcester City v Weymouth

15 January 1983
Altrincham v Telford United
Bangor City v Enfield
Barnet v Boston United
Barrow v Wealdstone
Bath City v Stafford Rangers
Dagenham v Yeovil Town
Northwich Victoria v Scarborough
Nuneaton Borough v Kettering Town
Runcorn v Maidstone United
Trowbridge Town v Frickley Athletic
Weymouth v Worcester City

22 January 1983
Boston United v Altrincham
Kettering Town v Frickley Athletic
Maidstone United v Bath City
Scarborough v Trowbridge Town
Stafford Rangers v Northwich Victoria
Telford United v Barnet
Wealdstone v Bangor City
Worcester City v Nuneaton Borough
Yeovil Town v Dagenham

29 January 1983
Altrincham v Boston United
Barrow v Kettering Town
Bath City v Maidstone United
Enfield v Scarborough
Frickley Athletic v Dagenham
Northwich Victoria v Yeovil Town
Nuneaton Borough v Telford United
Stafford Rangers v Wealdstone
Trowbridge Town v Worcester City
Weymouth v Runcorn

5 February 1983
Bangor City v Frickley Athletic
Barnet v Northwich Victoria
Boston United v Bath City
Dagenham v Barrow
Kettering Town v Stafford Rangers
Maidstone United v Worcester City
Runcorn v Trowbridge Town
Telford United v Weymouth
Wealdstone v Enfield
Yeovil Town v Altrincham

12 February 1983
Altrincham v Kettering Town
Barrow v Nuneaton Borough
Bath City v Bangor City
Enfield v Boston United
Frickley Athletic v Yeovil Town
Northwich Victoria v Maidstone United
Scarborough v Barnet
Stafford Rangers v Dagenham
Trowbridge Town v Runcorn
Weymouth v Telford United
Worcester City v Wealdstone

19 February 1983
Altrincham v Stafford Rangers
Bangor City v Worcester City
Barnet v Barrow
Boston United v Weymouth
Dagenham v Frickley Athletic
Nuneaton Borough v Scarborough
Runcorn v Bath City
Telford United v Trowbridge Town
Wealdstone v Kettering Town
Yeovil Town v Northwich Victoria

26 February 1983
Barrow v Dagenham
Bath City v Nuneaton Borough
Frickley Athletic v Maidstone United
Northwich Victoria v Boston United
Runcorn v Barnet
Scarborough v Altrincham
Stafford Rangers v Kettering Town
Trowbridge Town v Bangor City
Wealdstone v Telford United
Weymouth v Enfield
Worcester City v Yeovil Town

5 March 1983
Altrincham v Northwich Victoria
Bangor City v Wealdstone
Barnet v Scarborough
Boston United v Stafford Rangers
Dagenham v Trowbridge Town
Enfield v Bath City
Frickley Athletic v Barrow
Kettering Town v Weymouth
Maidstone United v Telford United
Nuneaton Borough v Worcester City
Yeovil Town v Runcorn

12 March 1983
Barrow v Barnet
Bath City v Altrincham
Nuneaton Borough v Enfield
Scarborough v Dagenham
Stafford Rangers v Runcorn
Telford United v Frickley Athletic
Trowbridge Town v Boston United
Wealdstone v Yeovil Town
Weymouth v Maidstone United
Worcester City v Bangor City

19 March 1983
Bangor City v Boston United
Barnet v Worcester City
Bath City v Scarborough
Dagenham v Nuneaton Borough
Enfield v Weymouth
Frickley Athletic v Kettering Town
Maidstone United v Barrow
Northwich Victoria v Altrincham
Runcorn v Stafford Rangers
Trowbridge Town v Telford United
Yeovil Town v Wealdstone

26 March 1983
Altrincham v Barnet
Barrow v Bath City
Boston United v Enfield
Kettering Town v Dagenham
Nuneaton Borough v Frickley Athletic
Scarborough v Yeovil Town
Stafford Rangers v Bangor City
Telford United v Runcorn
Wealdstone v Trowbridge Town
Weymouth v Northwich Victoria
Worcester City v Maidstone United

2 April 1983
Bangor City v Altrincham
Barnet v Kettering Town
Bath City v Weymouth
Boston United v Nuneaton Borough
Enfield v Dagenham
Maidstone United v Wealdstone
Runcorn v Barrow
Scarborough v Frickley Athletic
Stafford Rangers v Worcester City
Telford United v Northwich Victoria
Yeovil Town v Trowbridge Town

4 April 1983
Altrincham v Runcorn
Barrow v Scarborough
Dagenham v Maidstone United
Frickley Athletic v Boston United
Kettering Town v Enfield
Northwich Victoria v Bangor City
Nuneaton Borough v Stafford Rangers
Trowbridge Town v Bath City
Wealdstone v Barnet
Weymouth v Yeovil Town
Worcester City v Telford United

9 April 1983
Altrincham v Weymouth
Barrow v Boston United
Bath City v Wealdstone
Enfield v Yeovil Town
Frickley Athletic v Barnet
Kettering Town v Runcorn
Northwich Victoria v Dagenham
Nuneaton Borough v Maidstone United
Scarborough v Bangor City
Telford United v Stafford Rangers
Worcester City v Trowbridge Town

16 April 1983
Bangor City v Kettering Town
Barnet v Trowbridge Town
Bath City v Enfield
Boston United v Telford United
Dagenham v Runcorn
Maidstone United v Altrincham
Nuneaton Borough v Northwich Victoria
Stafford Rangers v Scarborough
Weymouth v Wealdstone
Worcester City v Frickley Athletic
Yeovil Town v Barrow

23 April 1983
Barnet v Weymouth
Barrow v Worcester City
Dagenham v Bangor City
Frickley Athletic v Bath City
Maidstone United v Stafford Rangers
Northwich Victoria v Kettering Town
Runcorn v Nuneaton Borough
Telford United v Enfield
Trowbridge Town v Altrincham
Wealdstone v Scarborough
Yeovil Town v Boston United

30 April 1983
Altrincham v Dagenham
Bangor City v Maidstone United
Bath City v Northwich Victoria
Boston United v Wealdstone
Enfield v Barrow
Kettering Town v Yeovil Town
Nuneaton Borough v Trowbridge Town
Scarborough v Telford United
Stafford Rangers v Barnet
Weymouth v Frickley Athletic
Worcester City v Runcorn

7 May 1983
Barnet v Bangor City
Barrow v Weymouth
Dagenham v Boston United
Frickley Athletic v Stafford Rangers
Maidstone United v Scarborough
Northwich Victoria v Worcester City
Runcorn v Enfield
Telford United v Bath City
Trowbridge Town v Kettering Town
Wealdstone v Altrincham
Yeovil Town v Nuneaton Borough

INTERNATIONAL AND CUP DATES 1982-83

All fixtures subject to alteration.

August
Sat. 21 FA Charity Shield

September
Wed. 1 FL Cup, first round, first leg
Sat. 4 FA Cup, preliminary round
Sat. 11 FA Trophy, preliminary round
FA Vase, extra preliminary round
FA Youth Cup, first qualifying round
Wed. 15 European Cups, first round, second leg
FL Cup, first round, second leg
Sat. 18 FA Cup, first qualifying round
Tue. 21 England v West Germany (UEFA Under-21 Competition – 1980-82 final, first leg)
Wed. 22 Denmark v England (European Championship)
Wales v Norway (European Championship)
Wed. 29 European Cups, first round, second leg

October
Sat. 2 FA Cup, second qualifying round
Sun. 3 FA Sunday Cup, first round
Wed. 6 FL Cup, second round, first leg
Sat. 9 FA Vase, preliminary round
FA Youth Cup, second qualifying round
Tue. 12 West Germany v England (UEFA Under-21 Competition – 1980-82 final, second leg)
Wed. 13 England v West Germany (Friendly)
Scotland v East Germany (European Championship)
Austria v Northern Ireland (European Championship)
Sat. 16 FA Cup, third qualifying round
Wed. 20 European Cups, second round, first leg
Sat. 23 FA Trophy, first qualifying round
Wed. 27 FL Cup, second round, second leg

October *(Cont.)*
Sat. 30 FA Cup, fourth qualifying round
FA County Youth Cup, first round
Sun. 31 FA Sunday Cup, second round

November
Wed. 3 European Cups, second round, second leg
Sat. 6 FA Vase, first round
FA Youth Cup, first round
Wed. 10 FL Cup, third round
Tue. 16 Greece v England (UEFA Under-21 Competition)
Wed. 17 Greece v England (European Championship)
Switzerland v Scotland (European Championship)
Northern Ireland v West Germany (European Championship)
Sat. 20 FA Cup, first round
Wed. 24 UEFA Cup, third round, first leg
Sat. 27 FA Trophy, second qualifying round
Sun. 28 FA Sunday Cup, third round

December
Wed. 1 FL Cup, fourth round
Sat. 4 FA Vase, second round
FA Youth Cup, second round
FA County Youth Cup, second round
Wed. 8 UEFA Cup, third round, second leg
Sat. 11 FA Cup, second round
Wed. 15 England v Luxembourg (European Championship)
Belgium v Scotland (European Championship)
Albania v Northern Ireland (European Championship)
Yugoslavia v Wales (European Championship)
Sat. 18 FA Trophy, third qualifying round

January 1983

Sat. 1	FA Vase, third round
Sat. 8	FA Cup, third round
	FA Youth Cup, third round
Sun. 9	FA Sunday Cup, fourth round
Sat. 15	FA Trophy, first round
	FA County Youth Cup, third round
Wed. 19	FL Cup, fifth round
Sat. 22	FA Vase, fourth round
Sat. 29	FA Cup, fourth round

February

Sat. 5	FA Trophy, second round
	FA Youth Cup, fourth round
Sun. 6	FA Sunday Cup, fifth round
Wed. 9	FL Cup, semi-final, first leg
Sat. 12	FA Vase, fifth round
Wed. 16	FL Cup, semi-final, second leg
Sat. 19	FA Cup, fifth round
	FA County Youth Cup, fourth round
Sat. 26	FA Trophy, third round

March

Wed. 2	European Cups, third round, first leg
	UEFA Cup, fourth round, first leg
Sat. 5	FA Vase, sixth round
	FA Youth Cup, fifth round
Sat. 12	FA Cup, sixth round
Sun. 13	FA Sunday Cup, semi-final
Wed. 16	European Cups, third round, second leg
	UEFA Cup, fourth round, second leg
Sat. 19	FA Trophy, fourth round
Sat. 26	FL Cup, final
	FA Vase, semi-final, first leg
Tue. 29	England v Greece (UEFA Under-21 Competition)

March *(Cont.)*

Wed. 30	England v Greece (European Championship)
	Scotland v Switzerland (European Championship)
	Northern Ireland v Turkey (European Championship)

April

Sat. 2	FA Vase, semi-final, second leg
	FA Youth Cup, semi-final
	FA County Youth Cup, semi-final
Wed. 6	European Cups, semi-final, first leg
Sat. 9	FA Trophy, semi-final, first leg
Sat.16	FA Cup, semi-final
Wed. 20	European Cups, semi-final, second leg
Tue. 26	England v Hungary (UEFA Under-21 Championship)
Wed. 27	England v Hungary (European Championship)
	Northern Ireland v Albania (European Competition)
	Wales v Bulgaria (European Championship)
Sat. 30	FA Vase, final
	FA Youth Cup, final

May

Sun. 1	FA Sunday Cup, final
Wed. 4	UEFA Cup, final, first leg
Sat. 7	FA County Youth Cup, final
Wed. 11	European Cup Winners' Cup, final
Sat. 14	FA Trophy, final
Wed. 18	UEFA Cup, final, second leg
Sat. 21	FA Cup, final
Wed. 25	European Champion Clubs' Cup, final

June

Wed. 8	Brazil v England (Friendly)

FOOTBALL AWARDS 1981-82

Footballer of the Year
The Football Writers' Association this year voted Steve Perryman (Tottenham Hotspur) Footballer of the Year. It was a popular choice, and makes Steve the third Tottenham player to win the award.

Past winners
1947-48 Stanley Matthews (Blackpool)
1948-49 Johnnie Carey (Manchester United)
1949-50 Joe Mercer (Arsenal)
1950-51 Harry Johnston (Blackpool)
1951-52 Billy Wright (Wolverhampton Wanderers)
1952-53 Nat Lofthouse (Bolton Wanderers)
1953-54 Tom Finney (Preston North End)
1954-55 Don Revie (Manchester City)
1955-56 Bert Trautmann (Manchester City)
1956-57 Tom Finney (Preston North End)
1957-58 Danny Blanchflower (Tottenham Hotspur)
1958-59 Sid Owen (Luton Town)
1959-60 Bill Slater (Wolverhampton Wanderers)
1960-61 Danny Blanchflower (Tottenham Hotspur)
1961-62 Jimmy Adamson (Burnley)
1962-63 Stanley Matthews (Stoke City)
1963-64 Bobby Moore (West Ham United)
1964-65 Bobby Collins (Leeds United)
1965-66 Bobby Charlton (Manchester United)
1966-67 Jackie Charlton (Leeds United)
1967-68 George Best (Manchester United)
1968-69 Dave Mackay (Derby County)
Tony Book (Manchester City)
1969-70 Billy Bremner (Leeds United)
1970-71 Frank McLintock (Arsenal)
1971-72 Gordon Banks (Stoke City)
1972-73 Pat Jennings (Tottenham Hotspur)
1973-74 Ian Callaghan (Liverpool)
1974-75 Alan Mullery (Fulham)
1975-76 Kevin Keegan (Liverpool)
1976-77 Emlyn Hughes (Liverpool)
1977-78 Kenny Burns (Nottingham Forest)
1978-79 Kenny Dalglish (Liverpool)
1979-80 Terry McDermott (Liverpool)
1980-81 Frans Thijssen (Ipswich Town)

PFA Player of the Year
The Professional Footballers' Association this year chose Kevin Keegan (Southampton) as their Player of the Year.

PFA Young Player of the Year: Steve Moran (Southampton)

Scottish PFA Footballer of the Year: Sandy Clark (Airdrieonians)

Scottish PFA Young Player of the Year: Frank McAvennie (St. Mirren)

Manager of the Year
Bob Paisley (Liverpool)
The outstandingly successful Bob Paisley was always favourite to win this award, having steered Liverpool to two more major trophies during the season. Bob won this award previously in 1976, 1977, 1979 and 1980, and has also been Manager of the Month on no fewer than nine occasions. The award is voted for by the Bell's Whisky panel.

European Footballer of the Year 1981
Karl-Heinz Rummenigge (Bayern Munich)

Previous winners
1956 Stanley Matthews (Blackpool)
1957 Alfredo Di Stefano (Real Madrid)
1958 Raymond Kopa (Real Madrid)
1959 Alfredo Di Stefano (Real Madrid)
1960 Luis Suarez (Barcelona)
1961 Omar Sivori (Juventus)
1963 Josef Masopust (Dukla Prague)
Lev Yashin (Moscow Dynamo)
1964 Denis Law (Manchester United)
1965 Eusebio (Benfica)
1966 Bobby Charlton (Manchester United)
1967 Florian Albert (Ferencvaros)
1968 George Best (Manchester United)
1969 Gianni Rivera (AC Milan)
1970 Gerd Muller (Bayern Munich)
1971 Johan Cruyff (Ajax)
1972 Franz Beckenbauer (Bayern Munich)
1973 Johan Cruyff (Barcelona)
1974 Johan Cruyff (Barcelona)
1975 Oleg Blokhin (Dynamo Kiev)
1976 Franz Beckenbauer (Bayern Munich)
1977 Alan Simonsen (Borussia Moench)
1978 Kevin Keegan (SV Hamburg)
1979 Kevin Keegan (SV Hamburg)
1980 Karl-Heinz Rummenigge (Bayern Munich)

IMPORTANT ADDRESSES

Football Association: E. A. Croker, 16 Lancaster Gate, London W2 3LW.

Scottish FA: E. Walker, 6 Park Gardens, Glasgow G3 7YE.

Irish FA: W. J. Drennan, 20 Windsor Avenue, Belfast BT9 6EG.

Welsh FA: Trevor Morris, 3 Fairy Road, Wrexham LL13 7PS.

FA of Ireland (Eire): P. J. O'Driscoll, 80 Merrion Square, Dublin 2.

League of Ireland: E. J. Dowling, 80 Merrion Square, Dublin 2.

Federation Internationale de Football Association (FIFA): Dr Helmut Kaser, FIFA House, 11 Hitzigweg, 8032 Zurich, Switzerland.

Union des Associations Europeenes de Football (UEFA): H. Bangerter, PO Box 16, CH-3000 Berne 15, Switzerland.

Football League: R. H. G. Kelly, FCIS, Lytham St Annes, Lancashire FY8 1JG.

Scottish League: J. Farry, 188 West Regent Street, Glasgow G2 4RY.

Irish League: W. J. Drennan, 20 Windsor Avenue, Belfast BT9 6EG.

Welsh League: J. T. Burrows, 16 Meyer Street, Thomastown, Tonyrefail, Glamorgan.

Alliance Premier League: P. D. Hunter, 24 Barnehurst Road, Bexley Heath, Kent DA7 6EZ.

Southern League: D. J. Strudwick, 49 Woodlands Way, Southwater, Horsham, Sussex RH13 7TF.

Northern Premier League: R. D. Bayley, 22 Woburn Drive, Hale, Altrincham, Cheshire WA15 8LZ.

The Association of Football League Referees and Linesmen: R. G. Warnke, 7 Ferndale Road, Binley Woods, Nr Coventry CV3 2BG.

Football League Managers and Secretaries Association: K. Friar, c/o Arsenal FC, Arsenal Stadium, Highbury, London N5.

Women's Football Association: P. Gregory, 7 Mayfield Road, London N8.

Universities Athletic Union: B. Byrne, 28 Woburn Square, London WC1.

English Schools FA: G. Evans, 4a Eastgate Street, Stafford ST16 2NN.

Professional Footballers' Association: G. Taylor, 124 Corn Exchange Buildings, Hanging Ditch, Manchester M4 3BN.

England Supporters' Association: R. Coates, Hill End House, Butlers Cross, Aylesbury, Buckinghamshire.